An illustrated handbook
of *BULBS* &
PERENNIALS

An illustrated handbook
of *BULBS &*
PERENNIALS

EDITED BY HUGH REDGROVE

CASSELL

Cassell Publishers Limited
Villiers House, 41/47 Strand
London WC2N 5JE

Copyright © Godwit Press Limited 1991

First published in Great Britain 1993
by arrangement with
Godwit Press Limited, Auckland, New Zealand

British Library Cataloguing in Publication Data
A catalogue record for this book is available from
the British Library

ISBN 0-304-34310-2

Printed in Singapore

Contents

Preface

I have been interested in perennial plants for over 60 years, both in Britain and in New Zealand, and consequently I am delighted that recently there has been a considerable upsurge of interest in these plants. However, the present system of retailing through garden centres has meant that these days there are very few plant catalogues produced, and it is the resulting lack of reference material that has encouraged me to edit this book, an expanded and updated edition of *A Handbook of Bulbs and Perennials for the Southern Hemisphere*.

In the course of my research, I have received help and information from many people, too numerous to name. In fact, without this assistance, the undertaking would have been considerably harder and the result less satisfactory. In particular, I would like to thank the following: Gordon Collier (Taihape), W.J. Dijk (Daffodil Acre), Ian Duncalf (Parva Plants), John van Eden (Tulip Farm), Gordon Evans (Dunedin), Jack Hobbs (Auckland Regional Botanic Gardens), Grant Iles (Bay Bloom Nurseries), Mrs May (Iris Society), Barry McKenzie (Topline Nursery), John Millichamp (Dunhampton Lilies), Mrs L. Neilson (Iris Society), Michael Perkins (Cottage Plants), Ranch Nurseries (Whangarei) and Mary Robertson (Horowhenua). I would also like to thank Carol Redgrove for typing the manuscript.

Hugh Redgrove
Auckland 1989

Unfortunately, Hugh Redgrove died shortly after completing the revision of this book. In the absence of an author, we have relied on a number of people for help in checking the text, verifying the numerous recent changes in nomenclature, and providing photographs to fill the gaps in Hugh's collection. In particular, we would like to acknowledge the contribution of Jack Hobbs, curator of the Auckland Regional Botanic Gardens, who spent many hours working on the manuscript and selecting photographs. Other people whose assistance is greatly appreciated include: Kerry Carman, Barbara and Ian Duncalf (Parva Plants), Keith Hammett (DSIR), Terry Hatch (Joy Plants), Grant Iles (Bay Bloom Nurseries), Rhonda Morgan (Pineland Perennials), Bryan Pollock (Green Leaf Supplies), Roger Price (Auckland Regional Botanic Gardens), Gordon Redgate, Bill Sykes (DSIR), and Mrs Jean Veal. We are also grateful to Gil Hanly for providing the photographs on pages 31, 45, 61, 90, 116, 144, 175, 205 and 277.

Godwit Press
Auckland, 1991

Introduction

The object of this book is to provide a reliable guide to the identification, selection, cultivation and propagation of over 350 genera of bulbs and perennials.

Perennials have become increasingly popular in recent years, and fashion has certainly played a part in this. For some years now there has been a renewed appreciation of cottage gardens and old-fashioned flowers, which include such well-loved perennials as pinks, primulas, salvias, violets and numerous kinds of daisies, as well as bulbous plants such as snowdrops, daffodils and hyacinths. More recently, there has been a move towards more formal, designed gardens, including carefully planned herbaceous beds and borders, and featuring perennials such as hostas and cannas, planted *en masse* for their architectural qualities.

Another reason for the recent popularity of perennials is their important role in 'low-maintenance' gardening. Few gardeners these days can afford to spend hours sowing and weeding borders of annuals—let alone pay someone else to—and perennials present a more permanent, consistently attractive alternative. Bulbs, particularly the hardier species, share this advantage, providing a seasonal show in return for minimal attention.

Perennials are an enormously variable group of plants. They range in size from low-growing ground covers to giants 5 m tall, with foliage and flowers in every conceivable shape and colour. There are perennials for any situation—sun, shade, dry banks, bog gardens, ponds, coastal gardens, containers—and this book will help gardeners to choose the right plants for the right spots, and to cultivate and propagate them successfully.

The entries that follow are arranged alphabetically by genus, and contain information on the natural distribution of the genus, its characteristics, requirements for cultivation, methods of increase, and notable pests and diseases. Numerous species and cultivars are described, many of which have only recently become available, and recent changes in nomenclature have been incorporated wherever possible.

A number of the plants described in this book do not come within the strict botanical definition of a perennial—some are shrubs or sub-shrubs— but because they are used horticulturally in the same way as perennials, and are often considered to be, or indeed sold as, perennials, it has seemed appropriate to include them.

This book is neither a botanical treatise nor a 'coffee-table' book. It is a practical, hands-on reference work for horticulturists, home gardeners and nursery workers, based on many years' experience in growing bulbs and perennials. Like its predecessors, it is dedicated to the gardening public.

Bulbs & perennials
A to Z

A

ACANTHUS
Acanthaceae   Bear's breeches

The genus comprises about 50 species, many natives of the Mediterranean region, the spineless *A. mollis* being the best known. This strong-growing, deeply rooted plant, happy under almost any conditions, is used largely for woodland planting or shady spots where few plants would survive. It is generally considered too vigorous in growth for the ordinary herbaceous border. The handsome, deeply serrated and veined, heart-shaped, dark green leaves are 30 cm (12 in.) across and 60 cm (24 in.) long. The 1 m (3 ft) tall, densely clustered spikes of light rosy purple bracts appear during summer and autumn.

A. spinosus has darker green leaves, deeply divided but not very prickly. It has bold spikes of white flowers tinted with purple, up to 1.2 m (4 ft) tall and freely produced.

Acanthus increases rapidly from root cuttings taken when the plant is dormant.

ACHILLEA
Asteraceae   Milfoil

Acanthus mollis

This is a genus of about 200 species, mostly natives of Europe, Asia and North America. As these plants belong to the same family as the common wild yarrow, which is usually a weed in light soils, it can be expected that even these 'educated' flowering species are inclined to be found out of bounds. Nevertheless, they are very easily controlled, and even in light, free soil they can be quickly reduced to a desirable size. If fresh rooted shoots from the outer parts of the clumps are removed each winter and planted again instead of the old root, better blooms will result. The colours range from white to pink, cerise and yellow, most varieties producing flattish heads comprising hundreds of miniature flowers.

A. filipendulina 'Gold Plate' is a selected form of a vigorous species, growing about 1.2 m (4 ft) tall, with pungent foliage, the stiffly erect stems being topped with 10–15 cm (4–6 in.) wide, flat, rounded heads of golden yellow. This is a valuable plant in the border and, along with a number of other forms in varying shades of yellow, is very popular in Europe. Another splendid hybrid form of this species is known as 'Coronation Gold'; while the heads are smaller and a bright golden yellow, the

Achillea filipendulina 'Coronation Gold'

whole plant is more branching, growing only 1 m (3 ft) tall. It produces valuable, long-lasting cut flowers, which retain colour and form when dried for winter decorations. *A. filipendulina* 'Moonlight' is deservedly popular. It has silvery filigree foliage, and in early summer it has flat, light yellow flower-heads, which are slow to fade.

A. millefolium. There are several brightly coloured forms of this common species, of which 'Crimson King' is the one generally grown, while 'Cerise Queen' is probably the most brilliant. Recent additions include pale pink 'Apple Blossom', glowing red 'Cherry Pie' and deep red 'Fire Beacon'. These are easily grown and very hardy, reaching 60 cm (24 in.) in height. Their flower-heads fade as they age and should then be removed to encourage further flowering.

A. ptarmica is a vigorous, spreading perennial, with white underground roots spreading quickly in light soils but easily kept in check. The best form is called 'The Pearl', with freely branching stems of small, double, pure white flowers like a giant *Gypsophila* 'Bristol Fairy'. A new selection called 'Terry's Double' carries larger, pure white flowers. The display commences in late summer and continues until winter, and the blooms are excellent for cutting and general florists' use. Plant in full sun to secure a maximum display.

ACHIMENES
Gesneriaceae

With brilliant-hued, miniature, gloxinia-like blooms and attractive foliage, these half-hardy plants from the tropical Americas are delightful subjects for large pots and hanging baskets. They are remarkably easy to grow, but will not stand heavy frosts and need shelter from adverse weather. Plants are therefore mostly grown in glasshouses or conservatories, except in very warm climates. They can also be grown in sheltered, well-raised, sunny beds outside. The longish, grub-like bulbs are easily broken and dry out quickly if left out of the ground for any length of time, so they are best left in their containers, unless they have become too crowded. Like begonias, they start into growth when the warm weather commences, growing rapidly and blooming freely all summer and autumn, and dying down later. They prefer to be kept dry, without any water, until the growth is ready to start again. Colours available are mostly lavenders, mauves and purples of velvety texture, but shades of pink, rose and even crimson also occur.

Propagation is from division, as plants increase rapidly if they are doing really well. Transplant during autumn, covering the roots about 5 cm (2 in.) deep.

ACIDANTHERA
Iridaceae

A little-known genus from northern and southern tropical Africa, *Acidanthera* comprises about 20 species. It is closely allied to the gladiolus, and some of the species used to be described under the headings of tritonia and sparaxis. Indeed this family has been pushed about from one genus to another in the past. Twice it has been classified as gladiolus and then again given generic rank.

A. bicolor was discovered in Tanzania and Ethiopia during 1896 and at that time was classified as a gladiolus. It was not until the taller and larger-flowered form *A. bicolor* var. *murieliae* was introduced about 1932 that these bulbs became generally popular. Most of the other species are only half-hardy, but *A. bicolor* and its taller form can be quite easily grown in temperate climates. The corms are dormant during winter, so that even in very cold districts plants can be lifted in the autumn, quickly dried to prevent soft rot, and stored in a dry, airy place until replanted in the spring. The species *A. bicolor* produces freesia-like corms up to 2.5 cm (1 in.) across, with numerous offsets, but the corms of the form *murieliae* are flattened like gladiolus and are often 5 cm (2 in.) or more across. Some growers experience more success by discarding the old corms, which seem to have a tendency to develop soft brown rot, instead sowing the numerous large cormlets, which all flower during the first season, in early spring.

A. bicolor grows only 45 cm (18 in.) tall, producing two to four creamy white, 5 cm (2 in.) flowers, with deep chocolate markings, on a loosely arranged, drooping spike. The taller-growing *murieliae* resembles a gladiolus in growth, having a straight flower-spike, with a dozen or more 10 cm (4 in.), white flowers, wide open and starry, with central blotches of maroon-black. Both are valuable garden plants and excellent cut flowers, the delicately fragrant blooms remaining fresh over quite a long period.

Some interesting hybrids have been raised between *A. bicolor* var. *murieliae* and some of the modern large-flowered gladioli. The main objective

Acidanthera bicolor

has been to develop hybrids that are perfumed as well as being first-class cut flowers.

The corms must be dried off quickly and thoroughly to prevent diseases developing in storage. Stocks can be raised from seed as well as the cormlets. Plant 10 cm (4 in.) deep, 15 cm (6 in.) apart over several months in spring for a succession of blooms.

ACONITUM
Ranunculaceae   Monkshood

This is an indispensable genus of over 60 species of hardy, autumn-flowering perennials, natives of Asia, Europe and America. They are easily grown in either sun or shade provided plants do not become dry during the growing season. The effect is delightful when plants are established in bold groups or in woodland conditions where they can be left undisturbed for years. Aconite, sometimes used in medicine, is obtained from the roots of the species *A. napellus*.

A. fischeri, a stocky, 90 cm (36 in.) tall, erect-growing plant, with solitary spikes of deep blue flowers held above rich green, glossy foliage, is one of the most valuable late-blooming perennials. Most blue-flowering plants are at their best in the spring, but this species will continue in flower throughout the autumn untouched by frosts. It is lovely when associated with the newer white shasta daisies and late-blooming helianthus. This species is also listed as *A. henryi* (syn. *A. californicum*), *A. columbianum* and *A. maximum*.

A. lycoctonum (wolf bane) is probably the best of the yellow-flowered species, of which there are a number. The form usually seen has smaller, primrose-coloured flowers produced freely on thinnish spikes. *A. lycoctonum* var. *pyrenaicum*, a form growing only 60 cm (24 in.) high, has larger, helmeted, yellow flowers in mid-summer. *A. lycoctonum* 'Ivorine' (syn. *A. septrionale* 'Ivorine') forms closely set, 90 cm (36 in.) spikes on well-foliaged bushes and has very attractive, ivory-white, hooded flowers.

A. napellus is the best-known and most popular European species, its thin, erect, unbranched stems reaching a height of 1–1.8 m (3–6 ft) tall. The terminal spikes of violet-blue, hooded flowers appear in

Aconitum fischeri

late summer. If grown from seed, purple or reddish purple forms sometimes appear as well as paler shades. Seedling-raised stock has given rise to several selected forms. *A. napellus* x *bicolor* has densely set, pale blue and white flowers; *A. napellus* 'Roseum' is a lower-growing, pale pink form, which is much less vigorous.

A. wilsonii is a vigorous Chinese species up to 2 m (6 ft) tall, sometimes confused with *A. napellus* but distinct in that the three-lobed leaves are more deeply pinnate. The 45 cm (18 in.) terminal spike carries a number of short side branches, and the 5 cm (2 in). long, violet-blue flowers are softly hairy. A selected form known as 'Barker's Variety' is very fine and deeper in colour.

All species can be raised from seed, but germination is usually poor and slow unless seed is sown as soon as it is ripe; old seed is worthless. Plants are easily increased by root division but when established are best left undisturbed for several years. Transplant in winter when dormant.

ACORUS
Araceae

This genus consists of only two species of grass-like plants suitable for growing near water.

A. calamus 'Variegatus' (sweet flag) has aromatic, erect, sword-like leaves with cream variegations, to 90 cm (36 in.). In spring the leaves take on a rosy tinge.

A. gramineus 'Variegatus' is smaller, with erect, dark green foliage with white variegations. The flowers are insignificant.

Propagation is by division of the rhizomes in winter or early spring. Plants should be divided every three or four years.

Acorus calamus 'Variegatus'

AETHIONEMA
Cruciferae

These are very free-flowering, evergreen perennials used mainly in rock gardens on light soils.

A. grandiflorum (syn. *A. pulchellum*) forms a large, compact clump to 30 cm (12 in.) tall, with elongated heads of pale pink flowers in spring and summer. It has narrow, blue-green leaves.

'Warley Rose' and 'Warley Ruber' are wide-spreading and 25 cm (10 in.) high, with pink and carmine flower-heads in profusion in late spring.

They must have perfect drainage and like a limey soil. Plants can be raised by seed sown in autumn or cuttings planted in spring.

AGAPANTHUS
Liliaceae

This genus, at one time thought to contain some 50 or more species, has been reclassified in South Africa and condensed into nine species. Some of these embrace a wide range of geographical forms, and vary in the height of the flower-stem from 40 cm to 2.5 m (16 in. to 8 ft). These types, growing as they do under widely differing conditions, reproduce true to type from seed and provide a most interesting study and opportunity for the hybridist.

In warmer countries the common species of these hardy South African 'lilies' are so prolific and easily grown that they are looked upon almost as weeds. Indeed, in many places they become naturalised in open fields and gullies, soon forming large clumps, while in mild woodland areas they seed down and can almost take possession of the undergrowth. Notwithstanding all this, the agapanthus is really a beautiful flower, and very useful for large decorations.

A. campanulatus is a hardy, deciduous species from Natal, and grows up to 90 cm (36 in.) tall, with medium to dark blue flowers, rather bell-shaped.

A. inapertus is one of the most interesting of all the deciduous species. It is considerably variable, ranging in nature over a wide area. As the name suggests, the flowers are pendulous in habit, hanging down from the 1 m (3 ft) stems. The narrow, tubed flowers, about 25 on an umbel, each 7.5 cm (3 in.) long, opening at the mouth in varying degrees,

Agapanthus inapertus

range in shade from near white through pale and bright blues to lilac, purple and deep violet. The predominating colour, however, is blue, and the form generally grown is deep violet. There is also a pale blue form called 'Cambridge Blue', which originated from seed from Wisley.

A. longispathus. This valuable species resembles somewhat the common form of *A. orientalis* but produces smaller heads of blue flowers in greater profusion. The spathe valves are also longer. The plant is completely dormant in winter.

A. orientalis. This is the common and best-known species, previously described under the name of *A. umbellatus*. It is evergreen and produces arching leaves up to 60 cm (24 in.) long. Umbels on 1–1.5 m (3–5 ft) scapes contain up to 100 blooms, each 5 cm (2 in.) long and wide.

Cultivars of agapanthus include:

'Albus'—a white-flowered form of *A. orientalis*.
'Albus Roseus'—as 'Albus' but flowers show a tinge

Aethionema grandiflorum

of pink with age.

'Blue Baby'—probably a cultivar of *A. africanus*, growing to 60 cm (24 in.), with light blue flowers on rather open heads in summer.

'Blue Nile'—massive heads of mauve flowers to 1.8 m (6 ft) and broad foliage typical of *A. orientalis*.

'Blue Skies'—good full heads of sky-blue flowers to 60 cm (24 in.) from mid-summer onwards.

'Flore Pleno'—a rare and interesting, lower-growing, double-flowered variety of *A. orientalis*; methyl-violet.

'Peter Pan—narrow leaves, heads of blue flowers to 50 cm (20 in.).

'Purple Cloud'—a very robust cultivar with tall heads of semi-pendulous, violet-purple flowers to 1.8 m (6 ft). The very strong, broad foliage is tinted purple at the base.

'Purple Splendour'—very similar to 'Purple Cloud', with slightly more rounded flower-heads.

'Queen Anne'—a compact form with mid-blue flower-heads to 60 cm (24 in.).

'Snowball'—a dwarf hybrid with pure white flower-heads 40–50 cm (16–20 in.) tall.

'Streamline' (syn. *A. minor*)—an outstanding cultivar with mid-blue flowers to 60 cm. The flowers appear continuously through winter to a peak display in late spring/early summer. Foliage is narrow but dense, so it makes an excellent ground cover planted at 60 cm (24 in.) intervals.

'Tigerleaf'—a form of *A. orientalis* raised by Hugh Redgrove, with striking foliage, green with broad bands of yellow on each side, and blue flowers.

'Tinkerbell'—a sport of 'Peter Pan'; narrow leaves conspicuously striped with white, heads of blue flowers to 50 cm (20 in.).

'Variegata'—an older variegated plant that has been slow to increase; grey-green leaves are up to 30 cm (12 in.) long, striped and bordered with white; blue flower-heads grow to 35 cm (14 in.) tall. This is a striking plant for a rock garden or the front of a border.

All agapanthus are easily grown in any reasonably well-drained soil and are useful as background plants for the herbaceous border or for edging a long drive. They are quite accommodating as tub plants;

This attractive perennial border features *Agapanthus* 'Blue Nile', a red form of *Achillea millefolium*, *Achillea filipendulina* 'Moonlight' (yellow), with *Stachys byzantina* (front) coming into flower.

when well established and root-bound, they seem to flower all the more freely, being most effective in full bloom. Stock or animals do not damage the plants naturalised in the open. Agapanthus increase readily from seed and should be transplanted during the winter months, although they are easily shifted at any time of the year.

AGERATUM
Asteraceae

This is a genus of annuals and biennials, some of which are more or less perennial in warmer climates. They prefer a sunny situation and fertile, well-drained soil.

A. houstonianum. In some countries this grows as an annual up to 30 cm (12 in.) high; in milder climates it is a shrubby plant 1 m (3 ft) high and even more across. The dull green, heart-shaped leaves are densely hairy and somewhat clammy at the back. The rounded, densely packed terminal heads of bloom are about 10 cm (4 in.) across, and the branching stems also carry several smaller side shoots. These finely rayed flower-heads resemble the well-known, cornflower-blue annual ageratum but appear on the bush continuously through summer and autumn. It is a useful cut flower, but the blooms do not withstand heavy winter frosts and it is therefore only suitable for milder climates if grown for this purpose. Plants are seldom killed outright by frost, and new spring growths produce a good display of blooms later. In any case, the bush is best pruned back heavily at the end of each winter. Increase is by seed.

AJUGA
Lamiaceae

These low plants are useful as ground cover in sun or shade for moist soil conditions.

Ajuga 'Jungle Beauty', 30 cm (12 in.), is notable for its large, rounded, very glossy, dark green leaves and its gentian-blue flowers.

A. pyramidalis has deep green leaves and dense spikes of gentian-blue flowers.

A. reptans is a popular ground cover in part shade; the purple-leafed form 'Atropurpurea' is at its best in some sun. 'Burgundy Glow' has wine-red leaves edged with white, and 'Variegata', with its green and white leaves, is striking in moist shade. Propagation is by division of established plants.

Ageratum houstonianum

Ajuga pyramidalis

ALBUCA
Liliaceae   Asphodel

This is a genus of 30-odd species of bulbous plants, which are natives of tropical and South Africa and, as can be expected, only half-hardy. Many are hardly worthy of cultivation, but the species *A. altissima* is probably the best known and is most often found in gardens where winter frosts do not exceed 15 degrees. It forms a large, flattish round, green-coated bulb, dormant in late autumn and winter. The bulb prefers to be placed on top of the ground with the fleshy roots penetrating deeply. The rosette of 45 cm (18 in.) long, lanceolate leaves surrounds the 60–90 cm (24–36 in.) tall, loosely arranged, tapering racemes, which carry 2.5 cm (1 in.) wide, six-petalled, white flowers tipped with green. These appear during spring, and the display is often prolonged into summer. The cut stems, sometimes two or three to a mature bulb, last well in water.

A. canadensis grows to 15 cm (6 in.) tall, with stiff, lance-shaped leaves and, in spring, loose spikes of tubular, yellow flowers with a green stripe on each petal.

Another desirable species, *A. nelsonii*, produces white flowers with a dull red stripe down the back of each segment.

Propagation is by seed sown in spring or by offsets removed when the plant is dormant.

Albuca canadensis

ALCHEMILLA
Rosaceae   Ladies' mantle

These are hardy, low-growing perennials suitable for the front of borders or for rock gardens.

A. alpina, 15 cm (6 in.), has attractive foliage, grey-green with silvery undersides and clusters of yellow-green flowers. It is best grown in crevices between rocks.

A. erythropoda is an excellent dwarf species, having close-growing, bluish foliage and sprays of sulphur flowers to 15 cm (6 in.).

Alchemilla mollis

A. mollis has wavy-edged, kidney-shaped and softly hairy leaves, which hold dew or raindrops for a long time. The flowers are small, in sprays of greenish yellow, rather like gypsophila. Ordinary well-drained soil suits them.

Propagation of all species is by seed or division in spring or autumn.

ALLIUM
Liliaceae

This is a genus of over 300 species native to Asia, the Middle East, North Africa and America. It includes onions, garlic and chives, and some of the garden varieties unfortunately carry the same pungent odour, a fact that affects their popularity; there are, however, quite a number of interesting species in which the objectionable smell is entirely absent. Many are delightful subjects for the rockery as well as for the herbaceous border, and some taller species reach a height in excess of 1 m (3 ft).

A. aflatunense. This useful species resembles *A. christophii*, with the rounded flower-heads on a smaller scale, the starry blooms more of a reddish violet and held erectly on wiry stems 45 cm (18 in.) tall.

A. caeruleum (syn. *A. azureum*) has flowers 60 cm (24 in.) tall and a pleasing shade of sky blue.

A. christophii (syn. *A. albopilosum*). This little-known species is one of the best of the stronger growers. The large, rounded-conical umbels, often 15–25 cm (6–10 in.) across on 60 cm (24 in.) stems, are composed of numerous, starry, pale violet flowers carrying a glistening metallic sheen. The interesting foliage is glabrous above and white-hairy beneath.

A. flavum. This evergreen, bulbous-rooted species forms a neat clump with narrow, grassy foliage, partly dormant in the winter. The dainty heads of bloom, pale yellow and appearing in mid-summer, make useful cut flowers.

A. giganteum is the strongest-growing species, growing 1.5 m (5 ft) tall, with large heads of violet-rose flowers and very ornamental foliage.

A. karataviense has broad foliage and dense umbels of pinkish mauve flowers on 22.5 cm (9 in.) stems.

A. moly forms a clump of broad, grey-green leaves. It flowers in summer, with stems up to 30 cm (12 in.) high of starry, yellow flowers.

A. neapolitanum is an early-flowering species, opening in early spring with 25–30 cm (10–12 in.) stems bearing pure white heads that are almost without the characteristic onion scent. They are quite useful as cut flowers. This species will seed freely, but if increase is not required, stems can be plucked before the seed is ripe.

A. pulchellum. This free-flowering bulb blooms from late spring till summer with successive scapes. It is long-lasting and has proven to be a good cut flower. The many-flowered umbels of pendulous, tubular flowers up to 7.5 cm (3 in.) across are bright reddish violet, topping thin, 60 cm (24 in.) stems. The whitish bulbs are oblong-ovate and nearly

Allium moly

evergreen.

A. roseum is somewhat similar in growth and habit to *A. moly* and grows about 30 cm (12 in.) tall. The rounded heads consist of numbers of small, pale pink flowers slightly tinged with purple. It is quite pretty when suitably placed in the rockery. Bulbs are naturally small.

A. sphaerocephalum. This tall-growing species blooms in late spring or summer, and the bulbs become dormant in late autumn. The 1 m (3 ft) tall, thin stems carry a terminal, tightly packed 7.5 cm (3 in.) wide ball of deep purple-crimson flowers. The heads are useful as cut flowers, remaining fresh over a long period, although eventually losing their colour.

Plant bulbs 5–10 cm (2–4 in.) deep and 5–15 cm (2–6 in.) apart during early and late autumn when dormant.

ALOPHIA
Iridaceae   Blue tiger flower

This genus of about 14 species of cormous plants, previously *Herbertia*, is closely allied to the tigridias, being natives of Texas, Chile and Brazil. Only one species is commonly known and grown, although some of the others are desirable subjects.

A. platensis is an interesting South American bulb, possibly a hybrid, which grows freely in almost any garden soil. It is, however, apparently happier

Alophia platensis

ALSTROEMERIA
Alstroemeriaceae   Peruvian lily

These most interesting and valuable hardy plants, all from South America, are among the finest of all perennials for cutting. About 50 species exist, varying in habit from miniature alpine plants only 10 cm (4 in.) high to robust-growing forms from the lowland meadows, 1–1.5 m (3–5 ft) tall. All are alike in their flower formation, resembling miniature trumpet lilies, six to 30 on an umbel, held on thin, wiry stems. Strangely enough, the dwarf or alpine species produce, as a rule, just as large blooms as the tall-growing ones.

All species are easily grown in free, loose soil, where they soon become established and form large clumps, bearing dozens of heads of flowers on strong stems. In very loose, moist soils, species may tend to overcrowd and become a nuisance, but most take a number of years to become established, and all can be easily controlled. They bloom freely from early to late summer.

A. aurantiaca is the most common and easily grown species, with heads of bright orange-yellow flowers spotted with maroon, freely produced on 1 m (3 ft) stems. A number of selected forms of this species are in cultivation, mostly with deep orange or bronzy orange flowers, the best known being 'Majestic' and 'Bronze Beauty'. An interesting form, raised in New Zealand and listed as 'Lutea', carries creamy yellow flowers tipped with pink. However, it is not the same as *A. aurantiaca* 'Lutea' offered in other countries and may be of hybrid origin.

A. hookeri. This is described as a dwarf-growing form of *A. ligtu*, but it is most likely a distinct species. The stems are only 22.5 cm (9 in.) high, carrying six to 12 large, soft pink flowers. It soon forms a neat clump with its attractive, greyish green foliage, and it is quite easy to grow provided drainage is good. It is not difficult to raise from seed.

A. ligtu was previously known as *A. chilensis*, but with the introduction of other strains we have a range of colours that have erroneously earned the name of 'Ligtu Hybrids'. The original colour was soft pink, spotted purple on the upper petals, but all shades from near white through to lighter and deeper pinks, salmon and orange-reds are now

in a light, sandy medium, where it soon forms a bold clump. The bulbs, which are 7.5 cm (3 in.) long and about 3 cm (1.5 in.) wide, are an interesting tango-orange shade when dormant during the winter months. The gladiolus-like leaves are heavily ribbed, also like the tigridias, and the thin, wiry stems, 1 m (3 ft) tall, slightly branched at the top, carry dozens of buds, which open up into glorious, china-blue, triangular flowers 7.5 cm (3 in.) across. Each bloom lasts one day only, but is replaced by another, day after day for several weeks. They are, therefore, not useful as cut flowers, but if planted in bold groups, the effect is most pleasing, the airy lightness and distinctive poise of the whole plant giving an effect that is quite arresting.

Increase is usually from seed, which germinates readily in the spring, blooming the second or third year, while mature bulbs multiply fairly quickly in light soil if undisturbed for two or three years. Transplant when dormant during winter and early spring. Bulbs should be lifted during the winter in colder districts.

Alstroemeria pulchella

found. From 10 to 30 lily-like flowers 5 cm (2 in.) wide and long are carried on 45–100 cm (18–40 in.) stems sparsely clothed with narrow, glaucous green leaves. Plants commence blooming in late spring and are most valuable for cutting. Although hardy and easily grown, they require a light, free soil or good drainage. The fleshy roots are dormant during autumn. Old roots resent disturbance once established, but stocks increase readily from seed, young yearling plants being the best for safe transplanting.

A. pelegrina. This lovely, little-known species has lilac-rose blooms splashed with purple. The flowers are quite large for a plant growing only 90 cm (36 in.) tall. This species, with its lovely, pure white form *A. pelegrina* 'Alba', is not at all difficult to grow when good sharp summer drainage is provided, but it will not stand heavy frosts and prefers semi-shade.

A. pulchella. This other well-known species is commonly called the parrot beak and is usually listed under the name of *A. psittacina*. It somewhat resembles in habit and bloom the *A. aurantiaca* group, except that the interesting flowers are dull rosy red tipped with green and with inner reddish

brown spots. It is also useful for cutting, and will grow and bloom freely from mid- to late summer, even in shade or woodland conditions, where it can be left undisturbed for years. The large, green seedpods are also very decorative.

A. violacea, also a desirable, little-known species, delights in loose, free soil in the semi-shade. The 45 cm (18 in.) stems carry 7.5 cm (3 in.), lilac-purple flowers in a five-rayed umbel on forked pedicels. A head of bloom resembles a spray of azalea in flower or a fine zonal pelargonium. A sheltered spot free from heavy winter frosts is essential for success.

A. 'Walter Fleming' is one of the few hybrids raised and is certainly an acquisition, having proved fairly hardy and easy to cultivate. It forms an erect-growing clump, otherwise similar in habit and growth to *A. aurantiaca*, which is obviously one of its parents. The 60–90 cm (24–36 in.) stems carry six to 12 wide-open, 7.5 cm (3 in.) flowers, ivory-white, winged, with smaller, bright yellow inner petals, these being streaked with chocolate and each petal tipped with lavender-mauve. The plant blooms in late spring and again in autumn if cut back, but odd heads will appear all summer until frosts begin. It is an excellent cut flower. Unfortunately, transplanting can be difficult and should be carried out when the plant is dormant, preferably in early spring. Much care should be exercised in breaking up the roots.

Alstroemeria 'Walter Fleming'

Another strain of attractive mixed colours is called 'Denver Hybrids'. These grow 30–40 cm (12–16 in.) high.

It is possible that a number of other little-known species are not grown because their requirements are not understood. Most alstroemerias come from areas where the seasons are well defined and the autumn is hot and dry. Some of these species are quite dormant throughout late summer and autumn, and the interesting fleshy roots, somewhat resembling bunches of white grapes, indicate a reserve supply against drought conditions. Such species resent rain or wet conditions during this resting period, and a premature starting into growth again results in a weakening of the plant.

Increase of alstroemerias is usually from divisions of older established clumps. This is best done in autumn soon after flowering; the new roots settle down before winter and bloom the following spring. Roots divided and replanted late or in winter, particularly in cold districts or in heavy ground, may become damaged and collapse. Fresh seed germinates freely, and plants bloom in the second season. When planting, the roots should be covered with about 5 cm (2 in.) of soil.

Althaea variety

ALTHAEA
Malvaceae Hollyhock

This is a genus of about 12 species, most of which are ornamental. *A. officinalis* is the common marsh mallow, a native of Europe and England, which grows wild in wet and boggy places. The 1–1.5 m (3–5 ft) long stems are clothed with soft, hairy leaves and numerous single, blush-pink flowers.

The species *A. rosea*, a native of Asia, grows to a height of 2 m (6.5 ft), with large pink flowers and roundish, rough foliage, and is the parent of our present-day hollyhocks. Both single-and double-flowered varieties are now available in a wide range of shades—white, cream, buff, pink, salmon, rose, scarlet, red and maroon—and these varieties reproduce true from seed. Seed should be sown in late spring or early autumn and plants set out before the winter so they can become well established before the spring growth, otherwise they may not bloom until the following summer. Old clumps or roots do not lend themselves to being divided up and resent disturbance.

As all these perennial, double-flowered varieties are tall growers, they are seen to best advantage as background material for a deep herbaceous border, against brick or rock walls, tall buildings or among low-growing shrubs. They can be grown successfully in almost any kind of soil, although, unlike their wild cousin the marsh mallow, they prefer reasonably good drainage and a position that tends to be dry.

The worst enemy to contend with is a brownish rust, which attacks the foliage, mostly of weak plants. Although this may not prevent blooming, the affected foliage is rather unsightly. Affected leaves are best removed and burnt, while the faded flower-spikes and stems should be cut off and destroyed, as the disease spores are carried over in the crown of the plant and if left will reinfect in the spring. A search for resistant or immune plants has so far met with no success. The safest way to retain a healthy stock is to raise fresh, young seedlings each season.

AMARYLLIS
Amaryllidaceae   Belladonna

The genus *Amaryllis* at one time included a number of bulbs such as crinum, habranthus, hippeastrum, lycoris, nerine, sprekelia, sternbergia, vallota and zephyranthes, all classed as different species of amaryllis. It is now considered that belladonna lilies, *A. belladonna*, are the only true amaryllis.

The old, common, pink form of *A. belladonna* is a delightful subject for naturalising, thriving in any open, well-drained space or even under large trees, as long as it is not too shady for the bulbs to ripen properly. The foliage is untouched by animals, so the plants readily adapt themselves to almost any position where heavy frosts do not occur. Permanent plantings can be made against fences, along drives, on poor, dry, sunny banks or in similar odd corners.

There are many desirable forms of belladonna besides the common pink and its taller variety 'Major', the colour of which is described as solferina-purple but is to most people deep pink. One of the best white-flowered varieties is known as 'Southern Cross'. The tall, white form 'Multiflora Alba' is a most desirable subject, producing 90 cm (36 in.) stems, with many white trumpets deepening to yellow in the throat. Another white form named 'Halthor' is larger and purer white, less reflexed and more trumpet- or lily-shaped, with a creamy throat. Corresponding deep pink forms of these taller-growing types are 'Multiflora Rosea', with cerise-red flowers and paler centres, and 'Rosea Superba', with its less-expanded trumpets, deepening or opening to almost wine-red when fully matured.

Amaryllis belladonna 'Multiflora Alba'

Another little-known variety is 'Mutabilis Rosea', with much-expanded and reflexed trumpets of a pleasing creamy salmon-rose shade. There is also a creamy white form of this variety. Many intermediate forms are found and these are no doubt seedlings raised from some of the above varieties.

Transplant bulbs when dormant in late summer and autumn. They should be partly buried with the necks protruding or half above the ground.

Amorphophallus rivieri

AMORPHOPHALLUS
Araceae   Devil's tongue

There is one species of this family that can be grown and will flower in warmer areas. The flower of *A. rivieri* comes up before the foliage, arum-like, to a height of 1 m (3 ft), with a spathe of blackish purple and a huge, tapering spadix to 50 cm (20 in.) long. A disagreeable odour is often emitted. The corms, which are quite dormant in winter and early spring, are used as a food crop in Indonesia and Japan. The foliage appears after flowering on a single, rose-marbelled stem, with three palm-like branches and numerous segments.

A. bulbifer has typical arum-like flowers in green, cream and pink on 30 cm (12 in.) stems. A rather similar plant belongs to the genus *Dracunculus* (q.v.).

ANAGALLIS
Primulaceae   Pimpernel

This genus includes annual weeds in both red and blue forms, but also *A. linifolia*, grown for its brilliant blue flowers of 1.5 cm (0.5 in.) diameter. This species requires a sunny, well-drained spot on a wall or rock garden. It can be propagated by seed or division in spring.

ANAPHALIS
Asteraceae   Everlasting

This genus of perennials from the alpine Himalayas grows well in colder areas. They do best in a sunny situation but should not be allowed to dry out. *A. triplinervis* var. *monocephala* is a low, tufted, grey-leaved plant, with heads of white flowers in late spring. If cut before they mature, flowers may be dried for winter decoration. Plants can be increased by division in winter or spring or by seed sown in autumn.

Anaphalis triplinervis var. *monocephala*

ANCHUSA
Boraginaceae   Forget-me-not

This genus consists of about 50 species, natives of Europe, North and South Africa, and western Asia. Most are annuals or biennials, with a few good, true perennials, which include strong, blue-flowered

Anchusa azurea 'Loddon Royalist'

plants that do not fade easily and are suitable for the herbaceous border.

A. azurea is the best-known species and is often listed as *A. italica*. The leaves are large, hairy and heavy, and the tall, much-branched flower-stems, attaining a height of 1 m (3 ft) or more, carry hundreds of loose forget-me-nots throughout summer and autumn. Although it offers nothing to commend it as a cut flower, nor are the individual blooms particularly attractive, the general effect is always pleasing, and the long flowering period is a decided advantage. This is a most variable species, and many selected forms, each of which produces plants reasonably true to type from seeds, have been isolated. One such is known as 'Royal Blue', with its abundance of deep gentian-blue flowers. 'Opal' is a very pretty, light blue form. A variety called 'Morning Glory' gives us a rich shade of lobelia blue, and 'Pride of Dover' is light azure-blue. Probably the best of all forms is 'Loddon Royalist', with the flowers set together more closely, providing a brilliant display. All these forms continue in bloom from spring until mid-summer, or even later if the older spikes are cut off as soon as they begin to fade, thus encouraging new side shoots and spikes to appear.

A. caespitosa is the most important introduction to this genus in recent years. There is considerable doubt as to whether the plant now in cultivation under this name has been named correctly, as it attains larger proportions than this species does in its native habitat. The form introduced makes a bushy plant up to 45 cm (18 in.) high, carrying masses of brilliant blue flowers, each centred with a white eye. The flowering period extends from spring well into summer, and it is therefore one of the most valuable blue-flowered, hardy perennials for the herbaceous border.

A. capensis, from South Africa, is not always perennial. It flowers in panicles of rich blue flowers only 45 cm (18 in.) high in mid-summer.

All species of anchusa can be easily increased from seed, blooming the first season; divisions or root cuttings will also readily establish themselves. All are easily grown in full sun in well-drained soil. With the taller *A. azurea* types, heavy soils often cause the roots to collapse. Transplant when dormant in winter.

ANEMONE
Ranunculaceae

The genus consists of about 70 species of flowering perennials, many with tuberous or rhizomatous rootstocks. Most species prefer well-drained soil and are happy in either sun or partial shade.

A. apennina is the wild Italian form of the woodland anemone. The soft, tender green, deeply cut foliage is always attractive, and the plants look really at home in the shade of big trees, or naturalised in open woodlands. The starry, single flowers, carried just above the foliage in spring, are usually in shades of pale and deeper blue, while pure white, lavender and pink forms do exist. They are slower to increase by division than other similar species but seed quite freely when really happy. They form a hard, thick rhizome, almost tuberous. This species, like *A. blanda* and *A. nemorosa*, will grow in dense shade, without any sun whatever, and should be only just covered with soil when planted.

A. blanda is a native of Greece and closely allied to *A. apennina*, both differing from the true woodland anemones in having hard, tuberous roots instead of the long, slender, brittle, creeping rhizomes so characteristic of *A. nemorosa* and its relations. This species, therefore, does not spread by root increase

into large masses, but under suitable conditions seeds freely, and if naturalised under trees, in shady, moist spots, the colony will enlarge, provided that the gardener is not too tidy, destroying the tiny seedlings while cleaning up around the larger plants. The single, starry, blue or pale blue flowers appear in the early spring, along with the winter aconites and snowdrops. A deep violet-blue variety called *A. blanda* 'Atrocoerulea' and a clear pink form, *A. blanda* 'Rosea', are desirable variations, while 'White Splendour' is a selected white form. A batch of seedlings will give all these shades as well as intermediate lilacs and reddish purples. Transplant during late autumn, setting the roots just below the surface of the soil.

A. coronaria is a spring-flowering perennial introduced to England from the Middle East in 1596. It grows to 25 cm (10 in.), with much-divided leaves and single, poppy-like flowers in red, pink, purple and blue. The brightly coloured, tuberous-rooted strains of this species are well known and commonly grown. The semi-double St Brigid strain has now become popular worldwide. The brilliant and varied colours include rose, mauve, purple, crimson, scarlet, deep and light blues, and all intermediate shades. Several selected types have been isolated and bred comparatively true from seed, the most popular being 'The Governor', with its brilliant scarlet flowers with conspicuous white centre. A strain of rosy lavender and rosy lilac shades is called 'The

Anemone blanda, white form

Admiral', while a mixture of rich blues is named 'Lord Lieutenant'. In Australia these three types are grown under the names 'Beacon', 'Amethyst Beauty' and 'Blue Admiral' respectively. The De Caen strain has single flowers in the same range of colours as the species. They are splendid for cut flowers and commercial growing. The best known and most popular variety is 'Scarlet Emperor' (syn. 'Hollandia', 'His Excellency'). A lovely giant-flowered blue is called 'Blue Bonnet' (syn. 'Mr Fokker'). 'Lilac Beauty' (syn. 'Sylphide') has rosy lilac flowers, and a most desirable pure white variety called 'The Bride' is valuable for floristry. For most general purposes and massed beds or borders, the mixed colours in either the single or semi-double strains are of great value.

To produce early blooms, it is essential to have tubers that have been harvested the previous year. They need a full six months' rest so they will start quickly into root action and grow rapidly. Tubers that have not had sufficient rest are very slow and variable in their growth. If kept in a cool, dry, airy spot in shallow containers, tubers will remain viable for two or sometimes three years.

Tuberous anemones will grow in any good, well-drained garden soil, but a mixture of decayed turf or compost with a little blood and bone and super-phosphate will give excellent results. Tubers are usually planted 15–30 cm (6-12 in.) apart and 5 cm (2 in.) deep. Do not retain tubers after the first year, because some will have become weakened through heavy blooming, thus becoming easy prey to rust and other foliage or fungoid diseases. Weekly applications of liquid manure when plants are coming into bud will greatly increase the size of the blooms and the length of stems.

A. x *fulgens*. This delightful winter- or early spring-flowering plant comes from Crete and is among the most brilliant of all flowers. In fact, a mass of blooms in a bowl or pocket of the rockery is almost painfully dazzling. The selected forms are grown from divisions of tubers, which when lifted resemble clusters of chocolate raisins. The best is probably the single-flowered form 'Annulata Grandiflora', with broad-petalled, vivid scarlet flowers with light yellow centres. The most prolific is 'Multipetala', a semi-double, finely petalled form very suitable for cutting. A double-flowered variety is also grown but is seldom available. Tubers can

also be raised from seed, blooming the second year, but poor or muddy forms usually occur. This is because *A.* x *fulgens* is not a true species but a natural hybrid between *A. pavonina* and *A. hortensis*.

A. x *fulgens* and all the selected forms are true perennials, coming up year after year if the situation is to their liking. Perfect drainage is essential, and the presence of lime is beneficial. A good, hot baking in the summer seems to help, but it is not necessary if the soil is light and the drainage is good. It is possible to naturalise tubers in lawns and grassy fields, where the brilliant scarlet blooms are seen at their best against a background of rich green. Try planting some in the rockery, in raised containers, and others at the foot on the sunny side of big deciduous trees. Many bulbs do well in this position, where drainage is always good, with no risk of wet feet in the summer. Plant 15 cm (6 in.) apart and 5 cm (2 in.) deep.

A. hupehensis has dark green, deeply divided leaves. The variety 'Splendens' is single-flowered and seldom exceeds 90 cm (36 in.) in height. It is compact in habit, with masses of deep rosy red blooms about 7.5 cm (3 in.) across in late summer and autumn. There are other selected forms of this species that are well worth growing, including 'September Charm'.

A. x *hybrida* (syn. *A. japonica*), the Japanese anemones, are hybrids between two species, one

Anemone x *hybrida*

being *A. hupehensis*. They have leathery foliage, dark on the surface and light green on the underside. The flower-stems, usually 60–90 cm (24–36 in.) tall, grow straight and erect from the centre of the plant, and bear many large, saucer-shaped flowers with a central cluster of yellow stamens in late summer and early autumn. Several double white, pink and rose forms exist. While admirably adapted to semi-shady conditions, woodlands or wild gardens, where they become firmly established and bloom freely each year, they are nevertheless quite at home in full sun in the herbaceous border and adapt themselves to almost any position. Some of the best varieties are:

'Bressingham Glow'—semi-double, ruby rose.
'Louise Uhink'—best semi-double, white.
'Margeurite'—full double, rosy pink.
'Max Vogel'—semi-double, clear pink.
'Prince Henry'—semi-double, rich claret-red.
'Richard Ahrens'—lilac-pink, soft pink inside.
'Snow Queen' or 'Whirlwind'—semi-double, white.
'Stuttgardia'—semi-double, rosy red, large blooms.

A. nemorosa is known as the woodland anemone of England. While somewhat resembling *A. blanda* and *A. apennina* in flower, it is quite distinct in foliage, and is easier to grow in warmer districts, thriving almost anywhere in shady, not-too-dry spots. The single, six-petalled flowers, which appear in late spring and early summer, are usually in shades of light and bright blue. Single- and double-flowered, white forms are also quite common. The wild, native form is usually white, slightly tinged with pink. When really happy, these lovely wild anemones increase and spread quite rapidly, eventually carpeting the undergrowth. The long, thin roots, which are brittle and easily damaged, should not be out of the ground longer than absolutely necessary, as they dry out quickly. They should be planted about 7.5 cm (3 in.) deep, and prefer a top-dressing each winter of decayed leaf mould. Transplant during autumn.

A. pulsatilla (syn. *Pulsatilla vulgaris*), the pasque flower, is one of the first of the perennials to bloom in the spring. Numerous cup-shaped flowers, described as bishop-violet, on 25–30 cm (10–12 in.), hairy stems, appear from the rootstock in early spring, before the attractive, fern-like foliage appears. This species is most variable, and several

Anemone pulsatilla

deeper-coloured forms exist, such as *A. pulsatilla* 'Rubra', with its ruby-red flowers. Soft pink and nearly red forms are now also offered, the best of which is named 'Red Clock'. This lovely species, when full grown and planted in bold groups, never fails to attract attention and favourable comment. The interesting seed-heads that follow are like balls of silken hairs. They remain on the plant for a long period and are useful for decorative purposes. Although easily grown in most places, *A. pulsatilla* and its forms love cool growing conditions, and require a semi-shady, moist spot in warm coastal districts. Plants can be increased from seed, but divisions or root cuttings should be taken from special colours.

A. vitifolia somewhat resembles the *A.* x *hybrida* and *A. hupehensis* varieties, though perhaps taller growing, with large, downy foliage and single, bowl-shaped blooms 7.5–10 cm (3–4 in.) across. A selected form, called 'Robustissima', is still more vigorous, with lovely orchid-pink blooms and a deeper shade of pink on the reverse of the petals. This species, like the *A.* x *hybrida* varieties, is easily increased by divisions of older established clumps during winter months, or larger quantities can be secured by taking pieces of roots 5–7.5 cm (2–3 in.) long and inserting them in boxes of sand until leaves appear on the tips. These smaller plants can be shifted out in the spring and will bloom just before winter.

ANIGOZANTHOS
Haemodoraceae   Kangaroo paw

There are approximately 10 species of these colourful and unique plants from Western Australia. Here they grow freely in the coastal bushlands and open areas, and seem to do best in rather poor, rubbly soil or broken shale rock. Plants are evergreen and do not die down in the winter, but a hot, dry autumn will toughen up the foliage and enable the plant to resist frosts.

A. flavidus is the best-known species and the easiest to grow. It is usually raised from seed, soon forming large, iris-like clumps, which develop until they are 30 cm (12 in.) or more across, with numerous, long, grassy or sword-like leaves. Later, stems 1.5 m (5 ft) high appear, with side branches carrying dozens of 7.5 cm (3 in.), bent, tubular, greenish yellow flowers tinged with red on the upper part of the tube. The flowers have a most uncommon,

Anigozanthos flavidus

woolly appearance and are long-lasting when cut. This is rather a variable species, and as it is apparently more easily grown than others, selected forms should be increased by division of roots. An equally vigorous form, with velvety, brownish red flowers, has been given the name of 'Rubra'. *A. flavidus* will grow quite happily on heavy soils. It has also been seen established successfully on banks of peaty drains, which seems to indicate that acid or peaty conditions are preferable. It will resist the black-leaf disease that affects most plants in wet climates, and can withstand up to 14 degrees of frost.

A. manglesii is the loveliest of all kangaroo paws. The 90 cm (36 in.) flower-stems are clothed with persistent velvety crimson down, and the 10 cm (4 in.) long, tubular flowers are vivid green with reddish tips. It is happy only in well-drained soil, preferably dry from late spring till winter. A wet summer can result in black leaf spot disease, which often destroys the plant. This species will withstand medium frosts only.

A. pulcherrimus grows to 80 cm (32 in.), with branched sprays of yellow flowers. It will grow well in average to light, well-drained soil in a sunny position free from weeds.

A. rufus grows to 45 cm (18 in.), with bronzy red flowers. It requires a gravelly, sandy soil and is difficult to maintain where rainfall is high.

Three hybrids—'Dwarf Delight', 50 cm (20 in.), bright flame colour; 'Joey Paws', 30 cm (12 in.), a miniature with pale green flowers on red stems; 'Red Glow', 1.8 m (6 ft), branching habit, dark maroon flowers—became available in the early 1980s, but they have largely been superseded by a hybrid group called 'Bush Gems'. These plants have been raised by tissue culture and tend to flower with shorter stems in their first summer. All are free-flowering, with numerous flower-stems on each plant. The best of the new varieties are very resistant to the fungus that causes black blotches on the foliage.

'Bush Baby'—50 cm (20 in.) tall, pale orange flowers with burgundy tips in spring/summer, old flowers retain colour; good container plant.
'Bush Dawn'—1.5–2 m (5–6.5 ft) tall, bright yellow flowers in summer, long flowering season; good cut flower.
'Bush Emerald'—75 cm (30 in.) tall, red stem and

Anigozanthos 'Bush Sunset'

ovary, emerald green perianth in winter and spring; good cut flower.

'Bush Glow'—75 cm (30 in.) tall, bronzy red and orange flowers in spring/summer, long flowering season.

'Bush Haze'—1.5–2 m (5–6.5 ft) tall, red stem and ovary, yellow flowers in summer; good cut flower and specimen plant.

'Bush Noon'—1.5–2 m (5–6.5 ft) tall, bronze stem, orange flowers in summer; good cut flower and specimen plant.

'Bush Nugget'—50–80 cm (20–32 in.) tall, branched, reddish stems, yellow flowers in summer; good cut flower and specimen plant.

'Bush Opal'—50 cm (20 in.) tall, branched, red stem and ovary, yellow-green flowers in winter/spring; good container plant.

'Bush Ranger'—50 cm (20 in.) tall, branched, bright red flowers in spring/summer, old flowers hold colour well.

'Bush Ruby'—1.5–2 m (5–6.5 ft) tall, rich, deep burgundy flowers in late spring/summer; good cut flower and specimen plant.

'Bush Sunset'—1.5–2 m (5–6.5 ft) tall, deep bright red flowers in late spring/summer; good cut flower and specimen plant.

ANTHEMIS
Asteraceae   Chamomile

There are about 200 species of *Anthemis*, very hardy, sturdy and easily grown, but few of them are of any value in the garden. They have finely cut foliage and bear masses of daisy-like, white or yellow flowers from summer until the first frosts.

A. cupaniana grows into a spreading mound of silvery foliage about 30 cm (12 in.) high, with white daisies throughout the summer.

A. nobilis 'Treneague' is the non-flowering form of chamomile that can be used as a lawn. It seldom requires mowing.

A. sancti-johannis is another species of interest. This much-branched, spreading plant, growing to a height of 50 cm (20 in.), gives us 5 cm (2 in.), solitary-headed flowers with rays of intense aureolin-orange and bracts of green, margined brown-black. The leaves are covered with shaggy grey hairs. Transplant freely during winter and spring.

A. tinctoria is the best-known and most-used species, the common type developing into a bushy plant 60 cm (24 in.) high and wide, covered in late spring and summer with 7.5 cm (3 in.) wide, creamy white, single daisies. Several distinctive forms have been named: 'Beauty of Grallagh', with its deep yellow flowers, larger than the type, is one of the best, while 'Grallagh Gold' is a bright yellow counterpart. Another earlier introduction called 'Mrs E. C. Buxton' has lemon-yellow flowers and is

Anthemis tinctoria 'Grallagh Gold'

well worth growing. All forms of *A. tinctoria* are easily grown in the poorest sandy or clay soils, even resisting hot, dry conditions. They are strong growers, and need constant cutting back and breaking up into smaller clumps each season. All are easily raised from cuttings or divisions, and should be transplanted during winter and early spring.

ANTHERICUM
Liliaceae

This genus consists of about 50 species, natives of Europe, America and sub-tropical Africa.

A. algeriense is similar to the more common *A. liliago*. It has grassy, grey-green leaves and erect stems with small, white, starry flowers with yellow stamens.

A. liliago, the common type, produces a rosette of narrow, kniphofia-like leaves and central, smooth, erect stems about 60 cm (24 in.) tall. These carry six to 12 starry, 5 cm (2 in.) wide flowers, almost transparent white with a delicate green spot on each of the five petals. The slightly superior form usually cultivated is called *A. liliago* 'Major'.

A. ramosum is a smaller plant growing 30–45 cm (12–18 in.) tall. It carries spikes of dainty, white flowers, and is best grown in groups of a dozen of more in light, sandy soil. Plants can be grown from seed.

The anthericums are completely hardy and easily grown in a open situation with free soil. The short rhizomes are thickly fibrous and are best divided in spring.

Anthericum algeriense

ANTHOLYZA
Iridaceae

A number of species once listed under this genus have now been assigned to other genera, and there is now only one species that correctly belongs—the little-known, solitary but interesting *A. ringens*. The dark green, heavily ribbed leaves, stiff and erect, are only 15 cm (6 in.) high, and the equally rigid flower-spike, carrying eight to 12 bright red, freesia-like flowers with a greenish lower lip, appears just a bit taller. This flower-spike terminates in a rigid, naked point without any bloom. This is said to have developed as a bird rest; the flowers are nectar-bearing, and the birds need this rest for pollinating the flowers. This species needs a sunny position, not too dry; otherwise it is easily grown. Corms are dormant in late autumn and should be planted out before winter, about 7.5 cm (3 in.) deep and 15–20 cm (6–8 in.) apart.

Antholyza ringens

AQUILEGIA
Ranunculaceae   Columbine

This is a genus of about 100 species of perennials with fibrous roots, distributed over temperate and mountain regions of the Northern Hemisphere. All species are hardy, many being very graceful, with fern-like foliage and attractive flowers. Some of the alpine species are delightful subjects for the rock garden, preferring a well-drained scree of shingly soil. They all seed freely and are easily increased this way. In fact, there is no other genus of plants in which the species intercross so freely, so it is difficult to maintain true stocks unless plants are more or less isolated.

Most gardeners know the various strains of *A. vulgaris* as the common columbine or granny's bonnet. This species is a most variable one, and many strains have been developed, including the different long-spurred aquilegias, double-flowered strains, and even selected colour series, which come reasonably true to type from seed. In the long-spurred strains, usually called 'Scott-Elliott's Hybrids', separate mixtures of blues, pinks, reds and coppery shades can be secured. A lovely variety called 'Crimson Star' gives us brilliant, velvety, crimson flowers with contrasting, central, white cups. A good strain of mixed, long-spurred hybrids will give a very wide range of colours and shades as well as two-toned combinations. Varieties and hybrids of *A. vulgaris* thrive particularly well in the shade. Plants should be set out in the spring or early autumn so as to secure good blooms the following spring.

Another improved strain, which embraces a very wide range of pastel shades and bi-colours, all with larger individual blooms, is called 'McKana Hybrids'. Still another strain with interesting, semi-double flowers is called 'Beidermeir'. The colours include rose, cream, blue and violet shades, and the blooms are shorter spaced. Both these strains are lower growing and the flower-stems are more branched than those of the usual long-spurred forms.

A. 'Nora Barlow' is a curiously attractive form with heads of fully double flowers in which red, pink and green are intermingled.

Some of the better wild species are worthy of mention, and plants or seed should be secured if and when available.

A. alpina grows only 30 cm (12 in.) tall, with sheaves of big, powdery blue and white, nodding flowers on leafless stems. The variety described as 'Hensoll Harebell' appears to be a very good form of *A. alpina*.

Aquilegia longissima

A. caerulea is a good blue-flowered species that is taller growing than *A. alpina*. The wide-open petals are in varying shades of light and bright blue, with contrasting white or creamy white central cups. It is also long-spurred, and grows about 50 cm (20 in.) high.

A. clematiflora is a spurless species, or possibly a strain, with spreading perianths of starry appearance. The colours are mostly in shades of pink and blue. Plants usually grow 1 m (3 ft) high and are quite attractive and distinctive in bloom.

A. longissima is the species with the longest spur. The blooms are canary yellow, sometimes shaded with rose, and are held gracefully on branching stems, displaying to advantage the 10 cm (4 in.), prominent spurs. The species has, no doubt, been used by hybridists in producing the various long-spurred strains offered today.

A. pyrenaica from the Pyrenees grows 10–30 cm (4–12 in.) tall, with small, lobed leaflets, and bright blue flowers in spring and summer.

Aquilegia pyrenaica

An interesting species called *A. skinneri* grows about 60 cm (24 in.) high, with glaucous foliage, the bell-like flowers being greenish orange, the sepals green, and the spurs bright red. It is quite an interesting summer- and autumn-blooming species.

All species or strains of aquilegia are easily raised from seed, which should be sown in the autumn or spring. Plants should be set out in ample time to become well established before the winter, otherwise they will not bloom the following spring or summer. The larger the clumps, the bigger the display the following season. Old plants do not readily divide up for transplanting, so a fresh stock of seedling plants should be raised now and again to replenish beds.

ARCTOTIS
Asteraceae

This is a genus of about 60 species from South Africa, closely allied to the venidiums. Considered half-hardy plants, they withstand much more frost and cold in dry, sunny or well-drained positions. In Europe they are usually grown as annuals, and even in warmer climates most species and varieties are comparatively short-lived, so fresh stock should be constantly raised from seed or cuttings. As most of them are semi-trailing in habit, they need to be

trimmed every six to 12 months. Some of the species are almost stemless, others grow into low-branching shrubs, but all produce large, open, daisy-like flowers somewhat resembling gazanias, mostly in shades of orange, yellow, pink or crimson.

A. calendulacea, now known as *Arctotheca calendula*, provides a very pleasing woolly foliage and variously coloured flowers, the best form being an orpiment-orange with a black centre.

A. revoluta is an attractive, spreading plant up to 60 cm (2 ft) across, with fine, grey foliage and cadmium-orange flowers produced from spring until late summer.

A. scapigera 'Hybrids', sometimes wrongly called *A. acaulis*, are really the result of crossings with various species. The true *A. acaulis* produces bright red flowers, sometimes yellow. Doubtless the pink-flowered, greyish-foliaged species *A. stoechadifolia* has had a major part in the production of the present-day hybrids, but several other species also show their influence. The best of these newer hybrids produce a wide range of colours, from white through lemon, yellow and bronzy red to lavenders and deep purples as well as pinks and rosy shades. These hybrids mostly display an attractive zone of a much deeper shade in the centre of the bloom, while others are enhanced by a different colour on the reverse of the petals. The solitary blooms, often 10–12.5 cm (4–5 in.) across on 25–30 cm (10–12 in.) stems, are freely produced throughout spring and summer and last a few days in good condition as cut flowers. Plants will continue in flower longer if the faded blooms or seed-heads are constantly removed.

Increase is best from seed if a good strain is

Arctotis 'Dreamcoat'

obtainable, but selected types or colours are quite easily raised from cuttings taken in the autumn or spring. In old, established plants it will be found that the stems near the base of the plant have already taken root, and these can be removed and shortened back for replanting. If sandy soil is sieved or scattered over the base of the plant, this will encourage the layering naturally. Plants can be set out almost any time of the year, although spring planting is the best in cold districts.

ARGYRANTHEMUM
Asteraceae

The genus *Argyranthemum* consists of 22 species of small shrubs or sub-shrubs, one of which is commonly included in the herbaceous border.

Argyranthemum frutescens, previously *Chrysanthemum frutescens*, the shrubby tree marguerite or Paris daisy, is an easily grown plant, particularly valuable for late autumn, winter and spring blooming, when frosts are not so severe as to damage the flowers. If plants are kept well pruned, blooms can be secured at any time of the year. The old single-flowered species, with large white flowers with yellow-brown centres, is a variety called 'Grandiflora', while a lemon-yellow-flowered form is known as 'Etoile d'Or'. Numerous forms have arisen, many with double or anemone-centred flowers in white, pink and yellow. 'Mary Wootton' is an excellent, pale pink double; 'Powder Puff' is a dwarf-growing, double pink'; 'Snowball' is taller, with attractive, fine foliage and double, white flowers; 'Twink' is very small and covered with little, single daisies, very attractive; 'Weymouth Pink' is the best single pink; and 'Crimson Pom Pom' is the best deep red. The first available double white introduced was called 'Mrs Sanders', while a small, full double-flowered variety with miniature blooms only 2.5 cm (1 in.) across is known as 'Snowflake'.

It appears that, apart from the single-flowered forms and the earlier-produced double whites, these most attractive, New Zealand-raised, coloured varieties have not as yet found their way to other parts of the world. There is little doubt that they would prove immensely popular, especially where they could be grown outside, as in California,

Argyranthemum frutescens 'Etoile d'Or'

Argyranthemum frutescens, single white

Australia, South Africa, and the warmer European countries. As pot plants they are most useful, and can be timed to bloom at any time of the year, even during the cold winter months. As cut flowers, all varieties have proved most valuable, and large quantities are grown in the southern parts of New Zealand for winter and spring blooms.

Plants are easily raised from soft, green cuttings, 7.5–15 cm (3–6 in.) long, taken almost any time of the year. Plants commence blooming in about six months.

ARISAEMA
Araceae

These are tuberous-rooted perennials from Asia and Africa, resembling the arum lily but with hooded spathes.

Arisaema candidissimum

A. candidissimum grows to 45 cm (18 in.), with white spathes sometimes striped with pink produced in mid-summer.

A. griffithii, from the Himalayas, flowers in early summer, with large, mottled brown and green spathes.

A. jacquemontii comes from Afghanistan and the Himalayas, and flowers in early summer with a green spathe.

Arisaema sikokianum

A. praecox is a small woodland species with striped, hooded flowers resembling small, brown otters, appearing in spring.

A. ringens, from China and Korea, commonly known as the cobra lily, grows 25–30 cm (10–12 in.) tall, with two erect, three-lobed leaves. In spring it produces hooded, green spathes with pale green stripes and edged with dark brown. As plants mature, they change sex from male to female.

A. sikokianum, from Japan, has five-lobed leaves and a brown spathe and large, blunt, club-shaped spadix. It flowers in late spring/summer.

These species are fairly hardy, but require a moist, shaded position. They can be propagated by seed sown in the autumn or spring or by offsets planted in spring. They die down in summer, when the tubers can be transplanted.

Arisarum proboscidium

ARISARUM
Araceae

This genus of tuberous perennials from the Mediterranean region has distinctive and unusual, hooded spathes.

A. proboscidium, popularly called the mouse plant, grows to 10 cm (4 in.), with arrow-shaped leaves. In late winter and spring, it produces long-tailed, hooded flowers with dark brown spathes.

A. vulgare also flowers in winter and spring, with small, striped, hooded brown spathes.

Propagation is by division of an established clump of tubers in autumn.

ARISTEA
Iridaceae   Blue brilliant

The aristeas are South African, fibrous-rooted plants with heavy, broad, iris-like foliage growing erectly 60–90 cm (24–36 in.) and correspondingly stiff flower-stems branching just above the foliage. Iris-like flowers of the loveliest bright sky-blue are produced over a long period. More than a century ago it was written that 'its profuse sky-blue flowers, the purest that ever fed on dew, open early in the morning and are gone before night, the next morning bringing a new offering of beauty.' All these species close their flowers in mid-afternoon.

A. cyanea is a dwarf with many 15 cm (6 in.) stems of the same vivid-blue spikes.

A. ecklonii grows to only 60 cm (24 in.), with similar foliage and numerous branching spikes of gentian-blue flowers

A. thyrsiflora (syn. *A. major*) now includes *A. capitata*, which is almost indistinguishable, although it has a more branching flower-spike. It has iris-like, evergreen foliage and erect flower-spikes to 1.8 m (6 ft). The flowers are vivid blue. Increase is best from seed, if available, as they are all easily raised; smaller seedling plants seem to transplant more readily in winter than older, divided clumps. The older roots seem to lack vigorous fibrous roots, and plants may collapse after shifting before new roots are formed. Little trouble is experienced, however, in light, free soils if they are firmly planted. Aristeas are apparently only half-hardy and are better grown as a pot plant in very cold districts.

ARMERIA
Plumbaginaceae   Thrift

The genus *Armeria* consists of over 50 species, mainly tufted perennials from Europe, Asia and North Africa. Many of the species are similar in

Aristea ecklonii

appearance, and much confusion still exists in their identification. These are very hardy, easily grown perennials, particularly suitable for light, free soils and resisting drought, salt spray and similar adverse conditions. The dwarf or pygmy forms, in both pink and white, are eminently suitable as edgings for herbaceous borders or formal gardens, producing neat, compact clumps and hundreds of round heads of small, pincushion-like flowers. The taller-growing forms provide a wealth of bloom throughout spring and summer, and the thin, wiry stems, often up to 40 cm (16 in.) in length, lend themselves to household decoration. Like many other plants that produce a tight cluster of basal leaves and stems, forming compact clumps, they resent wet conditions or heavy soils. Under such conditions, moisture lies in the clumps and causes them to rot, and such plants should be broken up or divided every second year.

A. maritima is the species commonly called the sea thrift, and perhaps one of the best of the old cottage-garden plants. It is also a variable species, ranging from white to rose, deep pink and crimson-rose, but the most common form is a purplish rose. Flower-stems are usually 15–30 cm (6–12 in.) high.

Dwarf, tufted varieties are often used for rockeries or edgings to flower borders. There are also some very fine miniature alpine varieties that are most desirable for the rock garden. One of the best of

Armeria pseudarmeria 'Snowball'

these is 'Vindictive', which has masses of reddish pink flowers. 'Bloodstone' is an excellent, compact grower to 10 cm (4 in.), with deep pink flowers.

A. pseudarmeria (syn. *A. latifolia*), is perhaps the tallest-growing and most popular armeria. It is a most variable species, ranging from pure white through pale pink, deep rose to fuchsia-purple. One of the best selected forms is known as 'Bees Ruby', with its 40 cm (16 in.) stems and terminal balls of ruby-red flowers, blooming from spring through to autumn. Another good form is called 'Glory of Holland', in which the flower-heads are a silvery pink, and which has a similarly long flowering period. A vigorous and large-flowered, pure-white form with strong, 45 cm (18 in.) stems is called 'Snowball', and is one of the best around.

Plants are readily increased from pulled-off cuttings taken in the autumn. When rooted, these can be planted out during winter or spring. Seed is easily raised but usually gives a mixture of forms and shades.

ARTEMISIA
Asteraceae

This is a large genus of aromatic plants and herbs, mostly from arid regions in the Northern Hemisphere. Valuable drugs are procured from some of the species.

A. absinthium 'Lambrook Silver', with its silvery white, feathery, strongly aromatic foliage and small, yellow flowers in globose heads, is most effective among the herbaceous border. *A. arborescens* is another excellent foliage species, with densely crowded, silvery grey foliage and growing 1 m (3 ft) tall and across.

A. lactiflora is the species most commonly grown here. It is a tall-growing, attractive Chinese species, which grows like a Michaelmas daisy or solidago, 1 m (3 ft) or more high, with many-branched heads of tiny, pale, milky white flowers in elegant panicles and with axillary side shoots, blooming in late summer. This plant is useful for associating with brilliant-coloured perennials and for separating the difficult shades of reds and crimsons, purples and pinks, providing a suitable counterfoil. The foliage is fern-like and aromatic.

A. ludoviciana (syn. *A. purshiana*) has willow-like foliage on 80 cm (32 in.) stems, very silvery and effective for months, but with insignificant flowers in late summer. It does best in poor soils.

Artemisia pycnocephala

A. 'Mori's Variety' forms a low carpet of silvery, fern-like leaves but has insignificant flowers. It is deciduous and grows best in full sun with good drainage.

A. 'Powis Castle' forms a broad, low, evergreen shrub with finely divided, silver-grey leaves, which are strongly scented. It is a hybrid of recent introduction and makes a fine border plant, growing 60 cm (24 in.) tall and 1 m (3 ft) wide.

A. pycnocephala (sometimes incorrectly referred to as *A. frigida*) is an aromatic perennial with woody rootstock, erect shoots of silky-hairy leaves to 40 cm (16 in.), and insignificant, yellow flowers.

A. 'Valerie Finnis' has upright stems of broad, white leaves, making a good clump for a mid-border position.

All artemisias are hardy and easily increased from divisions. They should be transplanted during winter.

ARTHROPODIUM
Liliaceae   Reinga lily

The genus comprises eight species, two of which are natives of New Zealand, the most attractive and best known being *A. cirratum*.

This is a fairly hardy plant, admirably adapted for growing under the shade of big deciduous trees, and with such protection should be able to stand quite cold winters. It will also grow in the open and requires no special attention, resisting dry and hard conditions.

It soon forms a neat, tufted, 60 cm (24 in.) clump, well furnished with single, light green, soft, flax-like leaves, which remain constant, not dying down in the winter. From a well-established clump, numerous thin, wiry, much-branched panicles appear in late spring, carrying hundreds of 2.5 cm (1 in.), starry, white flowers, tinted heliotrope with conspicuous yellow stamens. The flower-stems last quite well as cut flowers, and are very dainty and serviceable for most forms of decoration.

Increase can be made from seeds, which germinate freely, or from division of older clumps. It can be transplanted at almost any time of the year, but does not bloom until clumps are large and well established.

Arthropodium cirratum

A. milleflorum, the pale vanilla lily, has green or greyish foliage forming a grassy tuft to 50 cm (20 in.). It is fairly hardy, withstanding heavy frosts, but prefers a moist, well-drained soil and a position in full sun. In spring and summer it has small, white to mauve, vanilla-scented flowers.

A. minus, the small vanilla lily, is similar to *A. milleflorum* but grows to 30 cm (12 in.). It produces single, purple flowers in spring.

ARUM
Araceae

None of the well-known arum lilies are really arums at all. They are often called callas, but there is, in fact, only one species of calla in existence, and this is a floating water plant, not like a lily at all. Nor are they called richardias, as botanists have decided that this name, proposed by Kunth in 1818, cannot stand, as it had already been used for a genus of Rubiaceae. The correct generic name for the common white arum lily, as well as the yellow, pink and intermediate shades, is *Zantedeschia*.

The true arums are dormant in the summer, coming into growth early in autumn and blooming in the spring. About 15 species are known, all hardy and easily managed. They all form tubers and delight, during the growing season, in a rich, moist soil, yielding an interesting display of purple, yellow-green or spotted flowers.

The best-known species, commonly called lords and ladies, and often seen naturalised under trees or in grassy fields near old homesteads, is known as *A. italicum*. This plant bears rich green leaves, sometimes spotted purple, accompanied by greenish white, lily-like spathes and blades, also spotted purple. The flowers are followed by showy, scarlet, torch-like seed-heads, which colour after the leaves have fallen. It is not grown in gardens, as it is inclined to spread rapidly. The seeds are said to be poisonous.

The best-known garden species, generally listed as *A. sanctum* but correctly *A. palaestinum*, has bell-shaped spathes on 30 cm (12 in.) stems, and a 15–20 cm (6–8 in.) long spadix of dark purple or velvety black. Unlike some species that carry an offensive odour, this one is without perfume, and is hardy anywhere good drainage is provided.

Increase is from natural divisions of the larger tubers, and also from small offsets that form around the parent ones. Plant out from late summer to early autumn, setting roots 10–15 cm (4–6 in.) deep and 25–30 cm (10–12 in.) apart.

See also *Dracunculus* and *Amorphophallus*.

ARUNCUS
Rosaceae   Goat's beard

This genus is now separated from the spiraeas, and about 12 species are recorded, *A. dioicus* (syn. *A. sylvester*) being the best of them all. Its foliage, habit

Aruncus dioicus

and bloom resemble the astilbes, although the plant is stronger and even more imposing, blooming earlier in the spring. Established clumps produce an abundance of rich green, fern-like foliage, topped with immense, arching plumes of silky, creamy white flowers. A delightful form of this species, with beautifully incised foliage, lacy or almost thread-like, is called *A. dioicus* 'Kneiffii'. It is less robust, the drooping, creamy white flower-spikes seldom exceeding 75 cm (30 in.). The plant is most impressive even when not in bloom.

The aruncus are deservedly popular in England, where they are freely planted in woodland conditions, a setting where they can be seen to perfection. They revel in a rich, moist, deep soil, or conditions that suit the astilbes, preferably semi-shade. Increase is slow from seed or the division of the very hard rootstock during winter or early spring.

Asclepias tuberosa

ASCLEPIAS
Asclepiadaceae   Butterfly bush

Although there are over 100 shrubby, perennial and annual species, we will deal here with only the most outstanding.

A. pulchra, sometimes described as *A. incarnata* subsp. *pulchra*, is a hardy species useful for the herbaceous border. The flower-stems, which are covered with hairy down, are about 1 m (3 ft) high and carry crowded umbels of magnolia-purple flowers. If raised from seed, some interesting colours occur, from pale pink to light red. It is thought to be a natural hybrid.

A. tuberosa is considered one of the world's best herbaceous plants. It inhabits the sandy hills and sunny roads from Arizona to the Gulf of Mexico, and is easily grown in any free soil provided it is firmly planted. It produces flattish, composite heads of hundreds of brilliant, tangerine-red flowers; further side shoots appear during the summer and autumn. It is attractive to butterflies, and is altogether a plant commanding immediate attention. Some growers report interesting variations from seed, including deep yellow and orange-flowered forms. The dormant roots resemble a piece of dry wood cut in half, without any semblance of eyes or shoots. Nurseries supplying stocks often receive complaints that the top of the plant has been broken off. Established plants grow up to 75 cm (30 in.) tall.

Propagation is usually from seeds, which are housed in pods containing a kapok-like substance.

ASPHODELINE
Liliaceae   Asphodel

The name is a modification of *Asphodelus*. This genus consists of a dozen or more species, all of which are natives of the Mediterranean region. They are allied to the asphodelus, and are connected with and somewhat resemble the eremurus.

A. lutea is the only species commonly grown. It is a native of Sicily, growing wild in dry, poor, arid conditions, but flowering easily in any garden soil. It produces thick, fleshy roots, and rosettes of leaves 30 cm (12 in.) long, rough and spear-like. The flower-stems are 1 m (3 ft) in height, topped with up to 45 cm (18 in.) racemes of canary-yellow flowers, produced through spring and summer. There is a desirable double-flowered form called *A. lutea* 'Flora Pleno', whose blooms last in fresh condition over a long period. This is a very hardy, easily grown plant suitable for the background. Increase is from divisions in the spring, or from seed if available.

ASPHODELUS
Liliaceae

These are hardy, herbaceous, perennial plants with tall flower-spikes and tuberous roots. They are closely related to *Asphodeline* and require the same conditions—a sunny position in well-drained soil. They flower in spring and summer.

A. cerasiferus (syn. *A. ramosus*) has long, broad, grey-green leaves and branching spikes of white flowers to 1.5 m (5 ft) in early summer.

Propagation is by division in spring or by seed sown in autumn.

ASTER
Asteraceae   Michaelmas daisy

This genus of nearly 300 species of perennials and sub-shrubs with daisy-like flower-heads is distributed widely over Europe, North America and Asia. All species are easily grown, although some are more attractive than others. They vary in height from tiny miniatures for the rock garden to giants up to 2 m (6.5 ft) tall for the back of the herbaceous border. The leaves are sometimes dark coloured, sometimes hairy. The annual garden asters are really not asters at all but belong, strictly speaking, to the genus *Callistephus*.

All the asters are valuable, hardy garden plants, thriving in any well-drained soil, in sunny or semi-shady positions. The most vigorous types are best lifted every year, and two or three strong side shoots planted again. Larger and better blooms will be obtained by planting selected single shoots and training them like a single stem of chrysanthemums. Old or large clumps throw up a dozen or more flower-stalks competing for space and light, and unless well fed will last but a short time in bloom, with correspondingly smaller flowers. Because they are so easily grown, most people treat them casually, but few perennials will respond as well to kindly attention and good feeding as the asters. Well-grown and neglected plants raised from the same stock can appear to be different varieties. Under neglected or poor conditions, double-flowered varieties become singles, large flowers become small, and lasting qualities, either in the garden or as cut flowers, are at least halved.

A. alpinus is a species from the higher mountains of Europe and has been cultivated as a rock plant for several hundred years. The typical form grows about 22.5 cm (9 in.) high, with large, single-stemmed, violet-blue daisies arising from rosettes of grey-green leaves. Several forms, including one with purple flowers, others rosy mauve and even pink, have sometimes been offered but they do not seem to be generally available. This species prefers a poor, stiffish soil but is easy to grow in any but very light soil.

A. amellus and its varieties are the among loveliest of the perennial asters. The original species is distributed over southern Europe, and its history dates back a long way as a valuable herb and a 'cure-all' for many human diseases. The species and its varieties are very hardy and accommodating, not too tall, thus withstanding wind or exposure. They are slow to increase and never become out-of-hand. They flower over a long period and are quite useful for cutting. Many varieties are of dwarf, bushy habit, with many branched stems of single flowers 5–7.5 cm (2–3 in.) across. Often fresh shoots come up from the rootstock, thus prolonging the flowering period, which is usually from mid-summer till late autumn. The first outstanding improvement was 'King George', introduced in 1914 and still one of the best. It has large, bluish violet flowers with bronzy centres. 'Sonia' produces good-sized, lavender-pink flowers, and there are many other pink varieties, all excellent garden plants. Increase is from young growths as they appear in the spring; these root quite readily. Division from old, established clumps is also possible in spring, but plants are much slower to increase than the tall-flowering varieties and do not send out suckers or fresh shoots from the parent rootstock.

A. cordifolius is a lovely border species seldom seen

Opposite: Shades of pink, red and mauve blend pleasingly in this mixed perennial bed. Taller *Lavatera olbia* and *Penstemon* 'Garnet' have been planted to the right of the gravel path, together with *Erigeron karvinskianus*, while wallflowers (*Cheiranthus*), asters and other perennials are on the left.

in cultivation. The leaves are deeply heart-shaped, rough and hairy, and the tall, feathery sprays of miniature blue flowers are really delightful when massed or naturalised. Several selected types in distinct shades have been named. The best of these are 'Silver Spray', a pale lilac, and 'Elegans', pinkish lilac. Increase takes place readily from divisions or seed.

A. *dumosus* is common in sandy, dry places along the coast of North America, and is found in shades of violet, lilac and purple, and almost white. A selected, very dwarf-growing form called A. *dumosus nanus* was crossed with some of the tall *novi-belgii* varieties. The resulting hybrids have flowers that are much like the taller-flowering varieties, but the dwarf, compact plants, seldom exceeding 30 cm (12 in.) in height, form a solid ball of bloom in the autumn, and are therefore eminently suitable as border plants, edgings or for formal gardens. Plants are easily increased by division in spring.

The best cultivars of A. *dumosus* include:

'Buxton's Dwarf'—very compact to 15 cm (6 in.), with blue, button-like flowers.
'Lady in Blue'—25 cm (10 in.), bright blue flowers in late summer.
'Nancy'—30 cm (12 in.), light pink daisies.
'Pink Lace'—forms a rounded clump of lavender-pink, 30 cm (12 in.).
'Victor'—very compact, light blue, one of the original selections.

A. *ericoides* is an interesting species, with miniature flowers produced in great abundance on tall, branching stems late in autumn. Over 20 varieties have been listed, but few seem to be grown or available. This is a great pity as they are most desirable plants, resisting dry conditions and poorish soil more than most perennials. The best-known forms are in pale lavenders, rosy mauves and whites, while pale pinks and rosy shades also exist. The old English common names are 'farewell summer', 'mare's tail' and 'frost plant'.

A. *farreri*. The numerous, strong flowering stems are 30–45 cm (12–18 in.) tall, carrying single blooms 7.5 cm (3 in.) across, in a lovely shade of bluish violet. The finely rayed petals surround a central disc of bright orange. In habit of growth it is something like A. *alpinus*, the flower-stems arising from tufts of green leaves. This plant is easily grown in

Aster novi-belgii

any good soil. It increases freely from division.

A. x *frikartii*, a hybrid between A. *thomsonii* and A. *amellus*, is one of the finest dwarf-growing asters. For some reason this plant does not set fertile seed and continues in bloom over nearly three months. This free-branching plant, seldom exceeding 60 cm (24 in.) in height, has large, single flowers, bright campanula-blue in colour. Another selected form, 'Glory of Stafa', is clear sky-blue. Increase is very slow from division of the hardy, woody rootstock, and spring cuttings taken from the young shoots when 7.5–10 cm (3–4 in.) long are best. Do not transplant in winter.

A. *himalaicus* flowers early in summer with large, purplish blue daisies on unbranched stems to 30 cm (12 in.).

A. *novae-angliae*. Although somewhat resembling the more common *novi-belgii* group, the varieties derived from this North American species are readily recognisable. The typical form has stiff, woody stems covered with down, which is either greyish white or a brownish tint. The numerous, greyish green, woolly, narrow leaves clasp the stems, which are unbranched until 60–90 cm (24–36 in.) above the ground. The flowers of the wild species are a pleasing shade of violet-purple, very

Aster 'Magnet'

finely rayed and comparatively large. The plants are strong, vigorous and unusually free from disease, seldom suffering from wilt or mildew. The wild species does not seem to hybridise readily, so that relatively few new varieties have been introduced, but those listed are all outstanding garden plants. 'Barr's Pink' is a bright rose-pink, and 'Barr's Blue' is a purple-blue form. 'Harrington's Pink' is a lovely warm shade of salmon-pink, without any suggestion of violet or blue. It grows up to 1.5 m (5 ft) tall, well branched, and is a conspicuous and arresting plant when in bloom. 'Red Cloud' is perhaps the darkest-flowered of all asters, being a rich maroon-red. 'Survivor', rich pink, and 'Incomparabilis', bright purple-red, are among the best asters. Increase takes place slowly from divisions, as the rootstock does not sucker or branch out, but young, green shoots root readily in sand in the spring, blooming in the autumn if planted out in late spring.

A. novi-belgii. The vast majority of Michaelmas daisies grown nowadays are classified under this heading. The tendency today is towards larger flowers, full or semi-double, distinctive shades, and plants that do not grow more than 1 m (3 ft) tall. The result is that the modern Michaelmas daisy is worthy of a place in any garden. There are numerous culti-

vars, and the following are some of those being offered by nurseries:

'Blandie'—pure white, semi-double, 90 cm (36 in.).
'Climax'—lavender-blue, single, 1.5 m (5 ft); vigorous and late flowering.
'Coombe Violet'—large, semi-double, violet blue, 90 cm (36 in.).
'Fellowship'—creamy pink flowers in abundance, 1 m (3 ft).
'Harrisons Blue'—still the best mid-blue, 1 m (3 ft).
'Helen Ballard'—rosy crimson, semi-double, 1 m (3 ft).
'Magnet'—bright violet, 1 m (3 ft).
'Patricia Ballard'—large, semi-double, deep pink, 1 m (3 ft).
'Plenty'—large flowers of light blue, 1 m (3 ft).
'Royal Ruby'—semi-double, bright rosy red, 60 cm (24 in.).
'Sarah Ballard'—mauve-pink, semi-double, 1 m (3 ft).

A. sedifolius (syn. *A. acris*). Much is said in praise of this lovely, free-flowering plant, with its astonishing profusion of soft, starry, lavender-mauve flowers.

Aster yunnanensis 'Knapsbury'

Each stem, at almost every leaf joint, breaks up into a large number of thin, wiry branches, and when in full bloom the bushy plant, about 50 cm (20 in.) high, is a shaggy, wavy mass of colour. A dwarf variety only 25 cm (10 in.) high is called *A. sedifolius* 'Nanus', and is a lovely shade of lavender-blue, while a pale rosy mauve variety 'Roseus' is sometimes available. All types are excellent border plants, particularly suitable for massing or park display. Increase is from division.

A. tongolensis is from China and has pale blue daisies about 5 cm (2 in.) across. It is up to 30 cm (12 in.) high and flowers in early summer.

A. yunnanensis is another species somewhat similar in growth and habit to *A. farreri* but each stem carries several heads of fair-sized, lilac-blue flowers on 30 cm (12 in.) stems. The best selected form is 'Knapsbury'; the flowers are larger, produced on long stems, and the colour is a pleasing shade of deep, heliotrope-violet with a central orange disc. It is excellent for cutting.

Solidaster luteus (syn. *A. hybridus luteus*), the yellow aster, is a hybrid between an aster and solidago, producing dense heads of small, lemon-yellow flowers on 60 cm (24 in.) stems. It is a good perennial, lasting a surprisingly long time as a cut flower and associating well in the border with *A. amellus* and similar varieties. Readily increased from divisions, it is hardy and easy to grow.

ASTILBE
Saxifragaceae

This genus was once included with the spiraeas, and the connection still lingers in many minds, but the true spiraeas are now assigned to the family Rosaceae. The lovely hybrids available today are the result of crosses between *A. davidii* and other species forming a new group known as *A. arendsii*.

These most desirable, easily grown, hardy plants will thrive under average garden conditions in any place that is not too dry. Strictly speaking, they are best treated as bog plants, growing to perfection on the edge of ponds and in damp depressions. Under ideal conditions—that is, adequate moisture and semi-shade—the lovely fern-like foliage and beautiful, plumy spikes harmonise to perfection. In many varieties the young foliage is a beautiful, coppery red.

Astilbe roots are very hard and tough, and a very sharp knife or heavy, strong tool is required for dividing old clumps. Yearly winter top-dressings of rich compost will maintain vigour and richness, as astilbes delight in good soil.

The following are some of the best hybrids available:

'Amethyst'—light amethyst-violet.
'Betsy Cuperus'—creamy pink, drooping blooms.
'Bressingham Beauty'—many rich pink spikes, long-lasting.
'Cattleya'—lovely bright pink, long flowering, 1 m (3 ft).
'Diamant'—large plumes of pure white.
'Fanal'—garnet-red, bronze foliage, 60 cm (24 in.).
'Federsee'—huge plumes of deep carmine-pink, 75 cm (30 in.).
'Feuer'—coral-red, distinct shade, 60 cm (24 in.).
'Fuchsia Spangles'—tall spikes, fuchsia-pink.
'Gertrude Brix'—compact, carmine-red, 50 cm (20 in.).
'Granat'—deep crimson-red, taller grower, 75 cm (30 in.).
'Hyacinth'—plumy trusses, lilac-pink, 75 cm (30 in.).
'Prof. V. de Wielen'—tall, creamy white, arching sprays, 90 cm (36 in.).
'Red Sentinel'—intense brick-red, the darkest, 75 cm (30 in.).
'Serenade'—compact plumes of deep pink.
'Strausenfrieda'—arching stems of soft pink, 60 cm (24 in.).

A. davidii is one of the attractive parents of the modern hybrids. It is particularly valuable for semi-shady spots as well as wet or boggy positions. The bronzy green, fern-like foliage and reddish stems reach a height of 2 m (6.5 ft) and are topped with 50 cm (20 in.), plumy panicles of bright magenta flowers with purplish filaments and blue anthers. It blooms later than the hybrids mentioned and is more tolerant of imperfect conditions. A red-flowered hybrid, 'Joe Ophurst', shows this parentage but grows only 1 m (3 ft) tall, while 'Irene Rotseiper', a lovely, flesh-pink, is also of this type.

A. simplicifolia is a dwarf-growing species, but the true plant is no longer grown, several hybrid forms

Astilbe hybrids: 'Amethyst' (pink), 'Fanal' (red), 'Erica', (salmon)

about 45 cm (18 in.) tall being vastly superior. The best is *A. simplicifolia* 'Atro Rosea', a bright pink, while a salmon-rose called 'Praecox' and its pure white counterpart, 'Praecox Alba', are to be recommended. A lovely salmon-pink form with rich, purple-bronze foliage, 'Bronze Elegance', is a most elegant plant. These hybrids, splendid for the front border, are not as well known or grown as they should be.

A. taquetii is an outstanding, late-flowering species with much taller spikes than any other. The flowers open in early summer, about 1.5 m (5 ft), with long, narrow, rich pink plumes. A clone called 'Superba'

has rather deeper pink flowers. It is a splendid plant for moist soils or anywhere that can be irrigated during dry weather.

A wonderful effect in ponds and streams can be obtained by filling barrels with soil, planting six to nine roots on the top, and then lowering the barrels into the water, allowing the top to protrude 10–15 cm (4–6 in.) above the surface. As soon as the foliage is developed, the contour of the barrel is completely covered, and the delightful effect is of an island of astilbes just growing out of the water. The same procedure can be applied with similar effect by using *Iris ensata* and *I. sibirica* as well as other water-loving plants.

Propagation is by division, although new shades can be secured from seed. Transplant in winter.

ASTRANTIA
Apiaceae

This is a genus of perennials grown for their foliage and long-lasting flowers. *A. major* has curiously attractive, pinkish green flowers on leafy stems to 90 cm (36 in.). *A. major* 'Sunningdale Variegated' has striking leaves variegated with cream and yellow, less colourful from mid-summer. The erect, branching heads of white flowers grow to 60 cm (24 in.) in summer and autumn. *A. maxima* is charming with its glistening, light pink flowers. Propagation is by division in spring or by seed sown when fresh.

Astrantia major

AUBRIETA
Brassicaceae   Rock cress

This well-known border plant has been derived from the species *A. deltoidea* var. *graeca*. Although easily raised from seed, which yields a wide range of shades, the best results are obtained from named

Aubrieta deltoidea var. *graeca*

varieties raised from cuttings or divisions. These selected varieties are usually larger flowered, special or unusual shades, or else possess other outstanding features not present in mixed seedlings.

In addition to a selection of named varieties in blues, lilac, purple, violet, crimson and mauve, most attractive semi-double hybrids are available in various shades. One of the best is 'Barker's Double', which has luminous, plum-red flowers all spring. Other good cultivars include 'Blue Emperor', probably the best blue, 'Scholfields Double', rich crimson, and 'Mrs Rodwald', single crimson.

Aubrietas, when established, will withstand dry conditions and are suitable for planting on sunny banks, rockeries, stone walls and other exposed or coastal areas where many other plants would fail. A clump of aubrieta has been recorded growing on a sloping shoulder of a brick chimney, apparently without any soil, for over 30 years. Plants increase rapidly from autumn and winter cuttings, and divisions of old clumps, and are best planted out in the autumn so as to provide a display of bloom in the spring.

B

BABIANA
Iridaceae   Baboon flower

There are over 60 species of *Babiana* widespread through the central parts of South Africa's Cape Province and Transvaal.

These are brightly coloured flowers, easily raised from seed and also increased readily from bulbs. They grow freely in almost any soil, in open positions not subject to very heavy frosts, and are ideal border plants, or useful for filling bold pockets in the rockery. The colours available are mostly in self-shades of light and dark blue, purple, plum-red and also white. These are usually forms of *B. stricta* and *B. villosa*.

The species *B. plicata* is not at all common but is valued because of its strong and alluring carnation scent. The flowers, which are purple to pinkish mauve, are somewhat hidden among the 15 cm (6 in.) high foliage.

B. rubrocyanea is probably the most striking of all the species and is commonly known as the wine-cup babiana, because the bowls of the royal-blue flowers are stained rich crimson. The bulb produces two to four stems 15 cm (6 in.) tall, each carrying, during early spring, about six flowers to a spike, held well above the foliage. Many firms offer this as a form of *B. stricta*, but it is a distinct species.

B. stricta is the best-known species, usually seen with richly coloured, royal-blue flowers on 25 cm (10 in.) stems, held gracefully well above the foliage. Paler-coloured forms also occur, and a large-flowered, milk white to pale yellow form is called 'Sulphurea'. Some consider this a distinct species. Plant bulbs in autumn, 15 cm (6 in.) deep.

B. villosa. In this species the striking, cup-shaped flowers are a rich claret or wine-purple with black anthers. The flower-stems are up to 40 cm (16 in.) tall, held well above the slightly hairy, ribbed leaves.

Babiana stricta

The following species are quite uncommon: *B. ambigua* is only a few centimetres tall and has blue or mauve, 2.5 cm (1 in.) flowers with paler centres. *B. hypogea* grows 15 cm (6 in.) tall, with tufts of narrow, grey-green foliage in winter followed by attractive scented, blue flowers in early spring. *B. nana* has blue or pink, 2.5 cm (1 in.) flowers on stems about 10 cm tall. *B. pygmea* has pleated foliage 15 cm (6 in.) tall and 5 cm (2 in.) flowers of sulphur-yellow with dark maroon centres.

All babianas need deep planting, and the bulbs will often be found 15–20 cm (6–8 in.) below the surface. They are usually happy and long-lived on any soil in sun, and all are dormant in summer. Sow seed in autumn or spring, and set bulbs 5 cm (2 in.) apart and 15 cm (6 in.) deep in late summer and autumn.

BAPTISIA
Fabiaceae   False indigo

These are leguminous, herbaceous plants of North America. There are about 30 species, but the only one grown commercially is *B. australis*, sometimes listed wrongly as *B. caerulea*. It forms a strong, bushy, somewhat coarse-foliaged plant up to 1 m (3 ft) high and across, with deep sage-green, lupin- or ash-like leaves, and terminal spikes of campanula-violet flowers, 2.5 cm (1 in.) long, loosely arranged on thin racemes, partly hidden among the foliage. It is quite a useful hardy plant, particularly on account of the colour, which is poorly represented in hardy perennials. It blooms from spring until early summer. It increases rapidly from seeds and also from divisions of old clumps or spring-rooted cuttings, and should be planted out during the dormant period in the winter months.

BEGONIA
Begoniaceae

This genus includes perennials grown for their colourful flowers and ornamental foliage. Although begonias are not hardy enough to be grown outdoors permanently in many locations, some types are quite hardy and perennial in frost-free gardens. The begonia family has over 100 species in the tropics and sub-tropics, but those cultivated are mainly hybrids. Some begonias have tuberous roots and some have fibrous roots.

B. fuchsioides (syn. *B. foliosa* var. *miniata*) is grown as a succulent, shrubby plant about 80 cm (32 in.) tall, with oval, dark green, dentate leaves and small, single flowers. 'Coccinea' has red flowers, and those of 'Rosea' are rose-pink. They flower all through the year, and are excellent garden plants in semi-shade.

Begonia semperflorens

B. rex are usually grown as pot plants but can be used as a handsome ground cover in shade in frost-free gardens. They have a creeping rhizome, heart-shaped leaves, and pale pink flowers in early spring.

B. semperflorens is evergreen, with rounded, dark green leaves. It flowers all year round but predominantly in summer, and is extensively used as a bedding plant. Greatly improved strains are now offered by nurseries, some growing only 15 cm (6 in.), others up to 40 cm (16 in.); shades of white, pink and red are available.

The tuberous begonias include the giant-flowered specimens grown in greenhouses and sometimes grown outdoors in semi-shade. The 'Multiflora' strain is tuberous and is available in many shades of pink, scarlet, orange and yellow. They have masses of 5 cm (2 in.) flowers in late summer and autumn.

Propagation of tuberous begonias is by 7.5 cm (3 in.) cuttings from the started tubers, taken in late spring. Propagation from the minute seed is best left to the professional. Other species can be increased by stem cuttings, which root easily.

BELAMCANDA
Iridaceae   Leopard lily

There are two species belonging to this genus. *B. chinensis*, a native of China and Japan, is a summer-flowering species, little known but quite hardy and well worth growing. The sword-like foliage resembles that of the bearded iris, and the loosely arranged, branched, 60 cm (24 in.) stems carry a dozen or more 7.5 cm (3 in.), starry, bright orange flowers, heavily spotted with purple-brown, hence the common name. It is a shallow, fibrous-rooted plant, and demands good drainage, thriving particularly well in light or sandy soil. Increase is usually from the clusters of blackberry-like seeds, which germinate freely and normally bloom the second season. Because of these ornamental seed-heads, this plant is also called the blackberry lily. Older clumps can be divided up in autumn or winter. Although hardy in milder districts, it should be covered with leaves or some loose litter where frosts are severe. Several other coloured forms exist, including a pure, unspotted yellow.

BELLIS
Asteraceae

This is a genus of 15 species, including the common wild field daisy known as *B. perennis*. Full, double-flowered forms are well worth growing as hardy, front-border perennials or for edgings, blooming as they do from spring through summer. Several selected, named varieties are listed in Europe, including white, carmine-red, pink, and with rose-striped blooms. Although seed of *B. perennis* is available in mixed colours, and the resultant stocks are mostly double-flowered, these are not as good, nor are they as long-lasting, as the selected, named sorts. These plants are quite easily grown but will die out if allowed to become dry in the autumn. Increase is from divisions of older clumps or from root cuttings taken like those of perennial phlox.

Bellis perennis, double form

BERGENIA
Saxifragaceae   Elephant's ears

Listed previously under *Megasea*, but now given generic rank, this genus comprises six species with distinctive, thick, glandular leaves and stout, basal rootstocks. The best-known species, *B. cordifolia*, produces large, roundish, heart-shaped leaves, glabrous and toothed to the edges, and, during early spring, panicles of rosy red flowers on 30–40 cm (12–16 in.) stems. It is a most adaptable plant, thriving to perfection in shade or in the open border, but also quite useful for the larger pockets of rock

Bergenia 'Ballawley'

gardens. The blooms remain attractive over quite a long period and are very useful for cutting.

B. purpurascens (syn. *B. delavayi*) has reddish pink, bell-shaped flowers to 50 cm (20 in.).

Increase is from division of established, thick and fleshy rootstock, which lies on the surface during winter. Bergenia cultivars include:

'Abenglut'—glowing rosy red flowers to 30 cm (12 in.).

'Ballawley'—bright rosy red flowers to 30 cm (12 in.), deep green leaves.

'Bressingham Salmon'—handsome foliage and many arching sprays of salmon-pink flowers.

'Beethoven'—clear pink flowers carried on erect stems above good foliage.

'Flore Pleno'—large sprays of double, rose-pink flowers, 25 cm (10 in.).

'Morgenrote' (Morning Blush)—deep pink flowers in spring and sometimes in summer; an excellent garden plant with rounded leaves.

'Purpurea'—heads of pink flowers, foliage dark green turning maroon in winter.

'Silberlicht'—pure white flowers fading pink, dark green leaves 30 cm (12 in.).

'Smidtii Nana'—large, clear pink flowers to 45 cm (18 in.), large, toothed green leaves.

'Purpurglochen'—a small plant with rounded, puckered leaves and purplish flowers, fine for the front row.

'Stracheyi Alba'—a small plant from the Himalayas, with small, rounded leaves and short heads
of very white flowers.

'Sunningdale'—rich, deep pink flowers, glossy,
green leaves, maroon in winter.

BESCHORNERIA
Agavaceae

This genus of 10 species of Mexican plants is closely
allied to the aloes and agaves. The hardiest and only
species available commercially is *B. yuccoides*. A
mature specimen somewhat resembles a yucca
plant, with its rosette of green, rough-edged leaves
about 90 cm (36 in.) long and 7.5 cm (3 in.) wide. In
late spring heavy, unbranched, coral-red spikes
1–1.8 m (3–6 ft) long appear from the centre of the
clump, unfurling and displaying on short side stems
nodding, bright green, tubular bells 2.5 cm (1 in.)
across, enclosed in attractive, rosy pink bracts. The
whole spike is most interesting as it appears and
develops, remaining in an attractive condition,
either cut or on the plant, for six weeks or more. This
species seems quite hardy and is easily grown in
almost any soil except heavy clay, also withstanding
drought or dry autumn conditions. It seeds quite
freely in warm districts if two or more plants are
grown in close proximity. Seedlings a year old are
large enough for planting out permanently the following winter, usually blooming the third season.

Beschorneria yuccoides

BILLBERGIA
Bromeliaceae

There are over 50 species of billbergias, most of
which are greenhouse plants. They come from
southern Brazil and Mexico.

These easily grown bromeliads are for shady spots
in practically frost-free areas, but otherwise should
be grown as pot or conservatory plants. The hard,
somewhat yucca-like foliage suggests an ability to
resist drought. The most near-hardy species, *B.
nutans*, has pendant sprays of tubular flowers, bright
green edged with vivid blue, while the enclosing
bracts are rosy red.

Another species, much slower to increase and
seldom met with, is called *B. zebrina* on account of
the pretty, bronzy green foliage marbled with white.
The flowers, although larger, are similar in colouring but more of a salmon-rose shade. The overall
height when in bloom is about 75 cm (30 in.), while
B. nutans is smaller, seldom exceeding 45 cm (18
in.). Increase is from suckers or divisions of older
clumps, any time during late autumn and winter.

BLANDFORDIA
Liliaceae   Christmas bells

Four species of this genus are recorded. *B. grandiflora* (syn. *B. flammea*) is the largest-flowered of all
the species, each flower-stem 45 cm (18 in.) high,
carrying four to 12 campanula-like, drooping bells
of lovely rosy red to orange-scarlet, heavily bordered
with yellow at the mouth.

A smaller-flowered but possibly more brilliantly
coloured species is called *B. nobilis*, the flower bells
being more tubular, finely toothed on the margins,
and slightly reflexed at the mouth. This is the best-
known species, but all are really first-rank perennials, well deserving of the special attention
required.

These plants prefer acid soil, but they have been
successfully grown in any free, loose soil that is not
alkaline, or where rhododendrons and azaleas
thrive. It may be advisable to obtain some leaf
mould or peat to mix with the soil in order to get
them established. Plants seed freely and are not diffi-

cult to raise, usually blooming the second season after sowing. In habit, the clumps resemble miniature New Zealand flax bushes or tiny cabbage trees, the central flowers-spikes arising well above the foliage and blooming from summer into autumn. Transplant during winter and early spring.

BLETILLA
Orchidaceae   Bletia

Only one species from this genus of nine species is commonly grown. Previously listed as *B. hyacintha*, it is now correctly classified as *B. striata*. This well-known, half-hardy, terrestrial orchid can be quite easily grown in any reasonably good, loose soil not subject to wet conditions. While it seems to do best in a hot climate, even in full sun, it has been known to be successfully wintered in the open without any protection whatever, resisting up to 15 degrees of frost. It may withstand even more cold than this, as the fleshy roots are completely dormant in the

Bletilla striata

winter, with no foliage or green portion above the ground. It resents a severe check in the spring, once it has come into growth, but as the leaves do not

Phlomis fruticosa is an attractive perennial for borders

appear until late spring, there is only an occasional risk of damage.

The fleshy rootstock gives rise to long, single, heavily ribbed leaves, enclosing thin, wiry, 45 cm (18 in.) flower-stems, carrying exquisite, cyclamen-purple flowers 5 cm (2 in.) across, beautifully frilled and orchid-like. A rare form, *B. striata* 'Albo-Variegata', has pure-white flowers, and the leaves are striped with white as well. Both are front-rank plants that all keen gardeners should endeavour to possess.

Increase is usually from division of established clumps, broken up when dormant, preferably in spring just before the new growth starts. Plants seed freely in a hot climate but seem difficult to raise unless sown on finely chopped-up moss.

BOLTONIA
Asteraceae   False starwart

Somewhat resembling, and blooming at the same time as, the hardy perennial asters, this plant readily attains a height of 1.2 m (4 ft) and is admirably suited to the herbaceous border. The leaves are long, smooth, greyish and without 'teeth', and are thus distinguished from the asters. The hundreds of starry flowers, produced on freely branching side stems, provide a bold effect.

Boltonia asteroides

B. asteroides has white flowers, and *B. asteroides* var. *latisquama* is similar but produces an abundance of pinkish lavender or bluish violet blooms. It increases freely from divisions, and plants are easily grown in any position sheltered from heavy winds. Transplant during winter or spring.

BRACHYCOME
Asteraceae

This is a family of low-growing Australian plants, most of which are suitable for use as ground cover. The fern-like leaves form mounds and are continuously bespangled with blue daisies throughout the year.

B. iberidifolia grows fairly bushy to 30 cm (12 in.), with lacy, green foliage covered with lavender daisies.

B. melanocarpa 'Pibara', unlike others, grows a mat of bronze-green leaves that in time will cover a square metre. It is easy to grow in sun, and is covered all year round with daisies of an unusual crimson shade.

B. multifida has bright mauve-blue daisies to 30 cm (12 in.) high and continuously in flower. Its cultivar 'Break of Day' has blue daisies a shade deeper in colour. 'Pink Angel' is a new cultivar with a prostrate habit and covered with deep pink flowers all year around. All of these have lacy, green foliage.

B. nivalis is native to New Zealand and has large white daisies with golden centres over a mat of shiny, narrow leaves.

Propagation is by seed sown in spring. The grow-

Brachycome multifida 'Pink Angel'

Brachycome multifida

ing tips of young plants should be pinched out to encourage bushy growth.

BRAVOA
Amaryllidaceae   Twin flower

This is a genus of seven species, of which *B. gemini-flora* (syn. *Polianthes geminiflora*) is the best and only one grown. In root and growth, it is much like the tuberose, the 70 cm (28 in.), slender flower-stems carrying pendant, coral-red, tubular flowers about 5 cm (2 in.) long hanging in pairs. Free-flowering and easy to grow in any well-drained garden soil in full sun, the plant blooms during early summer, with odd spikes appearing during summer and until late autumn. The spikes are dainty and suitable for cutting, lasting quite a long time in water, the buds opening up in succession. Hybrids with the tuberose have been raised, but these seem to have been lost in cultivation. Bravoas are easily raised from divisions of clumps or from seed. Transplant when dormant in winter.

BRODIAEA
Amaryllidaceae

This genus originally consisted of over 40 slender-stemmed, bulbous plants from western North and South America.

B. coccinea (syn. *Dichelostemma ida-maia*), commonly known as the floral fire-cracker, is perhaps the best known and most attractive of the brodiaeas. (There is some debate about its correct name and classification.) It grows 60 cm (24 in.) or more, the thin, wiry stems supporting the top, which consists of a cluster of six to 24 pencil-like, 5 cm (2 in.) long, drooping flowers, deep crimson-red, the slightly expanded mouth being tipped with green. A group in full bloom is quite spectacular, and they last a long time either in the garden or as cut flowers. They usually bloom in late spring but die down soon afterwards. Although quite easy to grow in full sun, the situation must be well drained, preferably with gritty soil. It is a bulb that will withstand the driest of conditions. Seed sets freely, and this is the safest means of increase, although the 2.5 cm (1 in.) wide, rounded bulbs increase quite well if left undisturbed for a few years. Plant 5 cm (2 in.) deep, 7.5 cm (3 in.) apart during autumn.

B. laxa (syn. *Triteleia laxa*) is a very different species, looking more like a miniature agapanthus. The usual form has umbels of violet-blue flowers in early summer, but the plant is variable, and white, pink and pale blue forms are known. It grows to a height of 30–75 cm (12–30 in.) and can be propagated by seed or offsets in autumn.

Brodiaea coccinea

BRUNNERA
Boraginaceae

Three species of this genus are known, being closely allied to the anchusas and, until recently, included in this genus. The best species is known as *B. macrophylla*, a native of the western Caucasus, and sometimes goes under the name of *Anchusa myosotidiflora* or *Myosotis macrophylla*.

This is a most desirable hardy perennial for the front border, a semi-shady situation or woodland conditions. From neat clumps arise numerous branching panicles of 45 cm (18 in.) tall, forget-me-not-like, blue flowers with yellow centres. It flowers freely from the early spring onwards. It can be increased by division or from seed, and can be transplanted during winter and early spring.

A very striking variegated form has leaves that are strongly splashed with pure white.

Brunnera macrophylla, variegated form

Brunsvigia josephinae

the most attractive species are grown in gardens in their native country, only one seems to be generally cultivated in Australasia, *B. josephinae*. This species produces a large bulb up to 15 cm (6 in.) across, and a stem usually 75 cm (30 in.) tall, with a candelabra head of 20–40 narrow, bright cerise-red trumpets 7.5 cm (3 in.) long and about 2.5 cm (1 in.) wide at the mouth. These appear in late summer, but unless the situation is suitable, preferably in full sun, and hot and dry in summer, even full-sized bulbs do not bloom every year. Volcanic soils suit them well. They resent disturbance and may need two years to settle down and produce flower-spikes. Increase from offsets is slow, but may be the only method if seed is not available.

B. minor. Although not as tall as other species, it puts up a 22.5 cm (9 in.) wide, candelabra head of up to 36 tubular, rosy red flowers on erect, 30 cm (12 in.) stems. It seems to be as free-flowering as the common belladonnas.

B. orientalis, previously known as *B. gigantea*, is a desirable species, with immense bulbs sometimes weighing up to 4.5 kg (10 lbs). The large flower-head, comprising numerous dark crimson flowers,

BRUNSVIGIA
Amaryllidaceae

This is a South African genus of 11 species of bulbs allied to the belladonnas, which they closely resemble in growth and bulb. Although a number of

Opposite: This charming little rock garden separating the driveway from the lawn makes effective use of grey-foliaged plants such as *Artemisia pycnocephala*, dense with yellow buds, dianthus and lavender. The ground cover *Raoulia* forms a grey carpet, softening the rocks in the foreground.

measures up to 60 cm (24 in.) across. Unfortunately, the large leaves, which lie flat on the ground, are rather easily damaged by frost, but this species will stand more winter wet than others.

Several hybrids between forms of *Amaryllis belladonna* and *Brunsvigia josephinae* have been reported or offered for sale in different parts of the world. 'Beacon' is an interesting colour break, with the flowers opening up a brilliant scarlet-red with a startling white throat, changing with age to deep wine-red. It is similar to the ordinary *A. belladonna* type, very free-flowering, with four to 10 trumpets of 60 cm (24 in.) stems. The bulbs are smaller than the ordinary types and increase freely.

When not in flower the bulbs are difficult to identify. Usually the under-surface of the outer, papery skins of brunsvigias contains a shiny, shellac-like substance, while the belladonnas lack this and are more woolly under their skins. Transplant when dormant in summer or autumn, setting the bulbs almost on the top of the ground like nerines and belladonnas.

BULBINELLA
Liliaceae

There are at least a dozen South African species of *Bulbinella* and six in New Zealand. In bloom they resemble miniature kniphofias.

B. cauda-felis is a little-known species. It is entirely dormant during summer and autumn, but quickly develops grassy-foliaged clumps with the coming of late autumn rains. During late winter it produces numerous, small, poker-like spikes of creamy white flowers on 30 cm (12 in.) stems. These are very useful and long-lasting as cut flowers.

B. latifolia flowers in winter, with 1 m (3 ft) high stems with bright yellow, 15–20 cm (6–8 in.) flower-spikes held erect, and much broader leaves, as the name implies. It is a fine garden plant for coastal areas, and several plants should be grown in a group for best effect. It is excellent as a long-lasting cut flower.

B. nutans var. *nutans* (better known as *B.*

Bulbinella latifolia

Bulbinella nutans var. *nutans*

floribunda) is one of the showiest of the South African species, usually distinguished by its 45 cm (18 in.) long, tapering leaves, deeply grooved down the centre and almost folded in half. The 60 cm (24 in.) long flower-stalks, produced in early spring, terminate with 10 cm (4 in.), cylindrical flower-spikes composed of numerous, tiny, glittering, yellow flowers, the spike lengthening to 20 cm (8 in.) as it continues to open. This is a variable species, and rich orange and almost tangerine-red forms have been grown.

These South African bulbinellas seem to be quite easily grown in any loose, free soil, preferably acid with peat or leaf mould added. They are dormant from mid-summer until early winter, so can with-

Buphthalmum salicifolium

stand dry autumn conditions, although the fleshy roots may collapse if the soil is entirely devoid of moisture. They seem reasonably hardy and have withstood 15 degrees of frost without any apparent damage.

Increase is best from seed, which germinates freely and usually blooms the second or third season. Old clumps can be divided as soon as they are dormant during late summer, and should be planted with the top of the fibrous bundle of roots just under the surface of the soil. Some success can be achieved with root cuttings, which are the best way of increasing special coloured forms.

BUPHTHALMUM
Asteraceae

This hardy, showy, easily grown genus of seven species is usually considered to be rather second class, but it has its uses and is favoured by some gardeners. Heads of long-rayed, buttercup-yellow daisies and imbricated bracts are produced over a fairly lengthy summer-flowering period. The best-known species is *B. salicifolium*, sometimes listed as *B. grandiflorum*. It grows about 75 cm (30 in.) high and as much across.

Plants increase freely from divisions in autumn and can also be raised from seed sown in spring/autumn. Transplant during the winter months.

C

CALCEOLARIA
Scrophulariaceae

There are about 200 species of *Calceolaria*, many very beautiful, most natives of Central and South America. The shrubby species *C. integrifolia* produces soft green, heavily wrinkled, rather clammy leaves, rusty hairy beneath, and, during late spring and summer, crowded, many-flowered corymbs of 12 mm (0.5 in.) wide, brilliant daffodil-yellow flowers. There is also a brownish yellow-flowered form, and both forms are quite spectacular in full bloom. The plants grow to 75 cm (30 in.) high and across, but may die down to near ground level during very cold winters. The heavily laden flower-heads are rather brittle and therefore easily damaged by heavy winds. Plants need to be pruned back to half height each winter. Propagation is by softwood cuttings or seed.

Calceolaria integrifolia

CALLA
Araceae

There is only one species of the true calla. Plants that are commonly called calla lilies are now included in the genus *Zantedeschia*.

C. palustris is an aquatic plant native to the colder parts of the Northern Hemisphere. The leaves are cordate, the spadix short with upper flowers female and lower ones hermaphrodite, and stamens numerous and thread-like. These flowers are followed later by scarlet berries. This plant, which has become naturalised in England, is used for edging ponds, and the stems creep out of the water. Propagation is by division in spring or by seed sown in summer.

CALOCHORTUS
Liliaceae   Mariposa tulip

These dainty, western American natives are found along the Pacific coast and from Washington to Mexico, where they grow in open woodlands and on the banks of streams. They all belong to the lily family, and are closely connected with the tulips.

Perfect drainage is essential, and a deep, gritty soil and raised beds are recommended for successful growing. Most species are better grown in pots, in very gritty mix. Pots can be submerged in the garden. Summer rains are destructive to the bulbs unless drainage is sharp, and a situation that becomes hot and dry during the summer months is ideal for ripening the bulbs. Such conditions are often found under big deciduous trees, whose roots ensure the necessary drainage and carry away the surplus summer rains.

The 40 distinct species of *Calochortus* are divided into three groups. The first is the globe tulips, with

Calochortus uniflorus

long, shining basal leaves and slender stems, each carrying three to five globular, nodding flowers. These are woodland plants. *C. albus* is a lovely white-flowered species with beautifully frilled bells. A golden yellow-flowered species called *C. amabilis* is also reasonably easy to grow.

The second group is known as the star tulips. These are similar in habit, also producing thin, dainty, branching flower-stems 30–45 cm (12–18 in.) high, but in this section the blooms are held erect and are cup-shaped. The best species in this group is *C. caeruleus*, with variations of lavender, lilac-pink or violet-purple flowers, the three central petals being covered with soft hairs, thus earning it the common name of cat's ears. This species used to be known as *C. maweanus* while the larger-flowered species that used to be listed as *C. maweanus* 'Major' is now called *C. tolmiei*. *C. uniflorus* is another very easily grown species in this group. It is not a woodland bulb but grows in meadows that are quite wet in winter, even until after the flowering season. The wide-open, lilac-coloured blooms, often 3–5 on a stem, are freely produced, and it appears to be the easiest of all the calochortus to grow. It seems happy under almost any conditions, increasing rapidly from bulb division and also setting seed freely.

The third group comprises the true mariposa or butterfly tulips, of which the best known and most easily managed are *C. venustus* and *C. vestae*, the latter being apparently just a smaller-flowered form of the former. Bulbs start into growth early in autumn but do not bloom until early summer, so should not be allowed out of the ground for long. The thin, wiry, many-branched flower-stems often grow to a height of 60–90 cm (24–36 in.) and over a period of several weeks carry a number of 7.5 cm (3 in.) wide, bowl-shaped flowers, the three overlapping petals extending over the soft, reflexing rims. The predominant colour is creamy yellow flushed lilac, with dark maroon central base markings and rosy lilac exterior. This is a lovely, hardy bulb, which should be attempted by all who possess reasonably good drainage and shelter from heavy winds. A rich compost including fibrous loam gives good results.

Increase is usually from bulbs, which multiply if doing well, but seed germinates readily and plants usually bloom in the third season. Seed should be grown in boxes of coarse, gritty loam. Bulbs are planted in the autumn and set 7.5 cm (3 in.) deep and 15 cm (6 in.) apart.

CALTHA
Ranunculaceae   Marsh marigold

This genus of 20 species of perennial plants is native to the temperate and cold regions of the Northern Hemisphere. The shining, deep green leaves are more or less kidney-shaped, and in the better-known

Caltha palustris 'Plena'

species, *C. palustris*, the glistening, buttercup-like, golden yellow flowers make a pleasing contrast. These are held a short distance above the 25 cm (10 in.) foliage and appear in early to late spring. A non-seeding, double, yellow-flowered variety called *C. palustris* 'Plena' is the best one to grow, or a double-flowered, pale yellow form known as 'Pallida Plena'. An excellent white-flowered form is also available.

C. polypetala is a lush and robust species, with large leaves to 50 cm (20 in.) and bright yellow flowers.

All forms are suitable for establishing on the margins of ponds or streams, damp spots or shady corners. The smaller-growing species are very suitable for the rock garden, including the pale cream-flowered *C. novae-zelandiae*, a New Zealand native inhabiting shady alpine slopes. Increase is from seed or division of roots in the autumn.

CAMASSIA
Liliaceae

Camassia leichtlinii

Natives of western America from British Columbia to California, these six hardy, bulbous species are not as well known as they should be. They are mostly in lovely shades of blue, a colour often lacking in the herbaceous border, and their dainty, starry spikes of bloom add a note of charm to any garden. They are quite easy to grow in free, loose soil, resisting very cold conditions in the winter when the bulbs are quite dormant, and withstanding moist and even wet conditions. In their natural habitat they are seen growing in rich marshlands or on the banks of streams.

C. cusickii is the giant of the race and the queen of them all. It grows up to 1.8 m (6 ft) high, with strong kniphofia-like foliage and giant spikes of pretty, pale blue flowers. When raised from seed, deeper blue forms are often secured, while a pure white is known. This and all other species are most useful for indoor decoration.

C. esculenta (syn. *C. scilloides*) gives us numerous 60 cm (24 in.) spikes of rich, royal-blue, starry flowers. The calyx and unopened flowers give a greenish blue, electric effect, which is most pleasing and decorative. A less spectacular but interesting and useful creamy white-flowered form, known as

C. esculenta 'Alba', is sometimes seen in gardens. It is quite a strong grower, up to 1 m (3 ft) tall, and reproduces true to type from seed.

C. leichtlinii is a variable species, briefly described as a stout-growing form of *C. esculenta*, with 1–1.2 m (3–4 ft) stems and correspondingly larger bulbs. A type often grown is deep aconite-blue, but if raised from American seed, pure white, cream, blues and purples can be secured. *C. leichtlinii semi-plena* is a rare plant raised in Holland. It has double, cream-coloured flowers on tall spikes, but does not set seed, so increase is slow.

C. quamash is said by some to be another name for *C. esculenta*, but the stock sold under this name is quite different, having larger flowers a deeper ultramarine-blue, and growing about 30 cm (12 in.) taller. It may be just a selected form.

Camassias are best increased from seed, which germinates freely and produces flowering bulbs in two or three years. *C. esculenta* increases quite rapidly from bulb division, but the taller-growing species are slow to increase, the bulbs growing larger instead. Transplant when dormant in the autumn, setting bulbs 7.5–15 cm (3–6 in.) apart according to size.

CAMPANULA
Campanulaceae   Bell flower

This genus has over 250 species, most of which are hardy perennials distributed over the Northern Hemisphere, especially in the Mediterranean region. Many of these species are classed as rock and alpine plants, and are indispensable in a well-planned rockery. Unfortunately, a number of the most attractive species are outside the range of this book, and we therefore confine ourselves to some of the better-known, taller-growing species and varieties, all of which are particularly attractive.

C. alliatiifolia grows to 1.2 m (4 ft) from a rosette of foliage, with nodding, white flowers 2.5–5 cm (1–2 in.) long.

C. burghaltii has large, dangling bells of mauve-blue, which open in succession. This plant spreads freely on light soils.

C. carpatica comes from the Carpathians, as its name implies, and is the best known of the many desirable dwarf species. The plant forms a neat clump of smooth, ovate, cordate leaves, irregularly dentated, and during spring it throws up erect, wiry, branched stems of saucer-shaped flowers. The usual type grown produces masses of soft mauve-blue flowers, but there are several other named varieties ranging from white to blues, violet and purple.

Campanula burghaltii

There are also some very fine hybrids that have been derived from this species. *C. carpatica* is easy to cultivate, and is much used in rockeries or as a border plant, thriving in dry situations but preferring medium to light soils rather than clay.

C. glomerata is an erect-growing plant with flower-stems up to 60 cm (24 in.) high, usually single but sometimes branched. The ovate leaves are hairy, up to 7.5 cm (3 in.) long, forming a compact basal clump from which the flower-stalks arise in the spring. The terminal heads of funnel-shaped, somewhat hairy, veined flowers are usually deep violet-purple, a very rich and attractive colour. A selected form is grown and offered under the name of *C. glomerata* 'Superba'. Pure white, lavender and even double-flowered forms are also grown.

C. lactiflora is a strong-growing perennial attaining a height of 1.8 m (6 ft) when well established, and producing immense pyramidal spikes containing hundreds of starry, milky white blue bells, about 2.5 cm (1 in.) across. Selected forms include 'Loddon Anna', a pretty flesh-pink, 'Prichard's Variety', a deep blue, both 1 m (3 ft) tall, and a dainty little dwarf called 'Pouffe', which produces neat mounds of light blue flowers. A lower-growing and more compact variety of this species is known as 'Celtidifolia'. Plants bloom in early summer, and if cut back immediately, may produce a second crop of bloom in the autumn, particularly after a wet summer. Plants can be naturalised among light grass and will also thrive in the semi-shade.

C. latifolia has mauve-blue, tubular flowers on dense spikes to 90 cm (36 in.), and is very free-flowering and long-lasting. It often flowers a second time in autumn. *C. latifolia* 'Macrantha' is also vigorous and has handsome spikes of violet-purple. 'Superba' is another fine cultivar.

C. persicifolia is perhaps the best-known hardy, herbaceous campanula, with a spreading rootstock and 7.5 cm (3 in.), leathery, toothed leaves. Smooth flower-stems, almost devoid of leaves, carry dozens of large bells 2.5 cm (1 in.) or more across. The common type is blue, but possibly the best selected form, with large, silvery, china-blue bells, is one called 'Telham Beauty'. A deep blue-flowered variety is called 'Wedgwood', and a pure white counterpart is offered as *C. persicifolia* 'Alba'. Perhaps the most popular varieties in this variable

Campanula persicifolia 'Fleur de Neige'

heavy rosettes of leaves the first season, and tall, pyramidal, densely packed panicles of pale blue flowers with a deeper throat. A pure white-flowered variety also exists. It is a desirable and attractive plant, and fresh stocks are easily raised from seed.

C. rotundifolia is the European hare-bell with small, round leaves and numerous 30–45 cm (12–18 in.), thin, wiry stems of small blue bells, freely produced over a long period from new flower-stems arising from the abundant, spreading, underground roots. Easily naturalised in almost any odd corner, it has a tendency to spread rapidly, especially on light soils. *C. rotundifolia* 'Eden' is a New Zealand selection with shorter bells, freely produced in late summer.

C. sarmatica is a clump-forming perennial with erect flower-stems 30–60 cm (12–24 in.) tall, with nodding, grey-blue flowers.

C. trachelium grows to about 60 cm (24 in.), and the cultivar usually grown, called 'Bernice', has spikes set with fine, double, powder-blue flowers.

All campanulas are readily increased from divisions of old clumps, which should be broken up every two or three years, otherwise the ground becomes impoverished, with poorer blooms resulting from crowded clumps. Transplant during the winter months.

species are the double and semi-double types, of which we have 'Pride of Exmouth', a lovely soft double blue, and 'Fleur de Neige', a double white. 'Moerheimii' is another fine, very free-flowering, double white. A double violet-blue, with bells 5 cm (2 in.) across on strong, 1 m (3 ft) stems, is called 'Wirral Bell'. All forms of *C. persicifolia* are good for cutting, commencing to bloom in early summer. They will flower over a long period if the individual flowers are pinched from the upright stems as soon as they show signs of fading.

C. poscharskyana (sometimes wrongly labelled *C. garganica*) is low-growing and spreading, with sprays of mauve-blue flowers from late spring onwards. It will mound up to 20 cm (8 in.) and can be used as ground cover, on walls and in the front of mixed borders. Two good cultivars are 'E. H. Frost', pure white, and 'Stella', violet-blue.

C. pyramidalis is another tall-growing species, commonly called the chimney bell-flower. It is usually grown as a biennial, the plants forming

Campanula poscharskyana

CANNA
Cannaceae   Indian shot

This genus comprises about 50 species, natives of tropical America and Asia. The different varieties of cannas grown today are mostly the result of hybrids from many species, particularly *C. indica*, the flowers of which are pink spotted with red, and *C. lutea*, a most variable species ranging in colour from pale straw-yellow to orange. The older forms were grown almost entirely for their attractive foliage, some of which is beautifully marbled with deeper green and bronze, or is deep coppery red throughout. However, with the great improvement in the size of canna flowers in recent years, their value as a foliage plant has been almost entirely lost. In recent years, some very fine dwarf varieties, particularly suited to bedding, have been produced in Germany, and a set of larger-flowered, taller-growing hybrids called the 'Grand Opera Series' has been well received.

The following is a selection of dwarf cultivars:

'Alberich'—1 m (3 ft), apricot-peach, ruffled flowers, bronze foliage.
'Ambrosia'—80 cm (32 in.), apricot-orange with bronze foliage.
'Banner'—1 m (3 ft), rich golden yellow with green foliage.
'Cupid'—80 cm (32 in.), clear pink with green foliage.
'Gnome'—1 m (3 ft), huge heads of delicate pink.
'King City Gold'—1 m (3 ft), intense deep gold.
'Niagara'—1 m (3 ft), flame-red, widely margined with gold
'Perkeo'—1 m (3 ft), bright rose-red with green foliage.
'Rose Cavalier'—1 m (3 ft), massive heads of bright rose-pink.

Taller cultivars include:

'Ambassador'—1.2 m (4 ft), lovely moon-white, very showy.
'America'—1.5 m (5 ft), deep crimson-red, bronze foliage.
'Assault'—dazzling red dusted gold, bronze foliage.
'Goldbird'—1.5 m (5 ft), pure, soft golden yellow.
'La Traviata'—1.2 m (4 ft), lovely salmon-apricot.
'Madam Butterfly'—1.5 m (5 ft), large flowers, delicate creamy pink.

Canna 'La Traviata'

Canna 'Perkeo'

'Pfitzers Chinese Coral'—massive heads of salmon-pink.
'Pride of Holland'—1.8 m (6 ft), huge, rosy salmon flowers with bronze foliage.
'Statue of Liberty'—1.8 m (6 ft), large, brilliant orange, bronze foliage.
'Tiger Lily'—1.5 m (5 ft), pale lemon-yellow spotted with red.

Some of the little-known species are worthwhile,

being quite distinct from the varieties normally grown. One such is *C. iridiflora*, in which the pendant, open-mouthed, pink trumpets are 12.5 cm (5 in.) long; it grows 3 m (10 ft) tall and is a native of Peru.

While it is true that cannas will not stand heavy frosts, and collapse in the winter if left in the ground, it is not generally known that the fleshy roots can be lifted and stored in sand or similar material over the winter, just like dahlias. If winter frosts are not more than 16 degrees, the roots may be left in the ground without being disturbed. After the second frost has cut back the foliage, the tops and stems can be entirely removed and cleaned up, otherwise they look very untidy. In colder districts a covering of hay over the roots would provide the protection needed.

Cannas really need warmth, plenty of well-decayed manure, as they are gross feeders, and an occasional good soaking during the summer to prolong the flowering season. They are best grown in beds by themselves, with dwarf varieties planted in the outer row, then intermediate varieties, with the tallest in the centre. A carefully planned bed will give a continual display of bloom from late spring till autumn, or when the frosts come, but the peak of bloom will be during the hottest weather in mid-summer. While special beds are recommended, the canna, with its great range of shades, is an attractive addition to the herbaceous border. It should be remembered that they need full sun, and should not be shaded by adjoining plants, trees or buildings.

Increase is best from divisions, preferably in spring just as new growth is starting. Choose vigorous outer shoots for transplanting. New colours can be secured by raising seeds. However, the seeds are very hard and need to be filed through the skin to hasten germination.

CARDIOCRINUM
Liliaceae

This plant has previously been included in the genus *Lilium*. There are three species, only one of which is considered worth cultivating. *C. giganteum* is a woodland plant from the Himalayas and may be grown successfully in cooler climates. It prefers partial shade and deep, rich, moist soil. Bulbs should be

Cardiocrinum giganteum

Cardiocrinum giganteum and *Hosta sieboldiana*

planted just below the surface, and kept moist and mulched during warm weather. The stately spike may reach 3 m (10 ft), with up to 20 trumpet flowers, 15 cm (6 in.) long and usually slightly pendulous, occuring in summer. They are pure white outside, sometimes with red markings at the base. The leaves are large, bright green and glossy, arranged up the thick stem. Upstanding seed-pods are very decorative, and from the plentiful seeds new plants can be easily raised but take about seven years to flower. Mature bulbs are not suitable for transplanting; they die after flowering, leaving offsets that will take about four years to flower.

CATANANCHE
Asteraceae   Cupid's dart

This genus has five annual and perennial species, natives of the Mediterranean region. The herbaceous species *C. caerulea*, in its various forms, is the only one generally grown. The simple leaves are narrow or linear, confined in a tufted form to the rootstock, like the armerias. Numerous, thin, leafless stems, 60 cm (24 in.) tall, are topped with a solitary flower-head 5 cm (2 in.) across, each with several rows of petals, ragged or frilled at the edges. The pappus behind the flower is composed of five to seven slenderly tapered, papery scales, which are attractive dried when the flower has faded. The colour of the common type is a lovely shade of cornflower-blue, while a white with blue edge is called *C. caerulea* 'Bicolor'. A recently introduced, larger-flowered form of the usual type is called *C. caerulea* 'Major', and is preferable to the ordinary form. All these forms are extremely free-flowering, continuing in bloom most of the summer months. While quite hardy and easily grown in almost any type of soil, established roots often collapse in the winter if the position is inclined to be wet or poorly drained, or the soil rather heavy. Increase is either from seed or divisions of older clumps. Transplant during winter.

CELMISIA
Asteraceae

These lovely alpine daisies are almost entirely confined to New Zealand and the adjacent islands, with an odd species in Tasmania and one in Australia. In the South Island they are characteristic plants of the high mountain country, and are a wonderful sight when in bloom during mid-summer. Over 50 species exist, from tiny miniatures only a few inches high to strong-growing plants of 1 m (3 ft), with giant white daisies 10 cm (4 in.) across. Plants are easy to grow in cool, moist conditions that never become dry for more than a week or two at a time. Being alpine plants and bathed with mist almost every day, they cannot tolerate dry summers. The rich, leathery, green foliage of most species is handsome and distinctive, usually silvery underneath, hairy, and sometimes edged bronzy green. Quite a number of interesting natural hybrids exist. Most plants in cultivation in New Zealand have been collected from the wild, and if plenty of root is secured, they can be safely shifted any time. Good seed germinates freely.

   C. bellidioides is a mat-forming, evergreen perennial with rounded, leathery leaves and daisy-like flowers, 1 cm (0.5 in.) wide, with very short stems.

Catananche caerulea

C. spectabilis has thick, leathery leaves, the upper surface smooth and the lower densely hairy. White daisy-like flowers up to 5 cm (2 in.) across occur on stalks to 25 cm (10 in.) high.

C. traversii has sword-shaped, dark green leaves with reddish margins and cream undersides. In summer it has wide, daisy-like flower-heads.

Celmisia spectabilis

CENIA
Asteraceae

The South African species *C. turbinata* has a bushy habit and bears numerous, golden button flowers continuously throughout the summer. It needs a well-drained, light soil and a sunny situation, and is hardy in all but the coldest inland areas. It may not prove very perennial, but it is easily renewed from cuttings, and the stems often root where they touch the ground.

CENTAUREA
Asteraceae   Cornflower

This is a large genus of over 500 species of annuals and perennials, mostly natives of Europe, Asia and Africa. The sweet sultans and other hardy annual cornflowers are well-known garden plants, but there are a number of really useful perennial species that are worthy of a place in the herbaceous border. Plants of some of the species are a little inclined to sprawl too much or otherwise get out of hand, but if they are 'spring-cleaned' every now and again, they need not appear to be at all untidy. Most grow 60–90 cm (24–36 in.) tall, with graceful flowers, large thistle-like heads of numerous, finely rayed petals in shades of bright red, deep purple, blue and golden yellow. All are suitable for cutting.

C. dealbata is a very leafy plant, the foliage being greyish and very deeply cut. The 60 cm (24 in.) branching stems produce a mass of rosy pink cornflower heads from late spring onwards. A selected form known as *C. dealbata* 'Steenbergii' has larger, deep pink flowers, and is a very desirable hardy plant.

C. gymnocarpa is a silver-foliaged, shrubby perennial, very useful for lightening up the border during the dull or flowerless winter months. It grows about 75 cm (30 in.) high, forming a compact bush with doubly bipinnate, silver-grey leaflets. The rosy violet flower-heads, forming open panicles, are almost hidden by the dense foliage.

C. macrocephala is outstanding among the cornflowers, a handsome plant from the Caucasus

Cenia turbinata

Centaurea montana

Mountains, growing to a height of about 1 m (3 ft) or more. Early in the season the large rusty brown buds begin to appear and in due course open to reveal golden yellow thistle-heads, which may be 10 cm (4 in.) across. It is quite hardy and likes fairly moist conditions.

C. montana is the common or best-known species. It grows about 45 cm (18 in.) high, and blooms early in the spring, producing deep blue, rose or white flowers resembling the annual cornflower. Plants are usually raised from seed, although selected colours or types are increased from divisions.

C. ruthenica has foliage that is dark green and deeply cut, and the slender but erectly branching stems, up to 1.2 m (4 ft) tall, produce an abundance of very pretty, lemon-yellow heads. An easily grown plant of distinct merit.

Increase of all selected types is from divisions. Plants are quite easy to grow under most conditions and resist very cold winters. The species are usually increased from seed. Transplant during winter or spring.

CENTRANTHUS
Valerianaceae   Valerian

Often seen as a naturalised plant on dry banks, valerian can be used effectively in the garden, for the flowers have rich colouring and are long-lasting. *C. ruber* 'Coccineus' is the best variety, and has numerous heads of red flowers growing to 75 cm (30 in.) in late spring and early summer. White and pink forms are also grown. Good drainage is essential. Stocks can be increased by seed sown in autumn or spring.

CEPHALARIA
Dipsaceae

This genus consists of about 65 annuals and coarse, summer-flowering perennials, natives of Europe and North Africa. Only one species, *C. gigantea* (syn. *C. tatarica*), seems worthy of cultivation, and has a considerable appeal for the back of the herbaceous border. It is seen at its best in a wild or woodland garden, clumps growing up to 1.8 m (6 ft) high. From a hard rootstock it produces an abundance of deeply toothed, rich green foliage, and

Cephalaria gigantea

long, thin stems, topped singly with 10 cm (4 in.) wide, light yellow, scabiosa-like flowers, freely produced during late spring and summer. Increase is from seed, or division of old clumps in winter.

CERATOSTIGMA
Plumbaginaceae

From this genus, two perennial species are suitable for the border. *C. plumbaginoides*, which comes from western China, is a bushy plant, growing to 40 cm (16 in.) and covered with rich blue flowers in late summer. *C. willmottianum* is taller growing, up to 75 cm (30 in.), with darker blue flowers. In autumn the foliage is tinged with red. Some other species are grown as dwarf shrubs. All species succeed best in light soils, and are propagated from division or cuttings.

Ceratostigma plumbaginoides

CHASMANTHE
Iridaceae

These are South African bulbs, previously belonging to the genus *Antholyza*. *C. floribunda* has large, flattened corms, similar to watsonia corms, which

Chasmanthe floribunda var. *duckittii*

should be planted when dormant in late summer. The foliage is vigorous, again similar to that of watsonias but ribbed to 1 m (3 ft). Flower-spikes open in winter, with tubular, orange flowers arranged in opposite directions. Flowers can be damaged by frost and will need protection in cold districts. *C. floribunda* var. *duckittii* has yellow flowers and light green foliage, usually 5 cm (2 in.) wide, and flowers in winter also.

CHEIRANTHUS
Brassicaceae   Wallflower

This is a genus of perennials and sub-shrubs, some of which are best treated as biennials. They do best in fertile soil in an open, sunny position.

   C. 'Bowles Mauve' is a bushy plant to 75 cm (30 in.), with dark green leaves 5 cm (2 in.) long and small, deep mauve flowers in spring and summer.

C. cheiri is a shrubby plant, usually grown as a biennial. It has lance-shaped, dark green leaves and fragrant flowers in a wide range of colours—from white and yellow through to orange, bronze and red.

C. 'Harpur Crewe' is a deep yellow, double form, making a leafy bush to 40 cm (16 in.) tall.

C. linifolius is a bushy sub-shrub, the best form of which is 'E.A.Bowles', which has a long display of lilac spikes in late spring and early summer.

C. 'Moonlight' is a low-growing, pale yellow form with brown buds. It is probably better suited to rock gardens.

Many varieties are biennial and are increased by seed sown in spring. Selected forms are easily propagated by cuttings.

See also *Erysimum*.

Chionodoxa luciliae

Cheiranthus 'Harpur Crewe'

CHIONODOXA
Liliaceae   Glory of the snow

This genus consists of six species of lovely, spring-flowering bulbs, common and easily grown in England but seen less often in warmer climates.

They require a cool, shady spot, but in districts with cold, prolonged winters very little trouble will be experienced in growing them in almost any position, provided drainage is good. In warmer districts, bulbs should be planted up to 15 cm (6 in.) or more deep, as this helps to keep the bulbs cool; planted thus, they will grow much larger and produce more and better blooms than they do with shallow planting.

C. luciliae is the best-known species, with its brilliant blue, open-belled, starry flowers and white centres, four to 10 on a 15 cm (6 in.) stem. There are several light and deep pink forms of this species as well as a pure white one. A taller and larger-flowered variety is known as *C. luciliae* 'Gigantea', with its large, light blue flowers. A miniature-flowered variety seldom seen is *C. luciliae* 'Tmoli'.

C. sardensis is the other well-known species, and possibly the most desirable, a true gentian-blue colour without a paler centre. A splash of these on the rockery or naturalised under trees is most pleasing and arresting.

Natural increase of chionodoxas slows down or ceases in unsuitable conditions, but all species are quite easily grown. Increase is usually from seed, which is freely produced in large pods like hyacinths. Full-sized flowering bulbs are produced in three years. In Holland the seed is sown in trenches, and each year the trench is filled in as the bulbs become larger and stronger, until the soil is levelled off for the last growing season before lifting. This method results in bigger bulbs. Plant bulbs at a depth and spacing of 5 cm (2 in.) for massed effect during autumn.

CHLIDANTHUS
Amaryllidaceae   Sea daffodil

This genus consists of only one species, *C. fragrans*. Sometimes also called the perfumed fairy lily, this old-time but unfortunately not well-known South American bulb is worthy of much more attention. A coastal bulb, which delights in free, loose soil, resisting dry conditions in the autumn, it provides a display in the spring of delightfully fragrant, rich golden yellow trumpets 5–10 cm (2–4 in.) long, growing 30–45 cm (12–18 in.) tall. The glaucous green foliage is similar to that of narcissus, and this, together with the colour and to some extent the shape of the blooms, has earned it the common name of sea daffodil. Healthy bulbs are easily grown in well-drained soils, and it is a good subject as a cut flower.

Increase is from divisions, and bulbs increase rapidly when well established. In cold districts, bulbs can be lifted in autumn and stored over the winter, and will flower quite freely in the spring when replanted. Plant bulbs with the neck just below the surface of the soil, about 20 cm (8 in.) apart, while dormant during winter.

CHRYSANTHEMUM
Asteraceae

This genus has undergone considerable revision in recent times, and most species have now been assigned to other genera. The genus *Chrysanthemum* now includes three species of annuals, natives of Europe, North Africa and south-west Asia.

C. frutescens, the tree marguerite, is now classified as *Argyranthemum frutescens* (q.v.).

C. mawii should rightly be classified as *Tanacetum* (q.v.), although this does not appear to have been formally recorded.

C. maximum, commonly called the shasta daisy, is now classified as *Leucanthemum maximum* (q.v.).

C. parthenium, the herb feverfew, is now included, along with species of *Pyrethrum*, under *Tanacetum* (q.v.).

C. zawadskii var. *rubellum* (syn. *C. x rubellum*) is now classified as *Dendranthema zawadskii* (q.v.).

The numerous hybrid chrysanthemums grown by gardeners and for florists' and exhibition purposes are now classified under *Dendranthema*.

CIMICIFUGA
Ranunculaceae   Bugbane

This genus consists of 15 species of herbaceous perennials distributed over Europe, Asia and North America. They are valuable late-flowering, spikey plants for the back of the border, tolerating, if necessary, considerable shade. The tall, graceful spikes of bloom, reaching up to 1.2 m (4 ft), are well formed by mid-summer but do not open fully till the autumn.

C. americana grows about 1 m (3 ft) high, with long, erect spikes of closely set, ivory-white flowers.

C. racemosa has rather broader white spikes, growing to 1.5 m (5 ft). These are lovely associated with blue and yellow perennials.

Increase is from divisions when plants are dormant in winter.

CLEMATIS
Ranunculaceae

This genus has over 250 species, of which very few are in cultivation. Most people rightly think of clematis as climbers, but it is not generally known that there are also a number of quite attractive, shrubby, herbaceous species that are worth growing.

These are all easy to grow in full sun in any well-drained soil. Although the flowers are much smaller and petals not as broad as those of the climbing species, they are most attractive and, being nearly all blues and purples, help to add wealth to a rather poorly represented colour in the perennial border.

An excellent species, *C. fremontii*, grows only 45 cm (18 in.) high, with leathery, deep green foliage. It has violet-blue flowers of thick, fleshy appearance.

Opposite: The perennials in this cottage garden include grey-leaved artemisia, pink bergamot (*Monarda*), salvia in both green and purple-leaved forms, and red and yellow achillea.

Clematis recta

C. heracleifolia produces fragrant, tube-like blooms nearly all summer. The flowers are hyacinth-like, bell-shaped, pale blue or lavender blue in small clusters.

C. integrifolia, with its nodding, funnel-shaped, blue flowers borne on single stems and leathery, deep green foliage, is a plant that invariably attracts attention. *C. integrifolia* 'Hendersonii' is much the best form, with widely flared, blue flowers in summer, and growing to about 1 m (3 ft) tall, with scrambling stems that may need twiggy support.

C. recta grows erect about 1 m (3 ft) feet tall, with creamy white, fragrant flowers in mid-summer followed by fluffy, silken heads. There is also a double-flowered form of this species.

All clematis species and hybrids can be raised from seed, but unless freshly gathered and sown immediately, the seed will not germinate for about 12 months. Seed sown in boxes should be covered with sand and put away in a shady place until germination occurs. Large clumps can be safely divided up in the early spring, although no clematis, climbing or herbaceous, likes being disturbed.

CLIVIA
Amaryllidaceae

These plants are very easily grown, preferring semi-shade and thriving to perfection under the shade of trees, where they soon form strong clumps, with short agapanthus-like leaves and thick, fleshy roots. If a suitable, well-drained, warm position is chosen, either on the north side of big, overhanging trees or under the eaves of a building, plants will succeed without further protection in districts with frosts up to 10 degrees. In very cold districts they can be grown as pot or tub plants, blooming in the winter or early spring when few flowers are about.

C. gardenii has narrow leaves and reddish orange flowers. It is similar to *C. nobilis* but has fewer flowers, and these are without the green tips characteristic of the latter.

C. miniata is the best-known species, with its rich orange-apricot flowers, long-lasting when cut and therefore most valuable for winter decoration and florists' use. In Europe and America, the colour is usually bright scarlet with a light centre. A most desirable yellow-flowered variety, deeper in colour at the throat, is known as *C. miniata* 'Aurea'. Several other forms are known in shades of yellow, orange and red, and some lovely hybrids have been raised from these species. A superior cultivar, with bolder heads of scarlet and yellow flowers, is now readily available. Named *C. miniata* 'Grandiflora', it has

Clivia gardenii

Clivia miniata 'Grandiflora'

COLCHICUM
Liliaceae   Autumn crocus

About 60 species are known in this genus, distributed through the Middle East and the Mediterranean region and as far west as Europe, but many of them are hard to distinguish as they are very similar in appearance and bloom.

C. agrippinum blooms late in the season, with flowers of medium size with rather narrow, pointed petals chequered with lilac-purple on a ground of pale rosy lilac.

C. autumnale, with its rosy purple, crocus-like blooms, freely produced in the autumn, is among our best-known and most popular autumn-flowering bulbs. Each of the elongated, dark-skinned bulbs yields masses of flowers, sometimes two dozen or more, appearing before the leaves and roots start to grow. All species and varieties can be flowered inside a room or building without any soil or moisture being added, and are quite attractive and interesting subjects, particularly the larger-flowered ones. *C. autumnale* and its less common white form, 'Alba', are the most prolific in bloom and bulb increase, but the flowers are smaller, and not suitable for cutting. Double-flowered forms of *C. autumnale* are sometimes available. One of these is named 'Waterlily' and has a large flower with up to 20 warm rosy lilac petals. The flowers are so heavy that they tend to fall over soon after opening. The comparison with a small waterlily is apt.

C. bornmuelleri is a species often confused with,

larger flower-heads with 25–30 flowers and much larger foliage, up to 10 cm (4 in.) wide and 45 cm (18 in.) long.

C. nobilis is a smaller-flowered species often confused with *C. miniata*. It blooms during winter also, and gives us crowded heads, 40–50 on an umbel, blooms funnel-shaped and drooping, reddish yellow tipped with green. It is quite attractive and easily grown.

In hot climates, *C. miniata* is often seen growing happily without any special attention in the undergrowth of shrubberies where the roots are well-ripened in the autumn by somewhat hot and dry conditions. If too much moisture is given during the autumn, few flowers follow in the winter. Plants in pots or tubs are often partly dried off or tipped on their side for two or three months in the early autumn to enforce a rest and thus induce winter blooms.

Clivias have great possibilities as winter cut flowers. The three main essentials for success are protection from heavy frosts, shade for the foliage from direct sunlight, and dry conditions in the autumn.

Increase is from divisions of well-established clumps during winter or early spring. Seed sometimes forms under suitable conditions and is easily raised, although plants are slower to reach maturity.

Colchicum autumnale 'Waterlily'

Colchicum speciosum 'Album'

and close to, *C. speciosum*, but it blooms a fortnight earlier and with greenish white-tubed, large flowers opening almost white, later changing to rosy mauve with pale centres. Another distinguishing feature is that the large, elongated corm with long, tapering spur is covered with a membranous tunic.

C. byzantinum, a native of Turkey, is closely allied to, and often included under, *C. speciosum*. The lilac-rose flowers are much more numerous and of less substance, and the bulbs are larger. A similar species or selected form is listed under the name of 'Major Lilac' and may be a form of *C. byzantinum*. It is one of the earliest to bloom, with a great abundance of soft lilac-pink flowers.

C. luteum is a most desirable, spring-flowering species from western India but is seldom offered. It is the only yellow-flowered species known.

C. speciosum is possibly the best of all the species, with its large, beautifully formed, rounded cups of soft rosy purple, paling to white in the centre. Although forms approaching a rosy pink occur, the pure white form, *C. speciosum* 'Album', is certainly the most stately of them all and a lovely florists' flower. The lily-like cups, 7.5 cm (3 in.) across when fully open, are of purest white and, rising as they do straight from the ground without any foliage or

other signs of growth, are most arresting. Bulbs are very large, producing fewer blooms than the commoner *C. autumnale*, but this is compensated for by their chaste beauty, suggestive of marble.

There are several very fine hybrids or selected forms of species, including 'The Giant', which is large-flowered and deep mauve with a white eye, and 'Violet Queen', a deep purplish violet. 'Lilac Wonder' is a late-blooming hybrid in a uniform shade of violet-mauve.

All colchicums seem to thrive better in climates experiencing cold winters, and bulbs are seldom flowered successfully in warmer districts. Good drainage is essential, and they seem to be equally at home either under large trees or right out in the open. They are delightful when naturalised in bold groups or colonies where they can be left undisturbed for years, and are quite happy planted at the base of big trees. When bulbs become crowded and it is evident that the blooms are deteriorating, they should be lifted and divided up, preferably soon after the leaves have died down. *C. autumnale* and its various forms will naturalise readily in light pasture, where the flowers are most picturesque. In parts of Samoa, it can be seen growing wild by the thousand in open areas, which shows that this species at least is quite at home in a warm climate.

The strong, heavy foliage of all species appears in the spring many months after the flowers have finished, and it is difficult to reconcile such stout, robust growth and foliage with the delicate, fragile blooms of the autumn.

Increase of all species and varieties is from natural division of bulbs, although some species seed freely in their country of origin. Bulbs are transplanted from mid- to late summer, preferably before they have bloomed, but otherwise, they can be planted in late autumn. Set the bulbs with the long necks just below the surface of the soil, in groups 10–15 cm (4–6 in.) apart according to size.

CONVALLARIA
Liliaceae   Lily of the valley

Lily of the valley is a well-known, low-growing perennial, thriving best in semi-shady spots not too dry and with moderately rich soil. It does better in colder spots, blooming more freely after a hard, cold winter. The common species, *C. majalis*, produces single, thick, oblong leaves, remaining till late autumn, and the flowering crowns give us in the spring racemes of dainty, roundish bells rolled back at the mouth. The blooms are much prized for their delicate fragrance and last in water a long time. In many countries the flowering crowns are forced in glasshouses for early blooms, while sometimes the crowns are retarded in a cool store to provide blooms much later in the season.

Beds take a few years to become established, as plants resent disturbance, but if the situation is suitable the roots increase until they become a dense mass. When overcrowded, only a small proportion of the crowns will flower, in which case the bed should either be lifted or replanted, or strips 30 cm (12 in.) wide removed and filled up with good fresh soil. A top-dressing each winter of well-decayed animal manure is beneficial, resulting in larger blooms, while excellent results can be secured by piling fallen leaves—preferably oak leaves— on the beds, to rot down during the winter. Do not ever use walnut leaves, as they seem to be poisonous to most plants.

Several larger-flowered forms are known and grown in Europe under the names of 'Fortin's Giant', 'Berlin Variety' and 'Major', but the difference in these is not always apparent in the Southern Hemisphere unless they are particularly well grown. The so-called pink variety 'Rosea' is a weak grower, with small, lilac-pink flowers. It is interesting as a novelty but will never replace the white-flowered species. An interesting form has foliage striped with variegation and is called 'Variegata'.

Transplant during late autumn, setting corms 5 cm (2 in.) apart and 2.5 cm (1 in.) below the surface of the soil.

CONVOLVULUS
Convolvulaceae   Bindweed

One sub-shrub and one perennial of this genus are excellent garden plants. *C. cneorum* is shrubby to 60 cm (24 in.) or more, with very silvery leaves and pure-white, 5 cm (2 in.) flowers in late spring.

C. mauritanicus has trailing stems and profuse, 5

Convolvulus mauritanicus

cm (2 in.), open, mauve-blue flowers in summer. This species is excellent on walls and in hanging baskets.

Plants can be propagated by softwood cuttings in late spring and summer.

COREOPSIS
Asteraceae

This is a genus of about 120 species. Some attractive annuals are well known and freely used, but the perennials and their selected forms hold a strong and important position in the herbaceous border. They are not fussy as to soil, and seem to thrive along the sea coast and in poor or stony ground. In some parts of Australia, the common form of *C. grandiflora* has become naturalised.

C. auriculata 'Superba' is an attractive plant that produces blooms on shorter stems. It makes a splendid mass display, and the bright yellow daisies are enhanced by a brownish purple, central disc. Seed-heads of old flowers should be constantly

Coreopsis grandiflora 'Perry's Double'

removed to prolong the flowering period.

C. grandiflora is of robust, leafy growth, with a prolonged succession of 60 cm (24 in.), wiry stems topped singly with 5 cm (2 in.) wide, open flowers. The superior form 'Badengold' produces 7.5 cm (3 in.) wide, rich golden yellow, cosmos-like flowers on elegant stems and is most useful for cutting. This variety soon forms a strong clump 60–90 cm (24–36 in.) across and in height, providing a wealth of colour from late spring until winter. It seems to flower better in light, poorish soil otherwise the plant runs to foliage only. The double-flowered form of *C. grandiflora* is known as 'Perry's Double'. A more recent cultivar is 'Sunray', with full double petals that do not show any centre crown. The petals are attractively frilled and a rich golden yellow.

C. verticillata is a most useful species now deservedly popular with flower-lovers. The deep green, small but abundant foliage sets off to perfection the masses of 4 cm (1.5 in.) wide, golden flowers, each with a conspicuous black eye. A form called *C. verticillata* 'Grandiflora', the one usually cultivated, has slightly larger flowers, a little deeper in colour, and grows a few inches taller. A plant in full bloom has been aptly described as a yellow love-in-the-mist, the display often continuing from summer till early autumn.

The perennial coreopsis are seen at their best advantage when combined with white shasta daisies and a bold background of blue delphiniums. Plants suitably placed or grouped in this way are more attractive than if isolated.

Increase can be made from divisions of old clumps in the winter or spring, and also from spring cuttings. Seed of the hardy perennial species germinates freely if sown in autumn or spring, blooming the following summer. Selected types must be increased by divisions of old clumps in the winter or from soft cuttings rooted in the spring.

COSMOS
Asteraceae   Bidens

This is a genus of about 25 species of annual and herbaceous plants from tropical America and Mexico. The two species described here are the only ones generally in cultivation, and both are reasonably hardy. The foliage is pinnate, being divided into several segments. The tuberous roots resemble dahlias, and plants are often increased from soft spring cuttings in the same way. In very cold districts, these roots, when dormant, can be lifted and stored in sand or even dry, to be replanted in spring or when frosts are over.

C. atrosanguineus is commonly known as black cosmos. It is similar in habit and foliage to the fol-

Cosmos atrosanguineus

lowing species, except that the plant seldom exceeds 60 cm (24 in.) in height, and the smaller, single flowers are dark velvety red or maroon-crimson. This species is propagated from seed.

C. diversifolius (also known as *Bidens dahlioides*) forms an erect, bushy plant 60–120 cm (24–48 in.) high, the foliage being divided into five or seven lanceolate lobes. The thin flower-stems carry single, 5–7.5 cm (2–3 in.) wide, rosy-lilac, daisy-like flowers, each with a central yellow disc. These are freely produced throughout summer and autumn, and have some value as cut flowers. Like the preceding species, seed sets freely and germinates readily, blooming the first summer if sown early.

CRINUM
Amaryllidaceae

Gardeners will be surprised to learn that this genus comprises over 100 species, all of them highly ornamental, beautiful, flowering bulbs, easily grown and fairly hardy except in the coldest districts or wet places. The heavy, fleshy roots that penetrate deeply into the soil indicate that they are bulbs that experience or prefer hot, dry conditions in the autumn, and possibly in winter too. Bulbs are very large in some species, sometimes 15–20 cm (6–8 in.) across and 30 cm (12 in.) or more long including the neck, and weighing several kilograms. They prefer to be planted like belladonna lilies or nerines, with most of the bulb above the ground.

C. asiaticum is unlike other species. It has up to 50 white flowers with narrow, strap-like petals 10 cm (4 in.) long held in a large umbel on a stout stem.

C. bulbispermum is a most desirable species but seldom met with in gardens. It is the giant of the race, with big, trumpet-shaped blooms, either pink or white, on 1.2 m (4 ft) stems held well above the heavy foliage.

C. x *powelli* is the best-known, largest-flowered and easiest-grown variety, in either the pure white or soft pink form. It is a cross between *C. moorei* and *C. bulbispermum*. The heavy, kniphofia-like leaves are produced from the neck of the bulb, and the thick-stemmed scape comes from the centre, growing 30 cm (12 in.) or more above the foliage. The wide-open trumpets are 10 cm (4 in.) or more

across, neatly arranged and held six to ten on the bold flower-stem. They are useful for cutting and prized for bridal bouquets. The form known as 'Krelagii' has large, overlapping petals that are pink, flushed deeper in the throat.

C. moorei is similar to, and often confused with, *C.* x *powellii*. It has white flowers with a faint red flush and greenish tube.

C. scabrum grows to 60 cm and is white with red stripes on the petals.

Several interesting hybrids have been raised in California. The most colourful is a variety called 'Ellen Bosanquet', the blooms of which are a deep rosy claret shade, mostly trumpet- or lily-shaped, nearly as large and robust as the *C.* x *powelli* forms.

Bulbs are semi-dormant during winter, when they are are usually shifted. Well-established clumps root deeply into the soil and are difficult to remove.

Crinum x *powelli*

CROCOSMIA
Iridaceae   Montbretia

This genus from South Africa, comprising only six species, resembles in growth the small-flowered gladiolus, with its sword-like leaves. Two species, namely *C. aurea*, golden yellow tipped copper red, and *C. pottsii*, bright yellow flushed brick red, are the parents of the present-day, large-flowered montbretias. A natural hybrid between these two species, known as *C. x crocosmiiflora*, the flowers of which are orange-red, is recognised as the common montbretia, which now grows wild in some places or takes possession of old gardens.

The dainty *C. aurea* is a species worth growing. Some of the best varieties are 'His Majesty', orange-yellow and coppery red; 'Star of the East', pure orange; 'E. A. Bowles', soft carmine-red; and 'Tigridii', yellow with a brown centre. They have larger, wide-open flowers up to 10 cm (4 in.) wide when well grown, and they do not spread so readily, although seed-heads should be removed before they ripen.

C. masoniorum is a valuable introduction from South Africa. The blooms are much larger than *C. aurea*, 7.5 cm (3 in.) across, the colour being brilliant tangerine-orange shading to orange-flame at the edges of the petals. If raised from seed, a little variation in colour occurs, some plants being more of a reddish orange, but all forms are very brilliant.

About six blooms in pairs come out at once, held erect on stems to 75 cm (30 in.) but arching gracefully at the top. The stem usually carries two or more side branches, each with 20–40 buds, opening in turn and lasting several weeks in bloom. This species is a very desirable plant, possessing great possibilities for improvement and crossing with allied species or the existing hybrids in the large-flowered montbretias. It is also a most useful cut flower.

Plant corms 7.5 cm (3 in.) deep, 15 cm (6 in.) apart in winter, or later in the spring in very cold districts.

CROCUS
Iridaceae

This is a genus comprising over 80 species distributed over central and southern Europe, North Africa and western Asia as far as Afghanistan. Some of the species have been in cultivation for centuries, but the garden varieties seen today belong to the Dutch hybrids. Most of these have been derived from a variable species called *C. vernus*, in which white, lilac, blue and purple-flowered forms are known. These Dutch hybrids demand cool spring conditions and a climate with cold winters. A long, cool growing season for the foliage after corms have bloomed is necessary for the development of fresh corms. In warm districts, although newly planted corms flower quite well, the fresh corms produced each year become smaller until they disappear entirely. This is because the hot, dry spells in the spring ripen off the foliage prematurely before the corms have developed to full size. A semi-shady, cool spot should be chosen either in the rockery or on the south side of big trees.

The following varieties are some of the best of the named Dutch crocuses:

'Jeanne d'Arc'—extra fine, pure white.
'Little Dorrit'—soft china-blue, very free.
'Mammoth Yellow'—largest-flowered yellow.
'Purpureus Grandiflorus'—cup-shaped, purple-blue.
'Queen of the Blues'—soft ageratum-blue, lighter margin.

Crocosmia aurea 'Star of the East'

'Remembrance'—silvery purple, deeper base.

C. angustifolius (syn. *C. susianus*) is the cloth of gold crocus from Crimea and Caucasus. The roundish, lightly coated, straw-brown corms produce, in early spring, deep orange flowers feathered with deep brown. It seems a hardy, easily grown species, although not quite so happy in warmer districts, where it should be planted in the shade.

C. biflorus is commonly called the Scotch crocus. The flower tubes, 10 cm (4 in.) long, are silvery white to pale lilac, with yellow throat and out-segments buff, feathered with three to five fine, purple lines and blooming in early spring. The firm, flattened bulb is about 1 cm (0.5 in.) across, with a light brown tunic. It grows wild from Italy to the Middle East in lowland pastures and has long been in cultivation. There are nearly a dozen selected forms grown in Europe.

C. chrysanthus is a very fine species from Greece and Turkey, the cultivars of which can be grown successfully in cooler districts. Those usually available include:

'Blue Pearl'—purest blue ice.

'Cream Beauty'—pale creamy yellow of good size, very free-flowering.

'Lady Killer'—white, heavily marked outside with deep mauve.

'Snow Bunting'—white inside petals, outer are pure feathered with deep lilac.

'Sunshine'—golden orange, splendid large-flowered cultivar.

'Zwanenburg Bronze'—deep orange, heavily flushed outside with mahogany.

C. flavus (syn. *C. aureus*) is probably the best yellow-flowered wild species and is easier to grow in warmer climates than the popular 'Mammoth Yellow'. The flower-tube is 10 cm (4 in.) long, with an orange throat, bright orange-yellow segments, sometimes with a few faint grey lines near the base. It blooms profusely in early spring and increases freely from seed.

C. imperati. In this species, which is a native of Italy, the flower tube is 10 cm (4 in.) long, the throat orange, segments light purple and outside buff feathered purple. The smallish bulbs flower freely in late winter/early spring.

C. kotschyanus (syn. *C. zonatus*) is a native of Tur-

Crocus serotinus subsp. *salzmanii*

key and Lebanon. This species somewhat resembles *C. serotinus* subsp. *salzmanii* but blooms a month earlier with rosy lilac flowers, purple lined, and bright orange central spots. Corms are large and produce numerous small offsets.

C. ochroleucus. This is a prolific and easily grown, white-flowered species from the Middle East, quite happy in warmer districts where the larger-flowered Dutch hybrids would fail. A hundred or so bulbs planted in a group soon form a large colony, and provide an abundance of bloom in the late autumn. The 7.5 cm (3 in.) long tube is milk-white and suffused orange at the base, giving a general effect of creamy white.

C. serotinus subsp. *salzmanii* (syn. *C. salzmanii*) from Morocco and Spain is easily grown and quite happy in warmer districts. Under the ideal conditions of free soil and good drainage, corms grow up to 5 cm (2 in.) across, each producing, in the autumn, a dozen or more pale wine-lilac flowers, slightly feathered purple outside and with a yellowish throat. It is a splendid subject for planting under big deciduous trees and withstanding dry conditions. Bulbs increase rapidly and should be planted in late summer for autumn blooms.

C. sativus is the saffron crocus native to the region from Italy to Kurdistan; it seems to have been cultivated in Palestine in the days of Solomon. In some parts of England it has become naturalised. It blooms in autumn, with numerous, attractive, lilac-blue flowers shaded purple towards the base. The long, drooping stigmas of brilliant orange-scarlet are the source of the saffron of commerce. Bulbs are quite large for a crocus and increase readily.

Crocus tomasinianus 'Whitewell Purple'

obvious, however, that the autumn-flowering species must be planted in late summer in order to secure a good crop of blooms the first season. Set corms 7.5 cm (3 in.) apart in three rows for a border and cover with 5 cm (2 in.) of soil.

CUPHEA
Lythraceae

Two quite different species of this large family are grown. *C. ignea*, often called the firecracker, grows as a bushy sub-shrub to 60 cm (24 in.) and is covered all the summer and autumn with little tubular flowers about 2.5–5 cm (1–2 in.) long, bright red tipped with white.

C. micropetala is a sub-shrub up to 90 cm (36 in.) with 10 cm (4 in.) leaves and terminal, 2.5 cm (1 in.), tubular flowers of red, yellow and green. Plants are propagated by seed or cuttings in spring.

Cuphea ignea

CYBISTETES
Amaryllidaceae   Malagus lily

This beautiful South African bulb has 12–20 lily-like, fragrant, pink flowers at the top of thick stems in the autumn before the leaves appear. They grow

C. speciosus is claimed to be the best autumn-flowering species, with a number of attractive forms in shades of lavender, blue, purple and even white. The common type is violet-blue with orange-red stigmas, and globular flowers that are large for the size of the corms. This is a lovely species for the rockery or for naturalising.

C. tomasinianus is one of the best-known of the easily grown species, and one equally at home in the rockery or under big deciduous trees. It is a native of Dalmatia, where several forms exist. A number of these have been segregated, the best being 'Barrs Purple' and 'Whitewell Purple', the latter a rich reddish purple shade. The common type is pale sapphire-lavender with an exterior of silvery grey. Bulbs are quite round and small, and seldom more than 1 cm (0.5 in.) across. It blooms in early spring.

C. versicolor, the cloth of silver crocus, is a hardy, spring-blooming species from the Maritime Alps and has been in cultivation for centuries. Although a variable species, the type usually grown is known as *C. picturatus*, and is silvery white feathered with violet and with bright orange stigmas. The corms are 2.5 cm (1 in.) wide, pear-shaped tunics covered with parallel fibres.

Corms of crocuses should be planted in late summer if possible, although in colder districts spring-flowering varieties or species can be planted in late autumn and still give good results. It will be in winter, curving over and forming a rosette on the ground. The bulbs of *C. longifolia* will lose foliage in early summer and should not be watered after this. They do not multiply very rapidly and should be propagated from seed.

CYCLAMEN
Primulaceae

This is a genus of about 19 species, all natives of the Mediterranean region. Most are abundant in northern Italy. Although they are very hardy and, as may be supposed, withstand long periods of drought during summer and autumn, they prefer semi-shady conditions if available. They will all withstand cold winter conditions but require good drainage such as is found underneath large deciduous trees. In ideal conditions, the corms become larger each season and there is a corresponding increase in the number of blooms, until some species grow as large as big turnips or garden swedes, with a hundred blooms or more. The flower-stalks coil themselves into a spiral after the seed is set in the pod. This brings the seed down to soil level, for greater safety in germination.

C. africanum is a little-known species seldom offered in Europe, doubtless because it is only half-hardy. It is very happy in the Southern Hemisphere, soon developing large, flat-topped bulbs, which are dormant all summer and produce an abundance of 2.5 cm (1 in.) long, rosy-pink flowers, each with a deep carmine basal spot, during winter and spring.

C. coum is a lovely species with deep carmine-pink flowers, crimson at the base, and larger than most species, but shorter in the stem. The roundish, deep green leaves develop in the winter before the flowers appear in the winter or early spring. A delightful, pure white form with a startling crimson eye is known as *C. coum* 'Album'. Both are immensely popular in Europe, but are slower to become established than most other species.

C. cyprium is another rather tender species from Cyprus. The petals are white or pink, generally twisted, but smaller than *C. persicum*. It is autumn flowering and, like *C. persicum*, is scented.

C. hederifolium (syn. *C. neapolitanum*) is the best-known and easiest-grown species. It has pretty, marbled, heart-shaped leaves and, in autumn and winter, an abundance of cyclamen-pink blooms deepening to carmine towards the centre. *C. hederifolium* 'Album' is a lovely, pure white-flowered form that reproduces true to type from seed, and is even more easily established and prolific than the type. Both forms should be planted generously, as there are many places in an average garden where they can be grown to perfection with little attention.

C. persicum is the parent of our greenhouse pot plants, and is an excellent garden plant in warmer districts. The flowers are fragrant, and may be white, blush pink or occasionally carmine, borne on 15 cm (6 in.) stems well above the foliage. The petals are 2.5 cm (1 in.) long, narrow and twisted, and the leaves are variable in size and markings, sometimes round, sometimes ivy shaped.

Cyclamen persicum

C. purpurascens (syn. *C. europaeum*) is an easily grown species somewhat similar to *C. hederifolium*, the delightfully sweet-scented, carmine-rose flowers appearing in autumn and again in spring. Unlike most species, which root from the bottom centre, the corms produce roots all over and sometimes become very large. The leaves are green and not mottled.

C. repandum is probably the largest flowered of all species, blooming in the spring above the ivy-shaped leaves, which are somewhat silvery above and reddish beneath. The bright carmine flowers, deeper in colour near the tube, have much longer lobes and are more restricted than other species. Corms seldom exceed 2.5 cm (1 in.) across.

There are quite a number of other fine species, all of which are well worth growing, delighting in similar conditions. Increase of all species is easiest from seed, which must be fresh, as the germination falls off quickly, particularly if the seed is allowed to become dry. Plants will flower within a year if they are well looked after. They are best raised in a shady bed or in boxes under glasshouse benches. Some species, such as *C. graceum* and *C. persicum*, prefer to be planted deeply, but the corms of most other species rest on the surface of the ground. Late autumn is the best time to plant, although corms can be safely transplanted any time except when in full growth.

CYMBIDIUM
Orchidaceae

Although most orchids are suitable only for containers, it is possible in warmer climates to grow many cymbidiums outside if the right conditions are provided. Perfect drainage is their main requirement.

These orchids have long, narrow foliage, which is supported on conical or oval pseudo-bulbs resting on the top of the soil. The flower-scape emerges from the lower base of this bulbous formation, growing 30 cm to 1.2 m (1–4 ft), according to the variety or species, and each scape carries a number of flowers on short side stems.

C. grandiflorum has greenish flowers 10 cm (4 in.)

Cymbidium lowianum

across, with a straw-coloured lip and central purple-red blotches. *C. giganteum* is greenish yellow blotched red, and *C. lowianum* is also green, veined sepia-brown, with a whitish yellow lip and the front of the mid-lobe widely bordered crimson-red. These species and most of the other Indian cymbidiums are quite easily grown without any special attention, except correct potting mixture and partial shade in the hottest period of summer. This mixture should be composed mostly of open fibrous material; processed bark is now the basis of most of the orchid mixes available in garden centres. Light applications of a slow-action fertiliser once every three months will keep the plants in good condition. Ample drainage should be provided, with water supplied sparingly in the late summer.

It is not generally known that most cymbidium species are very hardy and will not be harmed in winter by medium frosts. In Australia, hybrid cymbidiums are grown outside in the garden like ordinary perennial plants, provided only with the necessary drainage, protection from bright summer light and heat, and shelter from winds. A summer house with 1 m (3 ft) walled sides to keep out ground draughts, and the remaining sides and flat top composed of split bamboo set 5 cm (2 in.) apart, provides a splendid shelter for growing these orchids and also other plants such as cyclamen, begonias and gloxinias. They can also be grown in a frost-free site in pots, so the plants are above ground level and the flower-stems can arch outwards in a natural manner. An alternative method is to make a planting box 75 cm (30 in.) deep, with scoria or gravel in the bottom, then filled with orchid mix. A site that gets sun for half the day is preferable, and if a tall, overhanging tree is nearby, so much the better. Plants should be watered twice a week in the hot weather. Each established plant will produce six to 10 spikes, which will last from four to six weeks, all through the winter. Choose some early cultivars and others to flower later. And when your orchid friends suggest the plants are ready for division, take no notice, because they will usually continue to flower every winter for 10 years.

Most orchids are surprisingly hard to kill, but once they have lost their root system through bad drainage, they are equally slow recovering normal health and flowering size. If it is found that the fresh whitish roots have become decayed, it is best first to cut away all such affected parts. Then take a large handful of fresh, clean sphagnum moss and pack it around the base of the then rootless plant, binding the moss very tightly in place with string. If these mossed plants are kept in a moist condition in a semi-shady spot, new roots will appear through the moss in three to six months' time, when the plants can be repotted in the usual mixture. Orchids should be repotted as soon as possible after they have bloomed.

CYNARA
Asteraceae
Cardoon, globe artichoke

Both the cardoon and globe artichoke, with their bold, grey foliage and purple, thistle-like flowers, are striking plants and can be used to good effect in the ornamental garden.

C. cardunculus, the cardoon, is a magnificent perennial, with long, silver-grey leaves that are pointed and divided, and stout stems bearing thistle-like heads. The foliage lasts well in water. This is a fine plant for the back of the border, and will take two years to reach its full height of 2 m (6.5 ft).

C. scolymus, the globe artichoke, grows 1–1.5 m (3–5 ft) high and has broader grey foliage and larger purple flowers, which are picked for culinary purposes before they open. This species also takes 2–3

Cynara cardunculus

Cynara cardunculus

years to produce a good crop. For best effect, grow plants apart from other tall plants so the architectural beauty of the foliage can be enjoyed.

Plants can be propagated by seed or division in spring.

CYPELLA
Iridaceae

This genus of more than 20 species is related to the tigridias and native to the cooler parts of South America. Bulbs produce much taller, branching, wiry stems, and dozens of dainty, triangular blooms 5 cm (2 in.) across, new flowers appearing each day over quite a long period. It is easy to grow but prefers light, free soil and full sun. It is quite attractive if planted in groups in the garden, but is not suitable for cutting.

C. herbertii, the best-known species, gives us flowers in a blend of tan, old gold and brown, and continues in flower nearly all the summer and autumn.

C. plumbea is similar in habit, but the flowers are a dull lead colour tinged with yellow. The bulbs, which are about 2.5 cm (1 in.) across and resemble a small gladiolus, can be lifted in the autumn and stored for spring planting without harm, and this

method is to be preferred in very cold and wet districts. Increase is usually from seed, which germinates freely and often blooms the first season. Bulbs are usually planted in winter, when they are dormant, and should be set 5 cm (2 in.) deep and 15 cm (6 in.) apart.

CYPRIPEDIUM
Orchidaceae   Hardy orchids

The so-called glasshouse slipper orchids that were at one time included in this genus have now been transferred to *Paphiopedilum*. Many of the hardy Northern Hemisphere ground slipper orchids are outstandingly beautiful. Most require an acid soil, thriving in shaded woodland conditions among rich leaf-mould, rooted logs or peaty loam. Some of the North American, Japanese and Tibetan species present very little difficulty once they have been acclimatised, but the roots are rather slow to increase.

C. calceolus var. *pubescens*, from North America, has large, yellowish brown flowers marked with darker lines, and a pale yellow lip. It grows to 60 cm (24 in.).

C. japonicum, from Japan, has solitary flowers on 25 cm (10 in.) stems. They are a pinkish colour, covered with red spots, and the lip is stained rose.

C. macranthum, from Tibet, has single, large, deep purple flowers, 5 cm (2 in.) long and 2.5 cm (1 in.)

Cypella herbertii

wide, on 30 cm (12 in.) stems.

C. montanum, from Oregon, has 30 cm (12 in.) stems, usually brownish purple, and flowers yellow spotted crimson. The white lip is striped red inside.

C. speciosum, from Japan, has 30 cm (12 in.) stems and large, bluish white flowers heavily veined rose.

Cypripedium species may be propagated by division of tubers in spring.

Cypripedium japonicum

CYRTANTHUS
Amaryllidaceae   Ifafa lily

This genus comprises over 50 species, closely related to the crinums, all being natives of South Africa, mainly from the east coast. Unfortunately, very little is yet known of many of these delightful species, and few of them are in general cultivation. They should take kindly to New Zealand and Australian conditions, where frosts are not severe. As none are

hardy in the colder parts of Europe and America, very little has been done to understand their requirements, or to raise new varieties in these countries. Many of the species intercross freely, and it is recorded that attractive hybrids between *C. sanguineus* and *C. elatus* have been raised.

C. breviflorus (syn. *Anoiganthus breviflorus*) produces a long-necked bulb. It is dormant during winter, with 30 cm (12 in.) long, narrow leaves, and during spring produces several stems in succession, each terminating with an erect umbel of bright yellow trumpets with flowers about 5 cm (2 in.) long and 2.5 cm (1 in.) at the mouth. This bulb is quite hardy and of easy culture, increasing freely from the small offsets. Full sun and good drainage are essential.

C. elatus is still widely known under its old name of *Vallota speciosa*. It is evergreen in mild climates, but loses its foliage in winter in cold areas. Good drainage is essential for successful cultivation, and plants do well in pots or tubs. Bulbs will grow up to 10 cm (4 in.) across but will bloom when half this size, flowering in summer with occasional extra spikes during the autumn. Each bulb produces one or more scapes with four to six bright scarlet, open trumpets, 10 cm (4 in.) across, on thick, 30–45 cm (12–18 in.) stems. Numerous small offsets appear around the parent bulb, and these can be separated

Cyrtanthus elatus

and grown on to flowering size. The variety 'Major' has large flowers, and 'Maxima Oculata' has flowers that are a brilliant flame-scarlet with a conspicuous white centre. There is also a pure white-flowered form, and a soft salmon-pink one called 'Delicata'. Transplanting is best done in winter, and bulbs should protrude half out of the ground, although in light soil deep planting is recommended.

C. mackenii is a well-known species, being prolific and easily grown. From four to 10 nearly erect, tubular flowers, 5 cm (2 in.) long, with slightly curved tubes, are held on 30–40 cm (12–16 in.) tall, soft, fleshy stems. A form often grown is *C. mackenii* 'Cooperi', with flowers a lemon-yellow shade, the type being usually white or nearly so. Several other lovely coloured forms include 'Roseus', soft pink, and 'Hermione', a pale apricot-salmon variety. All are most useful for cutting, the hardier form 'Cooperi' being grown commercially for such purposes.

C. obliquus gives us six to 12 pendulous, 7.5 cm (3 in.) long flowers, yellow, green and red, widening to 2.5 cm (1 in.) at the mouth. The 30 cm (12 in.) leaves are 5 cm (2 in.) wide and twisted at the ends.

C. o'brienii is a delightful species similar in habit and growth to the forms of *C. mackenii*, the narrow leaves being a dark green and the tubular flowers on 40 cm (16 in.) stems a bright scarlet.

C. sanguineus is a handsome plant, carrying two or three bright red flowers, 7.5 cm (3 in.) long, and widened to 2.5 cm (1 in.) or more at the throat. The leaves are sometimes glaucous and are 30 cm (12 in.) long, and the flower-scape is up to 40 cm (16 in.) or more.

C. tuckii carries as many as 15 nodding, curved flowers, 5 cm (2 in.) long, yellowish at the base, turning to blood-red above.

Most species seem to prefer sharp drainage, free soil and full sun, but some prefer shade. In fact, the clumps giving the best display of bloom have been grown in dry pockets in the rockery with a mixture of leaf mould and broken rock only. Bulbs should be planted like nerines, with the neck above the ground, and clumps seem to bloom more freely when crowded, bursting out into bloom in the autumn after a good rain, while the main crop of flowers appears in early spring. As pot plants they are easily managed, and can be bloomed in late winter or early spring. The flowers are excellent for cutting and are long-lasting.

Bulbs are usually damaged by frost exceeding 12 degrees. In very cold districts, if drainage is perfect, a technique that has proved successful is to bury the top of the bulbs 5 cm (2 in.) below the surface. Planted thus, bulbs are deciduous, losing their leaves in winter after frost or wet conditions, but in warm climates, or if grown in pots, they are nearly evergreen, and can be in bloom almost any time of the year if previously given a few weeks' rest or allowed to become dry. Increase is from divisions of bulbs in autumn or winter, or else from fresh seed, which blooms in the third year.

Cyrtanthus obliquus

D

DACTYLORHIZA
Orchidaceae

Marsh or spotted orchid

Members of this genus are tuberous perennials and can be grown outdoors in warmer parts of the Southern Hemisphere.

D. elata is the most handsome species, native to Madeira, growing 80 cm (32 in.) but often less, with broad, unspotted, iris-like leaves, developing violet-purple flowers in loose, cylindrical spikes. In nature it grows in wet meadows and bogs, and similar conditions must be provided.

D. fuchsii, known as the common spotted orchid, has leaves darkly spotted and requires semi-shade and a calcareous soil as it grows in open scrub and woodland margins over much of Europe.

D. maculata is another spotted orchid, which has smaller heads in dense, conical spikes up to 60 cm (24 in.) tall, pale pink although sometimes red to purple. The narrow leaf bracts are spotted and spaced up the stem.

D. saccifera comes from sub-alpine meadows in south-eastern Europe and also needs moist growing conditions. It has pink to purple flowers and plain, unspotted leaves.

Propagation is by division of tubers in spring.

DAHLIA
Asteraceae

This genus consists of 29 species, natives of Mexico, most with stout, erect, woody growth and tuberous roots. The dahlia was first introduced to various botanic gardens in Europe in the early nineteenth century. From this stock, the seedlings of which showed great variation, the whole range of garden varieties available today was derived.

Dahlias are easily grown in any good, well-drained garden soil. They form tuberous roots, and their basic requirements are a position in full sun, sheltered from heavy winds, and a soil that does not dry out easily. Either the sprouted tubers or rooted cuttings should be set out in the spring, when the danger of frosts is over and the ground is beginning to warm up. Sprouted tubers are preferred in colder districts where a comparatively short summer is experienced, but rooted green plants are quite satisfactory in warmer areas. Plants can be set out from spring until early summer and a good crop of bloom secured before winter. The growing plants are best supported by a stake as a safeguard against heavy winds. Old or faded blooms should be removed so as to help prolong the flowering season. Weekly applications of liquid manure, when plants have reached maturity, will be beneficial.

In cold districts, roots of dahlias should be lifted in the late autumn, after the foliage has been cut down

Dahlia 'Cheyenne'

Dahlia 'Elizabeth Hammett'

by frosts, and should be stored in a shed, under trees, or in any suitable place where they will not be damaged by winter cold or rot or dry out. In Europe, the roots are stored in cellars or sheds, and covered with straw. In late winter/early spring, these tubers are started into growth, in hot beds, frames or heated glasshouses. In dividing up large roots, it should be remembered that the tubers themselves do not produce buds, so they should be removed with a portion of the old stem attached.

Plants are liable to suffer from several diseases. In the virus group, tomato spotted wilt shows as concentric rings or wavy lines on the leaves; cucumber mosaic virus shows as mottling or vein bandings of yellow on the foliage. Any plants suspected of being virus-infected should be destroyed. Powdery mildew may cause trouble in the second half of the season and can easily be treated by the application of an appropriate fungicide. Among the insect pests, earwigs and thrips may need to be controlled.

The following is a classification of the various shapes and sizes, together with some recommended modern cultivars. (NB: Imperial measurements follow the classification and are not conversions of the metric.)

Giant decorative, over 25 cm (10 in.)—'Kidds Climax', 'Bonaventure'.

Large decorative, 20–25 cm (8–10 in.)—'Pineholt Princess', 'Polyand', 'Como Polly'.

Medium decorative, 15.5–20 cm (6–8 in.)— 'Alltami Classic', 'Formby Perfection', 'Alloway Cottage'.

Small decorative, 11.5–15.5 cm (4.5–6 in.)— 'Ruskin Diane', 'Nationwide', 'Lady Linda'.

Miniature decorative, up to 11.5 cm (4.5 in.)— 'Elizabeth Hammett', 'Christine Hammett', 'Abridge Taffy'.

Giant semi-cactus, over 25 cm—'Daleko Jupiter', 'Pink Jupiter', 'Rose Jupiter'.

Large semi-cactus, 20–25 cm—'Hamari Accord', 'Reginald Keene', 'Jim Branigan'.

Medium semi-cactus, 15.5–20 cm—'Jan Lennon', 'Eastwood Moonlight', 'White Moonlight'.

Small semi-cactus, 11.5–15.5 cm—'Cryfield Bryn', 'Lavender Athalie', 'Majestic Athalie'.

Large cactus, 20–25 cm—'Pacific Caroline', 'Jewel Eileen', 'Samantha'.

Medium cactus, 15.5–20 cm—'Banker'.

Small cactus, 11.5–15.5 cm—'Salmon Rays', 'Lady Kerkrade', 'Monk Marc'.

Miniature cactus, up to 11.5 cm—'Mersey Charm', 'Grace Candy', 'Mildura Gem'.

Giant fimbriated, over 25 cm—'Frontispiece', 'Show 'n' Tell', 'Amorangi Frills'.

Dahlia 'Cottontail', collarette type

Large fimbriated, 20–25 cm—'Poetic'.

Medium fimbriated, 15.5–20 cm—'Isobel Cox', 'Conquest Joy', 'Cheyenne'.

Small fimbriated, 11.5–15.5 cm—'Kaiwera Gold', 'Ambition', 'Otara Tolerance'.

Small ball, 11.5–15.5 cm—'Linda Mary', 'Risca Miner', 'Crichton Honey'.

Mini ball, up to 11.5 cm—'Nijinski', 'L'Ancresse', 'Kenora Fireball'.

Pompom, up to 5 cm—'Hallmark', 'Moorplace', 'Gordon Lockwood'.

Waterlily, up to 15.5 cm—'Figurine', 'Fern Irene', 'Cameo'.

Collarette, up to 11.5 cm—'Cherubino', 'Clair de Lune', 'Glenmark'.

Other types are anemone, single, peony and orchid dahlias, and many other cultivars will be found in trade catalogues.

DELPHINIUM
Ranunculaceae

Delphinium 'Blue Sensation'

This genus comprises about 200 species, of which less than 100 are known in cultivation. Delphiniums are herbaceous or semi-herbaceous in character, with some annuals, and are natives of the Northern Hemisphere, where they are found in Europe, Northern Africa, China, Tibet and North America. They display considerable variation in habit, ranging from species of tall stature to pygmies only a few centimetres high. The common name of larkspur, usually given to the annual types, originated from a fancied resemblance of the spur of the floret to the spur of a lark's claw.

The cultivation of delphiniums is well within the range of most gardeners, and they respond well to Southern Hemisphere climates. They prefer an open, sunny position and fertile, well-drained soil. Drought conditions are detrimental to delphiniums during growth, and it is better to plant on moist soils than on dry. Although they will tolerate a certain degree of acidity in the soil, any tendency towards sourness must be remedied by a dressing of lime in autumn. Planting is best carried out when the plants are dormant in autumn and winter. The best fertiliser is chicken manure that has been stacked or composted for at least six months. This should be dug into the soil two or three months after the application of lime. During the growing season plants should be watered and fed regularly, and the taller varieties should be staked.

In the colder climates, where delphiniums enjoy a long period of dormancy during winter, they appear to be of longer perennial duration than in warmer climates, where they tend to deteriorate after the first two years.

D. x *belladonna* and its forms are dwarf, branching plants, with sprays of florets, mostly single in form, usually of a pure blue colour with corollas of varied hues. They rarely exceed 1 m (3 ft) in height and are true perennials. There is a variety with semi-double, azure-blue florets tipped rosy-purple known as *D.* x *belladonna* 'Semiplena'. 'Blue Sensation' is a popular, New Zealand-raised and named variety, producing an abundance of real delphinium-blue flowers on unbranched, 1 m (3 ft) stems. Fresh

shoots from the base continue throughout the growing season, and clumps continue to bloom right up
till the winter. The freedom with which it blooms, if
the roots are not allowed to become dry during the
summer, may be due to the fact that the plants do
not, as a rule, produce seed. Clumps divide and
transplant readily in the spring.

D. 'Connecticut Yankees' is a comparatively new
American strain of bushy, wiry-stemmed, lower-
growing delphiniums of the D. x *belladonna* type, but
with larger flowers, and fresh heads of bloom
developing throughout the growing season. The
colours are mostly light to medium blue, purples,
lilacs and pastel shades, with a few whites. The
strain, which grows about 1 m (3 ft) tall, is excellent
for cutting, and is recommended for smaller gardens
and more exposed positions where the taller-
growing strains would be damaged by winds. Stocks
are usually raised from seed, although large clumps
can be safely divided during early spring.

D. *elatum* is a tall, erect, blue-flowered species and
the parent of most of the modern garden hybrids. It
has large, palmate leaves and spikes of semi-double
flowers in white and shades of blue, lavender and
purple. 'Pacific Giants' is a seed strain that breeds
true from seed. They are of biennial rather than
perennial habit, although in districts with cold
winters some of these hybrids have been known to
survive for a number of years. The following varieties are available; all grow to about 1.2–1.5 m (4–5
ft), with tall, tapering spikes of large flowers.

'Astolat'—from blush-pink to rose and mulberry-
    pink.
'Black Knight'—very bold spikes, violet-blue with
    black eye.
'Blue Jay'—rich medium blue with black eye.
'Galahad'—pure white, fine spikes.
'King Arthur'—huge spikes of royal-purple.
'Summer Skies'—light blue with white eye.

Large-flowered hybrids, also partly derived from D.
elatum, with single, double and semi-double flowers,
are in colours from white and cream through yellow
to light and dark blues and purples and pink.

D. x *ruysii* 'Pink Sensation' is a remarkable colour
mutation that originated from a chance seedling
among a batch of the scarlet Californian species D.
nudicaule, which gave rise to a race of scarlet, pink,
orange and yellow delphiniums. It has clear, pink

Delphinium 'Blue Jay'

flowers and resembles the D. x *belladonna* hybrids.
'Rose Beauty' is similar to but less vigorous than
'Pink Sensation'.

Certain wild species are worthy of note, although
few can be recommended for general garden cultivation. D. *grandiflorum* (syn. D. *chinense*), although
perennial in its native Asian home, is best treated as
an annual in some climates; its bright blue florets on
30–45 cm (12–18 in.) stems are valuable additions to
the flower border. There is also a pale blue form
known as 'Azure Fairy' and a pure white one. Their
flowering period extends over six months.

D. *sulphureum*, the yellow Syrian species, has produced effective spikes of sulphur-yellow florets with
apricot-coloured corollas to a height of 1.5 m (5 ft).
Its life, however, is brief. D. *leroyi* (syn. D. *wellbeyi*),
from Abyssinia, has fragrant, pale greenish blue
florets and flowers later than other species. It grows
and flowers well in Scotland, which suggests it would
do well in colder climates of the Southern Hemisphere.

D. tatsienense, a charming miniature of alpine character from Szechuan, China, has brilliant blue florets with long spurs, borne on gracefully branching sprays to a height of 45 cm (18 in.).

Protection from slugs is necessary; small slugs often eat out the eyes of dormant delphiniums, sometimes causing the plant to die. To avoid this, pile a heap of sharp sand 7.5 cm (3 in.) deep over each crown in late autumn. When new shoots develop they will be strong enough to survive when they have pushed through, but slug bait may still be required.

Diseases among delphiniums do not present any serious menace to their cultivation. Mildew can cause the foliage to become unsightly, but this, and *Bacterium delphinii*, a black spot disease usually found among plants in a confined or shaded position, may be controlled with a suitable fungicide. It is advantageous to choose a planting site with plenty of air movement but protection from strong gales. Maintaining youthful and vigorous stock is the best safeguard against disease.

Delphiniums may be propagated by means of seed, root division or cuttings. Seed retains its viability for a comparatively short period and should be sown either as soon as it is ripe, or under protection in winter or outdoors in early spring. If sown

Delphinium nudicaule

later, germination can be erratic. Root division may be carried out immediately after flowering or when growth begins in spring, but never when the plant is dormant. Cuttings are taken in spring when growth is not more than 7.5 cm (3 in.) high, and care must be taken to include a heel of the crown. Delphiniums from seed will vary considerably from the parent, but division and cuttings may be relied upon to produce true progeny. Set out fresh plants of delphiniums from late autumn until the end of winter, although late spring planting of seedlings will often provide a crop of bloom in the late autumn.

DENDRANTHEMA
Asteraceae

This is a genus of herbaceous perennials, sometimes woody at the base, with very short rhizomes. It consists of 20 species, most native to Asia but two of which are found in central and eastern Europe.

The numerous hybrid chrysanthemums grown by gardeners and for florists' and exhibition purposes, previously included in the genus *Chrysanthemum* but more recently classified as *Dendranthema*, have been derived over many years. Their ancestry includes *D*. x *morifolium* (syn. *Chrysanthemum morifolium*) and *D. indicum* and *D. zawadskii*.

Practically any reasonably good soil, provided it is not too wet, is capable of growing good hybrid chrysanthemums. A sunny, open position, plenty of humus or decayed animal manure worked into the surface, and ample watering during the summer and autumn are the first essentials. Set out plants when they are well rooted, pinch the heads out when plants are 15 cm (6 in.) high and again when these new shoots have made another 10 cm (4 in.) of growth. These early pinchings are necessary to secure a compact, free-branching bush. The first pinching is usually made in early spring and the second in early summer, but this depends on the condition of the plants at the time. If decorative flowers only are required, no further attention is necessary except staking, spraying and watering. Exhibition blooms are secured by allowing three main stems only and removing all side shoots, which diverts all the energy to the single terminal buds.

Increase of plants is from the new shoots that

appear around the base of the parent plants. When these are 7.5 cm (3 in.) long, they should be removed and rooted in sand or specially prepared beds, setting the plants out in their permanent positions from mid- to late spring. Very early planting is not recommended, particularly in cold climates, as adverse weather conditions often weaken plants and render them subject to disease.

Hybrid chrysanthemums are divided into classes, which include the following:

Anemone-centred: In this colourful section, the centre of the flower has a large or medium-sized, scabiosa-like cushion, usually in a contrasting shade to the outer ray florets. Some most attractive varieties are offered in this class.

Decoratives: These are the same as the preceding class except that they comprise varieties not more than 15 cm (6 in.) across. They are likewise incurving, reflexing or semi-incurving, and should be full-petalled, not showing a central disc.

Fantasies: This class embraces the daintiest of all chrysanthemums, deservedly popular for decorative work and garden display. They are full-petalled like the decoratives, except that the petals are fine and quilled, some being straight, others curved on the tips, giving a spidery effect. A wide range of types and forms now exist in this class.

Dendranthema, fantasy type

Dendranthema 'Vibrant'

Large-flowered exhibition: These are varieties with flowers over 15 cm (6 in.) in diameter and petals incurving, reflexing or semi-incurving. Examples of well-known varieties are 'William Turner' (incurve), 'Robert Eader' (reflex) and 'Edith Cavell' (semi-incurve). For show purposes, allow only three flowers to a plant to develop, but for general garden display or cut flowers, 20–50 flowers can be grown on a bush, though they are naturally much smaller.

Singles: Varieties in this section should carry three to five rows of petals, showing an eye in proportion to the length of petals.

Spoon or wheel: An interesting class, rather limited in the range of varieties available, in which the petals are slightly quilled for approximately half the length, the remaining part opening flat, terminating in a perfect miniature spoon, revealing a richly contrasting colour. These petals are arranged around the central disc like the spokes of a wheel.

Pom-pom: This section is one of the most free flowering, decorative, easily grown and long blooming of all the different classes. Very little attention is needed apart from early pinching to encourage bushy growth. Plants are covered with small, button-like blooms in autumn. A larger-flowered section with blooms up to 5 cm (2 in.) across is now also very popular.

The following are sub-sections of the above classes:

Cascade: A strain of miniature-flowered singles developed in Japan, grown in such a way as to produce a cascade effect. The plants are usually trained to hang down during the period of growth. They can also be stopped several times so as to form a bush covered with small aster-like blooms.

Charm: The plants of this type are low growing and compact in habit and growth, usually 60 cm (24 in.) in height and across, being covered with hundreds of small, single, daisy-like flowers characterised by narrow florets. They are most commonly grown in Britain as late-flowering pot plants.

Cushion mums: In bloom, these plants resemble a low-growing, bushy azalea covered with flowers. Plants do not need any attention in the way of pruning, soon forming a dense bush 30–45 cm (12–18 in.) high and as much across, being smothered with small flowers over several months in autumn. This type was developed in America, and cultivars have a range of flower types.

In recent years in New Zealand a range of cultivars has been bred which combines the most desirable characteristics of charm and cushion mums. They are easy garden plants and also make excellent bushy plants in containers and pots. Varieties include: 'Magic Sunset', red; 'Magic Noon', yellow; 'Magic Cloud', pink; 'Magic Dream', mauve; 'Magic Dawn', lemon; 'Magic Garden', yellow; and 'Statesman', rich crimson. A single plant may grow 60–90 cm (24–36 in.) in diameter and less than 60 cm (24 in.) high, simply smothered in bright, single flowers.

Dendranthema 'Magic Noon'

Dendranthema zawadskii, previously *Chrysanthemum zawadskii* var. *rubellum* (syn. *C.* x *rubellum*), is an interesting, hardy, free-flowering species. In its habit of growth it resembles a giant-flowered, loosely branched Michaelmas daisy, but the foliage shows the characteristic chrysanthemum features. It grows about 1 m (3 ft) high, branches freely, and the plant is smothered during the autumn with fragrant, single, pink flowers 7.5 cm (3 in.) across. The cultivar usually grown is named 'Clara Curtis'. Plants are very hardy, increase rapidly, and give a maximum display in the autumn. Roots should be broken up each season, preferably in early spring, and only the best outer shoots should be replanted. They increase rapidly in light soils. As cut blooms, they last well in water, remaining fresh longer during the cooler weather. Large heads or main stems are in themselves a giant bouquet, suitable for the decoration of large rooms.

DIANTHUS
Caryophyllaceae

The genus *Dianthus* is composed of over 300 species. The wild progenitor of modern carnations, *Dianthus caryophyllus*, has its home in central and southern Europe, and has long been naturalised in England, where it used to be commonly seen growing on old walls, in rocky places, and among the ruins of old buildings. Today the genus is divided into several

Dendranthema 'Statesman'

Dianthus 'Kiwi Gem' (top), 'Kiwi Frills' (middle), 'Kiwi Lace' (bottom)

sections, each with numerous varieties. Border carnations and pinks are suitable for gardens, but the taller perpetual and spray carnations are generally grown in glasshouses.

Border carnations and pinks

Border carnations come in a wide range of colours and colour combinations. The main distinguishing feature of this class is a broad-petalled flower, 7.5 cm (3 in.) across, nearly flat in appearance, with edges that are perfectly entire without serration. In some varieties the edges of the smooth, unspotted petals carry a narrow margin of some other bright colour, not diffused in any way into the ground colour of the rest of the petal. This is known as a picotee edge. Most of the varieties of border carnations carry a decided clove perfume. They are very free-flowering, the main crop being late spring and summer, with odd blooms during the autumn. Fresh plants should be propagated every two or three years by taking cuttings in late summer. Plants should be well established in their new quarters before winter.

A number of new cultivars have recently been bred in New Zealand by Dr K. R. W. Hammett, including:

'Auckland Star'—red self-colour.
'Crinoline'—maroon on white ground.
'C. W. Hammett'—magenta on pale pink ground.
'Enigma'—purple-grey.
'Filigree'—white with crimson picotee.
'Finnigan's Gold'—white flake on yellow ground.
'Greytown'—cerise segments on grey ground.
'Herald'— white self-colour.
'New Generation'—a lovely bicolour, scarlet on a white ground.
'Summer Sunrise'—apricot ground suffused with grey.
'Topline Supreme'—scarlet on yellow ground.

Garden pinks range in height from 30–45 cm (12–18 in.) down to rock garden varieties less than 10 cm (4 in.).

D. 'Allwoodii' represents a range of hybrids derived from a garden pink crossed with a perpetual-flowering carnation, and cultivars vary in height from 10 to 50 cm (4 to 20 in.).

Show pinks have been derived from *D.* 'Allwoodii' back-crossed with carnations, resulting in a strain of extremely free-flowering dianthus with perfect-shaped, smooth-petalled, double blooms, resembling miniature border carnations. As border or edging plants they are ideal, hardy, vigorous and bloom all summer. The following is a selection of popular pinks:

Dianthus 'Ian'

Dianthus 'Far Cry'

'Dad's Favourite'—an old variety, the white flowers edged with wine red.

'Doris'—(Allwoodii), lovely soft salmon-pink double, deeper in centre; long flowering habit.

'Glory'—smooth-edged, deep velvety red double.

'Highland Fraser'—single red, mottled with pink.

'Highland Queen'—single red, very free-flowering.

'Ian'—large, blood-red double with even deeper red centre.

'Kathryn'—pale pink, heavily laced with maroon, very free-flowering.

'Kiwi Frills'—deep pink petals edged and laced with red.

'Kiwi Gem'—white with maroon centre.

'Kiwi Lace'—pale pink petals, edged and laced with crimson.

'Lynette'—prolific, deep rose pink with deeper centre, early flowering.

'Mrs Sinkins'—well-known scented white, frilled petals, calyx split.

'Ripples'—double strawberry pink, laced edges and centre, rich pink.

'Snow'—smooth-edged double white of choice appearance.

'White Ladies'—pure double white, flowering continuously in mild weather, winter and summer.

The following is a selection of rock garden varieties:

'Counterpart'—a new cultivar with very compact growth and bright cerise blooms with darker markings.

'Far Cry'—a compact plant with large, single, pink blooms; flowers through the year in warm regions.

'Mars'—long established; ground-hugging plant with maroon flowers.

'Pretty'—forms compact mounds with two-tone pink flowers.

D. 'Rainbow Loveliness' is the name given to a unique strain of scented dianthus, normally raised from seed, in which the petals of the flowers are finely divided, giving the whole plant when in bloom a misty effect like a haze of colour over the border. This strain, growing 30–45 cm (12–18 in.) in height, embraces an intriguing range of colours and continues in bloom from late spring till late autumn. Cuttings can be taken from any particularly desirable plants.

Cultivation of dianthus in the garden is simple if it is remembered that all plants of this genus must be grown in full sunlight with perfect drainage.

Glasshouse carnations

Varieties in this section are generally too tall for garden cultivation and are primarily raised in glasshouses for the cut-flower market. They are increased from cuttings taken at any time of the year. These are best from side shoots in the middle of the flowering growths where the internodes are short. After planting, the young shoots should be pinched out. The blooms are usually high crowned in the centre and toothed or fringed at the edges, with more petals than a border carnation.

Spray carnations are a strain of perpetual carnations that has been developed to produce multiple flowers on a single stem instead of just one specimen.

DIASCEA
Scrophulariaceae

This is a small genus of perennial and annual herbs from South Africa.

D. rigescens grows to 45 cm (18 in.), with many spikes of tubular, rich pink flowers. The plants will send up new flower-stems for months, given sufficient watering. As no seed is set, propagation is from autumn cuttings, which root readily. Plants are not long-lived, and it is often advisable to root some cuttings each year.

D. 'Ruby Field' is smaller, to 25 cm (10 in.), and

Diascea 'Ruby Field'

has a long succession of deep pink, nemesia-like flowers in summer. It is often described as a cultivar of *D. cordifolia* or *D. barberae* but is actually a hybrid between these two species. It is an excellent rock-garden plant.

DICENTRA
Fumariaceae

About a dozen species belong to this genus.

D. eximia is an old favourite, not usually grown commercially but still found in old gardens. The greyish green leaves are many-lobed, and the drooping, 45 cm (18 in.), branching racemes carry numbers of reddish purple flowers. There is also a lovely, pure white-flowered form known as *D. eximia* 'Alba'.

D. formosa is a species closely allied to *D. eximia*, and, if anything, a better plant, with brighter pinkish red flowers and beautiful ferny foliage. It will thrive quite well in the shade and bloom over a long period if not too dry. *D.* 'Bountiful' is a delightful American hybrid, much like *D. formosa*, one of its parents, but the larger flowers are a more attractive shade of rosy red. If conditions are not too dry in the summer and autumn, it will continue in bloom for a period of nearly six months—hence the name. Increase is by division or soft spring cuttings.

D. formosa subsp. *oregana* is an old-time cottage favourite, the plant producing a tufted clump of coarsely toothed and lobed, silvery foliage. The short, nodding racemes of cream flowers, tipped with purple, appear in abundance during spring and continue till autumn if not too dry. The whole plant seldom exceeds 25 cm (10 in.) in height.

D. spectabilis. This old-time but still very popular perennial, commonly called bleeding heart on account of the reddish colour and heart-shaped flowers, is still a front-rank herbaceous plant that should be grown by all. It produces thick, fleshy roots designed as moisture storage for the hot, dry autumn of its native country, and is, therefore, essentially a spring-flowering plant. It rushes quickly into growth as soon as the warm weather starts, and within a few weeks produces numerous arched sprays of rosy red 'lockets' with white tassels. It continues in growth until early summer and then dies off quickly in the autumn, resting from then until spring, except in a moist climate, where the growth may continue for some time. Under ideal conditions, well-established clumps spread up to 1.2 m (4 ft) and grow 60 cm (24 in.) in height. This species is not long-lived in warmer climates. Seed is very seldom available, but stocks are increased from spring cuttings taken from the roots when about 7.5 cm (3 in.) long, and before plants bloom. Later summer cuttings will also root freely, but such plants must be encouraged into sufficient growth to produce a tuberous root, otherwise the plants will collapse in winter.

The individual flowers of *D. spectabilis*, like the aconitums or monk's hood, never fail to interest children—and even grown-ups! When taken apart they will reveal two rabbits, a harp, grandpa's

Dicentra formosa 'Alba'

glasses, and a bottle! Other common names are lady's locket or Dutchman's breeches, both suggested by the formation of the flower.

D. 'Boothmans Var.' is a new cultivar of great promise. It has beautiful, fern-like, glaucous leaves and 45 cm (18 in.) stems of deep rose, dangling flowers for many weeks. Give plants fairly sunny but moist conditions.

Generally speaking, all dicentras prefer light, fertile soils. Under suitable conditions, all will set seed, which is not difficult to raise, but which loses its vitality quickly. The most practical method of increase is by division in the spring of old, well-established clumps or by rooting soft spring growths as they appear. Transplant during winter.

DICTAMNUS
Rutaceae   Burning bush

There are only two species in this genus. D. albus is an old-world favourite that simply won't be hurried. Seed is slow in germination and plants require three or four years to reach flowering size. They also resent being disturbed when established, and are not easy to transplant except as young seedlings. In contrast to most perennials, which are short-lived or require constant transplantings, this subject is one of the longest lived of all plants and, like the herbaceous paeonies, can be left in the one place for 50 years or more.

The plant grows 45–60 cm (18–24 in.) tall, with odorous, glossy, leathery leaves, retaining their deep green colour right until the winter. The attractive spikes of flowers held just above the bushy foliage are either pure white, pink or purplish brown, and few plants surpass them as cut flowers. The purplish-flowered form is known as D. albus 'Purpureus'. The whole plant gives off a strong volatile oil, and the leaves or flowers will, when crushed, give a flash of light if a lighted match is held near them on a sultry summer evening. A bell glass with a hole on the top, if placed over the plant on a sunny day, will produce a continuous flame.

The rootstock is very hard and woody, retaining a firm hold in the ground, so that increase from divisions is difficult. Seed, if fresh, is not hard to raise,

Dictamnus albus 'Purpureus'

and year-old or even two-year-old plants are not difficult to transplant. It is a splendid, hardy garden perennial well worth waiting for. Transplant during the winter months.

DIERAMA
Iridaceae   Lady's wand

This genus of about 20 species of bulbous plants deserves much more attention than it receives.

D. igneum is a small, compact species with very narrow leaves, only 0.5 cm (0.2 in.) in width, 60–75 cm (24–30 in.) long. The flowers are held well above these, reaching to 1.2 m (4 ft), rosy pink and hanging gracefully. The buds are rather like ears of wheat, and are covered with small bracts.

D. pulcherrimum is the species generally cultivated. Above its bold sheaf of green, gladiolus-like foliage, it raises flowering stems 1.8 m (6 ft) high, which, bending over at the tips, put forth long, swinging tassels of tubular or bell-shaped blossoms up to 5 cm (2 in.) across and 7.5 cm (3 in.) long. The very slender but extremely tough and wind-proof stems sway in the breeze, so that a well-established clump

Dierama pulcherrimum

carrying hundreds of blooms 1–1.2 m (3–4 ft) above the foliage is extremely beautiful. The typical colour is lilac-purple, but a deeper and larger-flowered form called *D. pulcherrimum* 'Major' is richer in shade. A pure white form called 'Alba' and a pale lilac-pink form known as 'Moonlight' are both quite charming, while an extremely deep-coloured form, almost purple-maroon, listed as 'Nigra', is very attractive. These varieties or colours may be listed under different names. All are forms of *D. pulcherrimum*, and there is little doubt that, with some careful intercrossing and selection of seedlings, many desirable new shades could be secured.

Seedlings are easily raised and more readily transplanted than older clumps of bulbs broken up. The dormant period is very short, and in mild districts probably does not occur at all, but they can be safely transplanted during the autumn and winter. If this is done and the plants are established soon after flowering, they will bloom the following summer. This plant is very easily grown in full sun and well-drained soil, resisting adverse conditions including heavy frosts. Set bulbs 7.5 cm (3 in.) deep in groups 15 cm (6 in.) apart.

DIETES
Iridaceae

Three species of these iris-like plants from South Africa are commonly grown.

D. bicolor has 75 cm (30 in.) long leaves and 5 cm

(2 in.), flattish, three-petalled flowers, lemon-yellow with blackish brown spots.

D. grandiflora has leaves to 1 m (3 ft) and stems slightly taller, with flowers to 10 cm (4 in.) across, white to orange-yellow and blue in the centre of the flower. Both species flower at intervals throughout summer and autumn.

D. robinsoniana is from Lord Howe Island, off the coast of Australia. It has stems and leaves to 2 m (6.5 ft), and the flowers are 10 cm (4 in.) wide, pure white, and open in mid-summer.

All species will grow in semi-shade or sun on any well-drained soil. They are evergreen and permanent. Do not remove flower-stems, as they continue to flower for several years. Plants form short rhizomes, which can be transplanted in autumn, or they can be grown from seed.

Dietes grandiflora

DIGITALIS
Scrophulariaceae   Foxglove

This is a genus of over 20 perennial and herbaceous species, natives of Europe, North Africa and western Asia.

D. grandiflora (syn. *D. ambigua*) is a little-known true perennial. Like the common foxglove, with its large, greyish green, hairy leaves, it is happy in sun

Digitalis 'Mertonensis'

or shade. The 5 cm (2 in.) long yellow flowers, veined with brown, are 75 cm (30 in.) tall, and although not outstandingly beautiful, nevertheless always impress any who have not seen them before.

D. 'Mertonensis' is an interesting hybrid strain, being a cross between *D. grandiflora* and the common species *D. purpurea*. The spikes of bloom are a pleasing shade of cherry-rose to salmon-rose, and plants are up to 1.2 m (4 ft) in height. Seedlings reproduce true to type and bloom the following spring and summer if sown during early autumn.

The common foxglove is botanically known as *D. purpurea*. Two strains called 'Foxy' and 'Excelsior' give a wide range of shades from white through pale and deep pinks to light reds, with plain and also spotted throats, but the most outstanding feature is the great increase in the number of flowers, which in the 'Excelsior' strains surround the stem, instead of the usual one-sided, double row of blooms. They are ideal plants for the back of the herbaceous border or for naturalising in open woodlands, growing 1.2–1.8

m (4–6 ft) tall and withstanding fairly dry conditions. Seed should be sown in the spring or autumn and plants set out in early summer. These plants will bloom the following summer. Remove seed-heads after flowering to avoid plants seeding down where they are not required.

DIPIDAX
Liliaceae

This genus comprises four species, all from South Africa. Only one is in cultivation, namely *D. triquetra* (syn. *Onoxotis triquetra*), which seems to do well in almost any garden soil, but, unlike most bulbs, prefers damp or even bog conditions. The roundish, gladiolus-like bulb produces two leaves only, one a few centimetres above the ground and the other just below the flower-spike. The leaves are tubular, almost rush-like, and deep green. About eight to 10 wide-open, star-shaped flowers, blush-lilac with crimson-maroon nectaries at the base of the centre, appear on the thin, wiry stem, in all about 45 cm (18 in.) above the ground. Although some South African bulbs are poor as cut flowers, this one is splendid, keeping a long time in water, the flowers remaining open until the spike fades. In warm or sheltered spots, the flowers appear at the end of winter but continue to bloom until late spring. Plants will not stand more than 10 degrees of frost without some damage. Transplant bulbs 10 cm (4 in.) apart and 5 cm (2 in.) deep when dormant from late summer until autumn.

Dipidax triquetra

DISPORUM
Liliaceae   Fairy bells

This uncommon woodland plant originated in North America and Asia. It is a spring- and summer-flowering perennial that does best in a cool, shady position with rich soil. The erect stems arise during spring, with lance-shaped leaves.

An attractive form with variegated, 10 cm (4 in.) leaves is named *D. sessile* 'Variegatum'. It is a spreading plant and forms clumps to 45 cm (18 in.) tall. In spring it has bell-shaped, creamy white flowers.

D. smithii is a dainty, woodland plant with soft yellow flowers on arching stems to 60 cm. It spreads by stolons.

Propagation is by division in spring or by seed sown in autumn.

Disporum sessile 'Variegatum'

Opposite: White-flowered argyranthemum and yellow-flowered senecio provide quick-growing cover for a bank. The stone retaining wall is softened by the ferny foliage and delicate pink flowers of *Dicentra formosa* (left) and a mass of the ubiquitous annual forget-me-not (*Myosotis*).

DODECATHEON
Primulaceae   Shooting star

There are over 30 species in this genus, which comes from the mountain regions of north-west America.

These most charming woodland plants of the cyclamen family are very hardy, resisting the coldest of winters. However, they simply refuse to grow if not really happy. If planted in a mixture of peaty loam and sandy shingle or broken rock, in a cool, shady spot, they will thrive to perfection, with spikes up to 60 cm (24 in.) long carrying a dozen or more cyclamen-like, reflexed, drooping flowers.

D. integrifolium is a smaller-growing species and the most brilliant of them all, the predominant colour being deep crimson, the base of the petals white emerging from an orange-coloured cup.

D. meadia is the best-known species, with lovely scented, pink flowers suffused with rose, but it is variable in that pure white, lilac and even purple forms occur. *D. hendersonii* is similar to *D. meadia* but has deep crimson-purple tips.

Dodecatheon meadia

Increase is best from seed sown fresh after harvesting, and plants should be set out in their permanent position when only a year old, as big clumps divided up do not transplant readily and are slow to re-establish themselves. The plants form fleshy roots like primulas and are completely dormant in the winter. When a bed is properly established, a yearly topdressing of compost or well-rotted manure is desirable to keep plants in good health. They are all well worth growing, although they are seldom successful in warmer climates. Transplant year-old roots or divide old clumps when dormant in the winter.

DORONICUM
Asteraceae   Leopard's bane

This genus comprises about 30 species of perennials native to Europe and temperate Asia. All are yellow-flowered and daisy-like, many species being very similar in appearance.

D. plantagineum 'Excelsum', also known as 'Harpur Crewe', is the best-known and most popular cultivar. This most desirable and effective hardy perennial is particularly valuable because it can always be relied upon to produce a fine display of bloom in the early spring, before many other plants are in flower. The large, brilliant butter-yellow daisies, 10 cm (4 in.) across on thin 60–90 cm (24–36 in.), leafless stems, arise straight from the fleshy rootstock, which carries large, single, semi-prostrate leaves a few centimetres above the ground. The flower is not unlike the gerbera, except in colour, and is nearly as long-lasting as a cut flower, although the blooms close up at night. If conditions are not too dry, a second crop of bloom can be expected in the autumn. A double-flowered, deep yellow form called 'Spring Beauty' is strongly recommended. Best results are secured by replanting the most vigorous side shoots each season. 'Miss Mason' produces an abundance of 7.5 cm (3 in.), soft golden yellow daisies on 45 cm (18 in.) stems. It is a valuable front border plant.

A number of other attractive species are grown and worthy of inclusion, particularly as most of them are dwarf growing. Plant in full sun with good drainage, as they resent shade from overhanging

Doronicum plantagineum 'Excelsum'

plants; otherwise they are quite easy to grow. They are readily increased by dividing up the old clumps when dormant during late autumn and winter.

DRACUNCULUS
Araceae　　　　　　　　　　Dragon lily

This genus of two species is closely related to the genus *Arum*. *D. vulgaris*, sometimes commonly called the dragon lily, produces, from arum-like tubers, attractive, bright green leaves divided into 13–15 segments 15 cm (6 in.) long, held on a stalk 30 cm (12 in.) high. The central, unspotted pedicel is 30 cm (12 in.) or more long, and the arum-like spathe, about 7.5 cm (3 in.) long, is purplish white except in the mouth, which is striped purple. The extended blade is up to 30 cm (12 in.) long, purple-black, deepening at the margins. This is a plant rather more quaint and interesting than beautiful.

The dragon lily has specialised in getting carrion flies such as blowflies to take up the task of carrying the pollen from flower to flower and has developed 'a truly terrifying odour' for their delight. It is just as easy to grow as the well-known arums, the rhizomes being planted out when dormant during winter months, about 15–22.5 cm (6–9 in.) apart.

Dracunculus vulgaris

E

ECHEVERIA
Crassulaceae

These are succulents, the majority from Mexico. Most have fleshy leaves in rosettes, and some are richly coloured. *E.* 'Set-Oliver' has green rosettes from which grow 40 cm (16 in.) stems with heads of orange-red flowers tipped with yellow in midsummer. They are very showy in flower, and are suitable for sunny positions at the front of the border or on rock walls. Plants are quite happy in dry situations and can be propagated by seed in spring or autumn or by divisions or offsets.

ECHINACEA
Asteraceae   Cone flower

This genus has only three species, natives of North America.

   E. angustifolia is distinguished by its characteristic hairy stems and foliage, and drooping petals. Much has been done in the selection of superior forms, resulting in a strain with brighter tones and larger petals, which are held more erect instead of drooping.

   E. purpurea is the best known of the species. This valuable, autumn-flowering plant resists very dry conditions and helps to break up the monotony of the preponderance of yellow flowers in bloom at this time. It has rather dullish rosy purple, daisy-like flowers with a high central cone, stiff and quill-like, touched with gold. Selected forms such as 'White Swan', 'The King' and 'Beacon' are well worth growing. Plants grow 1–1.2 m (3–4 ft) tall with a stiff, erect habit. The flowers, which are zinnia-like in texture and 10 cm (4 in.) across, are useful for cutting, particularly if planted out in late spring or if a

Echeveria 'Set-Oliver'

batch of seedlings results in a crop of blooms in late autumn or early winter. Flowers last for a long period at that time of the year, while the plant itself can tolerate extremely dry conditions.

   The best method of increase is from divisions. If seed is saved, it must be from selected types, otherwise dull or muddy colours will appear. Transplant from winter until early spring.

ECHINOPS
Asteraceae   Globe thistle

This is a genus of nearly 100 species, native to Europe from Spain to India and also Northern Africa. Although several species are quite attractive and worth growing, the best of them all is known as *E. ritro*. This hardy perennial is something quite different and very interesting, rather similar in

Echinacea purpurea 'White Swan'

habit, appearance and culture to the eryngiums, commonly called sea hollies. The leaves are large, deeply cut and prickly, the stems silvery white, and the flowers either white or greyish metallic blue. The flower-heads are round like a ball, entirely covered with needle-like thistles. This is a useful perennial for the herbaceous border, providing something dis-

tinctive both in colour and appearance, and blooming throughout summer till late autumn. In this species the flowers are deep steel-blue, held on stiff, branching heads 1 m (3 ft) tall.

Another species worthy of mention, growing 2 m (6 ft) high and valuable for the back of the herbaceous border, is *E. sphaerocephalus*. The slightly wrinkled foliage is green above and felted white or grey beneath, while the flowers are silvery grey.

Increase is from seed or root cuttings, as described for eryngiums. Transplant during the winter or early spring months.

ECHIUM
Boraginaceae

These are hardy perennials, biennials and subshrubs, mainly from the Mediterranean region and the Canary Islands.

E. fastuosum is a branching, shrubby plant to 1.2 m (4 ft), with numerous spires, 30–60 cm (12–24 in.) long, of closely packed, deep blue flowers appearing in late spring.

E. pininana produces a huge rosette, up to 1 m (3

Echinops ritro

Echium fastuosum

ft) wide, of large, green leaves, and in spring to early summer this grows up to 3–4 m (9–12 ft) with a single, towering spike of blue flowers. It is biennial and will grow in half-shade. Several should be grown in a group if space permits.

E. pomponium is also biennial, with 40 cm (16 in.) basal leaves, 2 m (6.5 ft) stems, and a dense column of rose-pink flowers. This is probably the most handsome species.

E. scilloniensis is a hybrid recommended for its bright blue flower-spikes. It is similar in growth to *E. fastuosum*. If grown from seed, it is somewhat variable in colour.

E. wildprettii makes a lovely rosette of narrow, silvery leaves 60 cm (24 in.) across, which in its second season throws a single, bold spike, up to 2 m (6.5 ft), of rich coral flowers.

Echiums require a dry climate and well-drained soil for success. All species flower in spring.

ENDYMION
Liliaceae   Bluebell

These bulbous plants are often included in the genus *Scilla* but are now classified as a separate genus. The Spanish bluebell, *E. hispanicus* (syn. *Scilla campanulata*) is well suited to gardens. It has an erect stem 30–40 cm (12–16 in.) tall, carrying larger bells, usually blue but also white or pink. Selected forms with larger spikes include 'Excelsior', deep blue, the rosy lilac 'Rose Queen', and the pure white 'Alba Maxima'.

Endymion hispanicus 'Excelsior'

The English bluebell is a woodland plant named *E. non-scriptus*. Blue is the usual colour, but white and pink forms are also known. Flowers are bell-shaped and the top of the spike usually bends over. The Scottish bluebell is *Campanula rotundifolia*.

Plant bulbs in autumn, 7.5–10 cm (3–4 in.) deep.

Eomecon chionantha

EOMECON
Papaveraceae

This genus consists of only one species from China. *E. chionantha* grows 30–45 cm (12–18 in.) tall, bearing white flowers on branching stems in late spring. The grey-green, heart-shaped leaves are waved and fleshy. Plant the creeping rhizomes in winter in sandy peat in a sunny bed that is shaded from the afternoon sun.

EPIMEDIUM
Berberidaceae   Bishop's hat

While much valued in Europe and America as a low-growing foliage perennial for woodland conditions, this plant could be given a place in any garden and looks particularly well in a rockery setting as an undercover for azaleas and rhodo-dendrons. The leaves in the spring are soft yellow-green, and in some species they are veined and tinted bronze-red in the young growths. Autumn tints are very good during a wet autumn. The main stem divides into three sprays of leaves, and the whole plant has a neat, fresh and pleasing effect, soon spreading into large clumps, which can be left undisturbed for years. The small but dainty flowers are quite attractive, appearing with the first crop of leaves in the spring and lasting six weeks in water. The whole plant seldom exceeds 30 cm (12 in.) in height.

In all there are about 20 species and a number of hybrids; selected forms are cultivated and offered in European and American catalogues. Unfortunately, they are little known and rarely grown in the Southern Hemisphere. The following species and hybrids are worthy of attention.

E. grandiflorum (syn. *E. macranthum*) is a variable species, which if grown from seed will yield flowers from white to pale yellow, deep rose to violet. The best-known form is 'Rose Queen', with its deep carmine-red flowers, petals tipped white, six to 12 on 40 cm (16 in.) stems. Another form called 'Violaceum' produces blooms with pale violet petals.

E. pinnatum is an evergreen perennial, with clusters of small, pendant, yellow flowers in spring. The leaves are dark green, hairy when young.

E. x *versicolor* is a hybrid from *E. grandiflorum* and is sometimes offered as *E.* 'Sulphureum' or *E. pinnatum* 'Sulphureum', after the other parent. It has an abundance of soft yellow flowers in spring when the young leaves are soft bronzy red.

E. 'Warleyense' is a lovely hybrid with coppery, orange-red flowers, sometimes reddish streaked, with 20–30 flowers on a 30 cm (12 in.) raceme.

E. x *youngianum* 'Lilacinum' is also considered a natural hybrid, the pretty, deep lavender-mauve flowers appearing on 25 cm (10 in.) stems. There is a pure white and a pink-flowered hybrid in this cross.

All species and hybrids are easily divided and increased from the many-crowned clumps.

ERANTHIS
Ranunculaceae   Winter aconite

At one time classified as a helleborus, these tuberous, low-growing plants are among the first of all spring bulbs, opening their brilliant yellow, upturned cups in mid-winter. They are very hardy and are at home in half-shady places among shrubs or under trees, but they are essentially cold-climate bulbs and are not very happy in warm districts.

The brilliant yellow, sessile flowers, nestling in a rosette of leaves like an Elizabethan ruff, appear a few centimetres above the ground. These leaves expand somewhat when the flowers have faded. Corms that do not bloom produce ordinary leaves on short stalks. The best-known species is *E. hyemalis*, while another similar species, considered by some to be only a form of *E. hyemalis*, is *E. cilicica*. The latter flowers a few weeks later. A select variety raised in Holland, *E.* 'Tubergenii', is a cross between these two species, with larger flowers, and is a most desirable variety. Unfortunately, it does not set seed.

Epimedium pinnatum

Eranthis hyemalis

Increase is usually from seed, which will bloom the second or third year. If left undisturbed, drifts or colonies soon establish themselves by self-sown seed. These bulbs are lovely associated with galanthus and chionodoxas, or early-flowering crocuses and other early-blooming bulbs delighting in similar conditions. Set the bulbs in early autumn.

EREMURUS
Liliaceae   Foxtail lily

In all there are about 30 species in this genus, mostly from Turkestan, Siberia and the Himalayas.

All the eremurus produce a rosette of simple, strap-like leaves resembling kniphofias or agapanthus, and each crown yields one or more spikes of bloom, with strong stems 1.2–2.4 m (4–8 ft) tall and hundreds of starry flowers on a long, slightly tapering spike.

E. bungei is a low-growing variety, 1.5 m (5 ft) high, in a glorious, golden orange shade.

The pure white-flowered species *E. elwesii* 'Albus' is one of the most stately and lovely plants grown; there is also a soft pink form of this. Some botanists consider these to be forms of the species *E. robustus*.

E. robustus, with its noble 2.4 m (8 ft) stems of lovely peach-pink flowers, is the first to bloom in late spring.

A group known as 'Shelford Hybrids' may possibly be easier to grow than some of the species. This group embraces a wide range of colours, including pink, salmon, yellow, apricot and coppery tones, and it is claimed that they will bloom the third year

from seed, in contrast to most of the other species, which require six years or more.

Eremurus prefer a cooler climate. They require perfect drainage, as indicated by the large starfish-like roots up to 45 cm (18 in.) across, which feed on 15 cm (6 in.) of the surface soil only. These fleshy roots are drought resistant, and a good hot baking in the ground in the autumn seems essential. They are otherwise quite hardy, resisting the coldest of winters, remaining quite dormant from late summer till early spring.

Increase is from divisions. Some plants are propagated from root cuttings, or rather the 'legs' of the starfish-like roots, bedded in sandy loam and kept under fairly dry conditions until new crowns are formed. Seed is slow to germinate and requires pre-freezing or the cold of the winter to hasten growth. Transplant when dormant from autumn until early spring, resting the large, fleshy roots on a bed of sand or light shingle. Light, sandy loam or volcanic soil is preferred, and full sun and protection from heavy winds are essential.

Eremurus robustus

ERIGERON
Asteraceae

This interesting genus comprises over 200 species, most of which are hardy perennials and are natives of North America and Europe. They somewhat resemble dwarf Michaelmas daisies, and are indispensable for the front row of a mixed border. The herbaceous species and varieties form neat clumps of green or bluish green foliage, followed in spring and summer by numerous, loosely branched flower-stems, 30–60 cm (12–24 in.) high, of attractive, finely rayed daisies 5–7.5 cm (2–3 in.) across. Comparatively few of the species are in cultivation, as the modern hybrids are, in the main, superior. These hybrids have been derived mostly from the rich, violet-blue *E. speciosus*, its rosy purple form 'Quakeress' and the bluish violet *E. macranthus*, while the lovely but usually short-lived, burnt orange-yellow *E. aurantiaca* has had some part. The following are all desirable spring-flowering plants, growing 45–60 cm (18–24 in.) tall, hardy and easily managed anywhere.

'Dignity'—violet-mauve, deepening with age, giving a pleasing two-toned effect.
'Elsie'—orange buds, dainty pink, 30 cm (12 in.).

Erigeron 'Elsie'

'Foerster's Leibling'—crimson-carmine, semi-double.
'Pink Triumph'—robust semi-double, rosy pink.
'Prosperity'—brilliant semi-double mauve, 45 cm (18 in.).
'Vanity'—excellent clear pink, erect-growing, good cut.
'Violetta'—double lavender-blue, finely rayed flowers.
'Wuppertal'—large deep mauve, strong, 60 cm (24 in.).

E. karvinskianus (syn. *E. mucronatus*) grows about 30 cm (12 in.), with small daisy flowers of white and pink in profusion for months on end. It grows well on walls, seeding freely.

Propagation is by seed, softwood cuttings or division.

ERYNGIUM
Apiaceae   Sea holly

Over 100 species belong to this genus, which is native to South America and Europe. *E. maritimum*, the common sea holly of England, is practically the only coastal species generally in cultivation. The different varieties or forms offered for sale by nurserymen and generally grown seem to be derived from the species *E. amethystinum*, *E. giganteum* and *E. planum*, but all forms now bear the common name of sea holly, whether coastal plants or not.

All species and varieties, although quite hardy, insist upon good drainage, preferring a sandy soil. Plants have a tendency to collapse in wet, heavy ground during winter.

The spiny appearance of the highly coloured, thistle-like bracts that surround the central cone-shaped flower gives rise to the common name of 'holly'. The branched flower-stems, 30 cm (24 in.) or more in length, carrying a dozen or more violet-blue, greyish blue, or silvery blue flowers 7.5–12.5 cm (3–5 in.) across, are much prized for large decorations, and will last in a dried condition for a long period, although the bright colour fades.

E. amethystinum is a delightful free-flowering species, with deeply cut, spiny leaves, and branching heads carrying numerous, globular, prickly

Eryngium variifolium

heads of amethyst-blue flowers, to 75 cm (30 in.).

E. *giganteum* is sometimes short-lived but is free-seeding. The flowers are silvery blue, to 1.2 m (4 ft), and the foliage is silvery blue.

E. *tripartitum* has wide, branching stems, which carry small, blue bracts, growing about 60 cm (24 in.).

E. *planum* grows to 1.2 m (4 ft), with branching, blue stems and small, deep blue thistle-heads.

E. *variifolium* has silver, veined, evergreen foliage, which is attractive even in winter, and silver-blue flowers 60 cm (24 in.) tall. The latter three are all popular border plants.

E. 'Violetta' is probably the most popular variety grown, with dark violet-blue heads and bracts. The foliage is deeply cut and handsome, and the habit erect and neat. Plants grow to 75 cm (30 in.) tall.

E. *agavifolium*, E. *serra* and E. *yuccifolium* are all tall, to 1.5 m (5 ft), and have greenish white thistle-heads and narrow, spiny leaves.

Increase of the best forms is from root cuttings 7.5 cm (3 in.) long, inserted in sandy loam during the winter, and planted out in the late spring when the top growth appears. By taking cuttings each year in this way, a late crop of bloom can be secured, and the plants are sometimes a mass of flower through-out late autumn and early winter. All species are quite easily raised from fresh seed if available, but some variations from the best types are to be expected. Transplant when dormant in winter.

ERYSIMUM
Cruciferae

This is a genus of annuals, biennials and perennials closely related to *Cheiranthus*. Plants are suitable for borders, banks and rock gardens, and prefer light, well-drained, fertile soil and a sunny position.

E. *hieraciifolium* (syn. *Cheiranthus* x *allionii*), the Siberian wallflower, has toothed leaves and bright orange flowers. Varieties include 'Orange Bedder', a bushy plant with brilliant orange, scented flowers in spring.

E. *capitatum* makes a small bush, about 30 cm (12 in.) tall, with heads of cream flowers in late spring.

E. *linifolium* is a sub-shrub growing to 30 cm (12 in.). It has narrow, lance-shaped, blue-grey leaves and heads of small, pale violet flowers in early summer.   Propagation of all species and cultivars is by cuttings, which root very easily.

Erysimum capitatum

ERYTHRONIUM
Liliaceae

The species in this genus are natives of Europe as far as asiatic Russia and Japan, and also of North America.

These lovely little bulbs are called 'trout lilies' in California, where they grow wild in rich woodlands, under the trees or on the banks of streams in alpine meadows. They are very hardy, but resent dry conditions during the growing season, thriving best in cool, shady spots in warmer districts. They are apparently quite easy to grow in the open in districts experiencing cold winters and showery spring weather. They are truly lovely naturalised in colonies under trees or filling suitable pockets in the rockery, and every keen gardener should attempt to grow them. A mixture of leaf mould, decayed turf, chopped-up dried cow manure and sharp sand is a most suitable medium in which to grow these bulbs. The addition of fibrous material such as peat or bark is most beneficial.

E. californicum, the true species, is often confused with the common species, *E. citrinum*. The true species produces, on stems up to 45 cm (18 in.) tall, creamy white flowers with a chrome-yellow base, the segments not dilated, and mottled foliage.

E. citrinum forms large clumps furnished with dozens of 20 cm (8 in.) tall stems, carrying two to six flowers, white with a light yellow base and reflexed segments.

E. dens-canis, the true dog's-tooth violet, is a native of Europe and Asia to Japan. The broadly oval, green leaves, with a rounded base and pointed tips, are beautifully marbled purple-brown. The solitary, 5 cm (2 in.) wide, drooping flowers on 10 cm (4 in.) stems, are usually a purplish rose shade, but selected forms have been named and grown in Europe, such as 'Frans Hals', light reddish violet, 'Rose Beauty', deep pink, and 'Snow Flake', pure white.

E. hendersonii. Each bulb produces but two, narrow, dull green leaves, spotted purple-brown, and bell-shaped, 5 cm (2 in.), drooping flowers, pale lilac, spotted dark purple at the base. This species is not common, increase being usually from seed only.

E. oregonum (syn. *E. giganteum*) is the strongest growing and largest flowered of the genus. It is quite

Erythronium revolutum 'White Beauty'

easily grown and consistently provides a good show each spring, with four to six creamy white, orange-based, 7.5 cm (3 in.) wide flowers on 45 cm (18 in.) strong stems. Leaves are mottled light brown and white. Bulbs increase slowly, although plants seed and germinate freely.

E. revolutum is a hardy, later-blooming Californian species, with leaves faintly mottled brown and white, the creamy white flowers on 30 cm (12 in.) stems being tinged purple with age. Two selected desirable forms, 'Pink Beauty', pink with heavily mottled foliage, and 'Johnsonii', deep rose, should be secured if available. A lovely variety called 'White Beauty' has proved to be very easily grown, free-flowering and easily increased. The large, pure white, marbled flowers, two to six on 30 cm (12 in.) stems, carry a distinct central golden ring. The foliage, too, is beautifully mottled.

E. tuolumnense is one of the easiest species to grow, and is happy even in warmer climates. It has large, unmottled, rich green leaves, and 30 cm (12 in.) stems, carrying two to eight pure golden yellow flowers with reflexed segments, smaller than other species. In rich loam this species produces large, fleshy, elongated bulbs. Several hybrids have recently appeared.

Propagation is mostly from divisions, which increase if left undisturbed for two or three years.

Most species set seed freely if conditions are suitable during the flowering period. Treated like liliums, they produce flowering bulbs in three or four years. Many of the American species, particularly the brighter-coloured ones, increase very slowly by natural bulb division, so that the only way to increase stocks is from seed. A mixture of leaf mould and fine gravel is an excellent medium for raising seeds of most bulbous plants such as these, which are slow to germinate. If the seeds are scattered on the prepared surface and covered with fine chips, this keeps down weed growth, preserves the moisture and minimises 'damping off' when seed germinates. Bulbs are very brittle and easily broken, so they should be handled with care; they deteriorate quickly if left out of the ground for any length of time. If not replanted at once, bulbs should be stored in slightly damp sawdust, moss and coarse sand.

EUCHARIS
Amaryllidaceae   Amazon lily

This genus comprises 10 well-known species and several interesting hybrids. They are usually grown inside as pot plants. The best-known species is *E. grandiflora*, also listed as *E. amazonica*. The waxy, open, scented trumpets of sparkling purest white, 10 cm (4 in.) across, are held well above the luxurious, deep green foliage, two or four on 50 cm (20 in.) stems. This and other species are quite easy to grow as pot or tub plants. They prefer a semi-shady spot and ample water during the growing period, but this should be withheld and the bulbous roots allowed a

Eucharis grandiflora

dry resting period to encourage the formation of flower-spikes. Growth normally continues all the year round, but no flowers, or very few, will result unless an enforced resting period is provided. Two distinct crops of bloom can be secured, one in early summer and again during winter. However, it is safer to attempt one good crop only by resting the plant from late summer until early autumn, then watering and feeding, resulting in a good winter display. *E. grandiflora* is a really glorious subject, usually pot grown and transplanted any time during the resting period. Propagation is by offsets in spring, or by seed sown when ripe.

EUCOMIS
Liliaceae   Pineapple lily

The 14 interesting species in this genus, related to the scillas, form large, bulbous, fleshy roots. Although not quite hardy everywhere, these roots become quite dormant in the winter and can, therefore, be lifted in very cold districts and stored inside, then replanted in the spring. They also lend themselves well to being grown in pots or tubs.

E. comosa, sometimes listed as *E. punctata*, has highly attractive, purple-spotted, crinkled and waved, pineapple-like foliage, 45 cm (18 in.) long and 7.5 cm (3 in.) wide, produced in rosette form, enclosing a thick, tightly formed, cylindrical spike of flowers, cream and green, sometimes slightly tinted with pink. The seed capsules that follow the flowers are hidden deeply in tightly packed green bracts, the whole often topped with another foliage rosette, so that the thick spike looks like a green pineapple. When raised from seed, occasional pinkish or rosy purple-tinted forms occur, and these may be worth selecting to secure brighter-coloured varieties. Well-grown spikes of this species often reach 60–90 cm (24–36 in.) in height, with 30 cm (12 in.) or more of blooms. As a cut flower it lasts for nearly two months in an attractive condition, so it has possibilities as a decorative plant, besides never failing to arrest attention in the garden. There are some selections of this fine species with purple colouring on stems and flower bracts, but they are usually grown from seed and are therefore variable. These have been called the 'Gloria Strain'.

Eucomis pole-evansii

EUPATORIUM
Asteraceae

This genus consists of over 400 species of perennials and shrubs, most of which are American.

E. aromaticum is a robust plant for background planting in sun or light shade and moisture-retentive soil. It has loose heads of white flowers about 1 m (3 ft) high in summer.

E. cannabinum is a perennial for moist positions. The flowers are loose heads of reddish purple.

E. purpureum is a late summer or autumn-flowering plant suitable for the back of the herbaceous border, blooming as it does along with the Michaelmas daisies and solidago. The strictly erect, unbranched stems carry oval-lanceolate leaves, and are topped with a compound flower-head at least 15 cm (6 in.) wide and long, composed of numerous miniature, purplish pink flowers. An established clump will reach 1.5–2.7 m (5–9 ft) in height.

Eupatorium sordidum

E. pole-evansii is the giant of the genus, the immense spikes growing 1.2–1.8 m (4–6 ft) tall, the top 60 cm (24 in.) being encircled with soft green flowers, enhanced by the cream centres. The plant remains attractive over a long period, as do the spikes when cut.

E. zambesiaca is a delightful dwarf species, growing about 30 cm (12 in.) tall, with columns of pure white flowers. It will grow true from seed, taking about two or three years to flower, in late summer.

Eucomis is usually increased by dividing up old roots, removing any side shoots that may have developed around the parent. These side shoots or offsets will eventually become detached, but they usually have to be cut off if earlier increase is desired. Many of the species known are similar in the appearance of the flower-spike. Some produce plain green, unspotted or margined leaves; others have shorter, club-shaped, dense racemes of bloom. Transplant when dormant during winter.

E. sordidum has large heads, to 1.5 m (5 ft), of mauve-purple, fluffy flowers in late winter. It grows well in warm districts in semi-shade but is frost-tender.

Plants can be increased by seed sown in spring, by division in spring or autumn, or by cuttings taken in summer.

EUPHORBIA
Euphorbiaceae   Spurge

The genus consists of about 2,000 species, widely differing in habit, including the succulents that are natives of South Africa.

A number of the hardy perennial species are now in cultivation in the Southern Hemisphere, where previously only the well-known, shrubby, winter-flowering species *E. veneta* (syn. *E. wulfeni*) was grown. The early spring foliage and floral display of these species will quickly make them very popular.

E. amygdaloides forms a compact dome of velvety purplish maroon leaves, deepening as the summer advances. In spring it is covered with yellowish flower-heads, which make an interesting contrast, effective even in mid-winter. The cultivar name is 'Purpurea'.

E. epithymoides (syn. *E. polychroma*) is a brave little plant, producing very early in the spring a mounded, 30 cm (12 in.) high bush of fresh green foliage, topped with sulphur-yellow bracts, which later fade to green. The plant remains a perfect, neat ball throughout. The flowers last well when cut. Prune after flowering.

E. griffithii. In this delightful species the young spring growths are a soft, green-veined, dense red, and the 45 cm (18 in.) branches are topped with heads of copper-red bracts. A selected summer-flowering form, up to 60 cm (24 in.) tall, with even more brilliant spring growths, is known as 'Fire Glow'.

E. myrsinites is a most useful trailing species, with concave, light glaucous green leaves, in close spirals along the prostrate stems. It has composite terminal heads of bright yellow bracts in early spring, and increases readily from seed.

E. palustris is a handsome plant, growing to 1 m (3 ft), with larger, rounded, yellow flower-heads. It

Euphorbia robbiae

enjoys moist soil conditions.

E. robbiae grows to 45 cm (18 in.), with rosettes of dark green leaves and yellow bracts, and is very suitable as ground cover in shade and beneath shrubs.

E. sikkimensis is a handsome plant, valuable in the border. The young leaves and stems are almost a translucent, ruby-red colour in spring, followed by 1 m (3 ft) tall heads of rich daffodil-yellow bracts.

Plants are increased from young basal cuttings taken in spring, while seed sometimes sets on plants if the weather conditions at flowering time are suitable.

EURYOPS
Asteraceae   Paris daisy

The sub-shrubs in this genus grow well in warmer coastal areas and are often associated with perennials. They have attractive leaves and showy, daisy-like flowers, and prefer a position in full sun with moist, well-drained soil.

E. acraeus (syn. *E. evansii*) is more dwarf than other species and fully hardy, with silver foliage

Euryops acraeus

making a mound to 45 cm (18 in.), well covered with short-stemmed, yellow daisies in late spring.

   E. pectinatus has downy, grey foliage smothered throughout winter and spring with 5 cm (2 in.), yellow daisies.

   E. tenuissimus is similar except that the foliage is much divided and bright green. Prune both these species after flowering. Neither is hardy to very heavy frost.

   Plants can be propagated by softwood cuttings taken in summer.

F

FELICIA
Asteraceae   Blue marguerite

Although about 50 species of this genus exist, all hailing from South Africa, only one is commonly grown. *F. amelloides* is very popular in England for indoor decoration because it is seldom without bloom. In the Southern Hemisphere, grown outside, it is only half-hardy and will seldom stand more than 12 degrees of frost without damage to the foliage and blooms. Seedlings quickly form a low, bushy shrub up to 60 cm (24 in.) high, with roundish, alternate, deep green leaves and short-stemmed, sky-blue flowers about 2.5 cm (1 in.) across. It is useful for a small, formal hedge, if kept well trimmed, and will continue in bloom until frosts come. 'Santa Anita' is a larger-flowered form, with blooms nearly twice the size of the type. *F. amelloides* 'Gay' has the same blue daisies for many months, and the foliage is strikingly variegated green and white.

    F. amelloides and its forms are easily increased from cuttings taken in autumn or spring. Seed ger-

minates freely if sown in the spring, the young plants blooming the first season. Transplant from pots or boxes during the spring, or almost any time in warmer districts.

Ferraria crispa

Felicia amelloides 'Gay'

FERRARIA
Iridaceae   Starfish lily

This genus of bulbous plants was at one time included in the tigridas. These most unusual South African, dwarf-growing, fleshy-rooted plants, of which there are seven species, are surprisingly enough quite hardy if planted in a sunny, well-drained situation.

The only species generally cultivated is *F. crispa* (syn. *F. undulata*). It produces, during spring, numerous 5 cm (2 in.) wide, starry, frilly-edged flowers in a combination of slaty black and greenish white, each with conspicuous, central, orange stamens. These are held on erect, branching stems encased in wavy, iris-like foliage. The blooms open up in succession on fine days over quite an extended period. Stock can be increased by division when plants are dormant in late summer. In very cold districts, plant the roots up to 15 cm (6 in.) deep.

FESTUCA
Gramineae

This genus of some 100 annual and perennial grasses includes a number of ornamental-foliaged species, which, along with other attractive grasses, are popular for Japanese and scree gardens as well as rockeries. The only species generally cultivated is *F. ovina* 'Glauca'. As can be supposed from the varietal name, the foliage of this densely tufted, fine-leaved plant is an attractive glaucous or bluish green. It quickly forms a rounded clump about 22.5 cm (9 in.) high and 30 cm (12 in.) across. During early summer the plant throws up numerous seed-heads, which should be removed as soon as they develop, otherwise they are inclined to exhaust the plant, often resulting in collapse. Increase is from divisions during late autumn or winter.

FILIPENDULA
Rosaceae   Lace plant

This is a small genus of hardy herbaceous plants from the Northern Hemisphere, somewhat resembling and sometimes listed with the perennial spiraeas or astilbes. The attractive, deep-cut, fern-like foliage combines with showy panicles of white, purple or pink flowers, having a lacy or feathery appearance. They are very long-lasting, either outside in bloom or as cut flowers.

F. purpurea, better known to older gardeners under the name of *Spiraea palmata*, gives us large panicles of carmine-rose flowers on erect, 90 cm (36 in.), dark red stems, held well above the handsome, doubly serrate foliage. It blooms in early to mid-summer.

F. rubra (syn. *F. venusta*) was once listed as *Spiraea lobata* and is commonly known as 'Queen of the Prairie'. This species grows 1.2–1.8 m (4–6 ft) tall, the stiff, erect stems being held above the large seven-to-nine-lobed leaves, these in turn being deeply incised and toothed. The tiny, feathery, peach-pink flowers form a handsome, clustered panicle and are very pretty. An improved form, known as *F. rubra* 'Magnifica', is deservedly named, and is to be preferred.

F. ulmaria 'Aurea' (syn. *Spiraea*) is a yellow-foliaged form of the English native meadowsweet. The golden yellow foliage, to 45 cm (18 in.), makes it quite outstanding, and if its insignificant flowers are removed, it quickly becomes bright and leafy

Filipendula rubra 'Magnifica'

again until late autumn. It requires a moist place in full sun.

F. vulgaris (syn. *F. hexapetala*, *Spiraea filipendula*). From a neat clump of pretty, fern-like leaves appear erect, 60 cm (24 in.) stems, topped with crowded, flattish heads of ivory-white flowers. The double-flowered form, *F. vulgaris* 'Flore Plena', is the better one to grow. The lovely foliage remains attractive long after the summer flower-heads have finished. This is the only species that will tolerate fairly dry conditions, the others preferring situations that suit the astilbes.

Increase of filipendulas is from the division of the hard, fibrous and tuberous rootstock when dormant during winter.

FRANCOA
Saxifragaceae   Bridal wreath

Plants of this genus are natives of Chile. This large-leafed perennial is seldom seen, and is not considered hardy in England, except in very sheltered and well-drained spots. However, it is quite easy to grow in the Southern Hemisphere. There are three species known, the one usually met with being *F. ramosa* (syn. *F. glabrata*). The tall, much-branched sprays of small, white flowers, on 1 m (3 ft) stems, are most graceful, drooping down airily, well deserving the common name of bridal wreath or veil.

An attractive but little-known, pale pink-flowered species with dark green, oval hairy leaves is called *F. appendiculata*. This and *F. ramosa* are quite easily raised from seed, blooming within 12 months of sowing. Old clumps can be safely broken up any time during winter.

FREESIA
Iridaceae

This genus was introduced from South Africa in 1896. The form that was then discovered and named *F. refracta* bore fragrant blooms of a pale greenish yellow colour. In later years, what was thought to be

Freesia 'Burtonii'

a white-flowered form was discovered and named *F. refracta* 'Alba', but it is now considered to be a distinct species, the correct name of which is *F. lactea*. About the same time another pale citron-yellow form of *F. refracta* was discovered and then called *F. leichtlinii*. In 1898 a rose-pink-coloured species was discovered near Port Elizabeth, and a few bulbs were sent to Kew, where the name of *F. armstrongii* was bestowed in honour of the finder. The introduction of this vigorous species gave hybridists an opportunity to raise new colours and larger flowers. G. H. Dalrymple of Bartley, England, did much to improve the existing strains, and we still have what are known worldwide as the 'Bartley Hybrids'. American firms have produced some fine freesias including 'Elder's Giant White' and several double-flowered varieties. The latter have also been developed in Holland.

Australia and New Zealand have not been behind in their introduction of hardier outdoor strains. The popular, giant-flowered *F.* 'Burtonii', a chance sport, is not generally in cultivation outside New Zealand. The flowers are usually sterile and seed is very seldom seen, so stocks must be increased from divisions. It is a vigorous grower, the large bulbs producing in quantity flowers of pure creamy white with the yellow lower lip quite free from outer stain of purple or blue. Cultivars include the following:

'Ballerina'—giant white.
'Oberon'—deep red.
'Red Diamond'—double carmine-red.
'Romany'—double lilac.
'Rose Marie'—deep pink.
'Royal Blue'—blue.
'Rynvelds Gold', 'Corona'—double yellow.
'Stockholm'—red and rose.

Freesias are extensively grown for early cut flowers, either under glass or in sheltered spots. Although bulbs can be successfully grown in the open, larger and better blooms can be secured under glass or protected from adverse weather by glass frames. The earliest blooms can be secured only by raising a crop each season from seed. Freesias will bloom eight months after sowing, and if they are not allowed to become dry, they can actually be had in bloom at any time of the year. Named varieties of freesias or a special strain of hybrids can, of course, be increased by divisions only, as they will not come true from seed. It is not easy to flower these as early as seedlings, but if the bulbs have been well ripened the previous year, they can be started into growth in early autumn and gradually forced into bloom under glass to flower during the winter months. Bulbs affected with disease are readily discerned by dark marks on the outside and are best destroyed.

FRITILLARIA
Liliaceae

This genus of over 80 bulbous species is related to liliums and is widely distributed over the Northern Hemisphere. Unfortunately, many of the attractive, North American species do not take readily to cultivation. Stocks of plants or bulbs that are rather rigid in their cultural requirements are more easily established if raised from seed.

F. acmopetala is a native of Syria, and is happy in either cold or warm climates. It demands a free, loose soil with humus mixed in. The flat, depressed bulb is composed of two fleshy scales, from which arise, in spring, a single, unbranched stem 45 cm (18 in.) high, supporting about seven narrow leaves, and topped with one to three 5 cm (2 in.) long, drooping bells, olive-green on the outside, streaked purple-brown and shining yellow inside. The somewhat expanded mouth carries a transverse band of brownish purple. Plant 7.5 cm (3 in.) deep and 10 cm (4 in.) apart in groups of six to 12. This is a delightful rockery bulb.

F. imperialis, originally from Turkey, is one of the best-known European species, with its many forms. It is commonly called the crown imperial, on account of the whorls of bells on the top of the stem. Forms often grown include 'Aurora', a bronzy red; 'Lutea Maxima', yellow flowered; and 'Rubra Maxima', deep red. There are also intermediate shades and forms, and a double-flowered form is offered in Holland. *F. imperialis* and its varieties seem difficult to establish in warmer climates. The bulbs flower well the first season, then usually deteriorate gradually, either failing to flower or eventually dying out. Cold winter conditions and a moderately cool spring seem to be essential for success. Where these prevail, very little difficulty is experienced in growing them either in the open or semi-shade. Bulbs do not seem to be affected by any diseases. These large fleshy bulbs, 5–7.5 cm (2–3 in.) across, composed of two or three heavy, thickened scales, are easily bruised or damaged and, like all fritillarias, quickly deteriorate if left out of the ground for any length of time. Bulbs are best stored in damp sawdust, sand or moss if required for later planting. A large hole, often right through the centre or side of the bulb, marks the

Fritillaria imperialis

place of last season's flower-stem; this is not a defect, as many people suppose. In very wet climates, bulbs are best planted on their side in an envelope of sand, to allow good drainage and prevent water lodging in this hole and possibly developing rot.

Flower-spikes of established bulbs reach a height of 1 m (3 ft), with two or more whorls or crowns of bloom, one on top of the other. Although reasonably long-lasting as cut flowers, they are not used for indoor decorations on account of the rather strong and objectionable odour.

Increase is rather slow naturally from bulb division, although a reasonable number of small bulbs are found among old clumps. Seed takes four to six years to reach maturity, while outer scales taken from mature bulbs develop into flowering size in two or three years.

F. meleagris, commonly called the snake's head fritillaria, is plentiful in England and Europe, and grows in grassy meadows and semi-shady woodlands. This is the easiest species to grow and, although thriving in cooler districts, can be grown quite successfully in warmer parts. A free, loose soil not lacking in humus seems all that is needed, provided conditions are not too dry in the spring. Several forms occur, but the most common are white with green veins and a grey-purple, chequered form. The small white bulbs, up to 5 cm (2 in.) across, produce four to six basal leaves and 20–40 cm (8–16 in.) flower-stems, carrying one to three nodding bells, blooming during spring. Under favourable conditions, seed sets freely and should be sown in autumn, germinating in the spring and blooming the third year.

F. pyrenaica has bulbs up to 5 cm (2 in.) across, with flower-stems 30–60 cm (12–24 in.) tall, carrying two to four nodding bells 4 cm (1.5 in.) across, wine-purple with dull green spots, shining green inside and chequered reddish purple. This species seems happier in cold districts but is occasionally met with in warmer parts. The blooms, although attractive in the garden or rockery, particularly if planted in bold groups, carry a rather offensive odour, and are therefore not suitable for cutting. Increase is quickest from seed sown in the autumn and, like the varieties of *F. meleagris*, should be left undisturbed until the bulbs reach flowering size, usually in the third year.

All species and varieties of fritillarias should be replanted as soon as possible after lifting, as the uncoated and unprotected, fleshy bulbs wither and deteriorate rapidly.

G

GAILLARDIA
Asteraceae   Blanket flower

This genus consists of a dozen species of annuals and perennials. The annual varieties, both single and double flowered, are well-known and popular plants, particularly useful for sandy, free soils and coastal planting, thriving to perfection and blooming over a long period where other plants would fail. Others are biennial, and either die out after a year or two or else become scraggy. There are, however, a number of very fine, true perennial varieties, superior in size and bloom to most of the annuals grown, and embracing many distinct and unusual colour combinations and shades. All these newer perennial varieties, which have been derived from the wild species *G. aristata*, are excellent cut flowers and last quite a long time if the plants are not allowed to seed.

Gaillardia cultivar

Desirable cultivars include 'Kelway's King', a pure golden yellow without any other marking; 'Hughes' Red', a New Zealand-raised variety, vivid mahogany-red with outer petals tipped yellow; 'Judy Hughes', an attractive semi-double, brilliant red, the petals tipped with yellow. An attractive, self-coloured, rich coppery red variety, known as 'Wirral Flame', is worth securing if available, and is a splendid contrast to the pure yellow 'Kelway's King'. 'Burgundy' is another all-red cultivar.

Increase is usually from spring cuttings taken before the plants have bloomed.

GALANTHUS
Amaryllidaceae   True snowdrop

This genus comprises 20 species, natives of the Mediterranean region. We use the word 'true', associated with the common name, as the common snowflake or leucojum is often confused with these bulbs.

The success of these bulbs in Northern Europe is due largely to the long, cold winters and cool or showery spring conditions that follow. With a little thought and care, these essentials can be imitated fairly closely in warmer districts. Such conditions may be provided by selecting cool spots in the garden or rockery, perhaps sloping away from the sun, or by planting them in a shade-house.

G. byzantinus is perhaps the finest and least-known species, originating in southern Europe. It has broad, deep green foliage and bears, on long stems, well above the leaves, handsome, globular flowers, the inner tubes marked with rich green. It is even superior to the much sought-after *G. elwesii*, in that it blooms earlier on longer stems.

G. caucasicus is a desirable form, which blooms long before the common single and double varieties,

Galanthus nivalis

and has somewhat larger and more rounded flowers, sometimes two on a stem.

G. elwesii is a very fine snowdrop, the bulbs of which are several times larger than the common type, each providing several scapes of bloom. It has broad, grey-green leaves and white flowers with green markings on the petals. It flowers in early spring.

G. nivalis is the most common species of galanthus, with flowers white, tipped green in the petals, and blooming singly on 22.5 cm (9 in.) stems in early spring. A double-flowered form, *G. nivalis* 'Flore Plena', grows only 10–15 cm (4–6 in.) high, but provides an attractive display on account of the extra petals. The grey-green, strap-like foliage is quite distinctive. There are in all a dozen or more selected forms or geographical varieties of *G. nivalis*. *G.* 'Atkinsae' is a very vigorous form that will grow equally well in the open or in woodland. The flowers are large and globular on tall stems, and although they set no seed, they do increase freely. 'Magnet' is

a beautiful variety with notably long, slender pedicels, which carry flowers as if hanging from a fishing rod. 'Sam Arnott' has large, perfectly formed flowers and is vigorous, regarded by some as the finest garden variety.

G. plicatus has very large flowers with prominent green marking round the sinus of the inner segment. It is usually later flowering, and does best in partial shade.

Increase is usually from bulbs, which divide up like narcissus but are only about 1–2 cm (0.5–0.75 in.) across. The double form usually produces still smaller bulbs, while *G. elwesii* will often yield bulbs 5 cm (2 in.) across. All species can be increased from seed, except, of course, the doubles. Bulbs will bloom three to four years after sowing the seed.

GALTONIA
Liliaceae   Cape hyacinth

This genus consists of four species, the most attractive and best known being *G. candicans*. This hardy and handsome bulb is worthy of more permanent attention by the general gardening public. It produces large, roundish bulbs 5–10 cm (2–4 in.) across and, during summer, bold scapes 1.2–1.8 m (4–6 ft) high, with racemes of 30–50 pendant, fra-

Galtonia princeps

grant, pure white bells about 5 cm (2 in.) long, and 2.5 cm (1 in.) across at the mouth. Planted in groups of a dozen or more bulbs, they are most attractive in the herbaceous border, particularly if suitably associated with pink or blue perennials.

A remarkable new double white galtonia appeared in a New Zealand garden in 1982, in the middle of an established clump of *G. candicans*. It was named 'Moonbeam'. A single stem 1.5 m (5 ft) or more tall may carry over 40 flowers, with eight or 10 open at one time. These double flowers have many petals and no stamens, and are therefore long-lasting. The flowers are upward-facing on pedicels some 10 cm (4 in.) long, which makes the stems ideal for floral arrangements.

G. princeps is rather smaller than *G. candicans*, with petals more reflexed and tinged with green, but it is not often grown.   *G. viridiflora* grows to 45 cm (18 in.), with greenish white flowers.

Bulbs can be left undisturbed for years, but they increase slowly from divisions, usually growing larger each year instead. Plants, however, seed freely, and fresh stock is easily secured in this way, although it usually requires two or three seasons to produce mature, strong-flowering bulbs. Small bulbs, however, only 2.5–5 cm (1–2 in.) across, will usually bloom. Transplant when quite dormant, setting the bulbs 10 cm (4 in.) deep and in groups about 25 cm (10 in.) apart.

GAURA
Onagraceae

This is a genus of 25 species of perennials and annuals from North America, only one of which is worth cultivating—*G. lindheimeri*. It grows 1–1.2 m (3–4 ft) tall, with loosely branched stems covered with tiny hairs, and singularly beautiful, small, white flowers with rosy calyx tubes, giving the whole plant a misty pink appearance. In general effect, it can be compared with gypsophila. The plant is easily grown but prefers light sandy or free soil. It continues in bloom for about six months of the year, persisting until very late in the autumn. For this reason alone, it is a plant that deserves much wider popularity than it receives.

Increase is usually from seed, which germinates

Gaura lindheimeri

freely, blooming the first year if sown early, but old clumps can be divided during winter months. Cuttings 7.5 cm (3 in.) long, taken in the spring, root freely and bloom during autumn.

GAZANIA
Asteraceae

This genus consists of 16 species, all natives of South Africa.

Everybody knows the common, orange-yellow 'black-eyed Susan', which covers clay banks and otherwise impossible exposed dry spots in many cities and coastal towns. It serves to bind and hold crumbling banks and stop sand drifts. Resisting salt spray and extremely dry and poor conditions, it can still be relied upon to yield a wealth of colour during the spring months. This is probably the species *G. repens*.

G. nivea is somewhat less spreading. It has lovely silver foliage throughout the year and brilliant, golden yellow daisies throughout summer in sunny locations. A double-flowered form has been reported.

Hybridising has resulted in an ever-increasing range of new colours and combinations of colours. These hybrids are among the most popular of all low-growing perennials, providing a blaze of colour over a long period, bursting out again in full bloom after a good rain following a dry spell. Unfortunately, these new hybrids are not quite as hardy as the old species, but in coastal towns free from very heavy frosts little difficulty should be experienced in growing them. Good drainage and somewhat poorish soil give best results, but they can be successfully grown in almost any soil. If planted in good, rich ground, they make so much succulent growth and abundance of foliage that the clumps tend to rot after a spell of wet weather. Under such conditions, it is advisable to break up and replant old clumps every year, preferably in early spring or late autumn. If this is not done, the best of the old clumps will rot off just at the height of the flowering season, spoiling a good display.

The hybrids include many shades of wine-reds, brilliant purple-reds, pinks, orange, flame and lovely combination shades. There are also some attractive, anemone-centred doubles. By securing a collection of some of these colours, and allowing them to seed down in the autumn around the parent plant, many other new shades and colours can be secured. They readily intercross among themselves without artificial aid. Increase of any special colours can only be from divisions of old clumps, either in the autumn or spring. Even if not rooted, these divisions soon form roots if most of the foliage is removed and they are planted firmly. Rooted cuttings can be planted out at any time of the year, although spring and autumn are best.

GEISSORHIZA
Iridaceae

This genus of about 65 species was at one time included with the ixias, all being natives of South Africa, with one from Madagascar. All species produce tiny bulbs, some only as large as garden peas; others, even fully matured, are no larger than sweet pea seeds. An unfailing source of amazement is the quality and prolonged display of bloom produced from these tiny bulbs. The leaves are ribbed and hairy, and when young can be mistaken for blades of grass and accidentally weeded out. The branching heads of bowl-shaped flowers on 10–25 cm (4–10 in.) stems provide a brilliant display during spring.

G. erosa is a rich blood-red colour, unspoiled by any inner markings. It provides a bold splash of colour in the rockery.

G. radians (syn. *G. rochensii*) gives us deep blue flowers with pronounced bowls, and conspicuous, crimson blotches at the base.

G. secunda flowers in early spring, with tiny, bluish, cup-shaped flowers about 1 cm (0.5 in.) across, several atop each branching, slender stem. Plant the tiny bulbs close together and allow them to seed, and in a year or two there will be an attractive group.

G. splendidissima, with its vivid ultramarine-blue flowers, is lovely associated with the brilliant yellow *Hesperantha inflexa* var. *stanfordiae*.

Many gardeners refrain from attempting to grow plants that produce such tiny bulbs, as they eventually lose them in the soil, or they become scattered. A good plan is to plant such bulbs thickly in the

Gazania nivea

Geissorhiza erosa

desired soil in a small flower-pot, which is then buried just below the surface. When the plants are dormant, the pot can be lifted and the space filled with some showy summer annuals.

All the geissorhizas like a light soil in full sun, except *G. splendidissima*, which is quite happy on heavier soils. Increase is usually from seed, which germinates freely if sown in the autumn, blooming the second year. Plant bulbs from mid-summer until late autumn.

GENTIANA
Gentianaceae

The genus consists of 400 species, many of which are rock and alpine plants.

G. acaulis is perhaps the best-known and finest species, admirably suited for edgings or planting in pockets in the rockery, forming neat, compact, tufted clumps of glossy green, narrow leaves 4 cm (1.5 in.) long. The trumpets, borne singly on short, unbranched stems just above the foliage, are 7.5 cm (3 in.) long and up to 4 cm (1.5 in.) wide, turned back at the mouth, and are a glorious shade of rich, deep blue. Although an alpine plant, often bathed in mist and rain, the roots penetrating deeply into the loose moraines or rock rubble, it seems reasonably happy in most garden soils, except in warmer districts, if a deep root run is provided. Often gardeners report that they cannot entice their plants to bloom, and it is quite true that *G. acaulis* will not flower if it is not really happy. Working around the plants with one's fingers occasionally, giving the plant a light tug, encourages deeper rooting and results later in blooms. Full sun, even to scorching heat, with a deep, cool root-run seems ideal; place a few half-sunk rocks around newly set plants. Unlike the other species mentioned below, a light application of lime is beneficial. Increase is from divisions or from fresh seed. If seed is allowed to dry out, it may take a year or 18 months before it will germinate, but it will eventually grow.

G. asclepiadea, the willow gentian, grows 60–70 cm (24–28 in.), flowering in early summer with spikes of dark blue flowers. There is also an attractive white form. This species does best in cool climates.

Gentiana septemfida

G. lagodechiana and *G. septemfida* are two late summer-flowering species that are much easier to grow in warmer districts. Of similar growth, they are distinguished by the fact that *G. lagodechiana* bears its flowers singly on the end of new growth, whereas *G. septemfida* has terminal clusters of trumpets. The colour is rich, deep blue but can be variable. Both come from Eastern Europe and Turkey.

G. lutea is a handsome bog plant and will grow in semi-shade. It has broad, green leaves and a single spike of lemon-yellow flowers 1–1.5 m (3–5 ft) tall.

G. sino-ornata is a hardy, easily grown species of prostrate, spreading habit, with the flower-stems ascending at the tips. It is quite at home in the semi-shade, provided the position is not too dry in summer, and delights in an acid soil such as is suitable for rhododendrons. The open-mouth, campanula-like trumpets, 5 cm (2 in.) long, are deep blue, paler at the base, and banded purplish blue. Plants are easily increased by divisions of established clumps, and although not as impressive as the glorious *G. acaulis*, it is more easily managed and a most desirable plant. Plants of gentians are usually pot grown so they can be planted almost any time of the year. Old clumps should be divided from late autumn until early spring.

GERANIUM
Geraniaceae   Crane's bill

In all there are over 400 species of perennial geraniums, many of which are delightful rock or alpine plants. A large number of the perennial geraniums are unattractive, with dull pink or purple flowers, small and insignificant, but there are a few really front-rank subjects that should be in every garden.

G. cinereum grows to 15 cm (6 in.), with open, white to purplish pink, veined flowers, up to 2.5 cm (1 in.) across, on short stems. The lobed leaves are

Opposite: These parallel borders feature plants in a narrow range of colours but with widely contrasting forms and textures—hostas, irises, salvia, cardoon (*Cynara*), and annual forget-me-not (*Myosotis*). A clematis in full flower drapes the pergola on the left.

grey-green. 'Ballerina' forms a low tuft of leaves and almost continuous sprays of round, purplish pink flowers with darker veins. It requires a sunny spot with good drainage. *G. cinereum* var. *subcaulescens* is a striking plant. It grows to 15 cm (6 in.) high, with round, rich bright magenta flowers with black eyes appearing on spreading stems for months on end.

G. dalmaticum grows into a 25 cm (10 in.) mound of pink flowers in summer.

G. endressii is a bushy, almost evergreen plant with deeply lobed foliage and topped with cup-shaped, light rose flowers 5 cm (2 in.) across on 45 cm (18 in.), branching stems. *G.* 'Claridge Druce' is a hybrid of *G. endressii* that makes dense, leafy clumps in sun or part-shade, and flowers freely to 50 cm (20 in.) with lilac-pink flowers. 'Wargrave Pink' is a more pronounced pink than the species, while a variety with silvery pink flowers is called 'A. T. Johnson'.

G. himalayense (syn. *G. grandiflorum*) is one of the best species, with its branching heads of large, blue, single flowers veined crimson and with a reddish purple eye. It grows 45 cm (18 in.) high and is semi-prostrate in habit. A lower-growing form, 'Alpinum', has larger flowers.

G. incanum is a spreader from South Africa, with lovely grey-green, aromatic, filigree foliage, evergreen in most coastal gardens and ideal for wall plantings. It is well covered with mauve or lavender flowers in spring.

Geranium cinereum var. *subcaulescens*

G. macrorrhizum grows to 45 cm (18 in.), with flowers of deep pink, sometimes purple. There is also a white form.

G. maderense is a giant species that grows well over 1 m (3 ft) tall, holding itself erect on the wiry petioles of the leaves and producing, in its second or third year, a huge single head of hundreds of magenta flowers, which open in succession from early spring. Although monocarpic, this makes a fine foliage plant, quite happy in semi-shade on light to medium soils where frosts are not severe. It is easily raised from seed, which is usually dispersed around the plant.

G. palmatum (syn. *G. anemonifolium*) is a species from the Canary Islands, growing to 80 cm (32 in.), and similar in habit to *G. maderense* but not as spectacular.

G. pratense, with its deep purple flowers, often red-veined, and pretty, finely cut foliage, is also a worthwhile border plant. Desirable double-flowered forms include: 'Plenum Caeruleum', a light, powdery blue; 'Plenum Violaceum', rich, deep violet-blue; and 'Album Plenum', double white.

G. psilostemon is a strong-growing, striking species forming a bush 90 cm (36 in.) high and across, and well covered with masses of intense magenta-crimson flowers, each with a jet-black centre.

G. 'Russell Pritchard' grows about 30 cm (12 in.), with round-lobed, grey-green leaves and long sprays of carmine-red flowers. It forms a clump and is lovely on a wall.

G. sanguineum is a much-branched, hardy species, growing 30–60 cm (12–24 in.) tall and across, with five-to-seven-lobed leaves and slender stems carrying numerous, 4 cm (1.5 in.) wide, bright purple-crimson, notched-petalled flowers throughout late spring and summer. A dwarf-growing form more suited to rockeries or border edgings is called 'Lancastriense'; the flowers of this variety are pink veined with darker red.

G. wallichianum 'Buxton's Blue' is a fine border plant, with deep blue flowers growing up to 45 cm (18 in.) high.

G. traversii is an interesting species from the Chatham Islands, usually grown as a rock plant. It provides an attractive display of pure white, sometimes pale pink flowers, 2.5 cm (1 in.) across. The leaves are greyish green. A larger-flowered form, rather less floppy than the type, is called *G. traversii*

Geranium maderense

var. *elegans*. The blooms of this variety are soft pink.

Plants are not easy to divide unless they have formed old clumps, but most species can be readily increased from pieces of root cut 5 cm (2 in.) long and inserted upright in sandy soil until the green leaves appear. Transplant during winter.

GERBERA
Asteraceae   African daisy

This genus comprises over 70 species native to Africa and Asia, few of which are of any horticultural interest. The range of attractive colours, both single and double-flowered, has been derived from the Transvaal species *G. jamesonii*, also commonly called the Barberton daisy. This species, which in its wild state produces finely rayed flower-heads 7.5–10 cm (3–4 in.) across, held erect on 45 cm (18 in.) stems, is usually orange-red or flame-scarlet, although yellow and orange forms also occur. A small-flowered species, usually with dirty white flowers, called *G. viridifolia*, was thought to have been used at one time to give the present range of white, cream and pale-coloured forms.

The double-flowered gerberas first appeared in France, and hybridists now offer a full selection of colours and shades and also two-tone forms, either with the reverse of petals a darker shade or else the outer petals a lighter shade than the centre. Seed from doubles is seldom fertile unless hand-crossed; the resultant seedlings produce 50–75 percent double-flowered forms, the remainder being singles.

In the 1950s and 1960s an excellent strain of double-flowered gerberas was developed, with larger flowers and a wonderful range of colours from white and cream, through all shades of pink, cerise and crimson and yellow shades to orange and scarlet. Good broad-petalled, double flowers with strong stems have obviously been the aims of the hybridisers. The range includes the following:

'Autumn sunset'—double orange.
'Berlini'—double crimson.
'Copenhagen'—double light pink.
'Deep Tango'—scarlet red.
'Moonlight'—double cream.
'Princess'—salmon rose pink.
'Sheer Delight'—double gold.

Gerberas are not grown outdoors in Britain or northern Europe, and Dutch nurseries have grown them extensively under glass for cut flowers. They favour single or semi-double flowers, and their selections are mainly singles with several rows of petals and long stems. From these, more dwarf strains have been developed for use as pot plants, including 'Noonday Sun', golden yellow; 'Show Stopper', lilac-pink; 'Ferris Wheel', red with gold centre; 'Dream Girl', clear pink.

Unless particularly well harvested, seed of gerberas remains fertile for only a few months and should be sown as soon as ripe. A mixture of sandy loam with leaf mould seems ideal, and fresh seed germinates readily within 10–20 days of sowing. Water should be withheld or used sparingly as seedlings damp off very easily. Seedlings should be pricked out into boxes or beds when the second leaves appear, and these plants should be ready for setting out in the garden or nursery rows in late

Gerbera jamesonii hybrid

spring to bloom in the autumn. Plants can also be raised by cuttings from side shoots taken in summer.

Light volcanic or free riverbed soils seem ideal, but where the soil is heavy or of a clayish nature, specially prepared, raised beds are advisable. Gerberas have been successfully grown in pure sand only, watered occasionally with liquid manure.

Two foliage fungous diseases occur in the form of leaf spots, and although not really serious in that plants do not die, rather poor blooms are the result during the autumn, when infection is most prevalent. Once plants become affected it seems almost impossible to eliminate the trouble entirely. The most serious disease is a root rot, *Phytophthora parasitica*, which causes a blackening of the crown of the plant, soon resulting in complete collapse. This trouble is usually an indication of poor drainage or a weakened plant, but not always so, as it can become rampant and attack plants under ideal conditions. Badly affected plants should be destroyed. If the foliage of gerbera plants shows a tendency to wilt or turn a purplish colour on one side of the plant only, this is probably an attack of wire worm, which can be treated with an appropriate pesticide.

White rust is a serious disease that attacks gerbera plants. It manifests itself in small, round, white patches, usually under the leaves. It disfigures and weakens the constitution of the plants and results in a paucity of blooms.

Gerberas can be safely transplanted in warm districts any time from autumn until spring, but the best time in colder districts is in spring, just when new leaf and root growth are commencing. Some winter protection is necessary when frosts exceed 14 degrees.

GEUM
Rosaceae

There are nearly 40 species of this genus distributed over the world, predominating in temperate and cold regions. These old-time favourites of cast-iron constitution can always be relied upon to give a good show of blooms over a long period from late spring until early autumn. As with all other perennials, particularly those that set seed after blooming, a much longer flowering period can be secured by removing old or faded blooms, or cutting the flowers regularly for decoration.

Although quite a number of species are attractive and worthy of cultivation, practically the only taller-growing varieties we have are selected forms of *G. chiloense*. The two well-known varieties, 'Lady Stratheden', a pure double yellow, and 'Mrs Bradshaw', a double orange-scarlet, are still indispensable in the mixed herbaceous border. Both can be grown from seed and will produce plants true to colour.

There are several attractive, lower-growing species and natural hybrids worthy of a place in the rockery or the front of the herbaceous border. *G.* x *borisii* is a cross between *G. bulgaricum* and *G. reptans*, with bright orange flowers on 30 cm (12 in.) stems.

G. bulgaricum grows 35 cm (14 in.) high, with bright yellow, nodding flowers on long, feathery plumes.

G. x *heldreichii* is said to be a natural hybrid from *G. montanum*. It is a very showy variety with large, bright orange-red flowers produced during summer. Various forms have been selected, including a pure yellow.

G. heterocarpum is a rock-garden subject with a spreading habit and many heads of pale yellow flowers from late spring till summer.

G. japonicum is a good, robust border plant of 40–60 cm (16–24 in.), with erect stems and large yellow flowers.

Another good species is *G. montanum* and its various selected types. This produces a neat rosette of soft, hairy leaves and 22.5 cm (9 in.), erect stems of bright golden yellow blooms. It is a splendid rock garden subject.

An interesting autumn- and winter-blooming

species, native to Europe, is known as *G. rivale*. The pinnate foliage is roughly hairy, and the erect-growing, 45 cm (18 in.), nodding, coppery red flowers are somewhat incurved and not reflexed, although the flowers usually hang down, thus detracting to some extent from its value as a garden plant. Its interesting habit, together with the fact that it will bloom throughout the winter, makes it a plant worthy of consideration. 'Leonard's Variety' is a selected form.

G. sibiricum has charming yellow or coppery red flowers to 25 cm above a dense clump of foliage.

Other hybrids such as 'Fire Opal', brilliant flame-scarlet, 'Dolly North', a very large flower of light orange, and 'Red Wings', a luminous signal red, are well worth growing. In some cases these selected forms are hybrids with other species, producing numerous, branching, wiry stems 60–90 cm (24–36 in.) long, carrying an extended display of double or semi-double blooms 5–7.5 cm (2–3 in.) across.

All the species are easily raised from seed, producing blooms true to type, but the newer varieties are best increased from divisions, as seedlings show considerable variation. All of the geums are quite hardy and easily transplanted, either from divisions of older plants during winter months or from seedlings planted out in the autumn or spring.

GLADIOLUS
Iridaceae

The species of gladiolus probably number about 180, but many are not in cultivation. There have been numerous name changes as botanists have learned more about the genus, and several are incorporated in this book, based on the 1972 revision by Lewis, Obermeyer and Barnard, published in *Gladiolus* by Kirstenbosch (1972).

Gladiolus species
In contrast to the modern, large-flowered hybrids, which are all summer and autumn flowering, requiring to be planted out in the spring, most species of gladiolus are spring blooming and should be set out in the autumn.

G. alatus is a lovely miniature, suitable for the rockery, delighting in a sunny position with sharp drainage. Although easily grown, it simply will not tolerate wet conditions, but if a little thought is given to its simple requirements, there are few gardens where it cannot be grown happily. The 30 cm (12 in.) stems carry three to six wide-open, winged flowers, rich orange-red, with lower segments yellow at the base. Several lighter and darker forms are also known. Increase is from seed, or the numerous tiny cormlets that are attached to the base of the 2.5 cm (1 in.) wide, roundish corm.

G. angustus grows 25–50 cm (10–20 in.) tall, with funnel-shaped, creamy white flowers with a dark purple-brown marking on each of the three lower petals. In warmer districts it is persistent and flowers freely in a sunny position. It has sometimes been sold erroneously under the label *G. nanus* 'Nymph'.

G. byzantinus is a valuable, hardy species from the Middle East, easily grown anywhere, even in heavy ground. It appears to be free from any of the diseases that usually attack the corms of this family. The foliage is comparatively dwarf, up to 30 cm (12 in.)

Geum x *borisii*

high, and the slender flower-stems are up to 90 cm (36 in.). The flowers are about 7.5 cm (3 in.) across with four to six out at once. The colour is usually bright violet-purple with slight white markings, but a pure white form is also available. This species blooms in winter and is a useful cut flower. It increases readily from divisions of the parent corms, but also produces very large cormlets, which bloom the first season. Corms are dormant in late autumn and should be planted before winter, or in very early spring in cold districts. In coastal districts bulbs may be left undisturbed as they are hardier than the South African species. They should be transplanted in autumn when they are dormant.

G. cardinalis is one of the parents of the large-flowered hybrids. It has larger flowers, 7.5 cm (3 in.) wide, bright crimson marked with white on the lower petals, and growing on a stem about 60 cm (24 in.) long, which often leans towards the light.

G. carmineus is a very desirable and unusual species in that it flowers in late summer and early autumn before the foliage and seeds appear in late autumn. The flowers are up to 9 cm (3.5 in.) wide, a lovely deep pink, and are on short spikes about 30 cm (12 in.) tall. The two leaves that appear will grow 50–60 cm (20–24 in.) long and up to 1.5 cm (0.5 in.) wide, and will persist all winter. This species may be left in the ground in warmer districts.

G. carneus (syn. *G. blandus*) is sometimes known as the 'painted lady'. Although variable, it typically has pale pink flowers with wavy edges, growing 30–45 cm (12–18 in.), in spring.

Gladiolus cardinalis

G. x *colvillei*, often incorrectly known as *G. nanus*, are the baby gladiolus or painted ladies. They are the result of a cross between the red-flowered species *G. cardinalis* and the lemon-yellow *G. tristis*, which flowers at the same time. Well-known varieties include:

'Alba'—violet-coloured anthers.
'Amada Mahy'—orange-scarlet.
'Blushing Bride'—white with carmine flakes.
'Ne Plus Ultra'—carmine-red with white stripe, vigorous.
'Orangeade'—light salmon-orange.
'Peach Blossom'—pink, dwarf, wonderfully free-flowering.
'Rubra'—carmine-red blooms.
'Spitfire'—vermillion-scarlet with small violet flakes.
'The Bride'—pure white flowers and white anthers.

All varieties are easily grown and fairly resistant to pests and diseases. Corms should be planted in late summer or autumn (early spring in very cold districts) and they will flower the following spring or early summer.

G. natalensis (syn. *G. psittacinus, G. daleni*) is a summer-flowering form, with red to orange-yellow flowers often streaked or speckled with red. *G. natalensis* 'Hookeri' is cultivated only in mild or comparatively frost-free areas for its valuable winter

Gladiolus alatus

or early spring blooms. It is strong and robust in habit, preferring a free, loose soil and full sun, and soon forms large clumps or groups if left undisturbed. The spikes of brilliant-coloured blooms reach 1.5 m (5 ft). The plant dies down in spring and starts into growth again after a short rest. If not lifted, it commences to bloom from late autumn onward. The hooded flowers are rich yellow, thickly grained and overlaid with deep red, the general effect being a red and yellow bicolor. The flowers are 7.5 cm (3 in.) across, up to 24 or more on a spike, with four to eight open at a time. Flowers last a fortnight or more in water. Blooms will be damaged with any but light frosts, and can be cut in bud and opened up inside. Increase is from the large cormlets that form near the bulb or at the end of adventitious rootlets, thrown out 15–30 cm (6–12 in.) from the parent corm.

G. papilio (syn. *G. purpureo-auratus*) flowers in summer. The yellow-white blooms have a violet tinge and yellow patches on the lower petals. It may be left in the ground in warmer districts, and will increase by means of stolons.

G. primulinus, a wild species from tropical Africa, was not introduced into cultivation until 1900 but has quickly become the parent of a large number of the present-day hybrids. The colour is rich yellow, and the much-hooded flowers are formed so as to protect the pollen from being spoiled by the misty rains. It grows plentifully near the misty falls of the Zambesi River, where it was first discovered and

Gladiolus tristis

given the name 'maid of the mist'. These hybrids are preferred for indoor decoration to the large-flowered exhibition types. They are usually classed as miniature and butterfly gladiolus, and the hooded flowers of the *G. primulinus* varieties are superseded by cultivars with open, outward-facing flowers, often with ruffled petals of the butterfly class. These hybrids are available in almost every shade of the larger-flowered varieties. Corms can be planted from late winter until early summer to provide a succession of bloom, usually flowering 90 days after planting.

G. punctulatus grows 35–55 cm (14–22 in.) tall, with slender stems carrying smallish, mauve-pink, funnel-shaped flowers with a few reddish streaks on the lower petals.

G. tristis is a lovely species from Natal, worthy of much wider cultivation. It seems fairly hardy and prefers fairly heavy, deep soil but it is also successful in light soil provided it is not lacking in humus. The thin, rush-like foliage and flower-stems 60 cm (24 in.) high carry two to six delightfully fragrant, pale sulphur-yellow flowers 9 cm (3.5 in.) across. A clump in bloom will scent the whole garden with a magnolia-like perfume. The corms are smallish, up to 2.5 cm (1 in.) across, each producing an abundance of small cormlets. These will all bloom two or three years after sowing. It also sets seed freely, the resulting stock often yielding slight variations. Some forms often carry a band of purplish black stretching up the centre of each of the upper petals, but the most effective is the pure, unmarked sulphur-yellow that has been listed as *G. tristis* var. *concolor*. Some

Gladiolus x *colvillei* hybrids

efforts have been made to cross this species with the large-flowered hybrids in an attempt to raise a strain of scented gladiolus. The 2.5 cm (1 in.) wide corms are dormant in late summer and should be replanted again in autumn.

G. undulatus has long, narrow, green flowers on stems about 60 cm (24 in.) long and frequently spreading at an angle of 45 degrees if not supported. In some parts of New Zealand it is a roadside and garden weed on account of the profuse proliferation of cormlets, which will develop even on corms too small to flower.

Gladiolus hybrids

Very few species have been employed in raising the great range of modern large-flowered gladiolus available today. These species are natives of Europe, the Mediterranean region, and tropical and South Africa. Apart from the early-flowering *G.* x *colvillei* section, the present-day range of hybrids is divided into three classes: 'Primulinus' types, with slender stems, hooded flowers 6–9 cm (2.5–3.5 in.) across; 'Primulinus Grandiflorus' types, in which the stems are taller and stronger, upper segments horizontal or somewhat hooded, and flowers 9–11 cm (3.5–4.5 in.) across; the largest group, called 'Large-flowered Types', embraces ruffled and plain-petalled, exhibition and garden varieties, with blooms from 10–20 cm (4-8 in.) across or more.

For exhibition purposes gladiolus are classified into two types only: formal and informal.

Class I: Formal are those types that place their florets in a 2-2-2-2 arrangement, the petals of one floret overlapping the other, and completely hiding the stem and covering all gaps between florets.

Class II: Informals have a staggered arrangement of florets more openly placed on the spike. These are divided into two size groupings:
1. Large informals measure not less than 9.5 cm (3.75 in.) across the floret without stretching.
2. Small informals measure not more than 9.5 cm (3.75 in.) across the floret without stretching.

The culture of gladiolus is simple as they are not overly particular as to soils, but an open aspect, well-drained, sunny and protected from heavy winds, should be chosen. The ground should be prepared in the autumn by digging in well-rotted animal

Gladiolus natalensis

manure, or any green manure. About a month before planting the corms, the ground should be lightly forked over again. If stocks are to be increased from cormlets saved from the previous year, these can be sown first, towards the end of winter, in drills just like peas. The largest of them could be set out singly a few centimetres apart, like small corms. Full-sized corms, which are from 3 cm (1.5 in.) in diameter, are usually set 15 cm (6 in.) apart and 10 cm (4 in.) deep in rows or beds. Planting of corms in all sizes can be spread over the months from late winter until early summer, resulting in a succession of bloom as most gladiolus flower approximately 90 days after planting.

If the ground is reasonably rich in humus and prepared as described, there should be no need to add artificial manures. Good results, however, are secured with superphosphate, although a more balanced manure is four parts of superphosphate, three parts of bonedust and two parts of sulphate of potash. For exhibition spikes, liquid manure should be applied first when the flower-spike begins to show and continued at five-day intervals until the colour appears, when manuring should cease. Frequent stirring of the topsoil during the growing period is better than constant waterings, but if watering is necessary when the flower-spikes are developing, give the bed a real soaking, cultivating the surface of the soil as soon as possible afterwards.

Blooms should be cut with a slanting cut, running down the stem and giving it a twist at the required spot so as to leave all the foliage behind; this is necessary for the development of the corms. For inside decorations, best results are secured by cutting the blooms just as the first bud opens.

Unfortunately, diseases in gladiolus are more prevalent today than they were years ago, due no doubt to the weakening of resistance resulting from selective breeding. Many troubles can be avoided by drying corms quickly and storing them in an open, dry shed. It is advisable to check just before corms are set out to see if they are healthy. Thrips can give trouble in hot, dry weather, and at the first sign the foliage should be sprayed with an appropriate pesticide.

Corms should be lifted as soon as the foliage begins to turn yellow, and the tops cut off immediately, close above the corm. Dry thoroughly and quickly in the sun or an airy shed, removing the old wasted corm and roots as soon as they become loosened, in two or three weeks' time. The success of storing corms through the winter depends upon a quick and thorough drying to prevent the development of various scab diseases and rots.

GLORIOSA
Liliaceae   Climbing lily

Natives of tropical Africa, the gloriosas are truly lovely climbing members of the great lily family. They are easy to grow but require good drainage and freedom from heavy frosts. They are hardier than is generally considered, and even in districts with cold winters, success can be assured if they are planted in a very sunny spot sheltered from cold winds. The long, fleshy roots remain completely dormant for six months of the year and do not come into growth until late spring, when the ground is warm; hence there is little risk of spring frost damage. They grow quickly and bloom freely during the hot summer months. They are quite attractive as pot plants in very cold districts, requiring three to six tubers to a large pot. The single, lily-like leaves taper to fine points so attenuated as to become climbing tendrils, by which means the plant clings to any suitable support, such as netting, old stumps, or even shrubs.

The 7.5 cm (3 in.) flowers, which are produced singly at the axils of the leaves and stem, are lily-like, but the petals are curled and quaintly reflexed, with protruding stamens.

G. carsonii is an uncommon, free-flowering species, with the flower segments about 6 cm (2.5 in.) long and 1 cm (0.5 in.) wide, and a bright shade of red, shading to yellow in the centre. European firms list a form of this species with yellow flowers edged violet.

The best species, but unfortunately not particularly hardy outdoors, is *G. rothschildiana*, with flowers yellowish white near the base, deepening to ruby-crimson at the tip. The general effect is rich crimson, edged creamy yellow.

G. simplex, often listed as *G. virescens*, is more

Gloriosa rothschildiana

trailing or procumbent than other species and is rather variable in colour. The type commonly grown is usually a pale greenish yellow, but nevertheless quite pretty.

G. superba is the best-known and easiest-grown species, with its orange-yellow flowers deepening to red.

G. verschuurii is similar to *G. rothschildiana*, but the vivid red segments are not incurved, the flower being more open and less reflexed. It is more compact in growth and suitable for pot culture.

Increase is best from seed, which forms in large pods, and these are easily raised, blooming the second or third year after sowing. Much care should be exercised in lifting or handling the fleshy roots as they are easily broken, and even slight damage may cause them to rot. The new growth, as with the sandersonias, starts from the tip of the tuber so that if this is bruised or broken, failure to sprout and collapse of the root will follow. Shifting is best done in early spring, although the roots are completely dormant during the late autumn and winter, at which time, if plants are pot-grown, the soil should be allowed to dry out, or nearly so. Plant roots 15 cm (6 in.) apart and 7.5 cm (3 in.) deep.

GUNNERA
Gunneraceae

This genus of about 50 species of herbaceous perennials is widely distributed over most of the Southern Hemisphere.

G. chilensis (syn. *G. tinctoria*, *G. scabra*) is the species usually cultivated. It produces immense, coarsely rough, rounded, deeply veined and scalloped leaves, usually about 1.2 m (4 ft) across, on prickly stems up to 2 m (6 ft). The size of the leaves and length of stems depends on the richness of the soil and the amount of moisture available during the growing season. The plant dies down completely in winter. Grown in the right position, such as alongside a stream or pond, in a semi-shady place, it is a handsome plant, quite hardy and easily cultivated. The large, cone-shaped spikes or panicles of greenish yellow flowers, followed by green fruits tinted with red, provide some attraction but are usually hidden by the large foliage.

Gunnera manicata

G. manicata is the real giant of the genus, producing roots as large as a man's body, with immense, kidney-shaped leaves to 1.8 m (6 ft) across.

Although these two species are giants, there are several quite attractive miniatures, growing only a few centimetres high. Two such species, natives of New Zealand, are *G. dentata* and *G. monoica*, both mat-forming plants with hairy, heart-shaped leaves in rosettes, and also delighting in moist or boggy conditions. Other low-growing New Zealand native species are *G. prorepens*, which carries red, berry-like fruits in autumn, and *G. hamiltonii*, which forms tight mats of 5 cm (2 in.) rosettes of grey-green leaves. Both may be used as ground cover in moist places.

Increase of all species is either from seed sown in the spring or else from divisions of established clumps during winter or early spring.

GYPSOPHILA
Caryophyllaceae   Baby's breath

This genus comprises about 50 species, mainly from the eastern Mediterranean region. The well-known annual varieties of *G. elegans* are sometimes also called baby's breath or gauze flowers, on account of the dainty miniature flowers of misty grace.

A hardy and attractive, single-flowered species known as *G. acutifolia* is a native of Russia. The flowers are three times as large as those of the more common *G. paniculata* and occur in white and pale rose, with a greenish or reddish striped calyx.

G. 'Flamingo' is a tall-growing, autumn-flowering variety in rather a hard shade of light mauve-pink. This variety is considered by some to be a double-flowered form of the single pink-flowered species called *G. oldhamiana*, a native of Asia. It does not seem to possess any relationship with the *G. paniculata* varieties.

G. paniculata, with its sprays of tiny, single, white flowers, so useful for mixing with other flowers, is the best-known species. There is a good double, white-flowered form, 'Flore Pleno', which grows to about 60 cm (24 in.). This was the first double gypsophila.

Several double-flowered forms have been introduced, but the best of all the whites is the variety called 'Bristol Fairy'. If given plenty of space, this will grown to 1.2 m (4 ft) high and more across. This is now a front-rank herbaceous plant, and no garden is complete without it. An improvement called 'Bristol Fairy Perfecta' has larger flowers.

G. 'Lavender Lady' is a New Zealand-raised seedling, a cross between 'Bristol Fairy' and a semi-prostrate, single pink-flowered species known as *G. repens* 'Rosea'. The plant grows about 35 cm (14 in.) high, rather spreading in habit, with masses of double, pale lavender-pink flowers.

G. 'Rosy Veil' is the hybrid nearest to a true pink in the double-flowered forms, growing up to 75 cm (30 in.) tall, and more across. It was raised in Germany, where it was named 'Rosenschleirer', and is a valuable cut flower and garden plant. *G.* 'Pink Star' is a New Zealand-raised tetraploid break from 'Rosy Veil', with blooms twice the size of those on the parent plant.

Increase of 'Rosy Veil', 'Pink Star' and 'Lavender Lady' is from soft cuttings taken from the rootstock early in the spring, while the other two varieties are usually grafted on to pieces of roots, using the same type of shoots as for cuttings, when only 5–7.5 cm (2–3 in.) long. Grafts can be taken from last year's matured, unflowered growths or soft spring growths. All can be rooted from cuttings, but the use of plant hormones is desirable, and in some cases essential for success. Transplant when dormant during winter, or young grafted stocks as late as early summer, to produce bloom in late autumn or early winter.

Gypsophila 'Pink Star'

H

HABRANTHUS
Amaryllidaceae

About 20 species of South American bulbs form this genus, which is closely related to amaryllis, and which until recently included both hippeastrum and zephyranthes. The following two species of habranthus are easily grown and desirable subjects for the rockery or for group planting in the front of the border.

H. andersonii is a small, crocus-like plant with

Habranthus andersonii

yellow flowers with coppery exteriors, appearing on 25 cm (10 in.) stems in mid-summer. The flowers open in succession, with grassy foliage appearing later. Bulbs should be planted together in groups.

H. brachyandrus gives us 7.5 cm (3 in.), pale pink trumpets, blackish red at the base, two to four blooms on a 30 cm (12 in.) scape. The narrow strap-like leaves are about 30 cm (12 in.) long, and the bulbs are about 5 cm (2 in.) across.

H. tubispathus (syn. *robustus*) used to be listed among the zephyranthes, but possesses the true characteristics of the genus, with trumpet flowers 7.5 cm (3 in.) across and 10 cm (4 in.) long in a soft shade of pale rose, changing with age to almost blush-white. The bulbs are roundish, increasing freely, and blooming in summer.

Bulbs are partly dormant during late autumn and winter, when they can be easily transplanted. Free, loose soil with ample drainage is essential, but otherwise they are quite easily grown. Increase is from the bulbs or, if available, from seed, which produces bulbs of flowering size the third season.

HAEMANTHUS
Amaryllidaceae   Blood lily

There are about 50 known species of these half-hardy South and tropical African bulbs. They are hardy outside in warmer parts, and grow well and flower well in districts free from heavy frosts. The bulbs are large, forming heavy, fleshy roots like hippeastrums, so they prefer a free, deep root run such as is provided by friable, fertile soils.

H. albiflos. The 30 cm (12 in.) flower-stem carries a brush-like head of white, about 3 cm (1.5 in.) in diameter, with yellow stamens. The strap-like, leathery leaves are up to 12.5 cm (5 in.) long and 7.5 cm (3 in.) wide. This autumn-flowering species increases slowly.

Haemanthus coccineus

H. coccineus usually produces two large, broad, fleshy leaves, 15 cm (6 in.) wide and up to 90 cm (36 in.) long, lying almost prostrate on the ground. Later in the autumn, when the foliage has died down, 30 cm (12 in.), mottled stems appear, with a terminal cup enclosing a dense umbel with numerous, blood-red flowers about 5 cm (2 in.) long in the form of a brush. It is sometimes called the scarlet paint-brush.

H. rotundifolius has scarlet flowers similar to *H. coccineus* but with two leathery leaves, 15 cm (6 in.) long and 12.5 cm (5 in.) wide, almost round, lying flat on the ground.

H. katherinae, with tall stems and spreading foliage, has been transferred to the genus *Scadoxus* (q.v.) because of its very different growth habit.

Increase is from divisions or, more slowly, from seed, if obtainable. Transplant during early summer when bulbs are dormant, setting bulbs with the neck just below the surface of the soil. A semi-shady position suits best.

HEDYCHIUM
Zingiberaceae

The 50 species of erect, strong-growing perennials forming this genus are natives of south and east Asia, with the exception of one from Madagascar.

Although semi-tropical in origin, they are fairly hardy in most parts of New Zealand and Australia. They resemble the cannas in growth and foliage, and respond to similar treatment—good, rich soil and plenty of water during summer or when blooming. The broad leaves are spaced up the strong 1–1.5 m (3–5 ft) stem, which terminates in a cylindrical, many-flowered spike, 10 cm (4 in.) across. Most species are sweetly perfumed, all blooming in the autumn and lasting in an attractive condition over a long period.

The white-flowered, sweet-scented species *H. coronarium* is well worth growing.

A most desirable red-flowering species, *H. coccineum*, is worth securing if available. As this is a variable species, several shades of pink, rose, salmon and dull red may result from a batch of seedlings.

The best-known and easiest-grown coloured species is *H. gardneranum*, in which the flowers are rich yellow, with an orange patch in the centre at the base. In northern parts of New Zealand it is becoming a noxious weed, and should not be allowed to set seed, which is distributed by birds.

All species increase readily from divisions of old clumps, and should be divided or transplanted when dormant during the winter months. Seed germinates freely, and plants thus raised usually bloom the second season. Frosts will cut back the foliage if the plants are still growing, but, as with cannas, this will not damage the plants. As they bloom in the late autumn, plants should be cut down to the ground as soon as the flowers are finished or after the first frosts.

HELENIUM
Asteraceae   Sneezewort

This genus consists of about 40 species of perennials, which form a section of a large family of plants commonly called sunflowers. They are most valuable in the border during summer and late autumn, when they can be relied upon to give a vivid splash of colour. They are most accommodating and easy to grow.

The taller-growing varieties and species can be pinched back when the new growths are about 60 cm (24 in.) high so as to reduce their ultimate height,

Helenium 'Walstrand'

induce them to branch more freely, and thus avoid legginess.

H. autumnale is the common species from which many of our modern varieties have developed. The plant grows 1.5 m (5 ft) high, with terminal, branching heads composed of numerous, 5 cm (2 in.), yellow flowers, the petals being three cleft and somewhat drooping. The reddish brown form *H. autumnale* 'Rubrum' is the one more often grown, while 'Striatum' has golden flowers streaked with crimson.

Varieties include the following:

'Butter Pat'—a good, rich yellow, blooming very late in the season, continuing when others have finished; grows about 1 m (3 ft) tall.

'Copper Spray'—showy, coppery orange-red flowers on 1 m (3 ft) stems. The German name is 'Kuppersprudel'.

'Madam Canivet'—1 m (3 ft) high, golden yellow, listed by some growers as *H. pumilum* 'Magnificum'.

'Moerheim Beauty'—still the most popular in this shade; rich orange-reddish brown flowers on 1 m (3 ft) stems, dark-coloured foliage.

'Walstrand'—rich, coppery orange with velvety brown centre, to 1 m (3 ft); an excellent cut flower and border perennial.

'Wyndley'—bushy growth, very leafy and blooming over a long period; good-sized, orange-yellow

flowers flushed chestnut; grows 75 cm (30 in.) tall.

All species and varieties are freely increased by dividing up old clumps, the stronger, outer shoots being the best to retain.

HELIANTHEMUM
Cistaceae   Rock rose

This genus of about 100 species of small shrubs inhabits most parts of the Northern Hemisphere. Although the lovely selection of named varieties available are all strictly sub-shrubs and not true perennials, they are invariably included among the herbaceous plants in catalogues as well as in actual plantings.

Varieties have been derived from the species *H. nummularium*, a spreading, densely twigged shrub about 30 cm (12 in.) high, sometimes reaching up to 1 m (3 ft) across. The small, narrow leaves are usually greyish green with grey down beneath. During spring established specimens throw up numerous many-flowered racemes of 2.5 cm (1 in.) wide, single or double flowers, the display continuing over a considerable period. These plants are very suited for banks, hanging over walls, or for the front row of the herbaceous border. They will stand

Helianthemum 'Wisley Pink'

considerable drought, are quite hardy anywhere but are not long-lived. The weaker, single-flowered varieties sometimes become exhausted through heavy seeding, and non-seeding and more prostrate-growing, double-flowered varieties are often preferred. A good range of colours is generally in cultivation. Singles include pink, yellow, white, orange, scarlet, terracotta, chocolate-brown and crimson. 'Wisley Pink' is a lovely soft pink with a distinctive yellow centre. There are fewer colours available in doubles; 'Jubilee' is an excellent double yellow with dark, evergreen foliage; 'Mrs Earles' is a popular double red; 'Prima Donna' is double apricot; 'Rose of Leewood' is a good double pink. The double cultivars retain their flowers until evening, but the petals of the singles drop in the afternoon.

Increase is from 5–7.5 cm (2–3 in.) cuttings, taken in the early autumn. Some interesting colours can be secured from seed. Plants are best pot grown for safe shifting, unless they are transplanted when very small.

HELIANTHUS
Asteraceae   Sunflower

This genus of about 110 species is from North and South America. Most varieties and species produce an abundance of golden yellow, single blooms like miniature sunflowers, and as they bloom in the late autumn, when all the flowers are becoming scarce, they fill a useful place. All are very hardy and require no special soil or attention except that they prefer full sun.

H. decapetalus is one of the best species, forming a strong, compact rootstock and a leafy bush 1.5 m (5 ft) high, blooming in mid-autumn. As with many other tall-growing perennials, such as asters, helenium and rudbeckia, more compact plants can be secured by topping the new shoots when 30 cm (12 in.) or so high. Several forms are grown, superior to the type, such as 'Loddon Gold', which flowers in late summer with a fine display of very double, golden yellow blooms.

H. salicifolius (syn. *H. orgyalis*) is one of our showiest late-autumn-blooming perennials. Commonly known as 'Autumn Glory', it flowers when most other plants have finished. The rich, dark green,

Helianthus salicifolius 'Golden Pyramid'

shining leaves are willow-like, and the 1.2–1.8 m (4–6 ft), branching heads carry masses of 7.5 cm (3 in.), brilliant yellow, single daisies. It is lovely associated with late-flowering blue asters or salvias. A dwarf-growing sport of this species, named 'Golden Pyramid', forms a neat and very compact mound of rich green foliage up to 50 cm (20 in.) high, and during late autumn it is transformed into a pyramid of solid gold, entirely covering the foliage.

There are a number of other attractive, hardy species of helianthus, most of which are quite suitable for background plants for the herbaceous border. The common Jerusalem artichoke, *H. tuberosa*, belongs to this genus.

All helianthus are easily increased from divisions in the spring or by breaking up old clumps.

HELICHRYSUM
Asteraceae

This is a very varied genus of plants, some annual but also many perennials. All are sun-lovers and will grow on any average soil with good drainage.

H. angustifolium is the curry plant, a small shrub with very silvery, short leaves smelling strongly of curry in hot weather. Tufts of yellow, composite flowers appear in summer. It is not used for culinary purposes.

H. argyrophyllum is a dense ground cover with very silvery foliage and is excellent on walls, rooting as it spreads. It has yellow daisies (everlasting when dried) about 20 cm (8 in.) high in profusion in autumn, and is hardy in most districts.

H. baxteri is an Australian, small, shrubby plant to about 40 cm (16 in.), with narrow leaves and pure white, daisy flowers.

H. bracteatum is often grown as an annual for its multi-coloured, everlasting flowers, but there are also sub-shrubby forms with lemon-yellow and golden yellow daisies 5 cm (2 in.) in diameter on spreading bushes to 50 cm (2 in.). 'Dargon Hill Monarch' is the name of the golden-flowered form usually grown.

H. petiolatum is a hardy, spreading, shrubby plant with silvery grey foliage. If not controlled, it will climb up into shrubs or up a trellis. The flowers are white but not significant. More attractive is *H. petiolatum* 'Limelight', which has lime-green foliage that is almost yellow in good light. It has the same spreading habit.

H. retortum is a trailing shrublet with bright silver, heart-shaped leaves and large, papery white flowers in early summer.

H. selago is a small, evergreen shrublet of spreading habit, 25 cm (10 in.) high. It is native to New Zealand.

H. 'Sulphur Light' is also low-growing, with white, woolly foliage in a prostrate mass, followed by a profusion of sulphur-yellow flowers on 30 cm (12 in.) stems.

H. virgineum has masses of amber buds, which open to straw-like flowers 30 cm (12 in.) tall.

Propagation is by division or seed sown in spring.

HELIOPSIS
Asteraceae

Twelve species belong to this genus. This section of the autumn-blooming sunflowers contains some of our most valuable perennials. They are all quite easy to grow, being hardy even in adverse conditions. The flowers are heavy like zinnias and are therefore admirably suitable as cut flowers, particularly in large arrangements.

H. helianthoides subsp. *scabra* is the best-known variety, with rough, hairy leaves and flower-stems 0.6–1.5 m (2–5 ft) high. A selected form called 'Orange King' produces rich, orange-yellow, semi-double flowers, 7.5–10 cm (3–4 in.) across, the tips of the heavy-textured petals reflexing somewhat. Still another form known as *H.* 'Gigantea', rather taller growing, produces large, golden yellow flowers. In Europe several other interesting forms of this variable species are grown and much valued; 'Golden Plume', full double of perfect form, and 'Light of Loddon', a brilliant yellow with neatly

Helichrysum baxteri

Helichrysum bracteatum 'Dargon Hill Monarch'

Heliopsis helianthoides subsp. *scabra*

shaped flowers, are two of the best.

Further stocks are increased readily from divisions, which are transplanted during the winter months or early spring.

HELIOTROPIUM
Boraginaceae   Cherry pie

H. arborescens is a popular shrubby, bushy evergreen often used in mixed borders, especially for its pleasing scent. 'Lord Roberts' is the best cultivar available, with violet-blue flower-heads in which the open flowers fade to a lighter shade. It is hardy only in frost-free positions but grows well in containers to about 60 cm (24 in). Plants should be pruned to prevent them becoming straggly. Propagation is by cuttings taken in autumn.

HELLEBORUS
Ranunculaceae   Winter rose

Helleborus is also called the Christmas or Lenten rose. It is a genus of perennials, sometimes evergreen, with beautiful, open, cup-shaped flowers.

Plants prefer semi-shade and well-drained but moist soil.

H. foetidus grows 60–90 cm (24–36 in.) tall, with pale green, terminal flower clusters. It flowers in early spring, and does well in shade.

H. lividus (syn. *H. corsicus*, *H. argutifolius*), the Corsican hellebore, is a robust evergreen, with glaucous green, leathery, toothed leaves, growing up to 60 cm (24 in.) in suitable shady spots. Strong stems carrying 20–30 nodding, yellow-green, 5 cm (2 in.) flowers are held above the foliage and are most useful and long-lasting when cut.

H. niger and its selected forms are valuable florists' flowers. To produce earlier and finer blooms, the beds are usually covered with glass frames as soon as the buds appear. Under this protection the flowers develop longer stems and are neither damaged by adverse weather nor spotted by wind and rain. In New Zealand and Australia the plants thrive best in cold districts, or shady spots in warmer districts, and usually take a few years to become properly established. The name *niger*, meaning black, refers to the dark blackish rootstock, and not to the colour of the flower.

The common purple species of *H. orientalis* is well known, as is also the greenish white form, but

Helleborus lividus

Helleborus orientalis, white form

hybridisation has produced a much wider range of shades including soft pinks, rose, wine red and claret, some with deeper reverse colourings, and others beautifully spotted or splashed and marbled with other colours. In addition, the blooms have been greatly increased in size, substance and quality. All these hybrids are invaluable for inside decoration and florists' use.

H. 'White Magic' is a selection with similar flowers to *H. niger* but with more vigour. It was raised in New Zealand, and may be grown successfully in partial shade in warmer districts.

Increase is mostly by divisions of old clumps, preferably in the autumn or early spring. Seed germinates readily in the spring but should be sown as soon as ripe in summer. If sown too late in the season, they will remain dormant in the soil until the following spring. Seedlings should bloom two or three years after germination and thrive best in fairly heavy or moist soil in a shady spot, or even under big trees if not too dry.

HEMEROCALLIS
Liliaceae   Day lily

This genus has about a dozen species, most of which are natives of temperate eastern Asia. The best-known of these is *H. fulva*, a plant with scapes of rich

orange-red, funnel-shaped, reflexed flowers 7.5–12.5 (3–5 in.) across, with up to 12 on 1.2 m (4 ft) scapes. The leaves are 60 cm (24 in.) long, forming a strong clump of short, spreading rhizomes. This plant and a double-flowered form called *H. fulva* 'Flore Pleno' or *H. kwanso* 'Flore Pleno' have been in cultivation for centuries. Three other well-known species—*H. aurantiaca*, orange-flowered with a purplish flush, *H. citrina*, lemon-yellow, tinged brown on the reverse, and *H. thunbergii*, sulphur-apricot deeper in the throat—have been intercrossed and, with other species, used in the development of the great range of attractive-coloured hybrids now on the market. Colours range from pale yellow through orange, pinks, reds, coppery shades and purple-reds, many showing distinctive darker throat zonings or mid-petal bands.

These modern hybrids have been called lilies without disease. They are certainly the easiest of all plants to grow, resisting alike the driest of conditions and wet feet, blazing sun or semi-shade, and blooming over several months. The plants yield an amazing number of blooms, from 30 to 70 flowers, most scapes developing over a period of several weeks. However, they are not suitable for cutting unless the old flowers are removed each day. These hybrids lend themselves to many forms of garden ornamentation, and are equally at home in the herbaceous border, interspersed among shrubs or

Hemerocallis 'Glitter'

naturalised in grassy woodlands. The blooms are 10–15 cm (4–6 in.) across, carried on branching scapes 0.6–1.5 m (2–5 ft) tall, held well above the luxuriant, light green foliage.

Some cultivars are deciduous but others will retain their foliage through winter; varieties are marked D or E accordingly in the following selection.

Red shades: 'Bright Flame' (E), 'Cherry Festival' (D), 'Seventh Symphony' (D).

Salmon shades: 'Sari' (E), 'Dancing Beauty'.

Apricot shades: 'Aphrodite' (D), 'Soglio', 'Amazing Grace' (E).

Purple shades: 'Chartwell' (E), 'Russian Rhapsody' (E).

Lavender shades: 'Botticelli' (D), 'Buddy' (D).

Lemon or cream: 'Symphony of Spring' (E), 'Bells Appealing' (D).

Golden yellow: 'Aztec Beauty' (E), 'Glitter' (D), 'Gold Standard'.

Orange shades: 'Memories' (E), 'Katrina' (D), 'Polka Dot' (E).

Miniatures: These have smaller but more numerous flowers. 'Azrael', yellow (E); 'Golden Chimes', yellow (D); 'Little Business', raspberry-red (D); 'Baby Darling', purple (D); 'Curls', apricot (D); 'Stella d'Oro', golden yellow, continuously flowering (D).

Hemerocallis 'Cherry Festival'

Plants increase rapidly, soon forming strong clumps, which can be broken up any time during winter. Most of the species and hybrids are sterile to their own pollen, but if different varieties are crossed, seed-pods form readily, ripening in the autumn. The seeds are large and easily raised, the seedlings blooming the second year after sowing. This is a good way to acquire a large stock, possibly some new colours.

HERMODACTYLUS
Iridaceae   Snake's-head iris

This monotypic genus was at one time included amongst the irises. The only species, *H. tuberosus*, is really quite hardy, even in cold climates, and is not particular as to the type of soil, provided it is well drained. Although a native of the Mediterranean region, it has become naturalised in parts of England and Ireland.

Hermodactylus tuberosus

It produces fleshy, pronged roots about 5 cm (2 in.) long and, during late winter or early spring, 30 cm (12 in.) stems of solitary, greenish yellow, iris-like flowers, with contrasting falls of lurid purple. The plant is more interesting than beautiful, but as it blooms when few flowers are about, and also lasts well when cut, it is worthy of more attention. Some people consider the blooms most charming, and certainly they never fail to attract interest, being seen at their best when in bold groups or in a pocket of the rockery.

Roots should be planted 5 cm (2 in.) deep and 10 cm (4 in.) apart in the autumn, so they can become well established before winter. Increase is from seed if available, but more often from the natural division of the clusters of pronged roots.

HESPERANTHA
Iridaceae

Although this genus embraces 30 or more species, only two are commonly known and grown. These most interesting introductions from South Africa are very much like the sparaxias or tritonias in growth and flower, and just as easy to grow in any free, loose soil, with full sun, where frosts do not exceed 12 degrees. Bulbs are naturally small, and while moderate increase can be expected from natural bulb division, larger stocks are produced from autumn-sown

Hesperantha buhrii

seed, which germinates freely and blooms in the second year.

H. buhrii has two 36 cm (15 in.) flower-stems to each bulb, both carrying a number of side shoots, all of which yield numerous blooms. These do not open until the afternoon, but in the bud form are prettily marked with rose on the outside of the petals. Later they open up in glistening, pure white stars of dazzling brilliance. Associated with other bright-coloured spring bulbs, the effect is delightful.

H. inflexa var. *stanfordiae* is similar in habit and growth to *H. buhrii* but has bright butter-yellow blooms unmarked by any other colour, even at the base of the petals. The wide-open, 5 cm (2 in.) blooms displayed on numerous side branches give a rich splash of colour during spring. For startling effect, plant near the brilliant blue geissorhizas, either in the rockery in pockets, or an as edging.

HESPERIS
Brassicaceae

Hesperis is a genus of spring- and summer-flowering annuals and perennials. *H. matronalis*, sometimes called sweet rocket, has smooth, oval leaves and branching flower-heads rising to 60–90 cm (24–36 in.) tall, with white to lilac flowers becoming very fragrant on humid evenings. Plants are usually raised from seed but they can also be propagated by cuttings.

HETEROCENTRON
Melastomataceae

Native to Mexico and Central America, two species are commonly grown.

H. elegans (syn. *Schizocentron elegans*) is delightful when cascading over a wall or bank in a frost-free situation. In summer it is covered with purple flowers.

H. macrostachyum (syn. *Heeria rosea*), is a sub-shrub suitable for warm, frost-free locations. It grows up to 1.5 m (5 ft), with bronzy leaves on square, erect stems. The 2.5 cm (1 in.) flowers are rosy purple and appear in spring. Propagation is from cuttings.

Heterocentron macrostachyum

HEUCHERA
Saxifragaceae   Coral bells

This genus consists of about 70 species of perennial plants, natives of North America.

H. americana grows to 45 cm (18 in.), with bright red flowers in summer.

H. cylindrica is a tufted perennial to 75 cm (30 in.), making a round clump with spikes of greenish yellow to cream flowers in summer. 'Greenfinch' is probably the best cultivar of this species.

H. micrantha grows 60 cm (24 in.), with pale yellow flowers in summer. The best form, 'Palace Purple', has striking, rich purple foliage.

H. pubescens has 30 cm (12 in.), crowded flowers of deep pink variegated with yellow. The foliage is bronzy red in winter.

H. sanguinea, with its many forms and varieties,

seemed until recently to be the only one generally in cultivation. The bright red flowers of the type are small, bell-shaped or cylindrical, and carried loosely on panicles 45 cm (18 in.) tall, produced in abundance from established roots during spring and early summer. The lobed basal leaves are heart-shaped or roundish, while the thin, leafless flower-stems are covered with tiny spreading hairs. Pale and bright pink, white and cream, bright to deep red and intermediate shades occur from seed raised from this most variable species. As a rule, however, seed raised from any particular shade or colour will provide a batch of seedling plants with a heavy percentage of the same or similar colour.

Many of the so-called heuchera hybrids are derived from seeds saved from the different forms of the species *H. sanguinea*, although it is possible that some of the other little-known species may have been used in the raising of some of the better varieties. A number of selected forms or varieties have been named, and these are increased from divisions of the parent plants.

Cultivars available include 'Pink Fairy', which has dainty spikes of soft rosy pink bells in profusion. It has lovely compact, mottled foliage. 'Red Spangles' has crimson-scarlet flowers on stems up to 50 cm (20 in.) and is very free-flowering. The Bressingham hybrids are an English strain grown from seed from a choice range of modern cultivars and

Heuchera micrantha 'Palace Purple'

Heuchera sanguinea

contain many interesting colours.

Heucherella 'Bridget Bloom' is the result of a bigeneric cross between *H. sanguinea* and a closely related species, *Tiarella wherryi*. The result is a 45 cm (18 in.) plant with masses of starry, rose-pink flowers in late spring, with lesser displays during autumn. It is a useful plant and attractive, thriving in full sun or semi-shade.

All forms of heuchera are easily grown in any good, sweet soil not too heavy or liable to dry out in the spring. Plants prefer full sun, but will thrive quite well in the semi-shade, in sandy soil or coastal areas. Seed is easily raised and is the best means of quickly securing enough plants for a large border, but the best named varieties must be increased from division of old plants, preferably during the autumn or spring. It usually requires two or three seasons' growth before a border is sufficiently established to yield the desirable maximum display of bloom—hundreds of spikes all touching each other in a ribbon border 30 cm (12 in.) or so wide.

HIBISCUS
Malvaceae

This genus consists of about 300 species of herbaceous plants, shrubs and trees.

H. moscheutos, one of the few perennials com-monly grown, is a native of North America. The common form produces, between the axils of the leaves and the stem, light rose, single, hollyhock-like flowers, 10–20 cm (4–8 in.) across. The large, ovate, slender-pointed leaves, toothed at the edges and softly hairy beneath, are a light green colour and clothe the robust, unbranched stems, 1–1.5 m (3–5 ft) tall. The flowers are carried near the top of these stems and produced during late summer and autumn. In America, flowers have been produced with wider petals and full-open blooms, some of which measure 20–30 cm (8–12 in.) across. One such strain of *H. moscheutos* is known as 'Southern Belle', of which several named varieties are now offered, as well as the mixed colours. Other firms are offering separate colours, which reproduce reasonably true from seed, while another new dwarf strain called 'Disco Belle', which grows about 50 cm (20 in.) high, is valuable for smaller gardens.

These tall plants are very suitable for the back of the herbaceous border or for growing among ornamental shrubs. They are deep rooting, and when established withstand dry summer and autumn conditions; in fact, a hot summer is more or less essential to produce a good crop of bloom. The hard, woody roots are not easy to break up or divide, so

Hibiscus moscheutos

stocks are best increased from seed, although special colours should be increased either by division or else by the rooting of soft spring cuttings when the new shoots are 7.5 cm (3 in.) long. The range of colours includes white, pink, rose, claret and red, while some carry a deeper throat marking. Transplant when dormant during winter.

HIPPEASTRUM
Amaryllidaceae   Amaryllis

At one time this genus included the belladonnas, brunsvigias, crinums, lycoris, nerines, sprekelias, sternbergia and many others, but these have now been assigned separate genera. This genus, however, still embraces nearly 80 species, mostly very attractive bulbous plants, very few of which are commonly in cultivation. Hailing from tropical South America, most of the species are only half-hardy, requiring glasshouse conditions to be grown successfully.

H. advenum, also previously known as *Habranthus*, is a hardy, free-flowering bulb, easily grown in almost any situation or climate. The whitish bulbs, coated with a black skin, are about 4 cm (1.5 in.) across and 7.5-10 cm (3-4 in.) long, often irregular in shape. The trumpet-shaped flowers, 5 cm (2 in.) across, several on a 30 cm (12 in.) stem, are produced in late summer before any leaves appear. Colours of the forms grown include dull and bright reds and yellow. Set bulbs out 5 cm (2 in.) deep, 10 cm (4 in.) apart, during late spring or early summer when dormant, although they can be planted later in the autumn if they have been lifted before the leaves appear.

H. aulicum is a winter-flowering species from Brazil, easily grown and flowered in a frost-free location. It has rich orange-red flowers 15-20 cm (6-8 in.) in diameter, but the petals tend to be gappy.

What are commonly known as hippeastrums are mostly hybrids of *H. equestre*. In addition to the characteristic red and white striped forms, we have lovely self-colours in pinks, white, orange-red and crimson, and even approaching mauve and purple. The best strains and named varieties produce, on 60 cm (24 in.) stems, two to four wide-open trumpets

Hippeastrum 'Intokasa'

15-20 cm (6-8 in.) across, with large, overlapping petals. Named cultivars include the following:

'Blushing Bride'—rose-pink.
'Bold Leader'—intense crimson-red.
'Cocktail'—bright flame-red.
'Intokasa'—white with green throat.
'Majuba'—deep mahogany-red.
'Springtime'—soft rosy pink.
'Tangerine'—large orange-scarlet.
'Wedding Dance'—ice-white.

These hybrids are gross feeders and delight in a mixture of rich, turfy loam, well-decayed animal manure, leaf mould and coarse sand. In light, free soils, and districts with moderate frosts, bulbs can be easily grown and flowered outside in a sunny border. Mature bulbs, which are usually 7.5-10 cm (3-4 in.) across, should be planted with the neck protruding above the ground, while the fleshy roots should not be allowed to dry out after lifting. In colder districts bulbs are usually grown in pots or small tubs, and should be allowed partly to dry out during the resting period in late autumn. When grown in containers inside, bulbs should be planted like nerines, almost sitting on top of the soil. Flower-buds and stems appear out of the side of the neck of the bulb and usually two or more crops of bloom can be expected, beginning in early spring under glass with occasional flowers as late as mid-summer.

H. pratense (syn. *Habranthus pratensis*) is a native of Chile. Although a hardy bulb, it does not seem to be the easiest subject to establish, and many gardeners report failure or tardiness to bloom. Provided drain-age is good and the soil does not become hard through lack of humus, it seems to be a matter of patiently waiting until the bulbs become established before they will bloom. They resent being shifted as a completely new set of fleshy roots has to be formed. Bulbs bloom in the late spring with two to four trumpets on 30 cm (12 in.) stems, and are best trans-planted in autumn when dormant, set 5 cm (2 in.) deep. Two to four brilliant tangerine-red, lily-like trumpets are produced on 22.5–30 cm (9–12 in.) stems.

Increase is usually from the offsets removed from the sides of well-established bulbs, but the quickest way to obtain stock is from seed, which germinates freely in sandy loamy soil, reaching flowering size in three years' time. Young seedlings should be kept growing strongly, giving them more room as they develop, and potted up or planted in specially pre-pared beds as soon as bulbs are 2.5 cm (1 in.) or more across. As the first scape of bloom is formed in the bulb the previous growing season, mature bulbs are often sold when in flower.

HOSTA
Liliaceae   Plantain lily

These easily grown, hardy perennials prefer a moist, damp spot and are therefore eminently suitable for growing near water, on the margins of lily ponds, or in bog gardens. All produce, wide, decorative leaves from the fleshy, tuberous roots, some being hand-somely marbled or marked with white, while others are a bluish green. Forms with all-yellow foliage are also now available.

Hosta fortunei 'Aurea' (left) and 'Albo-picta' (right)

Hostas are good patio plants, doing well in large pots or planters. The range includes quite small forms as well as others with foliage up to 1 m (3 ft) high. The leaves and flowers last well in water and are popular in floral arrangements.

Interest in this genus is strong, and many new forms have originated. The following species and varieties are currently available.

H. crispula has leaves 20 cm (8 in.) long with white, irregular margins and tapering tips. It grows in a mound to 70 cm wide x 40 cm high (28 x 16 in.).

H. decorata has small, pointed, green leaves and narrow, cream margins. It forms a mound to 45 cm (18 in.). This species is stoloniferous and makes good ground cover.

H. elata has tall, wavy, dark green leaves to 20 cm (8 in.) wide, forming a mound to 75 cm (30 in.) wide. It produces a scape to 1.5 m (5 ft), and the flowers are pale purple with yellow anthers.

H. fluctuans 'Variegata' is a large specimen of upright growth to 60 cm (24 in.). It has wavy, oval leaves, pointed and margined bright yellow. The flower-scape is white tinted purple to 1.2 m (4 ft).

H. fortunei has leaves 15 cm (6 in.) wide and 30 cm (12 in.) long, and forms a mound to 35 cm (14 in.). It produces scapes of lavender flowers to 1 m (3 ft). 'Albo-marginata' has a golden margin on a dark green leaf. 'Albo-picta' has a bright yellow leaf with a dark green margin, slowly changing to all green by mid-summer. 'Aurea' has all-yellow leaves slowly changing to all green by mid-summer. 'Treasure Trove' has pale green leaves with irregular, creamy white variegation and is very showy. It was raised by the author.

H. montana 'Aureo-marginata' has huge leaves, 25 cm (10 in.) wide and 35 cm (14 in.) long, with wide, creamy white margins. In early summer it produces dense spikes of pale lavender flowers.

H. plantaginea has large, waxy, fragrant white flowers in late summer. The leaves are glossy and pale green with nine pairs of deep veins. Plants form a mound to 60 cm high x 90 cm wide (24 x 30 in.).

H. sieboldiana has large, round leaves, blue-green with a bloom that fades. It forms a mound to 75 cm high x 1.3 m wide (30 in. x 4.5 ft), and produces a short scape with white flowers in early summer. 'Elegans' is a recommended selected form grown from divisions. 'Frances Williams' has leaves 20 cm (8 in.) wide, 25 cm (10 in.) long, blue-green with irregular, wide, yellow margin. The flowers are pale lavender, 80 cm (32 in.) high.

H. sieboldii 'Kabitan' has narrow, yellow leaves edged with green. It is a small grower requiring good, fertile soil. 'Goldmine' is a seedling of 'Kabitan', with similar foliage but no green edge. It

is rather more vigorous than its parent and holds its colour well in the shade.

H. tokudama has excellent blue foliage. It is slightly smaller than *sieboldiana* 'Elegans', with very puckered, cup-shaped leaves, 22 x 20 cm (9 x 8 in.), and milky white flowers in early summer. *H. t. flavo-circinalis* has blue leaves irregularly margined with greenish yellow and deeply corrugated. 'Variegata' has blue leaves with the centres mottled with greenish yellow. It produces large spikes of white flowers in early summer.

H. undulata 'Albo-marginata' (syn. 'Thomas Hogg') has green leaves with creamy white margins, 15–20 cm (6–8 in.) long, mounding to 30 cm (12 in.). It produces a one-sided scape of mauve flowers. Var. *erromena* has leaves of medium green, about 20 cm (8 in.) long. It forms a mound to 50 cm high x 65 cm wide (20 x 27 in.), and has mauve flowers to 80 cm (32 in.). 'Univittata' has twisted leaves with a variable white centre stripe. It forms a mound to 45 cm (18 in.) high. Some leaves fade to all green in autumn. 'Variegata' is less vigorous, with twisted white leaves edged with green. It forms a mound to

Hosta ventricosa 'Aureo-maculata'

Hosta sieboldiana

25 cm (10 in.) high, and produces a scape of mauve flowers.

H. ventricosa has dark green, pointed leaves, and forms a mound to 60 cm high x 90 cm wide (24 x 36 in.). It is free-flowering, with stems to 1.2 m (4 ft) and 20–30 bell-shaped, violet flowers. The leaves of 'Aureo-maculata' have central variegations in spring then turn uniform dark green. The flowers are the same as the species. 'Aureo-marginata' has heart-shaped leaves with a unique twist and broad, irregular, yellow margins turning white. It forms a mound 45 cm (18 in.) high and 60 cm (24 in.) wide. Violet flowers to 80 cm (32 in.) appear in mid-summer. 'Variegata' has irregular cream margins on the leaves.

'August Moon'—large golden leaves and mauve flowers; needs some sun.

'Antioch'—pointed, green leaves margined with soft yellow; vigorous mounding habit, forms mound 25 x 15 cm (10 x 6 in.).

'Blue Cadet'—small, grey-green leaves to 11 cm (4.5 in.) long, gently undulating; scape 30 cm (12 in.) tall with mauve flowers.

'Francee'—leaves forest green with white margins, 15 cm (6 in.) long; forms mound to 60 cm high x 75 cm wide (24 x 30 in.); lavender flowers in late summer.

'Ginko Craig'—leaves long and narrow, thinly edged with white; wide, spreading, low growth.

'Gold Edger'—pale green leaves, 10 cm (4 in.) long, shading to a yellow edge; mounding to 25 x 30 cm (10 x 12 in.) wide; prolific lavender flowers.

'Golden Sceptre'—all yellow sport of 'Golden

Tiara'; a very striking plant of medium size.

'Gold Standard'—yellow leaves with green edges, the colour intensifying later; mounding to 60 cm high x 75 cm wide (24 x 30 in.).

'Golden Sunburst'—all yellow, a sport of *H. sieboldiana* 'Frances Williams'; the large leaves require some shade.

'Golden Tiara'—leaves light green with yellow margins, 10 cm (4 in.) long; mounding to 30 cm high x 40 cm wide (12 x 16 in.); purple flowers in mid-summer.

'Grey Piecrust'—leaves grey-green, margins deeply crinkled, 25 x 15 cm (10 x 6 in.); a very handsome plant with 60 cm (24 in.) scape of pale mauve flowers.

'Halcyon'—intensely blue-grey leaves; mauve flowers on 30 cm (12 in.) scape; one of the best small hostas.

'Honeybells'—a green-leaved hybrid with a good show of scented, mauve flowers in late summer, to 90 cm (36 in.).

Hosta ventricosa 'Variegata'

'Krossa Regal'—a large, handsome, grey-leaved plant, vase-shaped with lilac flowers; very vigorous, up to 1 m (3 ft) tall.

'Lemon Lime'—very small, yellow leaves, 8 x 4 cm (1.5 x 3.5 in.), with mauve flower-scape to 30 cm (12 in.); excellent small plant for the front of the border.

Propagation of hostas is generally by division. The species with green leaves may be grown from seed, but as they hybridise freely, it is not unusual for variations to occur. All special selections and variegated forms must be grown from divisions, taken while the plant is dormant in winter. Plants will not reach their full potential until the third season. Slugs and snails often damage the foliage, so it is wise to put down bait at the first sign of trouble.

HYACINTHUS
Liliaceae   Hyacinth

H. orientalis, the common wild hyacinth, a native of Syria, Greece and Turkey, is the only true species. The coloured forms often referred to as Roman hyacinths come from a group represented by *H. orientalis* var. *albulus* and var. *praecox*. These differ from the Dutch hyacinths in that instead of one or two large trusses, several loosely arranged flower-spikes are produced from each bulb. The common form is a deep blue, but pink and white-flowered forms are also available. Bulbs increase freely from natural division, a mature bulb being about 4 cm (1.5 in.) across.

Although hundreds of varieties have been grown in Holland over the years, today the list is narrowed down to a few dozen popular varieties. Unlike plants such as gladiolus or dahlias, in which form and shape of bloom play a large part, hyacinth flowers are all much alike in form and appearance, and colour is the most important factor. The double-flowered varieties were popular at one time, but because the heavy spikes are inclined to flop badly, they are fast disappearing. Varieties available include:

White: 'Carnegie', 'L'Innocence', both purest white.

Light blue shades: 'Blue Giant', 'Delfts Blue'.

Hyacinthus 'Jan Bos'

Dark blue: 'Blue Magic', 'Ostara'.

Pink shades: 'Lady Derby', 'Princess Margaret'; 'Orange Boven', rosy orange.

Red: 'Jan Bos', deep scarlet, medium spikes; 'Eros'.

Dark red: 'King of Night', deep maroon-red.

Violet: 'Amethyst', rich lilac.

Yellow: 'City of Haarlem', butter-yellow.

While clean, healthy stocks are absolutely essential, the perfection of the hyacinth flower depends largely on the strength of the root system. In Holland, hyacinths are grown in almost pure sand, indicating that perfect drainage and a free root-run are essential. This medium is then built up with well-decayed animal manure mixed with straw.

In beds, bulbs should be planted 15 cm (6 in.) apart and 5–10 cm (2–4 in.) deep, according to their size. The best plan is to remove 10 cm (4 in.) of top-soil, work up the under soil thoroughly and then press the bulbs into position, covering over again

with the topsoil. An even depth in planting and a uniform grade of bulbs will ensure simultaneous flowering.

Hyacinths can also be grown in pots or bowls. A mixture of loam and leaf mould combined with coarse sand suits best; broken crockery at the bottom of the pot will provide drainage. Bulbs that are firm but not too large should be planted in early autumn, 2.5 cm (1 in.) apart, with the tops of the bulbs covered by the soil, or just the apex appearing. Containers with bulbs and soil should be plunged under the ground in a cool, shady spot, or covered with 10 cm (4 in.) of soil for three months or more, until the roots have filled the container. This it to promote good root growth before the plants are forced into bloom. If brought inside or given warmth before the roots are firmly established, the flower-spikes will either fail or collapse, just when they should be at their best. Another method is to use an upturned flower-pot of the same size to help to keep bulbs dark and cool and from becoming too wet. Leave the pots in a cool spot, removing the inverted pot to allow more light as the spikes appear. This will slow the appearance of the flower-spikes but discourage undue leaf growth. When the spikes are about 7.5 cm (3 in.) above the ground and side leaves only a few centimetres, the pots or bowls can be brought inside the house and gradually into full light. The flower-spikes will then rapidly develop, opening up into full bloom, and lasting in good condition for several weeks. It is important to guard against slugs and snails or other insects when the plant is in bud.

Hyacinths can also be successfully grown indoors in glasses that are narrowed near the top so that the bulb rests on the rim. Large, plump bulbs should be chosen, and the glass filled up to the shoulder so the base of the bulb is in the water. The container should be kept in a cupboard or a reasonably dark, cool place until it is well filled with roots and the flower-spike is appearing from the neck of the bulb. When it is brought into the light the flower-spike will develop quickly and open up into full bloom. Bulbs cannot be treated in the same way the next season;

Opposite: This continuous border of variegated hostas is a most effective use of a versatile plant. The low-key colours of the flowers complement the restful shades of green in this secluded corner.

as soon as the flower-spikes have faded, cut them off, remove the bulbs from the container and allow them to finish their growth and ripen off in the ground.

The life cycle of a hyacinth is usually four years—it takes three years from a small 'pip' to full size, and in the fourth year the parent bulbs usually breaks up into several medium-sized or smaller bulbs. However, some varieties show natural increase each year. If flower-spikes of the single-flowered varieties are not removed when spent, they will usually ripen quite a good crop of seed. Hyacinths have been improved over a period of 200 years, almost to the point of perfection, which means that seedlings will give results as good or almost as good as named varieties. Although fairly large and easily raised, the seed does not produce a mature bulb in under five or six years, but small flower-spikes can be expected at the end of the third year. A fine range of colours and absolutely healthy disease-free stock can be obtained with seed.

Hyacinths are attacked by the larger narcissus fly, which lays its eggs in the foliage or neck of the bulb. Any softness, particularly at the neck of the bulb, should be suspected as caused by narcissus fly grub. The only satisfactory control is to immerse bulbs in hot water, approximately 110 degrees, for one hour. Most fungoid diseases in hyacinths develop about the time bulbs are ready for lifting. Stocks should be lifted when the foliage is turning yellow, the leaves should be broken off and the bulbs stored in open, airy trays, preferably with wire bottoms. Bulbs that have been recently lifted should not be subjected to direct sunlight for more than half an hour. When dried properly and matured, then a good sun-baking or direct sunlight seems to be quite beneficial, hardening up the skins and firming the bulbs.

HYMENOCALLIS
Amaryllidaceae   Spider lily

These bulbous plants, mostly from South America, Mexico and some from Africa, are quite hardy in the open in most parts of the Southern Hemisphere, although in Europe they are grown in pots like hippeastrums, nerines and other half-hardy bulbs. The curious lily-like flowers look as if some ambitious plant-lover had snipped the edges of the petals with

Hymenocallis macrostephana

scissors in an endeavour to improve on nature. All are delightfully scented and valuable for bouquets.

The bulbs are like narcissus but long-necked, although some are rounded. All produce heavy, fleshy roots, which suggests that in their native countries dry autumn conditions prevail. Indeed, this is borne out by the fact that unless they experience a decided rest in the autumn, plants often fail to bloom the following summer. In Holland, bulbs are lifted in the autumn and stored in warm conditions to encourage the flower-spikes to form in the bulb. As with most bulbs, the next year's flower-spikes are formed when the bulb is dormant, very soon after the foliage has died down, so that care in handling after lifting is important.

H. harrisiana is a very dainty, spidery lily, with four slender tubes on 30 cm (12 in.) stems carrying fringed, funnel-shaped cups and protruding filaments, earning the common name of fairy lily. It has a small, roundish bulb with glaucous green foliage.

H. narcissiflora (syn. *H. calathina*) is the best-known species, commonly called the sacred lily of the Incas. The large, long-necked bulbs, 5 cm (2 in.) across, produce six to eight strap-like leaves and central, two-edged scapes 45 cm (18 in.) tall, with two to five pure white trumpet flowers on an umbel. The tube is green, and the corolla, which is 10 cm (4 in.) long and across, is green striped. This attractive plant will grow in semi-shade but it needs a hot, dry autumn.

Hymenocallis narcissiflora 'Advance'

H. narcissiflora 'Sulphur Queen' has large, primrose-yellow trumpets with green stripes. 'Advance' is another cultivar with pure white flowers with white filaments. *H. festalis* is another hybrid with pure white, elegantly curled filaments. *H. macrostephana* is probably the most handsome, having white flowers with extra long filaments, 7.5–10 cm (3–4 in.) long, and leaves to 90 cm (36 in.) long and 7.5 cm (3 in.) wide.

Bulbs of all these species and hybrids increase quite freely when established. Transplant when dormant in the winter, setting the bulbs with the neck below the surface of the soil.

I

IBERIS
Brassicaceae   Candytuft

The genus *Iberis* includes annuals and perennials. All prefer a sunny position and well-drained soil, and many are excellent for the rock garden.

I. gibraltarica, Gibraltar candytuft, has pink flower-heads.

I. pruitii is an easier species to grow and maintain. It has masses of pink flower-heads, which turn white during spring.

I. sempervirens is an evergreen with prostrate habit to 25 cm (10 in.). 'Snowflake' is a fine cultivar, which covers itself in very early spring with heads of pure white flowers.

Plants can be increased by seed sown in spring.

Iberis gibraltarica

IMPATIENS
Balsaminaceae

Impatiens are succulent, perennial plants from the sub-tropics and tropics of Asia and Africa. They are extensively used for summer display and are often treated as annuals as they are frost tender. In frost-free gardens, many strains will survive the winter, and as they prefer shady areas, overhanging trees will often provide shelter.

Many strains have been developed, some growing only 15–20 cm (6–8 in.), others to 60–90 cm (24–36 in.), in a very wide range of colours, which breed true to colour, although mixtures are usually offered. Double impatiens in several attractive shades are available.

Seed must be raised under glass, and cuttings for propagation require similar protection. Plant after the danger of frost is over, in part sun or shade. Impatiens are excellent as house plants or as container and patio plants. New varieties are becoming available in an ever-increasing range of colours.

I. oliveri grows very bushy, to 2 m (6 ft), and is grown as a shrub in warmer climates. It has pale blue or pale pink, 6 cm (2.5 in.) flowers for most of the summer.

Impatiens oliveri

INCARVILLEA
Bignoniaceae   Pride of China

This genus consists of about a dozen species from Turkestan, Tibet and China.

I. delavayi is the best-known species, with handsome pinnate foliage, most attractive and somewhat fern-like, each leaf 30 cm (12 in.) or more long, divided into 15–20 dentate segments. From the semi-drooping rosette of leaves arise attractive scapes 30–60 cm (12–24 in.) tall, carrying two to 10 large, trumpet-shaped, rosy purple flowers, each 7.5 cm (3 in.) long and as wide at the mouth. They somewhat resemble the blooms of the hardy, deciduous climbing bignonias. A selected form of *I. delavayi*, called 'Bees Pink', is more of a rosy pink shade and not such a hard colour as the type. It comes true to type from seed.

I. mairei var. *grandiflora* is another desirable species, which differs from *I. delavayi* with its shorter, more rounded leaves and flower-scapes, carrying usually not more than two rosy red flowers. The blooms are larger, sometimes 12.5 cm (5 in.) across, yellow in the tube, and blotched white in the throat. Another variety of this species, *I. mairei* var. *mairei*, is often offered under the name of *I. brevipes*. The short-stemmed flowers are rich rosy red.

Although quite hardy, withstanding cold winter conditions, this is a family of fleshy-rooted plants that cannot tolerate wet feet when dormant, so a sandy or well-drained soil suits best. Provided conditions are not too wet, no great difficulty should be experienced in growing these really lovely plants. The heavy, deeply pronged, fleshy roots, often 5 cm (2 in.) thick, are very easily damaged or broken when being lifted and should be handled with care. These roots are really next season's stored energy, just like a bulb, and plants will flower freely the following spring if held in deep boxes of moist sawdust or moss. The roots will transplant quite readily without any loss or wilt, even when in bloom.

Incarvilleas die down very early in the autumn, and unless well marked they may have the tops of the roots and the growth buds cut off by the garden hoe. Increase is from seeds, which germinate quite readily in loose, free, sandy soil, the plants blooming the third season. It is very difficult to divide old clumps, but as old-established roots often collapse

Incarvillea mairei var. *grandiflora*

when they become too crowded, a fresh stock of seedlings should be raised every two or three years. Transplant from early autumn until early spring.

INULA
Asteraceae

This is a genus of hardy plants of the daisy family, mostly with glandular, hairy leaves and rather coarse growth. There are nearly 200 species found in Southern Europe, Asia and Africa, delighting in hot, sunny positions and blooming freely in the autumn. The flower bracts of most species are composed of many finely rayed petals, resembling those of the doronicums.

I. afghanica is quite the giant of the race, with heavy foliage and massive, branching stems, often reaching 1.8–2.4 m (6–8 ft) when well established, younger plants usually attaining only half this height. The brilliant orange-yellow flowers, over 10 cm (4 in.) across, are produced during summer and autumn, and are quite impressive. A selected form

Inula racemosa

called 'Magnifica' is the one usually grown.

I. ensifolia grows 30–60 cm (12–24 in.) tall, with a mass of yellow daisies on a bushy plant. It is a good front-row plant for the cottage border.

I. helenium grows about 2 m (6.5 ft) in good, moist soil, with leaves 40 cm (16 in.) long and stout, erect stems with large, yellow daisies, solitary or in clusters of three, in summer.

I. hookeri is a shaggy-growing species with downy leaves and finely rayed, lemon-yellow, slightly scented flowers, covering the 60 cm (24 in.) high bush. It is a desirable perennial, easily managed in any type of soil.

I. orientalis (syn. *I. glandulosa*) has finely rayed, shaggy blooms, wavy at the edges, 7.5 cm (3 in.) or more across, and a rich orange-yellow colour. It is a useful cut flower and a fine, hardy perennial.

I. racemosa may grow to 3 m (10 ft), with huge, ovate leaves up to 75 cm (30 in.), downy and arching. The flowers are 8 cm (3.5 in.), yellow daisies, opening in late summer towards the top of the stout stems, of which there will be several on older plants. Any good, moist soil is suitable, and propagation is usually from seed.

I. royleana is a lovely, silky-leafed species, unfortunately seldom seen in gardens. It carries, erectly on unbranched, 45 cm (18 in.) stems, huge, deep orange blooms, with rays so long that they droop at the edges. The large, tight buds are jet black and most impressive. This lovely species resents root disturbance and is not easy to divide; it is usually increased by seed, although good, fertile seed is seldom available, which no doubt accounts for its scarcity.

Increase of all species is from seed or divisions of old plants.

IPHEION
Liliaceae

Once included under *Brodiaea*, this is a genus native to South America. *I. uniflora* flowers early in spring, with pale blue, starry flowers on 15 cm (6 in.) stems and crocus-like foliage. It is fully hardy, succeeding well in light soil in a pocket of the rock garden, and may be left undisturbed for many years. Stock can be increased by offsets. Plant these or mature bulbs early in autumn, about 10 cm (4 in.) deep. A good white form is also available.

Ipheion uniflora 'Wisley Blue'

IRESINE
Amaranthaceae   Bloodleaf

This is a genus of sub-tropical plants, a few of which are grown for their foliage effect in summer bedding schemes. Only hardy in frost-free gardens, they are often over-wintered under glass.

I. herbstii has deep maroon foliage, and *I. herbstii* 'Aureo-reticulata' has green leaves heavily veined with yellow. Plants are easily increased from cuttings.

Iresine used in a bedding scheme

IRIS
Iridaceae

The genus *Iris* embraces about 200 species, nearly all from the northern temperate regions. Only the most commonly grown species and varieties are covered in this book. Irises are divided into two groups: bulbous and herbaceous.

Bulbous irises

Bulbous irises have hard, bulbous roots, which become dormant during the summer months, and mature bulbs or offsets are planted out or transplanted in the autumn. The Xiphium group, the Juno group and the reticulatas are all bulbous irises.

Xiphium group
This group includes the Dutch, Spanish and English irises, as well as early-blooming tingitanas.

Dutch irises are hybrids of *I. xiphium* from Spain, and are also derived from *I. tingitana*, resulting in a strain with larger blooms but without the temperamental shy-blooming characteristics of *I. tingitana*. A typical example of the influence of *I. tingitana* is that lovely, early-blooming variety 'Wedgwood', which has the same broad, glaucous green foliage and which flowers midway between *I. tingitana* and the Spanish varieties.

Dutch irises are the earliest of the three groups to flower. The following is a selection of varieties available:

'Belle Jaune'—large, clear yellow with orange-yellow falls.
'Blue Champion'—the largest bright, clear blue yet offered.
'Golden Harvest'—the most prolific and easiest deep yellow.
'Hildegarde'—very large, rich mauve flowers.
'Imperator'—tall, deep blue, blooming later.
'Joan of Arc'—large, creamy white, fine blooms.
'Le Mogol'—deep mahogany-bronze with yellow blotch.
'Lemon Queen'—citron-yellow, sulphur-yellow falls.
'Marquette'—icy-white with golden yellow falls.
'Princess Beatrix'—rich yellow with deep orange falls.
'Princess Irene'—pure white with deep orange, large.
'Professor Blaauw'—ultramarine violet-blue flowers, immense bulbs.
'Saxe Blue'—clear bright blue, yellow blotch.
'Wedgwood'—early soft blue, not as tall.
'White Superior'—snow-white, small yellow blotch.
'White Wedgwood'—equally early white, sometimes tinged with blue.

Spanish irises are also hybrids of *I. xiphium*. They range in colour from white through blue to deep violet, and include yellow and even bronze shades. They are very similar to Dutch irises but are more slender and flower slightly later. Varieties available include:

'Canary Bird'—bright creamy yellow.
'Delfts Blue'—lovely deep blue, yellow blotch.

Iris 'White Wedgwood'

'Enchantress'—lavender-blue with white falls and yellow blotch.
'Thunderbolt'—coppery orange flowers on tall spikes.

English irises, *I. xiphioides* (syn. *I. latifolia*), are not, in fact, from England but are native to the alpine meadows of the Pyrenees. The name English irises came about because the Dutch nurserymen who obtained their original supplies from England assumed they were an English species. They are the last of all the bulbous irises to flower, blooming in early to mid-summer. In their native habitat, the meadows are frozen during winter, and in the growing season the roots are kept moist from the melting snows. Root growth continues from autumn right through the winter, so bulbs should be planted out in late summer to early autumn, the earlier the better. The thick, fleshy shoots do not appear until the early spring, the foliage developing quickly into rigid, deeply channelled leaves, curving outward and

somewhat resembling leek plants in growth. The robust flower-stems, each developing two flowers, grow to a height of 75 cm (30 in.), but often only 45 cm (18 in.) tall in warm districts, or where lack of late spring moisture results in shorter growth. The wild type is a rich purple with thin, central, yellow lines on the blade of the falls. The most common form is a dark purple-blue called 'King of the Blues', but a good range of shades can be secured from seed, which takes about five years to bloom.

Cultivars include:

'Mont Blanc'—pure white.
'Prince Albert'—silver-blue.
'Prince of Wales'—marine-blue.
'Tricolour'—mottled orchid.

Dutch, Spanish and English irises are quite hardy and easily grown in almost any type of soil not entirely lacking in humus and with reasonably good drainage. Bulbs need not be lifted each season, but when lifted, it is advisable to dip them in a fungicide before replanting, as a safeguard against fungoid foliage troubles, which sometimes develop later. Stimulating manures should be avoided as they encourage foliage diseases, but a complete fertiliser low in nitrogen should be applied.

The bulbs of English irises are larger than most of the Dutch or Spanish varieties, and they are rather soft and easily damaged, particularly if the loose, outer husks are removed. Bruised or otherwise damaged bulbs often quickly develop disease, deteriorate or collapse, and stocks affected in this way should be dipped in a suitable fungicide before planting to prevent soft rot.

A fungoid foliage disease sometimes causes premature ripening off of the leaves, and an eventual dying off of all green foliage and stems. The resultant bulbs are small and underdeveloped, the flower-spikes poor and the general appearance unsightly. Some varieties, particularly those derived from *I. tingitana*, are subject to virus infections, which cause the foliage to show yellowish streaks, the blooms to have darker patches, and the whole plant to be dwarfed. The infections are spread by aphids or, more commonly, by cutting clean stock with the same knife or secateurs that was used for infected plants. There is no cure, and all infected stock should be removed and burnt as it becomes evident.

I. juncea is a brilliant yellow-flowered iris from

North Africa and Sicily, somewhat resembling the Spanish or Dutch varieties in bloom, although seldom exceeding 60 cm (24 in.) in height. The flowers, two on a stem, are a most vivid yellow without any touch of gold or light shades to dull their brightness. The round and rush-like foliage is a dull, glaucous green. The bulbs are distinct from all other irises in that the peculiar hard, dark brown skin splits into long fibres at the neck. This lovely iris must have good drainage and thrives particularly well in silty or gravelly soils. It is fatal to attempt to grow it in heavy or clay soils with poor drainage, and it will not stand very heavy late-spring frosts. Bulbs should be lifted and replanted in the autumn every second year.

I. tingitana, from North Africa, grows and increases prolifically, but is the joy and despair alike of many gardeners. Even the plumpest of bulbs sometimes fail to yield a single bloom. In nature, where this iris blooms freely, the bulbs grow in a reddish clay soil and are subject to a severe summer baking during the dormant season. It seems necessary, therefore, that during the summer or the early stages of growth the bulbs experience severe conditions or some sort of check in order to induce the internal embryo flower to fully develop. Lifting and baking the bulbs for some weeks in the sun, and planting them shallow like shallots, are measures that have proved successful. In any case, a wet climate or a district subject to heavy winter frosts is not recommended, this iris preferring a hot, dry situation. While the foliage is fairly winter-hardy, the flower-spikes are usually spoilt by severe frosts. Virus can also be a problem. The 10 cm (4 in.) wide, soft lilac-blue flowers, held on 50–60 cm (20–24 in.) stems, resemble the Dutch irises, but they are even larger and bloom during late winter or early spring.

I. tingitana var. *fontanesii* is similar to the species but more slender and blooms later in the season.

Juno irises

This is a group of species from the Mediterranean and Middle East, including Iran, Iraq and Afghanistan. Fleshy roots maintain the bulbs during the long, dry summer in their native countries. The bulbs resent disturbance, and must be handled carefully if it is necessary to move them. They require a fertile, well-drained soil in a position that is in full sun and gets a good baking in summer. Seedlings

Iris juncea

take four years to reach flowering stage.

I. bucharica is a hardy iris and the easiest to grow of the Juno group. The characteristic, large, thick-necked bulbs are coated with a brown tunic, and the much-branched flower-stem resembles in growth dwarf maize, usually 45 cm (18 in.) high. The foliage is bright, shiny green, strong and vigorous. The topmost spathe of the stem opens first, followed by buds produced between the axil of the stem and the leaves, continuing in succession until eight to 10 have bloomed. The standards, crest and style arms are white, and the rounded falls bright yellow. This valuable and attractive garden plant blooms during spring. Good drainage or deep, free soil and a dry autumn are essential to secure good blooms. In autumn the bulbs put out thick, white, fleshy roots, sometimes as thick as, and resembling, white radishes. Much care is needed in lifting the bulbs, as these roots are easily broken off. While new roots appear each growing season, those produced the previous year are important in quickly establishing

Iris bucharica

the bulb again in its new position. Without some of these roots attached, bulbs sometimes 'sulk', coming into growth late in the season, and do not become established until the following season. Bulbs should be planted out during the early autumn.

I. orchioides has shining, golden-yellow flowers up to 70 cm (28 in.) high. The standards are small and drooping, and the strap-shaped falls are deep yellow touched with green.

I. persica is a low-growing iris, 5 cm (2 in.) tall. It comes in various colours but is usually greenish blue with a dark patch on the fall and a yellow crest.

I. sindjarensis (syn. *I. aucheri*) is charmingly perfumed, with bright green leaves and lovely, pale blue flowers. It is about 30 cm (12 in.) tall, and flowers in early spring, with up to six flowers appearing from the leaf axils. The plant re-roots quite early in the autumn.

I. x 'Sindpers' is a fairly dwarf hybrid between *I. sindjarensis* and *I. persica*. It is free-flowering, with porcelain-blue flowers tinted with sea-green and yellow.

Reticulata irises

These are early-flowering irises, which grow well in an open, sunny situation with good drainage. The round bulbs are covered with a net-like tunic.

I. histrio, a native of Syria and Asia Minor, is somewhat similar to but smaller flowered than *I. reticulata*. It is the earliest to bloom, opening its slender, lilac-blue flowers in mid-winter. It is not as robust a grower as *I. reticulata* but it is very hardy and quite easy to grow, provided winter drainage is good. Plant bulbs 5 cm (2 in.) deep early in the autumn.

I. histrioides is a little-known but lovely winter-flowering iris. The rounded blooms, 7.5 cm (3 in.) across, are carried on a 10 cm (4 in.) tube and are a rich shade of ultramarine-blue. The buds appear above the ground in mid-winter, each bulb producing several blooms. No leaves are apparent until the flowering season is almost finished. These leaves, when developed, grow to a length of 60 cm (24 in.) and, like all bulbs of this group, need to be carefully protected from damage or weed competition, as the next year's crop of bloom depends on the health of the foliage. Bulbs are best lifted and replanted each season, not later than mid-summer.

I. reticulata is a native of the Caucasus, where the predominant shade is a reddish purple. The form generally offered world-wide is a violet-blue shade, a colour seldom met with in its natural habitat. *I. reticulata* and its various forms are lovely subjects for planting in bold groups, or for filling pockets in the rockery. The bulbs bloom in winter when few flowers are out. The stems are only 15–30 cm (6–12 in.) high, and the blooms are very dainty, faintly scented, and last in fresh condition for several days

Iris x 'Sindpers'

Iris reticulata

in water. Bulbs can also be grown in a container indoors. Set close together, the effect of the crowded heads of blue among the glaucous foliage is very pleasing. Bulbs should be replanted soon after lifting, as they deteriorate quickly.

The following forms are worth obtaining:

'Cantab'—a lovely pale blue.

'Clairette'—striking, with erect petals in sky-blue contrasting with deep blue falls.

'Harmony'—a lovely uniform sky-blue with a yellow ridge; a good variety for growing in pots.

'Hercules'—a reddish purple-flowered form, but the flowers are rather spoilt by the strong-growing foliage, which tends to hide the blooms.

'Jeannine'—clear violet-purple with a prominent orange ridge, and sweetly scented.

'Pauline'—violet-purple flowers with a white blotch.

'Springtime'—blue standards and violet falls tipped with white and a yellow rib.

It is generally believed that *I. reticulata* prefers a climate with a cold winter, a decided spring, and a hot, dry summer, but it has been grown successfully under a variety of conditions, including a frost-free climate and in heavy ground. It appears that a healthy stock of bulbs is the most important consideration. Its success in colder climates may be due to the fact that colder winters retard or eliminate cer-

tain diseases, the worst of which is one commonly called ink disease. Once infection sets in, the whole stock will eventually be destroyed if the trouble is not arrested. Its presence will be noted by a premature dying of the foliage, and when lifted the bulbs will have black sooty patches, while with some, probably affected the previous season, only the husks will be left remaining. To treat affected bulbs, lift and dry them and then dip in a strong fungicide solution. Store in a dry, open shed, and dip in the solution again before replanting in late summer.

Herbaceous irises

This section includes bearded and beardless irises with rhizomes or fibrous roots. Beardless irises covered here include members of the evansia, Japanese, Pacific Coast, sibirica and spuria groups as well as other species. Propagation of herbaceous irises is by division.

Bearded irises

Bearded irises are the most widely known and most popular group of irises. They are rhizomatous, and are so-named because they have a 'beard' along each fall. Three main types are recognised: tall, medium and dwarf. Modern hybrids are derived from various species of mainly Euro-Asian origin and have arisen from a multitude of crosses. The same cultivation notes apply to all three types.

Good sharp drainage, an open, sunny spot and an alkaline soil are essential for the successful growing and flowering of bearded irises. Rhizomes should be planted out as soon as possible after blooming, preferably in mid-summer, but they can be planted as late as autumn. Although very hardy and easily transplanted, the earlier planting ensures good heads of bloom the following spring, while very late plantings may cause flowering to fail until the next season. Plant the rhizomes firmly but with the top portion just above the surface of the soil. It is advisable to keep the top soil stirred and never allowed to become hard, sodden or rain-settled. A light dressing of dolomite lime in the winter will be beneficial; feeding with complete but low-nitrogen fertiliser should be carried out in both autumn and spring. Fresh animal manures should be avoided as they are likely to cause rot and foliage diseases.

When the foliage has faded in the autumn and partly died down, remove all these old leaves to

Iris pumila 'Meadow Court'

allow the sun to keep the rhizomes dry and healthy. A good autumn sun-baking helps to promote a better crop of blooms in spring.

Rhizome rot is a serious disease that affects bearded irises. It can be recognised by the evil-smelling, white pulp in the rhizome, and earlier by the yellowing of the leaves on the affected root. It is present where there is a lack of good drainage, where the soil is over-rich in nitrogenous manures, or where the position is too shady. In light, well-drained soils, poor ground and sunny, dry positions, it never occurs. Affected portions should be cut away and nearby leaves removed; a dusting of lime is also helpful.

A huge range of new and beautiful varieties are appearing each year in almost every country where these irises are grown, and it is not practical to make recommendations.

I. pallida grows to 90 cm (36 in.), with light green, pointed leaves and pale lavender, fragrant flowers. *I. pallida dalmatica* is a free-flowering cultivar with lovely light silvery blue flowers. It is easily recognised by the white, papery covering on the buds. Two variegated cultivars are grown, although they are quite uncommon. *I. pallida* 'Variegata' has green and white leaves, and *I. pallida* 'Aureo-variegata' has similar variegated leaves tinged with yellow.

I. pumila (syn. *I. chamaeiris*) is commonly called the dwarf bearded iris and is largely used for massed plantings, either in beds, large groups, the sunny side of large, deciduous trees, or as permanent edgings. Plants are not out of place in the rockery, and are quite at home on sunny, dry banks, where they soon form a solid mass of rhizomes. The known forms of *I. pumila*, in yellows, white, blues, purples and even pinkish tones, all produce stems 15–30 cm (6–12 in.) in length. Cultivation is the same as for bearded irises, good drainage and full sun being essential. Rhizomes, usually in small clumps, are best transplanted in the autumn but they can be shifted at any time of the year except when growing strongly.

Evansia group

This group is also known as crested irises because they have crests instead of beards. They have broad, flat leaves, and in general are happy in the same conditions as bearded irises.

I. cristata is a very dwarf and delightful iris from eastern North America, flowering at about 12.5 cm (5 in.) high, after which the leaves will grow somewhat taller. The flowers are a clear lavender-blue with white crests and eye. In cooler districts it may be grown in full sun, but in hotter climates it should have partial shade. It does not need lime, but good compost will be beneficial. A white form, 'Alba', is also known.

I. gracilipes is a little crested iris from Japan, a very dainty plant growing up to 30 cm (12 in.), with flowers about 2.5 cm (1 in.) across, lavender-blue and marked with white. It should be grown where it will be protected from the heat of the summer sun, and in leafy compost and preferably volcanic soil. Transplanting or division should be done very carefully.

I. japonica (syn. *I. fimbriata*, *I. chinensis*). The long, dainty, many-flowered sprays of this lovely crested iris, a native of Japan and China, rival the choicest of orchids. Although very easily grown and quite hardy, except in the very coldest districts, it does not always bloom freely. In its wild state, this iris grows in open, damp woodlands, so it prefers some shade. It is shallow-rooted and cannot sustain a prolonged drought without harm. Plants have abundant deep green, strap-like foliage, and numerous, creeping rhizomes resting on the surface of the soil. In late winter or early spring, 60 cm (24 in.)

spikes carrying six to 12 blooms appear just above the foliage and continue their display over a period of six weeks. The wide-open, pale lavender, frilled blooms, 6 cm (2.5 in.) across, are white-crested in the centre, surrounded by a few purple dots.

I. lacustris is very similar to *I. cristata* and grows little more than 7.5 cm (3 in.) tall. It grows well in a shady situation where the soil does not dry out.

I. tectorum. Although a native of China, this iris was first introduced from Japan, where it is grown on the ridges of the thatched roofs of houses. The plant produces an abundance of thin, creeping rhizomes and 7.5 cm (3 in.), broad, shining green leaves drooping over at the top, as do most of the other species of the crested irises. The 45 cm (18 in.) flower-stems carry several flat, upturned, 7.5 cm (3 in.) blooms, crisped at the edges in a shade of lilac blue, veined slightly with a deeper lavender shade and the central crest being white and lilac. Plants in bloom somewhat resemble a small-flowered, double Japanese iris. A pure white-flowered form is known as *I. tectorum* 'Album'. These irises will tolerate dry conditions during summer, but clumps soon exhaust the organic matter in the soil and need replanting every few years, preferably in autumn or else soon after blooming in the spring.

I. wattii is another fine iris belonging to this section and somewhat resembling *I. japonica*, but with 10 cm (4 in.) blooms, up to 50 on a stem. It is a splendid iris for a shady position sheltered from heavy winds.

Iris wattii

Japanese irises

I. ensata (syn. *I. kaempferi*), are lovely, moisture-loving, clematis-flowered irises simply indispensable for the water or bog garden. They can also be grown reasonably well in any good garden soil or situation that does not become dry until mid-summer, when plants finish flowering. Losses in transplanting these irises, which have given rise to an impression that they are difficult to grow, are usually due to plants drying out before the new roots have appeared. This iris throws up a number of sword-like leaves in the spring straight from the hard, fibrous root, and the sustaining new roots do not appear until a month or six weeks later. It is at this critical time that newly planted roots need watching and watering if a dry spell is experienced. For this reason *I. ensata* are best planted in the autumn or during the winter before new growths appear. Very firm planting is also essential, mainly because any disturbance through weeding or cultivation will break the new delicate roots.

These irises have been cultivated in Japan for centuries so nobody is quite sure of the parents of many of the newer varieties. We are told that three distinct classes have been raised in different parts of Japan, and one of these classes is called Higo irises. American hybridists have bred varieties that appear to be even superior to what have so far been produced in Japan. They are certainly larger flowered than the older types, sometimes measuring 25 cm (10 in.) across, with three to six broad petals, some of which are beautifully frilled or waved at the edges. The range of colours is mostly confined to light and dark blues, purples, ruby-red, violet and misty blues, while the elusive shades of soft pink are now appearing. Many are beautifully veined and netted with deeper markings, while others carry distinctive borders around the petals in lighter or darker shades and often pure white. These irises are lovely for cutting, and as other buds on the stem open up in water later, they remain effective over a good period.

Japanese irises are seen at their best in bold groups on the edge of ponds. They are quite happy in these conditions during the growing and flowering period but not during winter. Clumps should be divided and roots planted from autumn through until early spring. Plants are easily raised from seed, but only singles or three-petalled flowers result as a rule.

Iris ensata 'Royal Robes'

Cultivars include:

'Botan Sakura'—1 m (3 ft), soft lavender-pink, deeper veining.

'Dawn Ballet'—1 m (3 ft), large, single, plum-red with white petalettes.

'Enchanted Melody'—1 m (3 ft), large, ruffled flowers of orchid-pink with lavender crest.

'Machayo'—large, double flowers of pure snow-white.

'Midsummer Revelry'—white with lavender-mauve segments.

'Oriental Glamour'—much-ruffled, large double flowers in violet and purple.

'Reign of Glory'—ruffled white with blue edges and stippling; early.

'Royal Robes'—huge, dark royal-purple shading to rich blue centre.

'Summer Storm'—very dark purple with ruffled black styles; late.

'Worlds Delight'—lovely clear lilac-pink; outstanding.

Pacific Coast irises

This is a group of rhizomatous Californian species and hybrids, which prefer a location in sun or partial shade and acid soil.

I. douglasiana is a strong-growing species, soon forming large clumps up to 60 cm (24 in.) across, carrying hundreds of blooms on 60 cm (24 in.) stems, produced just above the coarse broad foliage in the spring. Colours include lavender-blue, lilac, purple and violet shades, as well as creamy white and almost pale apricot. This species has been crossed with *I. innominata*, resulting in some excellent varieties.

I. innominata. Although known for hundreds of years, growing wild in profusion in the state of Oregon, USA, it was not realised until comparatively recently that this species had never been botanically recorded, hence the paradoxical name of *innominata*, which means 'not named'. In the lovely forms available, we have a most valuable addition to our gardens, and a plant adaptable to almost any conditions, including cold and wet, provided drainage is reasonably good and plants are set out in full sun. Plants are evergreen with abundant narrow, grassy leaves soon forming neat clumps, each producing for a period of six weeks dozens of flowers on 25-40 cm (10–16 in.) stems, very suitable for cutting. The hybrids raised by crossing with an allied species, *I. douglasiana*, give a range of flowering times throughout spring.

The roots of these irises are fine and thread-like, making them rather difficult to transplant, the divisions from older plants sometimes collapsing before the new white shoots appear. Seedlings or young plants are always in a vigorous state so little difficulty is experienced with these, but plants should be broken up or shifted in the autumn or spring just after blooming. Plants established in pots can be transplanted safely at any time. Seed saved from a collection of named varieties or good seedlings will yield a high percentage of good colours and forms. This should be sown in the autumn and is easily raised, usually blooming the second season. No animal manure or lime should be applied to beds of these or other Pacific Coast irises. If browning occurs in a clump, cut out the diseased leaves and rootstock, and treat the remainder of the plant with a fungicide dip before replanting.

Sibirica group

This group takes its name from *I. sibirica*, a moisture-loving species that will form a large clump at the edge of a pond or bog. Unlike the Japanese irises, the blooms of this iris are rather more like the bearded group, except that the stems are longer, thinner and less branched. They soon form bold clumps with neat, deep green, grassy foliage, supporting in a stately way the numerous flower-stems that arise 60 cm (24 in.) or more above the leaves. The narrow, wiry rhizomes are closely set in a tight, compact clump and are entirely covered by the abundant foliage. The colours available are mostly light and dark blue, purple, violet and white with intermediate shades. They are usually in pure self-colours, although some of the light blues are prettily veined with deeper tones. Newer colours include near pinks, lavender and reddish violet. This species likes the same conditions as the Japanese irises, but they are much easier to transplant in the spring and losses very seldom occur. For preference, transplant when dormant during winter.

I. delavayi is one of the tallest growing in this section, reaching a height of 1.5 m (5 ft) or more. The distinguishing features are the larger flowers up to 10 cm (4 in.) across with rich violet, spoon-shaped, perpendicular falls, and horizontal standards and style arms, the haft being marked with a splash of white. This plant will grow in very wet conditions and can be readily transplanted during autumn and winter.

I. forrestii can be briefly described as a fragrant, yellow-flowered *I. sibirica* with narrower foliage and 45 cm (18 in.) stems. However, it is not as robust as some other species, resenting dry conditions in the summer. The falls of the bloom are a deeper shade of yellow than the standards. Plants are easily raised from seed, blooming the second season, and some interesting variations in shades can arise. Roots can be divided up and transplanted during autumn or winter.

I. wilsonii somewhat resembles *I. forrestii* and it is the only other yellow-flowered iris of the sibirica group. It was introduced from western China in 1912 but is still not common. The 1 m (3 ft) flower-stems carry two blooms 9 cm (3.5 in.) across, the standards being pale primrose and the falls somewhat deeper with light brown veins at the centre. It is easily grown in most garden soils and should be transplanted when dormant during late summer or winter.

Iris sibirica 'Helen Astor'

Spuria group

This group of irises grow well in sun or semi-shade, and prefer moist soil. They tend to flower better after a good hot summer.

I. graminea is a very dwarf iris, growing to 30 cm (12 in.) high, with dark, narrow, strap-like leaves and vari-coloured flowers of deep lilac, red-purple and china-blue. They have a delightful scent. This species prefers full sun, but in hot climates some partial shade is desirable.

I. monnieri. This lovely, hardy iris is often confused with *I. ochroleuca*, which is understandable as some authorities consider it to be just a yellow-flowered form. It is similar in appearance but it is less robust in growth, the flower-stems seldom exceeding 1.2 m (4 ft) in height. The soft yellow blooms, two to four on a stem and produced in early summer, are also useful for cutting. A deeper yellow-flowered variety called *I.* 'Monaurea', which is a hybrid between *I. monnieri* and a rare species called *I. aurea*, is more common than the true species. Both are easily grown in any situation not too dry, but plants should be set out in the mid-autumn before the new leaf growths appear, otherwise they suffer a severe check and do not bloom again for some time.

I. ochroleuca. This hardy, strong-growing species is one of the best waterside irises, suitable for the moist border or for naturalising in open woodlands. The strong flower-stems, rising to a height of 1.2–1.8 m (4–6 ft), are topped with large white flowers, each with a splash of gold on the falls. Several short, lower branches, hugging tightly to the stem, prolong the flowering season, each bud opening up in succession in water. Plants bloom in early summer and are transplanted from autumn until late winter.

Other species of herbaceous irises

I. alata is a lovely, autumn-flowering iris seldom seen nowadays. The flower-stem branches into three or four side shoots, each carrying soft, 10 cm (4 in.), blue flowers, beautifully ruffled and waved, enhanced by a ridge of bright orange. It is a native of southern Spain and north Africa, and grows wild on the slopes of Mount Etna and in Sicily, preferring a hot, dry early summer.

I. cretensis has grass-like foliage and grows barely 12.5 cm (5 in.) high. The flowers, in lavender-violet shades, have fine petals and are very dainty and

Iris ochroleuca

attractive. It is a gem for the rock garden but it has a relatively short flowering season.

I. foetidissima is an evergreen species for growing in the shade of big trees, with deep shining green foliage and attractive pods of scarlet seeds in autumn and winter. The plant itself easily becomes naturalised in large woodland areas, and is not generally grown in cultivated gardens. The flowers are insignificant but the clusters of heavy seed-pods split open and reflex to display rows of scarlet seeds, which remain attached to the outer skins. If cut and hung in a shed to dry, these showy pods become valuable for colourful winter decorations. *Foetidissima* means stinking, referring the rank odour of the foliage when crushed. A striking, creamy-white, variegated foliage form is now very popular and useful for scree gardens.

I. fulva (syn. *I. cuprea*) is a native of North America. The 7.5 cm (3 in.) wide flowers are small for an iris growing 75 cm (30 in.) tall, yet the colour is quite arresting, no other species possessing such a rich tangerine-brown shade. Both standards and falls hang down and the style arms hold horizontally, thus resembling a small-flowered Japanese iris. A hybrid from the species, *I.* 'Fulvala', growing only

50 cm (20 in.) high, produces bronze-purple flowers of a rich velvety texture. The narrow, woody rhizomes of *I. fulva* and the thicker but very rough-looking ones of *I.* 'Fulvala' can be readily transplanted from mid-autumn until early spring, the flowering period being just after the bearded irises have finished in late spring.

I. louisiana. These irises have been bred from wild species from Louisiana and Florida. The clumps have hard, rhizomatous, brownish deep green roots, which lie on the surface of the soil, and drooping gladiolus-like foliage. During late spring, 0.6–1.2 m (2–4 ft) tall, zig-zag stems carry six to 12 triangular flowers, 10–15 cm (4–6 in.) across, opening in succession over a period, and also in water when cut. They revel in heat, moisture, and an acid soil, succeeding best in moist soils rich in compost and in full sun. They are well suited to warmer climates but are quite easy to grow in most gardens, increasing more rapidly where conditions are ideal. The cut stems are most useful for indoor decoration, and regarded by some as even more beautiful than the lovely Japanese irises. The following is a selection of modern hybrids and indicates the range of colours:

'Amber Goddess'—frilled flowers of honey-amber, yellow signals.

'Blue Shield'—rich velvety purple-blue self, orange signals, wide petals.

'Carmen'—rich chrysanthemum red, wide frilled petals.

'Charlie's Michelle'—ruffled amaranth-rose, golden signals, super form.

'Clyde Redmond'—true medium blue, green crests, dwarfer growth.

'Delta Star'—deep purple, petals with yellow star, flattish flower.

'Dixie Deb'—light yellow with orange signals, prolific, long-flowering.

'Freddie Boy'—deep rose with rose-red falls, very pretty, early.

'Full Eclipse'—blackish violet flowers, very striking, tall, large flowers.

'Plantation Beau'—milky violet with turquoise.

'Rue Royale'—rich yellow with gold signal, good form, branching.

'Uptight'—primrose-yellow, orange signal, tall to 1.2 m (4 ft).

I. pseudacorus is a hardy iris, the flowers being flat and rich golden yellow. In England it is commonly called the yellow water flag. It resents lime but is easily grown in any garden soil that is not too dry. It requires full sun, although it is happiest in boggy or wet spots and is very suitable for planting around the sides of large ponds or lakes. The ribbed, sword-like leaves and heavy spikes of bloom 1.5 m (5 ft) high lend themselves to bold indoor decorations. It is considered by some to be too common for general garden culture and is often seen naturalised in open fields and wet depressions. Transplant during autumn or winter.

I. susiana (mourning iris). The huge crepe-like blooms, 15 cm (6 in.) in depth if well grown, are pale cream, so heavily veined with greyish purple as to give the blooms a sombre appearance. Although introduced from Turkey hundreds of years ago, this iris has never become plentiful as it is seldom really happy, few gardens providing the conditions required. Perfect or sharp drainage is absolutely essential, while a hot, dry summer providing a long dormant period is also needed. The safest way is to lift the roots when they die down in early summer and store them in a dry, open shed until late autumn. Some success has been achieved by planting roots on the sunny side of the house and under

Iris pseudacorus 'Variegatus'

Iris louisiana 'Clyde Redmond'

wide eaves, where natural rainfall is much reduced. Stony, volcanic or sandy soils are usually quite suitable, particularly if beds are raised. A heavy dressing of lime is beneficial.

I. unguicularis (syn. *I. stylosa*) is quite a common iris in most gardens but is seldom grown to perfection, because the flowers and buds are either hidden in the massive grassy foliage and never seen, or finally eaten by slugs or snails. It is admirably suited for growing in the shade or under big trees, but is equally at home in the full sun. The most effective use of this iris we have seen was its employment in holding up a clay bank. It eventually became a solid wall 1.5 m (5 ft) high and 30 m (100 ft) long, and because of the poorness of the soil the foliage was sparse, thus allowing the flowers to be seen to advantage. The best way to secure good undamaged blooms for winter display or decorations (they are lovely cut flowers) is to remove all the foliage about 15 cm (6 in.) above the ground with a pair of shears in the early autumn, before the flower-spikes or buds have formed. No fresh leaves will appear before late spring, and the flowers will stand out and can easily be seen and readily picked. Furthermore, slugs and other insects, which are fond of these dainty blooms, find little protection or shelter for their onslaughts. They have lavender-mauve flowers, and there are several forms with large or smaller flowers. Cultivars include 'Speciosa', with larger flowers, and 'Alba',

which has white flowers and yellow blotches. 'Mary Barnard' has deeper, bluer flowers, and 'Walter Butt' has sky-blue flowers.

I. versicolor is a fairly vigorous grower, reaching 1 m (3 ft). The foliage is usually a pale green, almost yellow-green, and the flowers are white through lavender or violet-blue to quite deep red, often with darker veining. Naturally a plant of bogs, this species will grow quite happily in an ordinary, compost-rich garden soil if it has adequate water. It gives six weeks of bloom in late spring and early summer.

ISOPLEXIS
Scrophulariaceae

There are about five species in this genus of evergreen, semi-woody shrubs, allied to the foxglove, from the Canary Islands and Madeira. They are hardy in most coastal districts but not where heavy frost is experienced. They prefer a medium to light soil.

I. canariensis may grow to 1.5 m (5 ft), with large leaves, the flower-spikes carrying orange-yellow, tubular flowers in a dense spike. *I. sceptrum* is somewhat smaller, to 1.2 m (4 ft), with smaller leaves and terminal spikes produced very freely in mid-

Isoplexis sceptrum

summer. The spikes are also smaller, yellow with brown shading. This is an excellent garden plant for the warmer districts, of attractive but unusual colouring. It is easily propagated from seed or from cuttings, and should be pruned in early spring.

IXIA
Iridaceae   African corn lily

A genus of 30 or more species belonging to the section of the iris family to which the sparaxis and babianas also belong, these hardy and half-hardy South African bulbs are among the showiest of spring-flowering plants. They all prefer good drainage, and the drier the conditions after blooming, the better the bulbs will mature, ensuring a good crop of flowers for the following season. Although there are numerous varieties offered today, many of the original species are still among the best.

I. campanulata (syn. *I. crateroides*) is a valuable, stocky-growing species, with short, broad basal leaves and 45–60 cm (18–24 in.), slender stems, carrying 24–30 bell-shaped, scarlet-red or carmine flowers during spring. Corms are covered with distinctive, netted fibre.

I. dubia is a delightful, early-flowering species, growing about 30 cm (12 in.) tall, with comparatively large flowers on slender stems, golden yellow with a small black eye. It is worthy of much wider cultivation.

I. latifolia (syn. *I. capillaris*, *I. incarnata*) is a distinct species and probably the earliest to bloom in the spring. The branching stems produce masses of small, papery, soft gentian-blue flowers, which are delicately perfumed.

I. maculata is a semi-dwarf species, growing up to 60 cm (24 in.), with closely packed heads of large, wide-open, yellow flowers, each with a purple-black centre. Other shades include cream with reddish brown, lilac-mauve and brownish centres, and orange and black.

I. paniculata (syn. *Morphixia paniculata*) is a very distinct, late-flowering species, providing a lovely display in early summer. It produces numerous buff-pink, starry flowers on 45 cm (18 in.) stems, the 7.5 cm (3 in.) long tubes being reddish brown at the base, and is a desirable species, effective when massed.

Ixia maculata

I. viridiflora is the most popular and sought-after species, with its wide-open, sea-green flowers with conspicuous blue-black throat. It grows best on sandy or volcanic soils, and it tends to die out on heavy soils, whereas the other species will grow well in any soil in a sunny position.

There are some very fine colours among the named hybrids available today, and these should prove very popular in well-drained, hot, spring gardens, where it is not possible to grow many summer or autumn plants.

'Afterglow'—orange-buff with dark eye.

'Conqueror'—deep golden yellow with coppery orange reverse.

'Elvira'—pale eggshell-blue, late flowering; quite distinct and very pretty.

'Gem'—lemon-yellow with conspicuous purple-bronze eye; strong growing.

'Golden Glory'—beautiful, rich orange-yellow, self-coloured variety with large, wide-open blooms; somewhat dwarf in habit.

'Rosalind'—cherry-red; tall, robust variety.

'Rose Wonder'—double cerise-red; very attractive.

'The Bride'—pure white; 1 m (3 ft), with strong, free-branching stems; vigorous, disease-resistant form.

'Venus'—brilliant wine-red.

'Vulcan'—brilliant coppery orange, shaded scarlet; one of the best and richest in colour.

Ixia paniculata

The fatal disease that attacks the green ixias, and also most other species and varieties to a lesser degree, is known as *Sclerotium rolfsii*, which becomes apparent during warm weather. Virus-affected corms, identified by the streaked appearance of the flowers, should be destroyed, as there is no known cure.

All ixias are increased from division of parent bulbs, but if a larger increase is required, the tiny bulbils or 'spawn' attached also to the larger bulbs can be saved and sown in beds. Many species and varieties ripen seed, which should give a wide range of colours and perhaps some new shades worth segregating and increasing separately. Plant bulbs from mid-summer until autumn, 5–7.5 cm (2–3 in.) apart and 5 cm (2 in.) deep.

IXIOLIRION
Amaryllidaceae

The name means ixia-like lily, referring to the shape of the flowers. There are three species of this hardy bulb from central Asia, and they are among the loveliest of small-growing spring flowers, preferring cool winter, moist spring and hot, dry summer conditions.

I. tataricum (syn. *I. pallasii*, *I. montanum*) is the best-known species. It produces bulbs up to 2.5 cm (1 in.) across, 5 cm (2 in.) long, and, during winter and spring, loose tufts of green leaves followed by umbels of wide-open, bright blue flowers on 30 cm (12 in.) stems. Under ideal conditions, the bulbs will throw stems up to 60 cm (24 in.) long. Stock can be raised from fresh seed, which germinates readily and blooms the second or third year. Bulbs should be planted in the autumn.

J

JASIONE
Campanulaceae

The genus consists of about a dozen perennial species from the Mediterranean region, of which *J. perennis* appears to be the only one generally grown. It forms a tufted clump of narrow, greyish green, rather hairy leaves, and during summer produces numerous, erect, unbranched, naked stems 30 cm (12 in.) tall, each topped with a semi-globose head of 5 cm (2 in.) wide, soft blue flowers, somewhat resembling a scabiosa. It is an attractive, hardy perennial, easily grown in full sun in well-drained soil, and deserves to be more popular. Plants are increased readily by the division of old clumps during winter or early spring.

Jasione perennis

K

KNIPHOFIA
Liliaceae   Red hot poker

The genus has about 24 species, natives of South and East Africa and Madagascar. The old species *K. uvaria*, known in old-fashioned English gardens, is a fiery scarlet torch with yellow or greenish yellow lower flowers. A number of other interesting species have been introduced from South Africa and these have been inter-crossed by hybridists, resulting in a variety of newer colours and types, ranging in height from only 60 cm (24 in.), with dainty slender stems, up to giants 2 m (6.5 ft) high, with stems as thick as one's wrist. Plants are easy to grow under almost any conditions, and they are also useful for naturalising in grassy fields as the plants are not touched by animals. Whether species or hybrids, kniphofias will add much wealth to the herbaceous border, as they can all be relied upon to make a brilliant display over a fairly long period.

K. caulescens grows to 1.5 m (5 ft) and is especially good in milder districts where late frosts are infrequent. It produces roundish heads of greenish yellow, rosy-tipped flowers in late winter or very early in the spring. A cultivar named 'Charles Reader' has creamy yellow flowers that develop from green buds.

K. x *corallina* is one of the best, showiest and most popular hybrids. In late spring and summer it produces elongated, closely packed spikes of deep coral-red flowers on 1-1.2 m (3-4 ft) stems, and is very brilliant and effective.

K. galpinii is a pretty little species, with grassy foliage and slender, 75 cm (30 in.) stems, topped with drooping, loosely packed heads of apricot-orange flowers, produced in abundance over a long period.

K. gracilis is another grassy-foliaged species, with dainty, one-sided, arching heads of lemon-yellow flowers on 60 cm (24 in.) stems. It blooms over a long period if conditions are not too dry.

K. macowanii (syn. *K. triangularis*) is very dwarf and distinguished by the triangular section of the flower-stems, which only grow to 40 cm (16 in.), with orange-red flowers in summer. This species is small enough for the larger rock garden.

K. praecox (syn. *K. zululandiae*) is by far the best winter or early spring-flowering species, producing a brilliant display during the dull, cold months. The cultivar 'Winter Cheer' produces 20 cm (8 in.) long, closely packed heads of bright orange-red flowers on 1-1.2 m (3-4 ft) stems. In areas with mild winters and only light frosts, a fine display will commence in mid-winter and continue well into spring. The plant itself is near hardy, but very severe frosts will damage the first flower-spikes.

K. uvaria 'Grandiflora' is a variable plant and commonly grown. It has tall spikes 1.5-2m (5-6 ft), and orange-scarlet buds opening to yellow flowers in late summer and autumn.

The following are selected kniphofia cultivars:

Kniphofia caulescens 'Charles Reader'

Kniphofia uvaria 'Grandiflora'

'Apricot Torch'—a distinct variety with handsome spikes of pure orange-apricot; 2 m (6 ft); early summer flowering.

'Bright Lass'—neat, compact spike of deep but bright orange-red, overlaid terracotta; 1 m (3 ft).

'Ernest Mitchell'—elongated spikes of citron-yellow; 1.5 m (5 ft).

'Gold Else'—semi-dwarf, lemon-yellow; 1 m (3 ft).

'Jubilee'—distinct shade of salmon-buff; 1 m (3 ft).

'Little Maid'—low-growing to 60 cm (24 in.), with a long succession of light yellow flowers fading to ivory.

'Maid of Orleans'—fine, creamy white, elongated spike; 1 m (3 ft).

'Orangeade'—true orange with compact spikes; 1 m (3 ft).

'Pencil'—buds bright green opening to creamy yellow; foliage dies down in winter; 90 cm (36 in.).

'Pinkette'—attractive, salmon-pink fading to creamy white; to 90 cm (36 in.); summer flowering.

'Stately'—spikes green opening to creamy yellow; 90 cm (36 in.).

'Winter Gold'—rich golden yellow, well-frilled, 22.5 cm (9 in.) torches on 1.2 m (4 ft) stems; autumn flowering.

'Yellow Spire'—a handsome plant, with tall spikes of bright yellow; 1.8 m (6 ft); late summer flowering.

All kniphofias are best increased from divisions, preferably in the spring. It is not advisable to break up clumps until well established, otherwise the new shoots will not have produced fresh roots, and will be lost. Seedlings raised from hybrids will yield some interesting shades, but these usually require two or three years to bloom.

L

LACHENALIA
Liliaceae

This genus consists of about 65 bulbous species, all natives of South Africa. They are valuable, half-hardy, winter and early spring-flowering bulbs, particularly suitable for light, free soils with good drainage. They also grow well in containers, and are easily grown inside or under glass in cold or very wet districts where outside cultivation would fail.

L. aloides (syn. *L. tricolor*) is the best-known and most variable species, resulting in a number of forms that are grown and often wrongly considered distinct species. The species produces lemon-yellow, tubular flowers, tipped green, and reddish brown at the base. It is usually the last to bloom in the spring. 'Aurea' has bright orange-yellow flowers on 22.5–30 cm (9–12 in.) stems, and the taller-growing form, 'Aurea Gigantea', has well-covered spikes, sometimes reaching 45 cm (18 in.). 'Quadricolor' grows naturally in a limestone area and is happier under

Lachenalia contaminata

such conditions. It is the first to bloom, the shorter, 10–15 cm (4–6 in.) spikes appearing in mid-winter, with 2.5 cm (1 in.) long, tubular flowers, red at the base, greenish yellow in the middle, with outer segments tipped green and inner tube reddish purple. Perfect drainage and freedom from heavy frosts are essential. If happy, the bulbs produce large quantities of 'spawn' around the base.

L. bulbiferum (syn. *L. pendula*)·is the so-called red lachenalia much used for bedding and cutting. It produces a round, flattish, clean, white bulb, sometimes up to 5 cm (2 in.) across, colouring up to purplish red if exposed to the sun when lifted. This species, if really happy, is more prolific than any other, producing numerous small bulbs just below the surface of the soil. In sunny, frost-free positions, plants also seed freely, while leaf cuttings taken about flowering time and inserted in sandy loam to half their depth will result in hundreds of small bulbs like peas forming on the base of these cut portions. This species is a robust grower, with dark green, usually unspotted foliage and erect, graceful racemes of deep coral-red flowers, up to 16 on 15–30 cm (6–12 in.) stems. It blooms in early spring, sooner in sheltered spots, or during mid-winter under glass. 'Scarlet Bloom' is a hybrid of *L. bulbiferum* parentage which is very vigorous and increases readily on rich, light soil. The spikes are large and a somewhat brighter and lighter coral-red colour, eminently suitable for bedding.

L. contaminata is easy to grow and late flowering. The stems grow to about 12.5 cm (5 in.), with closely set white flowers, which have a fluffy appearance because of the dainty, brown-tipped stamens.

L. glaucina grows to 30 cm (12 in.) tall, with sturdy stems carrying bluish mauve flowers. *L. glaucina pallida* has yellowish green flowers, which appear during spring.

L. liliflora has a good white spike, only 15 cm (6 in.) tall and quite long-lived, but it is very late in

Lachenalia glaucina

flowering. Increase is slow.

L. longibracteata has 30 cm (12 in.) tall spikes of creamy yellow flowers. It is not as showy as other yellow species and is rather uncommon.

L. mutabilis is an interesting and valuable species, popular as an early spring cut flower. The small, open bells, recurved at the tips, are loosely arranged on a 22.5–30 cm (9–12 in.) stem, and first open up sky-blue, with inner segments dull yellowish green with a purple-brown blotch near the tip, becoming crimson-brown with age. A clump of bulbs in full bloom, displaying spikes at different stages of development and colours, is quite arresting. This species requires perfect drainage and will not withstand frosts more than eight degrees.

L. orchioides has small, fragrant, multi-coloured bells on the many-flowered, densely set spikes. The colours range from whitish to yellow and tinged with red or blue, and the bells are closely set on a spotted scape.

L. 'Pearsoni' is reputed to be a cross between a good golden-yellow form of *L. aloides* and the coral-red *L. bulbiferum*, but there seems no evidence of the influence of the latter species. It is, however, a fine plant and probably the best orange-yellow-flowered form, being taller growing, with more flowers to a spike, the buds and base of the bloom being reddish orange. One of the distinguishing features of this variety, which is sometimes confused with taller-growing forms of *L. aloides* 'Aurea', is that the stems are mottled with purple-brown. It is a splendid cut flower, blooming several weeks earlier than 'Aurea'.

L. reflexa is very distinct in having three to six upturned, yellow flowers on a short spike, about 10 cm (4 in.) tall. It flowers in spring.

L. rosea and *L. violacea* both have rather slender spikes; the former is pink tinged, and the latter has flowers of a bluish green tipped with purple. Both grow about 18 cm (7.5 in.) tall.

There are many other interesting species, most of which are worth growing and are easily raised from seed. However, it must be stressed that perfect drainage and a situation rather on the dry side are absolutely essential for success with these species. Failures in growing or flowering lachenalia successfully are due either to frost damage or excessive wet conditions resulting in fusarium attacking the base of the bulbs. Affected stock has a pinkish discoloration at the base of the bulb and should be lifted when dormant and destroyed. All lachenalia bulbs should be kept absolutely dry and fully open to the air or even subdued sunlight. Bulbs stored in bags or closed boxes soon deteriorate or develop soft rot. All the species should be planted as soon as possible after they have died down, preferably from mid- to late summer.

LAPEIROUSIA
Iridaceae   Scarlet freesia

This genus of 60 species of bulbous plants from tropical and South Africa is allied to the watsonias and now includes *Anomatheca*.

L. laxa is a hardy, pretty little plant. It is easily grown from seed but is more often increased by bulbs in milder climates. It is like a freesia in foliage, growth and bulb, with wide-open, somewhat starry flowers, rosy-scarlet in colour, with deep maroon

Lapeirousia laxa

throat markings, on thin, wiry, 30–45 cm (12–18 in.) stems. Bulbs are easily grown in loose, free soil, and are suitable for naturalising under larger deciduous trees, where they seem to thrive quite well. If left undisturbed, the bulbs seed down freely, soon forming a nice colony. A pure white-flowered form, 'Alba', is less vigorous and naturalises less readily. If grown from bulbs planted in the autumn, plants usually bloom in the spring, but if seed is sown in the spring, the bulbs flower throughout the summer. Plants are hardy in all coastal areas if planted about 7.5 cm (3 in.) deep, and if frosts are heavy, a mulch will usually protect them adequately.

LATHYRUS
Fabaceae

Most of this genus are perennial climbers.

L. latifolius is often known as the everlasting pea and, given support, can climb to a height of 3 m (10 ft). The species has bright carmine flower-spikes in profusion, and good selections are 'White Pearl' and 'Rose Queen', the latter having attractive pink flowers. They may be grown on trellis or other support, flowering for many weeks of summer.

L. vernus grows 30–40 cm (12–16 in.) tall, a bushy plant with purple flowers in spring. A selection called 'Spring Delight' has charming, creamy pink flowers above the greenery. All are fully hardy and perennial everywhere. Propagation is from seed.

Lathyrus vernus

LAVATERA
Malvaceae   Mallow

This genus includes annuals and shrubs, which do not qualify for inclusion, but two are sub-shrubs and good for the perennial border.

L. cachemiriana grows 1.5 m (5 ft) and has pale rose flowers in the summer.

L. olbia grows to 1.8 m (6 ft), with rosy lilac mallow flowers for most of the summer.

L. 'Barnsley' is a beautiful new variety that grows 2 m (6.5 ft) tall and is smothered with pale pink flowers, fading to deeper pink.

All species like hot, dry positions but are otherwise easy to grow. They should be hard pruned early in spring. Propagation is by softwood cuttings in early spring or summer.

LESPEDEZA
Fabaceae

There are about 100 species of these shrubby or herbaceous plants, but the best and most cultivated one is known as *L. thunbergii* (syn. *L. sieboldii*). From a hard, woody rootstock, it produces strong, wiry shoots up to 1.8 m (6 ft) tall, semi-drooping at the top, something like the wands of the dierama or fairy bells. The top half develops into loose, drooping sprays containing hundreds of rosy purple, pea-shaped flowers in late summer. It is seen at its best trailing over a wall or associated with some of the autumn-flowered perennials. This plant does not seem to be much grown, but it is well worth a place in the garden. The roots penetrate deeply into the ground and are hard to break up or increase, but fresh roots can be secured by taking cuttings in the spring when the new shoots are 7.5 cm (3 in.) long. Established plants will stand very dry conditions. Transplant when dormant during winter.

LEUCANTHEMUM
Asteraceae

This is a genus of about 25 species of perennial, or rarely annual, herbaceous plants, from Europe, North Africa and south-west Asia.

Lavatera cachemiriana

Leucanthemum maximum 'Phyllis Smith'

Leucanthemum maximum, previously *Chrysanthemum maximum*, commonly called the shasta daisy, is a robust perennial 60 cm (24 in.) or more in height, with strong stems carrying solitary flower-heads of single, white daisies 10 cm (4 in.) across. Many improved and selected forms have been introduced, and one of the first to command attention was a variety with nicely frilled petals, called the chiffon daisy. 'Esther Read', which was the first full double, creamy white, is still considered a good herbaceous plant, excellent for cutting and florists' use. Some of the more recent introductions in double-flowered forms have immense, frilly blooms up to 15 cm (6 in.) across. Two of the best are 'Edgebrook Giant', and 'Wirral Supreme', both of which are excellent cut flowers, their blooms being held erect on strong stems. An exceptionally tall and free-flowering, single white is called 'Exhibition'. It flowers in mid- to late summer and is over 1 m (3 ft) tall. 'Cobham Gold' is fully double, but the name is an exaggeration, the flowers being cream with a touch of yellow in the centre. 'Phyllis Smith' has several rows of narrow petals and is free-flowering to 80 cm (32 in.). This variety is popular as a cut flower. 'Snow Lady' grows only 30 cm (12 in.) tall, small enough for the front row of a border. The comparatively large, glistening, white flowers are very effective.

All the shasta daisies are of great value in the herbaceous border, and are particularly attractive associated with blue or yellow flowers, while they also serve as a foil between groups of hard colours such as reds and purples. All are increased readily by division during winter or early spring.

LEUCOCORYNE
Amaryllidaceae   Glory of the sun

The genus consists of about five bulbous plants and is allied to *Triteleia* and *Brodiaea*, all being natives of Chile.

L. ixioides is temperamental but this may be due to conditions it experiences in its natural environment, where occasionally the short autumn rainy season that starts the bulbs into growth may fail entirely, with the result that the bulbs remain dormant in the ground a whole year without growing at all. Bulbs in cultivation have been known to 'sulk' for two years, remaining firm and sound and coming away freely the next season. It seems to thrive well under conditions that suit freesias or other South African bulbs, preferring a warm climate with a long, dry summer rest. In some places it may be best grown in pots or boxes under glass, or in a conservatory.

When really happy, each bulb produces one to three spikes 45 cm (18 in.) tall, topped with four to eight glorious, gentian-blue flowers, about 5 cm (2 in.) across, with a white centre, somewhat resembling a giant head of *Chionodoxa luciliae*. As a cut flower they are unsurpassed, providing every feature that could be desired. The stems are thin and wiry, the dainty, wide-open flowers are prettily waved and deliciously scented, lasting fresh in water two weeks or more.

Bulbs are increased from seed only; the mature bulb, which is round and about 1 cm (0.5 in.) across, does not increase by division. Seed germinates readily the first season, throwing up a single, grasslike leaf; two leaves appear in the second season, and a few bulbs bloom the third year. Bulbs are best planted 15 cm (6 in.) deep in the late autumn but can be left without lifting if the situation is hot and dry. This may seem very deep planting for bulbs so small, but bulbs have been known to re-establish themselves at a depth of 25 cm (10 in.) in light soils when drainage is perfect.

LEUCOJUM
Amaryllidaceae   Snowflake

There are 12 species of the common spring-flowering snowflake, of which *L. aestivum* is the best known. These bulbs are quite often confused with the true snowdrop, which is, however, a galanthus. The snowflake is not cultivated much in gardens in the Southern Hemisphere, as it is so prolific and considered common, but it is very suitable for naturalising in bold groups in open fields, under big trees, or even in lawns. Animals do not touch the foliage, and the bulbs seem quite capable of fending for themselves without any attention.

A larger-flowered form of the common snowflake is called 'Gravetye Giant', and this is well worth obtaining. Its flowers are twice the size of the common species, and it grows to 30 cm (12 in.) tall, flowering early and continuing long after the usual form has finished. Unfortunately, it does not set seed, so it is still scarce. The leucojums are quite happy in partial shade. Transplant from mid-summer until autumn.

Leucojum aestivum 'Gravetye Giant'

LIATRIS
Asteraceae   Gay feather

This genus consists of 40 species. It is a rather odd plant, but nevertheless very attractive in the garden, a desirable cut flower and a good bee plant. The peculiarity of the liatris is that the blooms open up from the top downward, instead of the lower flowers

Liatris spicata 'Goblin'

opening up first, as with most other plants. The lower stems, densely covered with narrow, grass-like leaves, somewhat resemble certain liliums in growth. The cylindrical heads of bloom, sometimes up to 60 cm (24 in.) long, are composed of numerous finely rayed rosettes surrounding the stem.

L. pycnostachya grows 1 m (3 ft) or more tall, the dense spikes of intense purple-rose flowers being very good for cutting.

L. spicata (syn. *L. callilepis*) is a low-growing species up to 60 cm (24 in.) high, found growing along water courses. The flowers are generally lilac-purple, but there is a pure white form in cultivation. A real dwarf called *L. spicata* 'Goblin' has short, stocky spikes growing 30 cm (12 in.) high. 'Kobold' has the flower-stems seldom exceeding 75 cm (30 in.) in height and spikes that are full and large. The colour is deep lilac-purple. The taller forms of this species will need staking in an exposed position.

The liatris are all easy to grow in almost any climate, preferring a position not too dry, and doing quite well even in wet places or semi-shade. The hardy, woody root, somewhat resembling a bulb, is quite dormant in the winter, without any roots at all, so apparently plants are not affected in any way by adverse conditions during the resting period. The unusual appearance and brilliant colours of this family make them desirable and attractive border plants, favoured by butterflies and bees. Increase is

usually from seed, which germinates freely in the spring, the plants blooming the following autumn. Division of old roots is difficult. Transplant when dormant during winter.

LIBERTIA
Iridaceae

This is a genus of 10 species of perennials with short, creeping rhizomes, fibrous roots, and numerous thin, narrow leaves at the base of the stems.

L. caerulescens grows to 60–90 cm (24–36 in.) with stiff, narrow green leaves and pale blue flowerheads.

There are four recognised species native to New Zealand. All are easily grown, evergreen, herbaceous plants with stiff, narrow, attractive, brownish green foliage.

L. grandiflora produces tall, wiry, lightly branched flower-stems up to 90 cm (36 in.) high, with dainty,

Libertia caerulescens

white flowers, elegantly arranged. These are followed in the autumn by golden brown seed capsules, which are quite useful for decoration.

L. ixioides, from its tufted clump of leaves, produces numerous, smaller, white flowers on 30 cm (12 in.) stems.

A popular species now used in Japanese or scree gardens is known as *L. peregrinans*. The stiff, erect foliage is an attractive yellowish green, with a prominent orange-brown mid-rib. It is easily increased from seed or divisions during the winter months, and it will spread slowly.

L. pulchella is a dainty little species growing only 22.5 cm (9 in.) high.

Increase of all species is by division in spring, but plants can also be raised by seed sown in autumn or spring.

LIGULARIA
Asteraceae

This genus consists of about 150 species of herbaceous perennials with striking foliage and handsome flower-heads, natives of Europe, Asia and Africa north of the tropics. This genus is closely allied to the *Senecio*, and the species described below were until recently classified under this heading.

L. dentata (syn. *L. clivorum*) is perhaps the most striking species in its different forms. The attractive, 25–40 cm (10–16 in.) long leaves are kidney-shaped and coarsely toothed at the edges. The 1 m (3 ft) flower-stems terminate in a loose corymb of orange-yellow, daisy-like flowers, 7.5 cm (3 in.) across, with a central yellow disc 2.5 cm (1 in.) wide. A larger-flowered, bright orange variety is called 'Orange Queen'. 'Desdemona' is a handsome cultivar with dark purple stems and leaves.

L. hodginsii is very similar to *L. dentata*; it comes from Japan, growing to 1 m (3 ft), with heads of orange flowers and large, rounded leaves. All forms delight in moist or damp spots and are happy situated at the edges of ponds or semi-shady, moist spots. Plants are, however, very easily grown anywhere except dry situations.

L. macrophylla 'Aurea' grows up to 1.8 m (6 ft) and has large leaves up to 60 cm (24 in.) long and panicles of yellow daisies.

Ligularia dentata

L. stenocephala (syn. *Senecio przewalskii*) has handsome foliage and imposing, black-stemmed, narrow spikes of bright yellow flowers to 1.5 m (5 ft). The cultivar usually grown is 'The Rocket'.

L. tussilaginea is a subtropical plant from Japan, hardy in frost-free gardens. The form known as 'Aurea-maculata' is often grown as a foliage plant. It has bold, rounded leaves heavily marked with large, round, creamy yellow spots. Another striking form has the leaves variegated with white and is named 'Argentea'. Both forms have light yellow flowers, and may be grown in shady situations or on patios where frost does not reach them.

L. veitchiana may grow to 1.5 m (5 ft), with leaves 30 cm (12 in.) long and spikes with 30 cm (12 in.) heads of numerous bright yellow flowers.

Increase is from divisions of the fleshy-rooted clumps while dormant during winter. Fresh seed germinates readily, with plants flowering the second year.

Opposite: Grey and green foliage plants are used together to good effect in this formal garden. A variegated hosta thrives in the shade of a weeping pear, a low box hedge and lavender cotton (*Santolina*) edge the path. White dianthus, campanula, irises and foxgloves (*Digitalis*) harmonise with the garden's subtle colours.

LILIUM
Liliaceae

There are over 80 recorded species belonging to this genus, all of which are natives of the temperate regions of the Northern Hemisphere. Unlike other families of bulbs or corms such as narcissus or gladiolus, where a general cultural rule covers them all, each species of lily has its own peculiar and distinctive character and charm, its likes and dislikes. With perhaps a few exceptions, liliums as a class are easy to grow, and provided a few simple basic instructions are followed, a very wide range of varieties can be grown in almost any garden.

The most important thing for successful lily growing is to provide perfect drainage, and this is not difficult on volcanic, sandy and gravelly soils, but a combination of clay soil and high rainfall can be fatal to most lilies. On heavier soils, lilies should be planted on raised beds, and sloping ground is an advantage. Preparation on heavier soils should include the addition of organic material such as old sawdust, leaf mould and compost.

Most lilies, except *L. candidum*, grow stem roots just below the surface in the growing season, and it is important to mulch plants well to prevent them drying out in hot weather and to prevent weed growth. A good handful of a balanced fertiliser will help the lilies keep healthy and strong.

Bulbs should be planted with 10 cm (4 in.) of soil above the bulb, and unless the soil is light, a good handful of sand can be placed in the hole on which to bed the bulb. Smaller bulbs could be planted less deeply. Lilies need sunlight, although some varieties keep their colour better in semi-shade. A sunny, open spot is less likely to become too wet in winter than a shady position among trees, although groups of lilies associated with low-growing, fibrous-rooted shrubs can look superb. Bulbs are best planted or shifted in the autumn, as soon as possible after flowering, but preferably in time to establish a fresh root system before the winter conditions set in. When once established, lilies should be left undisturbed for years, and the general rule is to leave them alone until they show signs of overcrowding.

Most liliums increase naturally by division of the parent bulbs, also from small, stem-rooting bulbs produced above the larger ones. Others such as *L.*

Lilium auratum 'Platiphyllum'

tigrinum, *L. sulphureum*, *L. sargentiae* and *L. bulbiferum* form stem buds between the axils of the leaves and the stem. These bulbils when mature drop off or are readily detached in the autumn. They should be planted immediately in light, free soil, and will usually bloom the second or third year. Propagation from scales is the usual method of increasing bulbs commercially. Flower-stems can also be removed and heeled into half the length of the stem at an angle of 45 degrees, and by the winter, numerous small stem bulbs will have formed up the length of the submerged stem.

If lilium seed is obtainable, this is probably the best, if slowest, form of increase. Larger quantities can be raised in this way, and, unlike other methods of propagation, diseases are not carried over, as long as conditions are suitable. Seed of most species germinates in a few weeks' time if sown in autumn, but species such as *L. auratum* usually take at least 12 months before the leaves appear above the ground. As soon as they are large enough, usually 12 months after sowing, or two years in the case of slower-growing species, the small bulbs should be lined out or planted up in their permanent position.

Before discussing the three main diseases affecting lilies, it should be mentioned that many failures with lilies are not due to disease at all but are caused by unsuitable growing conditions or a general lack of good health; it is surprising how apparently diseased or weak-looking bulbs recover and respond to correct feeding and a suitable root-growing medium.

The dreaded virus disease can be recognised by yellowish streaks in the foliage, distorted flowers and a general sickly appearance, with a corresponding weakening of the bulbs. The trouble is generally spread by insects, such as green fly, passing from affected flower-heads to clean bulbs, and also by contact when bulbs are grown closely together, or are placed together in the same box when lifted or being transplanted. All affected bulbs should be destroyed as they will never recover again to full health. The second disease is fusarium, which is a basal rot. In affected bulbs, the scales are usually found to be loosened from the main bulb and blackened at the juncture, as also is the base of the parent bulb. Fungicide preparations dusted in the hole before planting will cure the problem, and even badly affected bulbs should be perfectly healthy next year. Botrytis attacks the foliage and stems only, and is recognised by the presence of large, rust-coloured spots or blotches on the foliage. These later turn whitish or bleached looking, developing a grey mould. This disease can attack at any time during the growing period and affects all species of liliums, whether in the wild or in cultivation. It usually appears after late frosts, hail or wind damage, which allows the spores to gain an entrance into the bruised portions. Affected foliage should be removed to minimise the spread of the trouble and the tops sprayed with a fungicide. Usually the bulbs appear quite healthy the following season.

Lilium species

The following species and varieties are easily grown under normal conditions.

L. auratum, the golden-rayed mountain lily of Japan, probably created a greater sensation than any other plant when introduced in 1862. Millions are grown and exported to all parts of the world, yet few really happy clumps are seen. It is not particular as to soil, providing no lime is present, but the secrets of success are healthy stock and perfect drainage. Vigorous young bulbs 5–7.5 cm (2–3 in.) across, carrying healthy roots and no loose scales, should prove to be suitable. They are to be preferred to large over-fed bulbs, which, although attractive to buy, are usually disappointing. A position among low-growing shrubs, where the top and flower-head meet the sun, is usually ideal. There are many desirable forms of this lilium: L. auratum 'Platy-

phyllum' has larger flowers, broader leaves and is more robust than the type; 'Crimson Queen' carries a broad band of red shading to pink at the edges, some forms varying in intensity; while 'Rubro-vittatum' is somewhat similar but the yellow central band down the petals gives way to deep red or crimson, the rest of the flower being more heavily spotted. L. auratum 'Virginale' is pure white, unspotted, with a central, golden yellow band. It has been extensively hybridised with L. speciosum.

L. candidum, the beautiful, pure white Madonna lily, is probably the oldest and best-known of any cottage garden lily. Unfortunately, it is a lily that is rather subject to botrytis, but with healthy stock and a suitable situation, it is one of the easiest and hardiest lilies grown. Bulbs should be planted with the top only about 2.5 cm (1 in.) below the surface in light soils and barely covered in heavier, and will succeed better with sharp drainage and a hot, dry summer and autumn.

L. chalcedonicum, the brilliant scarlet-flowered

Lilium auratum, pink

Lilium formosanum, white form

Turk's cap lily, also known as the scarlet martagon, is a glorious lily, with its strong, recurved, brilliant flowers, 7.5 cm (3 in.) across, two to eight carried on stems 60–90 cm (24–36 in.) tall. A more robust form, lightly spotted with purple, is called 'Maculatum'.

L. davidii (syn. *L. pseudo-tigrinum,* *L. sutchuense*). This elegant and graceful species, with its numerous cinnabar-red, reflexed flowers, is in some respects similar to *L. tigrinum* var. *splendens* but is more choice and refined. It is a prolific grower, forming numerous small bulbs on underground stems; these small bulbs often bloom the first year after removal. A selected form is known as *L. davidii* var. *macranthum,* and is superior to the type in every respect, the colour being more of a bright orange-red shade. Plant bulbs 15 cm (6 in.) deep.

L. formosanum is a popular, strong-growing lily, which reaches a height of 1.5–2 m (5–6.5 ft) or more if well grown. The narrow trumpets, 22.5 cm (9 in.) long, are reflexed at the mouth, pure white, creamy in the throat and flushed purple-brown on the exterior. A most desirable pure white-flowered form is known as 'Wilsons White'. An alpine form called

L. formosanum 'Pricei', growing only 60 cm (24 in.) high, with one or two blooms to a stem, is more suitable for florists' use. All forms are easily raised from seed if sown as soon as ripe, bulbs often blooming the following autumn. Yearling or small two-year-old bulbs are better than older bulbs, as this is a lily that loses health once it reaches maturity.

L. hansonii seems to be one of the few lilies that is not subject to the various diseases that affect other species. It belongs to the *L. martagon* group, with partly reflexed, pleasingly fragrant, orange-yellow flowers, spotted brownish red, usually six to 12 carried on stems 1 m (3 ft) tall. Good drainage and cold winter climates seems to be preferred.

L. henryi. This hardy lily is sometimes called the orange speciosum. Although lacking the refinement of some other lilies, it is a valuable, easily grown, late-blooming species, and when really happy, produces enormous bulbs with flower-stems up to 2 m (6.5 ft) tall. The nodding, reflexed, unspotted flowers, an orange-yellow colour, carry a prominent green, central line.

L. longiflorum. There are many forms of this well-known Christmas lily, but the oldest and best-known is *L. longiflorum* 'Harrisii', also called *L. eximeum,* and generally known as the Bermuda lily. 'White Queen', known in America as the 'Croft Lily', is another variety worth growing. A desirable, quickly maturing form known as *L. longiflorum praecox* will bloom within 18 months from seed sown.

L. martagon. This hardy lily is popular and easily grown in England but is not so happy in warmer climates, where a cool, shady spot should be chosen. The common type grows to a height of 1–1.8 m (3–6 ft), with numerous, glossy, purple-red, much-reflexed blooms of waxy substance, 10–50 on a stem. Several most desirable wine-red, purplish black, claret-red and even pinkish forms are grown, and these colours can usually be secured by raising a batch of seedlings from good types. The lovely, pure white *L. martagon* 'Album' is also a most desirable and easily grown lily. Attractive hybrids between *L. martagon* and *L. hansonii* vary in colour from citron-yellow, through bronzy orange to light purplish yellow, all with reddish spots.

L. pardalinum, the panther lily of California and Oregon, with its many forms, is one of the hardiest and most dependable species. It will thrive in almost any soil or position, is not averse to heavy clayish soil, and is happy on the edge of streams, ponds or in open woodlands. The type carries loosely branched heads of rich orange, recurved flowers, flushed to red on the tips of the petals. The form known as 'Giganteum', which some authorities consider to be a natural hybrid, will grow to a height of 1.8 m (6 ft), the prevailing colour being rich vermillion-red, passing to orange-red at the tips of the petals, the centre of the flower being deep gold and covered with purple spots. Another form with bright orange-yellow flowers and broad, almost glaucous leaves is called *L. pardalinum* 'Pallidifolium'; still another richly coloured variety is known as 'Johnsonii'. Bulbs, which are rhizomatous, increase quickly by division, but they can be raised from the small scales.

L. pumilum (syn. *L. tenuifolium*) is a charming little lily, with slender stems and narrow, grassy leaves, the neat, reflexed flowers being of the brightest vivid scarlet. The bulbs are small, seldom exceeding 2.5 cm (1 in.) across, so that to secure the desired effect either in a pocket of the rockery or in the front border, a dozen or more bulbs should be planted in one group. The flower-stems usually grow about 45 cm (18 in.) high, carrying four to 12 blooms, although if really happy in a sandy loam with a mixture of leaf mould, this lily will reach 1 m (3 ft) or more. A lovely, golden-orange form is called 'Golden Gleam'. Stocks are easily raised from seed,

Lilium pyrenaicum

bulbs blooming the second season but reaching full size the third year.

L. pyrenaicum. Although not as common as it might be, this lily is easily grown and disease resistant. It is commonly called the yellow Turk's cap, on account of its marbled, reflexed, yellow flowers, spotted black. A brownish red form, equally hardy and easily grown, is called *L. pyrenaicum* 'Rubrum'. The flower-stems, carrying six to 10 blooms and growing to a height of 75 cm (30 in.), are densely covered with rich green, fine, narrow leaves. The blooms carry a rather strong perfume, rather precluding their use for indoor decorations.

L. regale. This splendid lily has proved to be the hardiest and most popular lily grown. The slender, wiry stems, 0.6–1.5 m (2–5 ft) high, carry from four to 30 or more large, funnel-shaped flowers, more or less wine-coloured on the outside, pure white and lustrous on the face, and clear canary-yellow within the tube. A pure white-flowered form known as *L. regale* 'Album' is grown, as are other selected forms.

Lilium pardalinum

L. speciosum, also sometimes referred to as *L. lancifolium*, is one of the most popular and best-known species. The two most plentiful forms, 'Rubrum' and 'Album', are often called by the rather misleading common names of pink or white tiger lily. A superior, glistening, white-flowered form with a green central stripe down each petal is called 'Kraetzeri', while a ruby-red-flowered variety much deeper in colour than the common pink forms is known as 'Magnificum'. All forms of *L. speciosum* are valuable, autumn-flowering lilies and are among the last to bloom. Increase is usually from natural division and the small bulbs formed on the top of the parent bulbs, as well as from scales.

L. testaceum, commonly known as the nankeen lily, is thought to be a natural hybrid between *L. candidum* and *L. chalcedonicum*. It grows up to 1.5 m (5 ft) tall, with yellow-orange flowers.

L. tigrinum, the well-known tiger lily, is perhaps the oldest lily known in cultivation, and never fails to provide a bold display in the autumn. The common type produces large heads of reflexed, deep orange-red flowers, heavily spotted with purple. The double-flowered *L. tigrinum* 'Flore Pleno' is also plentiful and attractive. Most forms of *L. tigrinum* grow to a height of 1–1.5 m (3–5 ft) and are readily increased from the numerous stem bulbs, which should be planted in the autumn as soon as they become detached. These bulbs flower the second year, reaching full size the third year.

L. umbellatum is the name for the brilliant orange, orange-red and flame-red, erect-flowering cottage lilies. There are at least 20 or 30 forms, from the lovely 'Alice Wilson', with its lemon-yellow, upturned flowers, 10 cm (4 in.) across, to 'Early Dazzler', broad petalled, deep red, and 'Grandiflorum', a rich orange shaded to red at the tips. Most bloom in late spring.

L. wilmottiae is a hardy, easily grown lily, with pyramidal heads of recurved, rich orange-red flowers, 10–30 on a stem. The slender, grassy foliage of rich green covers the stem, which attains a height of 1.2 m (4 ft). Several forms are known, a number of which appear in catalogues as *L. maxwill*, *L. davmottiae* and others. This lily is now considered to be a geographical form of *L. davidii*.

Lilium hybrids

The Royal Horticultural Society and the North

Lilium longiflorum

American Lily Society have classified the hybrid lilies as follows. Under each group, we list some of the best cultivars currently available.

Division 1: Asiatic hybrids
These are stem rooting and grow to 75–100 cm (30–40 in.). They include the mid-century hybrids raised by Jan de Graaf in Oregon, and a wide range of hybrids is now available. Some are upward facing, other outward facing, and a few have pendant flowers. All are hardy everywhere, but in warmer districts they are not so long-lived. 'Enchantment', orange-red, and 'Fire', flame-red, are two well-known varieties, but there are at least 30 more, including:

'Guardsman'—upward-facing, brilliant, wine-red flowers on a well-spaced stem with up to 18 buds; 1 m (3 ft).
'Firecracker'—deep cherry-red, upward facing; a very good cut flower; 70 cm (28 in.).
'Golden Wonder'—upward facing, soft yellow; very early flowering; good in the garden and for cutting; 1 m (3 ft).

'Miss Alice'—upward facing, soft red flushed with cream in the throat, wide petals open flat; 1 m (3 ft).

'Misty Moon'—ivory-cream flowers of good texture lined with red-brown on the petals; 75 cm (30 in.).

'Sarah Aimee'—white flowers flushed with gold; plenty of flowers on the stem; 1 m (3 ft).

'Sweetheart'—clear, pale pink without spots or markings, a new and lovely colour; 1 m (3 ft).

'Trade Winds'—this tall lily has striking, golden-yellow flowers, almost spotless; excellent for the back of the border; 1.5 m (5 ft).

Division 2

These are the hybrids of *L. martagon* and *L. hansonii*. They are woodland plants so they like a natural or acid soil and light shade.

'Bunting'—a selection with deep pink buds opening to shell pink fusing into cream, with tiny maroon spots; summer flowering.

'Dalhansonii'—dainty Turk's cap flowers with darker markings; early flowering.

'Nepera'—a martagon lily with bright, rusty-orange flowers with darker markings.

Division 3

This group covers *L. candidum*, the madonna lily, and hybrids and forms. Transplant when necessary in autumn, with no more than 2.5 cm (1 in.) of soil above the top of the bulb. Leaves will quickly follow, and flowers will appear in early summer.

Division 4

These are hybrids of the North American lilies, mostly the progeny of *L. parryi* and *L. pardalinum*. They are tall lilies up to 2 m (6.5 ft), with many pendant, reflexed flowers on a stem, and they come in yellow, orange and red shades. The Bellingham hybrids are popular and easy only in colder districts.

Division 5

This section includes any hybrids and selections of *L. longiflorum*, called the Easter lily in the Northern Hemisphere and the Christmas lily in the Southern. 'Dutch Glory' is a hybrid that has extra vigour as long as virus-free stock can be obtained. The F1 hybrid form of *L. longiflorum* has wonderful vigour and grows to 1.8 m (6 ft) tall, flowering in mid-summer. The pure white trumpets are magnificent.

Division 6

These are trumpet lilies derived from various Asiatic species, and are known as Aurelian and Olympic lilies. They are stem rooting, so should be planted with 10 cm (4 in.) of soil over the bulb. Some have pendant flowers, many have wide-open trumpets in a variety of colours. Popular cultivars include:

'Bright Star'—tall spikes of reflexed, white flowers with orange centres.

'Copper King'—rich, coppery orange trumpets.

'First Love'—sunburst form in melon-tangerine shades; 1 m (3 ft).

'Golden Splendour'—brilliant golden yellow trumpets.

'New Era'—well-formed but smaller trumpets of pale cream; late flowering.

'Pink Perfection'—magenta-rose trumpets, paler in the throat.

'Waireka'—deep apricot trumpets; a very fine hybrid.

'White Perfection'—sparkling white trumpet, lemon throat.

The strains grown from seed can be recommended.

Lilium speciosum hybrid

Lilium 'Waireka'

Division 7

These are known as Oriental hybrids and are derived from *L. speciosum* and *L. auratum*. All are stem rooting and need 10 cm (4 in.) of soil above the bulb. These lilies grow especially well in the warmer areas and on light soils. They are arranged in two groups according to flower shape.

Auratum hybrids have bowl-shaped, very large flowers.

'Caesars Robe'—carmine-red, edged pure white.
'Emerald'—white tinged with green, spotted.
'Erebus'—enormous open flowers, dark red.
'Journeys End'—flat flowers, slightly reflexed, all red.
'Kim Pink'—huge, luminous, carmine-pink.
'Red King Melford'—very large, clean bright red; 1 m (3 ft).
'Rose Queen'—rich pink shaded salmon, white edges.
'Wildfire'—somewhat reflexed, deep plum with dark spots; 2 m (6.5 ft).

Speciosum hybrids have reflexed flowers.

'Black Beauty'—vigorous, very dark maroon; 2 m (6.5 ft) stems.
'Dawnette'—lovely pastel pink, spotted deeper pink; 1.2 m (4 ft).

'Shooting Star'—large star-shaped, brilliant cerise-red, edged white.
'Ushida'—rosy crimson with fine white edge
'White Opal'—large, pure white, open flower; light, pale lilac spotting.

Division 8

All other hybrids. All the species are in this group, and those generally grown in gardens are described in previous pages.

LIMONIUM
Plumbaginaceae   Statice

This genus has about 300 species of annuals, perennials and sub-shrubs.

L. caspium is a European species without much garden value, but some hybrids of it are very popular with florists. These include 'Misty Blue', 'Misty Pink' and 'Misty White'. They have a profusion of tiny flowers on slender spikes 1.5 m (5 ft) tall on established plants. Plant in groups on a well-drained site in full sun.

L. incanum is probably the best-known species, the dried cut flowers of which are very popular. The plant forms a flat rosette of leaves, from the centre of which arise stiff, erect stems, densely branching at the top to form flattish heads of tiny, flesh-pink

Limonium perezii

flowers. The type is variable if raised from seed, so better selected forms should be increased from pieces of root. 'Dumosum' is a desirable form, growing about 50 cm (20 in.) tall.

L. latifolium, although not so attractive, is useful on account of the delicate, misty appearance of the dried flower-stems, which can be mixed with other flowers. The much-branched, leafless stems, up to 60 cm (24 in.) high, carry hundreds of tiny, pale lavender-blue or bluish white flowers. A selected form called 'Violetta' has deep lilac-violet flowers, and another variation, 'Rosea', shows more of the pinkish tone. It is a deep-rooting plant and it often covers a considerable area. It forms a plant 60–90 cm (24–36 in.) across and half as tall, with deep green, leathery leaves 7.5 cm (3 in.) long and half as wide, preferring free soil and full sun. Increase is from seed sown in the spring or from pieces of roots, 5 cm (2.5 in.) long, inserted upright in sand until the foliage appears. Transplant during winter and early spring.

L. peregrinum (syn. *L. roseum*) is a shrubby species that grows well in coastal, sandy soils. Spreading terminal panicles on 15–25 cm (6–10 in.) stems carry numerous bright pink, starry, kalmia-like flowers, much larger than those of any other species. When cut and dried, these retain their attractive colour over a long period, sometimes for years, and are most decorative. The plant is reasonably hardy, withstanding frosts of at least 12 degrees, although it needs protection the first season or when young. Full sun and good drainage are essential for success with this lovely plant.

L. perezii is the giant of the race and one of the finest species grown, but unfortunately it is half-hardy and will not withstand frosts over six degrees, unless in sheltered sunny spots. It can be grown as a pot plant in colder districts. It has large, ovate, shining, deep green leaves and broad trusses of rich violet flowers with a few white ones intermingled. These are produced very freely in early summer and continuously in warmer areas. Light soil and good drainage in full sun will give the best results. The flowers can be dried for winter decorations. Increase is from fresh seed if available, or else by layers. Cuttings are not easy to strike, but the lower side shoots root more readily than the main tips.

Other perennial species worth growing are *L. gmelinii*, with its rosette of basal leaves and 60 cm (24

Limonium caspium 'Misty Blue'

in.), thinly branched scapes of small, tubular, coral-pink flowers, and *L. caesium*, growing only 30 cm (12 in.) high, with stout, much-branched panicles of pink flowers in spring.

Plants of all species or varieties of limonium are best increased from seed although stocks of special forms or colours can be increased from root cuttings of the herbaceous varieties and top cuttings of the sub-shrubby species. They are best transplanted during winter or early spring.

LINARIA
Scrophulariaceae　　　　　　　　　　　Toad flax

In addition to annual species, there are several good perennials, which generally prefer a well-drained soil in the sun.

L. genistifolia has tall spikes of citron-yellow flowers similar to snapdragons, growing to 90 cm

(36 in.), with glaucous foliage. *L. genistifolia* subsp. *dalmatica* (syn. *L. macedonica*) is another erect perennial, with racemes of primrose-yellow flowers in summer and autumn, growing 60–90 cm (24–36 in.) tall.

L. purpurea is the purple toad flax, but the most popular form is 'Canon Went', with slender spikes of pink snapdragon flowers. Established plants may be divided in autumn or spring.

LINUM
Linaceae   Perennial flax

This genus of about 230 species, distributed widely in temperate regions, embraces a number of splendid hardy perennials.

L. arboreum is a desirable species forming a bush of rounded, blue-green leaves, with heads of bright daffodil-yellow flowers the size and shape of the common periwinkle. It is deservedly valued in England but seldom seen in the Southern Hemisphere.

L. flavum is a compact-growing species up to 40 cm (16 in.) tall, with bluish grey leaves and good-sized, transparent, golden flowers covering the much-branched heads.

L. narbonense produces numerous, erect, thin, wiry stems, very much branched, clothed with small, narrow, deep green leaves, and arching over at the top. During late spring and summer, the plant carries an abundance of 3 cm (1.5 in.) wide, open, funnel-shaped, bright blue flowers. A selected form known as 'Six Hills' is a lovely sky blue. This is probably one of our best true blue perennials, forming a neat bush up to 60 cm (24 in.) tall, blooming over a long period.

L. perenne (syn. *L. sibiricum*) is the most vigorous of all the species, forming a shapely, bushy plant up to 45 cm (18 in.) tall, and well covered with light blue flowers. A pure white form, 'Alba', is also available.

All the species are quite easy to raise from seed, cuttings or pieces of root taken during winter. Full sun is necessary, and they prefer a light free soil. Transplant from late autumn till early spring.

LIRIOPE
Liliaceae   Turf lily

Of the six species recorded in this genus, *L. muscari* is the one most commonly grown. It used to be known as *Ophiopogon spicatus*. This interesting plant from Japan is suitable for grouping under trees, where it will stand considerable dryness and shade, while it has its uses as an edging or border plant. It is grown as a pot plant in Europe, being not quite hardy outside. Broad, grassy foliage, always neat

Liriope muscari

Liriope muscari, variegated form

and tidy during spring and summer, is followed by spikes of lilac-purple flowers in the autumn. It always arrests attention, as the immediate impression is that it is a grape hyacinth blooming out of season. A number of selected forms are grown, including one with attractive, silvery, variegated foliage. It is quite useful as a cut flower.

The plant does not exceed 45 cm (18 in.) in height. If plants are raised from seed, some interesting varieties occasionally occur, from deep purple to bluish white. The roots are somewhat tuberous and are drought-resistant. They are readily divided and transplanted in winter and spring.

LITHODORA
Boraginaceae

L. diffusa (syn. *Lithospermum diffusa*) is a prostrate, shrubby plant, popular on account of its small but vivid blue flowers throughout spring. It is an excellent wall plant in any position that is not excessively hot and dry in summer. Popular cultivars include 'Heavenly Blue', gentian blue, and 'Grace Ward', which has slightly larger flowers.

Plants should be trimmed back after flowering. Propagation is by cuttings taken in mid-summer or by seed sown in autumn.

LITTONIA
Liliaceae

This genus of only two species is related to the gloriosa. *L. modesta* is a semi-climbing plant, attaining a height of 1 m (3 ft) or more, with bright, shining green leaves so extenuated as to become tendrils. The 5 cm (2 in.), bell-shaped flowers are bright yellow, produced singly on a short pedicel between the axil of the leaves and stem. Although the stems are reasonably strong, some support is needed to prevent the tops drooping during the flowering stage in the autumn. If planted in groups among the low-growing shrubs, which provide this light support, the effect is quite pleasing. The flowers are followed by large seed-pods, which when ripe split open, revealing bright orange-red seeds. These germinate

Littonia modesta

freely if sown in autumn or spring, resulting in flowering-sized roots the second season. Like the gloriosas, the interesting, fleshy tubers are often two-pronged and, being entirely devoid of fibrous roots during winter, can be lifted and stored out of the ground like dry bulbs. Although it is not generally considered to be hardy, *L. modesta* can be successfully grown in a climate with a very cold winter if the roots are lifted when dormant in the autumn, stored during the winter and replanted in spring. If left undisturbed, roots will not withstand more than 12 degrees of frost, preferring a sunny, well-drained situation.

LOBELIA
Lobeliaceae

This genus of over 200 species comprises annuals, perennials and shrubs. The numerous varieties of blue annual lobelias are well-known and deservedly popular border plants, but the perennial species, while revealing the relationship in the shape of the blooms, are entirely different in habit.

Lobelia x *vedrariensis*

All the perennial lobelias, being very shallow-rooted, cannot tolerate dry conditions for more than a few weeks, so they need to be planted in a moist spot. A cold, semi-shady position may give quite good results if there are no overhanging plants or shrubs nearby.

L. cardinalis, the cardinal flower, is the true species, seldom met with in gardens. It usually has green foliage, and the terminal spikes of brilliant scarlet flowers on 1 m (3 ft) tall scapes are one-sided. It is a variable species in height and colour, and some interesting types can be secured if raised from seed.

L. laxiflora is an interesting sub-shrub or perennial, in which the new flower-stems continue to appear throughout the year in milder climates, the plants being seldom without some bloom. It forms a strong bush, abundant with erect, lightly branched, thin stems, well clothed with lanceolate, slender-pointed, sharply toothed leaves, and carrying 5 cm (2 in.) long, open-mouthed flowers, red and yellow,

produced on long axillary pedicels. These appear at the tips of the branches, interspersed among the foliage. At no time does a spectacular display occur, although the greatest show appears during late spring. This plant can be readily increased by division at any time.

L. siphilitica is the hardiest species known. The light green leaves are closely set and form a leafy spike up to 75 cm (30 in.) tall, studded with light blue flowers in the autumn. It prefers moisture and semi-shade, but is generally easily cultivated.

L. splendens (syn. *L. fulgens*) is the best-known and most popular perennial species. A hardy plant, hailing from the mountain states of eastern North America, it is found growing wild in swamps, wet places and stream sides, but always in the open, as it quickly collapses if overshadowed by other plants. In its wild state it is valued for the colour of the flower, which is usually a bright red although sometimes pink or white, and also for its foliage, which is generally brilliant green. The selected form grown in gardens has 60–90 cm (24–36 in.) spikes of brilliant scarlet-red flowers and rich, shining, bronzy red foliage, with very little variation in colour if raised from seed. A hybrid called 'Queen Victoria' produces brilliant scarlet-red flowers and a still deeper bronzy purple foliage. This form is usually offered wrongly under the name of *L. cardinalis*.

Some interesting hybrids have been raised in England in various shades of pink to purple. In New Zealand a hybrid named 'Flamingo' has proved excellent, growing over 1 m (3 ft) tall, with good spikes of deep salmon-pink and green foliage. Some dwarf strains called 'Dwarf Gallery' are now available.

L. tupa is an interesting and little-known species from Chile. It is a giant of the race, established clumps often producing flower-spikes over 2 m (6.5 ft) in height. The stems are thick and shrub-like at the base, the oval, pointed leaves are soft and downy, and the terminal spike-like racemes 1 m (3 ft) long are composed of hundreds of reddish scarlet flowers, produced in the late summer, continuing until April. An established clump throws several of these stems and lower spikes, producing an attractive display for the back of the herbaceous border. The plant prefers a hot, dry autumn and good winter drainage, but otherwise it is hardy and easy to grow. It is a plant that resents disturbance when once established, and the only practical method of increase is from seed.

L. x *vedrariensis* is an excellent border plant. The erect scapes of bloom, usually on unbranched stems 1 m (3 ft) or more, are a rich shade of violet-blue, but there is a wide range of selected colours now available. It demands full sun but a situation that never becomes very dry.

Increase of perennial lobelias is usually from divisions of established clumps, which should be broken up in any case every two or three years, as quite often the central, fleshy roots develop a rot that spreads through the whole of the plant. Seed is very tiny but germinates readily in damp soil or on finely chopped sphagnum moss. Transplant from late autumn until early spring.

Lupinus polyphyllus, Russell strain

LOTUS
Fabaceae

This is a genus of perennials and sub-shrubs from the Canary Islands. One species is grown—*L. berthelottii*—which has sprays of coral-coloured pea flowers on silvery foliage to a height of 40–60 cm (16–24 in.). This attractive, spreading plant requires a fairly sunny situation on light or sandy soil, but it is suitable for warm coastal gardens as it is not very frost hardy. Propagation is by cuttings taken in summer or seed sown in spring or autumn.

LUPINUS
Fabaceae

Over 300 species of this genus have been described, and many hybrids have been raised. Most are natives of western North America, where annual, shrubby and herbaceous species are frequent. The well-known and popular herbaceous lupins grown in gardens today have been derived from *L. polyphyllus*, which in its wild state produces racemes of bloom in deep blue, purple, a reddish colour, yellow and white.

The Russell strain of lupins has entirely superseded all earlier varieties in the size of blooms and spikes. The main distinguishing feature between the Russell lupin and the older forms lies in the standard or upper part of the flower. In the older varieties this upper standard was closed, often revealing the naked stem. In the Russell varieties, this standard is broad, spreading and shield-like, and thereby gives greater substance to the spike, entirely hiding the central stem. Seed from guaranteed stocks of the Russell strains yields a high percentage of first-class plants, while a big range of named varieties is also offered now for sale.

The modern herbaceous lupins, like the present delphiniums, are comparatively short-lived unless

Lotus berthelottii

clumps are divided every two years in warm districts, or three to four years in cold climates. When roots become large they are often attacked by a root rot known as *Sclerotinia sclerotiorum*. In light, poor or pumice soils, very little of this trouble occurs. Lupins are acid-loving plants and will not tolerate lime in any form, nor will they grow well on heavy, clay soils. When grown in warmer climates, they often flower with a single spike, whereas in colder areas plants may have eight or 10 spikes. In some areas of New Zealand they have even become naturalised.

Plants should be set out during winter or spring. Cuttings from parent plants should be removed close up against the rootstock when the new shoots are 2.5–5 cm (1–2 in.) long. They should be potted up or inserted in boxes of sand, and kept in a shady place until rooted. Cuttings must be given plenty of air and shaded from direct sunlight, and are best held in bush or lath houses, not under glass, otherwise they quickly damp off. Rooted cuttings planted out in spring will bloom freely in the autumn.

Plants are best raised from seed, if good seed from selected parents or named varieties is available. Of course, the very best plants will be the named varieties, which have been raised from cuttings or divisions.

LYCHNIS
Caryophyllaceae   Campion

This is a large and variable genus.

L. chalcedonica is the best-known species, commonly called the Maltese or Jerusalem cross, on account of the shape of the four-petalled blooms. It is one of the oldest hardy perennials grown and is still a popular border plant. It forms a compact clump from which arise thin, hard stems 60 cm (24 in.) long, with rounded, phlox-like, terminal heads of brilliant scarlet or brick-red flowers. There is a very fine, double red-flowered form called 'Rubra Plena', which remains in bloom over a longer period than do the single-flowered varieties as it does not set seed. Single pink, rose and even pure white varieties are known.

L. x *arkwrightii* is a cross involving *L. chalcedonica* that produces 30 cm (12 in.) tall heads of vivid, deep

Lychnis x *arkwrightii*

orange-scarlet flowers, each 5 cm (2 in.) across, continuing its display from late spring until early autumn. The other parent, *L.* 'Haagiana', itself a hybrid, produces varying shades of salmon, flame and scarlet, with slightly smaller flowers. Both are very showy garden plants but unfortunately they are weak growers and usually short-lived. As they reproduce readily from seed, a fresh stock should be kept coming along each year.

L. coronaria is a desirable species, with silvery, woolly, densely leafed, non-flowering shoots at the base. It produces during early summer flower-stems 45 cm (18 in.) high, headed with starry, laciniated, single flowers 5 cm (2 in.) across in shades of pink, white or purplish red. This species is often grown as a silver edging or border plant for its foliage alone. A selected form known as 'Abbotswood Rose' is preferable to the variable seedling-raised stock. This variety produces an abundance of vivid magenta-crimson flowers, covering the compact, 60 cm (24 in.), rounded bush. As has been suggested by others, the name 'Abbotswood Brilliant' would have been more appropriate. *L. coronaria* 'Alba' is an excellent 60 cm (24 in.), white-flowered plant.

L. flos-jovis is a well-known, old-time favourite, mostly grown for its thick, woolly, silvery foliage, although it is not unattractive when in bloom, the masses of purple or red flowers being carried on 60 cm (24 in.) stems. It is a useful foliage plant for brightening up the herbaceous border at a time when few other plants are in bloom.

L. fulgens is a species similar in habit to *L. chalcedonica* but its stems are usually shorter and woolly, with leaves rather thick and the flower-heads purple or scarlet.

L. viscaria 'Splendens Plena' forms a neat, densely tufted clump resembling the armerias, with single leaves somewhat longer and usually bronzed at the tip during winter. The flower-stems are 30–45 cm (12–18 in.) long and the blooms are arranged in a raceme. In the double form they closely resemble a miniature head of double-flowered annual stock, in an attractive shade of rosy pink, paler at the centre. This plant forms a suitable edging for a large herbaceous border, as the uniform tufts of bronzy green foliage are attractive at all times, while the massed display of bloom is also impressive. Unlike the other less-attractive species, it never seeds down to become a nuisance in the garden. Full sun and good drainage are preferred, otherwise plants may collapse in the winter or during wet spells.

All the lychnis species are easily raised from seed sown in the spring or autumn, and old clumps can be divided up during winter or while dormant. Increase of selected forms and varieties must be from divisions of older clumps. Late autumn or early winter planting is preferable if a good crop of bloom is desired the first spring.

Lychnis coronaria 'Alba'

LYCORIS
Amaryllidaceae   Spider lilies

These handsome, bulbous plants are closely related to the nerines. There are about 17 distinct species, all natives of Japan and China.

L. africana (syn. *L. aurea*), the golden spider lily, is a lovely species, with its large umbels of bright yellow flowers on 40 cm (16 in.) stems, but it is happy only in warm districts and under ideal conditions. It is a very choice subject for the connoisseur. It will grow and flower well in a shady, well-drained spot protected from heavy winter frosts, and it will also do well in pots. It demands a decided rest during the dormant season. As is the case with all half-hardy bulbs of the amaryllis family, the autumn and winter foliage must not suffer damage at all, as new leaves will not appear or be replaced until the next season. Good rich foliage sustained over a long growing period, free, sharp drainage, and a decided summer rest—the drier the better—will result in fat bulbs and good blooms. *L. incarnata* is similar in habit but much hardier, with large, pale flesh- to rose-coloured flowers, and as with *L. aurea*, the segments are prominent and not much waved or reflexed.

L. radiata, commonly called the Japanese spider lily, is the most common, easiest grown and hardiest species. During early autumn the scapes appear, 40 cm (16 in.) in height, and carry four to six flowers with waved and recurved segments. The numerous stamens, protruding as much as 7.5 cm (3 in.) from the centre, give the fascinating spidery appearance. The colour is best described as a dull scarlet-red, and the leaves, which are strap-like, resembling nerines, follow when the flowers have faded. Although easy to grow and withstanding quite heavy frosts, it is a subject that must have free drainage and prefers a good hot baking in full sun when dormant during late spring and summer. The number of flower-scapes produced in the autumn seems dependent upon such conditions prevailing, as few blooms follow a wet summer. There is also a little-known, creamy white-flowered form of this species called *L. radiata* 'Alba'.

L. squamigera is a hardy species, which produces a large bulb, 5–7.5 cm (2–3 in.) across, and a strong fleshy root system. During summer it throws up 60

Lycoris radiata

cm (24 in.), naked stems, topped with four to seven fragrant, trumpet-shaped, rosy-lilac flowers, glistening and silvery in appearance. A darker-flowered form called *L. squamigera* 'Purpurea' has deeper lilac-purple blooms. This desirable bulb unfortunately does not bloom very freely except in ideal conditions provided by good drainage and a hot, dry summer, but the flower-scapes are singularly attractive, well worth waiting for and good for cutting.

Increase is from bulb offsets, which should be planted early in the autumn, either before or after flowering.

LYSICHITON
Araceae

This genus consists of two robust marsh plants, one from eastern Asia and the other from North America. The striking and ornamental yellow or white spathes, produced in early spring, are followed by tufts of bold arum-like foliage, which arise from a creeping rhizome. These are hardy perennials for the bog garden or damp spots. They are easily raised from seed but are almost impossible to divide.

Plants grown from seed will reach flowering size the third season. They do not grow well in warmer areas, apparently requiring a cold and frosty winter climate.

L. americanum produces roundish spathes of pale yellow, 10 cm (4 in.) wide and 15 cm (6 in.) long, but unfortunately yields a rather offensive odour. *L. camtschatcense* is pure white with narrower and longer spathes, blooming a month later than the American species.

Lysichiton americanum

LYSIMACHIA
Primulaceae   Loosestrife

This genus consists of over 100 species of perennials and a few shrubs, scattered throughout the world. Several interesting species of hardy, herbaceous perennials are in cultivation. All species enjoy moist soil conditions, and are easily grown and freely increased from divisions of old clumps.

L. clethroides is an erect-growing, seldom-branched, downy-foliaged perennial, the stems of which are clothed with ovate-lanceolate leaves up to 15 cm (6 in.) long, which take on deep crimson and orange-scarlet colourings in autumn before dying down. The slender, arching spikes of milk-white flowers, to 1 m (3 ft), drooping at the tip, resemble

Lysimachia ephemerum

a small kniphofia head. These appear during late spring and summer, and are very useful cut flowers. The plant grows to about 1 m (3 ft) and is a very useful subject for the herbaceous border, soon forming a strong clump. The roots should be divided up and replanted every second season.

L. ephemerum is a clump-forming perennial that grows to 1 m (3 ft) high. It has leathery, grey-green leaves and erect spikes of starry, white flowers.

L. nummularia (creeping Jenny) is a low ground cover, the yellow form of which makes an attractive patch of colour in summer in semi-shade.

L. punctata, sometimes known as the yellow loosestrife, is also an erect-growing perennial. The 60 cm (24 in.) stems are lightly branched at the top and carry, in mid-summer, a great massed display of brilliant yellow, starry, 2.5 cm (1 in.) wide flowers, produced in whorls near the top of the stem.

LYTHRUM
Lythraceae   Loosestrife

About 30 species of this genus are recognised, mostly inhabiting swampy, marshy ground, some even growing in water. They take kindly to culti-

vation and thrive well in almost any soil without requiring moist conditions.

L. salicaria is the common purple loosestrife, which makes a leafy bush up to 1.2 m (4 ft) high, with woody lower stems and tapering 'fingers' of reddish purple bloom, 22.5–40 cm (9–16 in.) long. Several selected forms in better colours are grown and are popular hardy perennials. 'The Beacon', with its bright rosy red colour, is the most spectacular. Others worth growing are 'Lady Sackville', deep pink, 'Morden's Pink', and 'Robert', both good pinks in different shades.

L. virgatum is not so tall, with smaller, dark green leaves, and branching flower-heads up to 1 m (3 ft). The form usually offered, and superior to the type, is called 'Rose Queen', a lovely rich pink with a tinge of purple. This is one of the showiest and most reliable summer-flowering, hardy perennials. Another form called 'The Rocket' provides a fine display, with deeper pink flowers.

The roots of lythrum, being hardy and woody, are difficult to divide, but stocks are readily increased from cuttings, removed when a few centimetres high. Transplant during winter months.

Lythrum virgatum 'Rose Queen'

M

MACLEAYA
Papaveraceae   Plume poppy

This genus of two species was until recently classified under the name of *Bocconia*. It is considered distinct because of the palmate appearance of the leaves, the seed formation and herbaceous habit. Both species are very hardy, easily grown perennials, which are recommended for naturalising or filling up odd corners where nothing else will grow.

M. cordata, (syn. *M. japonica*), from China or Japan, reaches a height of 1.5–2 m (5–6.5 ft), with large, attractive, heart-shaped leaves, much lobed, glaucous, and deeply veined, and carries terminal, plumy flower-spikes of cream, tinted with pink. It is one of the most attractive foliage plants available for the herbaceous border.

M. microcarpa is more common than *M. cordata*. It has large, prominently veined leaves, and the plumy flower panicles, borne erect, are a bronzy shade; the

Macleaya microcarpa

buds are pink. This species can be very invasive, but surplus roots are easily removed in winter if they prove to be too prolific. Transplant when dormant during winter or early spring.

MALVA
Malvaceae   Mallow

This is a genus of hardy perennials from Europe.

M. alcea fastigiata is a strong-growing bush to 1.2 m (4 ft), bearing quantities of pink or red, open flowers.

M. moschata is bushy to 1 m (3 ft), with profuse pink flowers in summer. The white form, 'Alba', is the most popular.

M. sylvestris is inclined to be biennial, and has purple flowers on bushes to 1 m (3 ft).

Propagation is by seed, but selected forms must be increased from cuttings.

MECONOPSIS
Papaveraceae   Himalayan poppy

This is a genus of nearly 40 species of herbaceous plants. Most of the species in cultivation are annuals or biennials, and others are true perennials only under ideal conditions.

M. betonicifolia is a woodland species, and except in cool climates, must be grown in semi-shade and moist conditions. If really happy, the flower-stem will reach 1.2 m (4 ft) in height, with up to 30 wide-open, 10 cm (4 in.), saucer-shaped flowers of the purest sky-blue imaginable. The flowers are satiny in texture and enhanced by a central tuft of yellow stamens.

The seed, which is very fine, must be fresh, and

Meconopsis betonicifolia

sown in the early spring on finely chopped moss or sandy loam. Plants should be pricked out twice, kept from direct sunlight, and planted into their permanent position as soon as large enough before the end of spring, or else kept in deep boxes of sandy loam and leaf mould until the following spring. The rich green, hairy leaves will not stand direct sun or drying winds, so the plants need shelter as well as shade. They do not need coddling, but for success must have a cool root run, shelter from wind and sun, and free, moist soil. The plants do not bloom the first season, but if half a dozen or more large, healthy leaves have developed throughout the previous summer and autumn, fine heads of bloom can be expected the following spring. They die down completely in the winter, each plant leaving a fat, pointed crown just above the surface, often 7.5–10 cm (3–4 in.) across and deep, something like the crown of *Primula denticulata* when dormant.

Most people who have never grown this plant before apparently expect the luscious green leaves to

continue through the winter, until blooming time. The winter in Tibet is very cold, and the plant grows in open woodlands at an altitude of up to 3,000 metres, so the crowns are quite dormant until the rush of spring growth occurs. They are monocarpic usually, although occasionally perennial if conditions are ideal; the old crown dies out but side shoots continue, although seldom bloom the second year in succession. A fresh crop of young plants should be raised and set out each season to be sure of yearly displays. Transplant when roots are dormant during winter.

M. cambrica is the Welsh poppy, easily grown in any well-drained soil in full sun, where it may colonise itself from seed. The flowers are rounded, yellow or orange poppies of 4 cm (1.5 in.) diameter. The leaves are deeply cut and hairy, and grow up to 60 cm (24 in.). There is a double form called 'Flore Pleno', which is increased by careful division in early spring.

M. grandis has larger, rich blue flowers to 1.5 m (5 ft), and is considered to be an easier plant to grow, usually perennial. 'Branklyn' is similar and still more perennial.

M. integrifolia has buttercup-shaped, 8 cm (3.5 in.) wide flowers in a lovely soft yellow, carried bunch fashion on stout, 45 cm (18 in.) stems, the leaves being grey and fluffy. *M. napaulensis* produces nodding flowers, usually reddish purple or blue, on stout stems up to 2 m (6.5 ft) high. Like the preceding species it is monocarpic, but before flowering

Meconopsis regia

it forms a very beautiful rosette of brown-haired leaves for nearly a year.

M. regia is more perennial, the silky-haired leaves being decorative even in winter. In summer the branching stems of large, golden yellow poppies reach to 1.5 m (5 ft). These and other desirable species are easily raised from seed, the plants themselves being very hardy.

Transplant young growing plants in the spring and dormant roots from autumn until late winter.

MELASPHAERULA
Iridaceae

M. ramosa (syn. *M. graminea*) is a South African bulb with freesia-like foliage, flowering in early spring with slender, branching stems to 60–70 cm (24–28 in.) tall, festooned with small, cream flowers. These produce an effect similar to gypsophila, and are long-lasting and delightful in a vase. The bulbs are very small, black corms, dormant in winter, which should be planted in autumn in a sunny situation. It naturalises easily from seed.

Mertensia virginica

Melasphaerula ramosa

MERTENSIA
Boraginaceae

This genus consists of about 50 species, mostly from the cooler parts of North America. The most popular is the Virginian lungwort or blue bells, known as *M. virginica*. It is among the loveliest of all blue spring flowers, providing a constant supply of bloom for several months, or even longer in cold, shady spots. It bears smooth, oblong, green foliage of a rich metallic lustre when young, and 30–45 cm (12–18 in.) stems with clusters of rich, blue, tubular flowers about 2.5 cm (1 in.) long, 20 or more on a semi-drooping raceme. Large established clumps give a wealth of bloom at a time of the year when there is little in flower, providing a pleasing contrast to the yellow of the daffodils and polyanthus. Although this plant will grow quite well in the sun, it prefers semi-shade, and is seen at its best naturalised in woodlands or alongside banks of streams. It is commonly called the Virginian cowslip.

Although there are a number of other attractive species, many of them are classified and grown as rock plants. *M. primuloides* is a delightful border or front row plant. Growing only 15–30 cm (6–12 in.) high, it produces numerous short-stemmed, dense racemes of indigo-blue flowers, providing a lovely splash of colour in the rockery. It is essentially a spring-flowering plant, and the foliage dies down soon after flowering. Increase is from fresh seed, or divisions of clumps in the autumn or early winter.

MIMULUS
Scrophulariaceae   Monkey flower

The perennial species of this genus from the temperate areas of the Northern Hemisphere are easily grown and usually have a spreading habit. They all need moist soil in sun or shade.

M. 'Andean Nymph' has hairy leaves and rose-pink flowers with pale yellow tinge and deeper pink spots. It grows to about 20 cm (8 in.) in height and has a spreading habit.

M. cardinalis grows 30–60 cm (12–24 in.) tall with red flowers.

M. guttatus has yellow flowers spotted with red, 30–45 cm (12–18 in.) tall.

M. lewisii flowers in late summer with red or white flowers to 45 cm (18 in.).

M. luteus has yellow flowers to 45 cm (18 in.) in profusion.

Planting is usually in spring, and propagation is from seed or cuttings.

Monarda didyma

MONARDA
Lamiaceae   Bergamot

This genus consists of about a dozen species, annuals and aromatic perennials, all native to North America. *M. didyma*, with its various forms, seems to be one of the most useful. It has rather coarse foliage, with large heads of gaping, wide-mouthed flowers of brilliant scarlet on 1 m (3 ft) stems. A selected scarlet-flowered form is called 'Cambridge Scarlet'. All varieties of this species have rather shallow roots and resent very dry summer conditions. It is not very successful on heavy soils, preferring light or gravelly soils where the roots can spread easily. Nevertheless, it is easy to grow in most gardens not lacking in humus, and under ideal conditions such as moist free soil, it rapidly forms large clumps 60 cm (24 in.) across in a single growing season and, therefore, needs lifting and replanting when crowded. A shade in soft rose is called 'Croftway Pink'; 'Fire Beacon' is a brilliant light red;

Mimulus 'Andean Nymph'

'Prairie Glow' is a distinct salmon shade of pink, and delightfully scented, while the best in the deep rosy purples is called 'Prairie Night'. 'Snow Maiden' is a white-flowered cultivar but is rather less vigorous. Plants increase rapidly from divisions any time during winter.

MORAEA
Iridaceae

Moraea villosa

This is a genus of about 100 species of bulbous or herbaceous plants, Africa's contribution to the iris family. The sub-section with hard, rhizomatous rootstocks instead of corms is usually called dietes or the butterfly irises, but strictly belong under the heading of moraea. They differ from dietes in that they have small corms while the dietes have rhizomes. They have iris-like flowers with three large lower petals and three small upper petals. A number of most interesting bulbous species have been intercrossed, with the result that some attractive strains are available. Even in the *M. villosa* hybrids there is an amazing range of shades, and it is a pity that these lovely bulbs are not better known. They are not difficult to grow, but seem to prefer a free soil with a heavy pan or hard lower soil in which the bulbs bed themselves. Good drainage in full sun is essential.

M. edulis produces one long, thin leaf in the winter, and during spring throws up a single stem, which carries thickly clustered sprays of flower-buds. These buds open up during early summer, one or two blooms to each spray, lasting the day only, with fresh buds maturing the next day. The wide-open, 5 cm (2 in.) flowers are very showy, with a smooth texture and iris-like refinement. The colours vary from softest pale blue to deeper blues. They continue in flower about a month and set seed freely.

M. ramosissima grows to a height of 90 cm (36 in.), branching all the way and bearing pale yellow flowers on every branch, each flower about 40 cm (16 in.) across. Unfortunately, each flower opens only for the afternoon. Plants prefer semi-shade and are very suitable for planting among shrubs. They die down in summer.

M. spathulata is often mistaken for a yellow iris, with its strap-like leaves, often 1 m (3 ft) or more

long. It is a valuable early-blooming species, flowering in late winter in mild districts. The bright golden yellow, 10 cm (4 in.) flowers on 60–90 cm (24–36 in.) stems, held just above the foliage, which bends over at this point, are most attractive and suitable for cutting. The main disadvantage of the plant is the abundance of these long leaves, which bend over about 45 cm (18 in.) above the ground and trail over the soil. Transplant corms in late summer.

M. villosa is sometimes listed under the name of *Iris pavonia* or commonly called the peacock iris. The small, round bulb is encased in a reticulated, netted, fibrous coat, apparently intended by nature to preserve it from excessive moisture. In the well-known type, the 5 cm (2 in.) blooms on 30 cm (12 in.) stems comprise rounded petals of pale slatey blue with prominent, dark peacock eyes. Other colours raised from seed include light and dark blues, pink, orange, old gold and bronzy shades. All carry the distinctive, iridescent, peacock-blue blotch on the three rounded petals, this in turn being outlined with purple, black or other contrasting colours. These colours are usually offered as *M. villosa* hybrids, but strictly they are just mixed coloured forms of the one species.

New plants can be raised by seed sown in spring or autumn. This will produce flowering corms the second season. Transplant during autumn.

MORINA
Dipsaceae

M. longifolia is an evergreen Himalayan plant with attractive rosettes of prickly leaves and 60 cm (24 in.) spikes of curiously shaped pink and white flowers in summer. The foliage is fragrant and the stems are attractive when dried. Increase is by seed sown in early autumn or by division after flowering.

MUSCARI
Liliaceae   Grape hyacinths

All muscari are hardy, spring-flowering bulbs, of which there are about 50 species, separated from the hyacinth group mainly by the fact that the individual flowers or bells are constricted at the mouth instead of expanded or reflexed.

M. armeniacum is the common grape hyacinth, of which the old variety 'Heavenly Blue' needs no introduction. The common form gives us a prolonged display of rich cobalt-blue flowers on numerous, 10 cm (4 in.) spikes. A pretty Cambridge blue variety is known as *M. armeniacum* 'Cantab', and a double-flowered form is called 'Blue Spike'.

Muscari azureum

M. azureum (previously *Hyacinthus azureus*) differs from the other species in that the perianth segments are flared instead of incurved. This little-known but most desirable early spring-flowering bulb is very suitable for a rockery. Dense heads of miniature, tubular bells, resembling elliptical balls of bright azure-blue, bloom before the other muscari species are even showing bud. There is also a white-flowered form. This species increases readily from seed and flowers the second year. Plant bulbs in autumn, 5 cm (2 in.) deep and 7.5 cm (3 in.) apart.

M. botryoides is the true grape hyacinth, more dwarf than *M. armeniacum*, with spikes of deep sky-blue flowers produced on numerous racemes. A charming, pure white-flowered form, most sought after and nearly as prolific, is *M. botryoides* 'Album'.

M. comosum 'Plumosum', the feathered hyacinth, is a most desirable bulb. When really happy, with good drainage and rich compost, the large, feathery plumes of violet-coloured filaments, up to 25 cm (10 in.) long and 5–10 cm (2–4 in.) across, remain in an attractive condition over a long period. It has, therefore, proved to be a valuable cut flower. The species *M. comosum*, known as the tassel hyacinth, grows 35–50 cm (14–20 in.) high, the greenish flowers having whitish lobes, changing to purple on the tops. Still another form, *M. comosum* 'Monstrosum', produces bluish violet, feathery plumes in a dense, loose tuft of slender branches.

M. neglectum is an interesting species sometimes met with and useful in the rockery. Racemes 5 cm (2 in.) long on 20 cm (8 in.) stems are composed of 30–40 deep blackish blue bells, freely produced. This species usually spreads freely.

M. tubergenianum. This species is now commonly known as the Oxford and Cambridge muscari, because when it is in full bloom, the top of the spike is bright clear blue and the bottom half deep Oxford blue. The buds are a most distinctive turquoise-blue shade, quite unlike any other species. It is easily grown, producing numerous spikes 15–20 cm (6–8 in.) tall.

All grape hyacinths increase rapidly from bulb division, and from the abundance of small offsets clustered around the parent bulbs. *M. comosum* and its varieties do not produce many 'pips'. The dormant period of the grape hyacinths is often very short, bulbs starting into root action in late summer, particularly after a hot, dry spell followed by warm

Muscari comosum 'Plumosum'

cm (24 in.) high, carry large, terminal, dense corymbose heads, 15 cm (6 in.) across, of bright blue flowers somewhat paler at the edges. Older plants form a long, thick, cylindrical rootstock, which lies on the surface of the ground, and being shallow rooted, this should not be disturbed. These old clumps are inclined to die out, but young plants re-establish themselves readily from the large, winged seeds or nutlets. These germinate freely where they fall. It is a plant that prefers semi-shade and must never be allowed to become dry at the roots. It blooms during late spring and early summer, when the rich blue flowers and shining green leaves add a note of distinctive freshness to the garden. A pure white-flowered form called *M. hortensia* 'Alba' reproduces true to type from seed.

Many people are not successful in growing this lovely plant, and this seems to be because conditions are too dry for the shallow roots, the position is too sunny, or the soil is lacking in humus. Plants can be set out almost any time of the year, but preferably in the spring so as to become established before blooming the following season. From seed sown in the autumn, blooms can be expected in 18 months. Young plants will not stand more than about 12 degrees of frost without damage.

rains. If beds or borders require lifting or transplanting, this should be done as soon as the foliage has died down. When once lifted and dried, the bulbs can be kept out of the ground in good healthy condition for planting as late as winter, but autumn planting is recommended to ensure a good spring crop of flowers.

MYOSOTIDIUM
Boraginaceae

This is a monotypic genus in which the species, *M. hortensia*, is confined to the Chatham Islands off the coast of New Zealand. The large, attractive leaves, deep green and glossy, if well grown are nearly as large as rhubarb. The stout flower-stems, up to 60

Myosotidium hortensia

N

NARCISSUS
Amaryllidaceae

This genus embraces a considerable number of species and natural hybrids, most of which occur in the Northern Hemisphere and Europe. The better known attractive species are briefly described under a separate heading. It is not our intention to cover more than brief cultural notes, recognition and control of diseases, and to provide the modern classification, as revised in 1977.

Most narcissus will grow and bloom freely in any well-drained soil not devoid of humus, while many of the stronger-growing varieties can be freely naturalised in grass. Rather stiffish or heavy soils usually produce better-quality blooms, but light, free soils usually produce healthier stocks as diseases spread less readily during wet weather.

Among the pests that affect narcissus, *Merodon equestris*, commonly called the narcissus fly, is one of the most injurious, also attacking amaryllis, galanthus, habranthus and hyacinths, as well as a number of other bulbs. The adult is a large, two-winged fly about 1 cm (0.5 in.) long, resembling a small, hairy bumble-bee. There is considerable colour variation in the individuals, some being yellowish and others brown, and the bodies are often banded. The flies appear in summer, more abundant on sunny days, and are easily recognised in flight by their peculiar droning sound. If a close watch is kept, the flies can be trapped and destroyed with a butterfly net. The female lays her eggs singly, either low down among the foliage or on the soil near the neck of the bulb; a favourite place is any crack in the soil formed by decaying foliage or stems. Egg-laying may be prevented to some extent in the vicinity of the bulbs by earthing up around the necks of the bulbs or by consolidating the soil by treading or rolling as the foliage is dying down. The newly hatched maggot passes

Narcissus bulbocodium 'Early Gold'

down into the ground and enters the bulb through the basal plate, then begins to feed on the inner scales until the bulb is completely hollowed out, the interior becoming a mass of decaying wet frass. Some bulbs survive the attack, but the growth the following season is usually poor and spindly. When fully fed, the maggot leaves the bulb and pupates in the soil. The lesser narcissus fly, *Eumerus tubercalatus*, lays several eggs in one spot and usually three or more maggots will be found in a bulb.

Any soft-necked bulbs should be suspected as being affected, and a few specimens should be examined by cutting the bulbs open. The maggots in affected stocks can be destroyed without damaging the bulbs by immersing them for one hour in water kept to a constant temperature of 110 degrees — or up to three hours if eelworms are also present.

The eelworms that attack narcissi are small, almost microscopic, nearly transparent, roundish worms. They spread through the soil during the wet weather, infection being much more rapid in heavy soil than light and sandy ground. Areas affected with bulb eelworm should not be planted again with bulbs for three or four years.

The worst disease other than insects affecting narcissi is known as basal rot, usually beginning and becoming more serious when bulbs are lifted and in store. The fungus responsible is *Fusarium bulbigerum*, and the signs are chocolate or reddish brown rot, usually at the neck and travelling downwards. Poor storage conditions, especially dampness, will encourage the spread. If valuable, affected bulbs should be planted in light, sandy or otherwise well-drained soil, where recovery may be expected. The trouble will disappear if drainage is good and bulbs are well dried when lifted.

The only other disease likely to cause much concern is known as stripe. It is generally considered to be a virus of some kind and manifests itself as mottling or striping of the foliage, usually a paler green or yellowish green. Affected bulbs do not suffer to any great extent and seldom collapse, but the flowers often show a breaking in colour, light greenish patches or streaks. The only method of control is to remove and destroy affected bulbs as they are identified.

Narcissus species

We give brief descriptions, mainly for identification purposes, of the best-known and most popular miniature or otherwise desirable wild species. Plant bulbs fairly close together for massed effect and 5–10 cm (2–4 in.) deep, according to the size of the bulbs.

N. asturiensis, which used to be known as *N. minimus*, is a comparatively rare and much sought-after species. It is the smallest-flowered trumpet narcissus known, rich golden yellow on 10 cm (4 in.) stems. It is usually confused with *N. minor*. It is rather slow to increase from bulb divisions but seeds freely.

N. bulbocodium (hoop petticoat daffodil). This most variable species, ranging over a wide area of southwest Europe, and North Africa, is difficult to define in the different forms as it is hard to tell where one ends and the other begins. Some record nearly 30 subspecies or varieties, but even thus divided, considerable variation exists.

N. bulbocodium var. *citrinus*. As the name implies,

Narcissus cyclamineus

the cup is pale yellow or citron, and is more expanded than the type, with greenish petals. The bulbs divide slowly, but it seeds freely and is best increased in this way.

N. bulbocodium var. *conspicuus* is the commonest variety and the easiest to grow. The cup is deep yellow, rather long and slightly restricted at the mouth. The usual form produces numerous, erect, narrow leaves and single blooms on stems 10–15 cm (4–6 in.) tall. Some stronger-growing types with larger flowers grow 22.5–30 cm (9–12 in.) tall.

N. bulbocodium var. *foliosus*. In colour and form this resembles the common type, but the milk-white cups are smaller and daintier, held on 15 cm (6 in.) stems. The narrow, grass-like foliage remains green nearly all the year, increasing rapidly, and the longer, narrow bulbs are constantly dividing up into smaller offsets. This form crossed with *N. b.* subsp. *romieuxii* has given us *N.* 'Nylon', the only worthwhile hybrid so far. It is the first of all to bloom, and masses of frilled-edged, milk-white flowers appear in mid-winter. It increases freely.

N. bulbocodium var. *monophyllus* (syn. *N. cantabricus*) is the pure white counterpart of the common form, but with more expanded cups like *N. b.* subsp. *romieuxii*. It commences to bloom in late winter and continues for several weeks with a succession of bloom. Unfortunately, it is not easy to grow, a well-drained, semi-shady spot in the rockery being most suitable.

N. bulbocodium subsp. *romieuxii* is a form from the Atlas Mountains, with widely expanded, pale yellow cups, charmingly waved at the edges. The blooms appear very early in the spring on 10 cm (4 in.) stems and stand up to 20 degrees of frost without damage. It appears easier to grow than *N. b.* var. *citrinus*, and likewise increases freely from seed.

N. cyclamineus has a reflexed perianth. It is earlier flowering than most species and has clear, yellow flowers on 15 cm (6 in.) stems. Like most of the miniature daffodils, it prefers a moist, light, sandy soil. Bulbs are small and slow to increase except in suitable conditions. It is a native of Portugal. There have been a number of splendid hybrids raised from this species, and although larger flowered and with longer stems than the type, they inherit a strong constitution and are, therefore, easier to grow. A selection is listed under Division 6 below.

N. x *gracilis* is sweetly scented, with two-toned, sulphur flowers on 30 cm (12 in.) stems—a real charmer. It flowers much later than any other narcissus.

N. jonquilla is a slender, graceful plant about 45 cm (18 in.) high, with narrow, rush-like foliage and scapes of usually three, fragrant, slender, cylindrical yellow cups and greenish yellow tubes. It blooms in early spring, and is more plentiful and more easily grown than most other species. A desirable dwarf-growing form is sometimes offered as *N. jonquilla* 'Minor', but it is such a shy bloomer that it is of little value horticulturally. The single- and double-flowered forms of *N. jonquilla* are often confused with the taller *N.* x *odorus* (syn. *N. campernelli*), but the former can be distinguished by their very strong, distinctive perfume as well as their lesser height.

N. juncifolius is a true miniature, with quite round, rush-like foliage, bearing several bright yellow flowers on 15 cm (6 in.) stems.

N. minor. This lovely miniature, with erect or ascending trumpets on 15 cm (6 in.) stems, is readily identified because it is really a bicolor, the segments being sulphur-yellow and the trumpet bright yellow, slightly longer than the segments.

N. nanus is somewhat similar in appearance to *N. asturiensis* (*N. minimus*) but is larger in all its parts, growing to a height of 15 cm (6 in.). The nodding trumpets, which are faintly scented, are usually held at an angle of 45 degrees to the ground and appear later in the spring. A double-flowered form resembling the ragged blooms of a dandelion, more interesting than beautiful, is called *N. nanus* 'Pumilis Plenus', or commonly known as Rip van Winkle.

N. x *odorus* has bright yellow flowers 6 cm (2.5 in.) wide, usually two to four on 45 cm (18 in.) stems, produced freely in late spring. The narrow, linear foliage is channelled down the face. This is a very hardy and easily grown species, common in old gardens and often seen naturalised in the grass. A small-growing form called *N.* x *odorus* var. *minor* has flowers only 2.5 cm (1 in.) wide and 22.5 cm (9 in.) high.

N. pumilus is the tallest grower of the miniature trumpets, with scapes about 22.5 cm (9 in.) long. The bright yellow blooms are slightly scented, and the glaucous green foliage is rather twisted and semi-prostrate. This species used to be wrongly listed as *N. minor*. It is the most common and plentiful of the miniature trumpets.

N. tazetta (syn. *N. canaliculatus*) is the bunch-flowered species to which the popular *N.* 'Soleil D'or' belongs. This miniature throws flower-scapes about 10 cm (4 in.) high, with eight to 12 small, yellow cups and white perianths. Although it increases rapidly, it does not often flower freely.

Narcissus 'Nylon'

Narcissus 'Hawera'

Bulbs seem to need a good hot summer baking and light, dry soil. The true species grows only 10 cm (4 in.) high, but there is a taller-growing form up to 30 cm (12 in.), identical in other respects.

N. triandrus, commonly called angel's tears, carries clusters of elegant, creamy-white flowers, distinguished by a roundish cup and reflexing perianth, on a slender, round scape. It is a truly lovely species, growing 15 cm (6 in.) high, and gives a fine display of bloom if really happy. A pure white form is known as 'Albus'. A larger-flowered, pure white form is known as *N. triandrus calathina*. Some variation occurs from seedlings raised, but this is the best way to maintain a healthy, vigorous stock. There is also a small group of delightful hybrids derived from this species. All are lovely, producing several flowers on a stem. These are described under Division 5.

N. watieri. This attractive, scented miniature, a native of Morocco, is easily grown, producing solitary white flowers on 10 cm (4 in.) scapes about 2.5 cm (1 in.) across, with an expanded, shallow, cup-shaped centre.

There are quite a number of hybrids of miniature trumpets, few of which seem to be commonly available. 'Bambi', a Dutch-raised bicolor 22.5 cm (9 in.) high, has white petals and a golden trumpet. It is valuable because it flowers very early. 'W. P. Milner' has a 15 cm (6 in.) miniature trumpet, opening greenish yellow and fading to primrose. It increases prolifically and blooms freely.

Narcissus varieties

For horticultural purposes, the different varieties have been classified into 12 divisions. The following is the 1977 Royal Horticultural Society classification. There are hundreds of good cultivars, and those listed below are a selection of proven varieties.

Division 1: Trumpet daffodils of garden origin; one flower to a stem; trumpet or corona as long or longer than the perianth segments.

Yellow—'Golden Rapture', 'Temple Gold', 'Golden Horn', 'Arkle'.
White—'Empress of Ireland', 'Glacier', 'White Prince'.
Bicolor—'Outward Bound'.

Division 2: Long-cupped daffodils of garden origin.

Yellow—'Camelot', 'Butterscotch'.
Yellow with red cup—'Falstaff', 'High Fire', 'Red Mission'.
White—'Castle of Mey', 'Canisp'.
White with red cup—'Masquerade', 'Hotspur'.
White with pink cup—'Salmon Trout', 'Rainbow'.
White with yellow cup—'Irish Minstrel', 'Canterbury Fair'.

Division 3: Short cup.

'Audubon'—white perianth, rosy coral cup.
'Little Jewel'—white perianth, pink-rimmed crown.
'Merry King'—yellow perianth, deep red cup.
'Snowcrest'—pure white perianth, lemon-green cup.

Division 4: Double daffodils of garden origin.

'Acropolis'—white with small red central petals.
'Golden Ducat'—large golden yellow.
'Tahiti'—golden and orange-red.
'Tonga'—yellow with orange-red in centre.
'White Lion'—white with soft yellow.

Division 5: Hybrids of *N. triandrus* of garden origin. The species is listed in Division 10.

'Hawera'—tall, soft yellow, three flowers to a stem.
'Liberty Bells'—lemon yellow.
'Rippling Waters'—creamy white.
'Silver Chimes'—all white.

Division 6: Cyclamineus hybrids of garden origin. *N. cyclamineus* is listed in Division 10.

'Beryl'—primrose-yellow, reflexing perianth and small, globular, orange cup; 20 cm (8 in.).
'February Gold'—early; slightly reflexed, yellow perianth and golden orange trumpet; 30 cm (12 in.).
'February Silver'—milky white.
'Jack Snipe'—creamy petals and primrose cup.
'Jenny'—creamy white.
'March Sunshine'—yellow perianth and long cups of pale orange.
'Peeping Tom'—intense deep yellow; characteristic reflexed perianth; 30 cm (12 in.).

Division 7: Jonquilla daffodils of garden origin. These have the characteristics of *N. jonquilla*.

'Cherie'—dainty, delicate pink cup, white petals.
'Lintie'—dainty, butter-yellow cup and orange petals.
'Pippit'—lemon-yellow turning white.

Narcissus 'Jack Snipe'

'Trewithian'—two or three pale yellow flowers per stem.

Division 8: Tazetta daffodils of garden origin.

'Canaliculatus'—dainty, three to five scented flowers of white with yellow cups.
'Minnow'—several creamy flowers with yellow cups on each stem.

Division 9: Poeticus daffodils of garden origin.

'Actaea'—pure white perianth, red/yellow crown, early.
'Cantabile'—sparkling white with red/green crown.
'Cantata'—very white perianth.

Division 10: The wild species detailed above.

Division 11: Split-corona daffodils, which have their corona split for at least a third of its length.

'Colorama'—dark orange collar, golden yellow perianth.
'Mistral'—white perianth, lemon-white collar, early.
'Parisienne'—white perianth with deep orange corona.
'Top Hit'—perianth sulphur-yellow, light orange collar.

Division 12: Miscellaneous cultivars.

'Jessamy'—a bulbocodium hybrid of milk-white with wide crown.
'Little Gem'—miniature, golden yellow trumpet.
'Little Beauty'—dainty little bicolor trumpet.
'Nylon'— a hybrid of bulbocodium form, creamy white, usually flowering in mid-winter; increases well in warm climates.

NEOMARICA
Iridaceae

This genus contains about a dozen species of iris-like perennials, with creeping rhizomes and tall, leathery, deep green leaves. The best-known species, a native of Brazil, is called *N. caerulea*, producing tall, straight, sword-like leaves, and 90 cm (36 in.) scapes of 10 cm (4 in.), triangular, sky-blue flowers with three smaller central petals, and

Neomarica caerulea

yellowish claws barred with brown and orange. Each flower-stem yields an amazing number of blooms, which open up day after day like the tigridias and cypellas. A bold clump in full bloom is always arresting, but it is essentially a garden plant as the flowers are not suitable for cutting.

There are a number of other interesting species worth securing if seed or plants become available, including *N. brachypus*, in which the yellow flowers are barred red at the base, and *N. gracilis*, which gives us pale bluish flowers marked deeper at the base and spotted reddish brown. All the species are best increased from seed as divided plants from older clumps do not, as a rule, transplant readily, except in light, free soil or when firmly planted. All species seem to be reasonably hardy and have withstood frosts exceeding 15 degrees without apparent damage. Transplant from late autumn until early spring.

Opposite: This mixed planting includes a number of perennials—yellow coreopsis and achillea, purple and white irises, pink bergamot (*Monarda*), a large-leaved gunnera—as well as a selection of annuals and shrubs. The vibrant pink rhododendron is underplanted with self-seeding cinerarias, contributing to an exuberant display.

NEPETA
Lamiaceae Catmint, catnip

This is a genus comprising over 150 species of perennials and annuals, distributed over the Northern Hemisphere, but very few are of any garden value.

N. x *faassenii* is the catmint grown in gardens, and now established as being a natural hybrid between *N. mussinii* and *N. nepetella*. It is a useful, hardy border plant, eminently suitable for loose, free soils, resisting dry conditions and some degree of salt spray or adverse coastal conditions. It has small, wrinkled, grey-green foliage, and the numerous flower-stems carry hundreds of small, pale violet-blue flowers produced all summer and autumn. The foliage yields a pleasant, pungent odour, evidently much appreciated by cats, hence the common name. In late autumn, the plants, which have produced a spread of 60 cm (24 in.) and reached 30 cm (12 in.) in height, should be cut back to the ground, otherwise they will become ragged in appearance. A selected form with somewhat larger and brighter flowers is known as 'Six Hills Giant'.

N. grandiflora 'Souvenir d'Andre Chaudron' is the best form so far raised, with jagged spear leaves and nearly 60 cm (24 in.) spikes of clear lavender flowers, produced from late spring till autumn. In good strong soil the plant will grow to 1.2 m (4 ft)

Nepeta x *faassenii* 'Six Hills Giant'

high and across, and is a useful border plant. American growers have renamed this plant 'Blue Beauty'.

N. nervosa is another interesting species from Kashmir, suitable for the front of the herbaceous border, having dense, cylindrical, 35 cm (14 in.) spikes of clear, wisteria-like, blue flowers. It commences blooming in late spring, continuing until mid-summer.

Plants increase freely from divisions, the old clumps broken up in the winter or spring yielding an ample supply of planting stock. Cuttings taken in the autumn or winter root freely.

NERINE
Amaryllidaceae Spider lily

This genus of 30 or more species, all natives of South Africa, is closely allied to the amaryllis and was at one time included in this genus. Nerines are among the finest autumn-flowering bulbs and deservedly popular as cut flowers, remaining in a fresh and attractive condition for seven days or even longer.

In England and America, these bulbs, with the exception of the hardy species *N. bowdenii*, must be grown under glass, as they will not withstand heavy frosts on the foliage. If grown in pots or containers, the soil should be a mixture of fibrous loam, coarse sand, decayed manure and leaf mould. The bulbs should be set with the necks above the soil and, whether established or just newly potted, water should be withheld until the flower-spikes appear, then plants should be freely watered during the growing season until late spring, when the foliage begins to turn yellow. Bulbs should be left in pots in full sun or under glass without any water at all until flower-spikes again appear.

These same conditions are ideal for outside cultivation, and that is why these bulbs do so well in parts of Australia, where a Mediterranean type of climate is enjoyed, with practically no rain from spring till autumn and high day temperatures. Nerines rather resent being disturbed or, more correctly, will not bloom as freely as they do when they become crowded.

N. bowdenii is one of the most important bulbs in this family. Unlike other species, this one is dor-

Nerine sarniensis hybrid

mant, or nearly so, during the cold winter months and is, therefore, hardier than other species. In districts with hot, dry summers, the foliage sometimes disappears or yellows off during late summer before the flower-buds appear, but in moist districts or with freshly planted stocks, the foliage persists right up to the flowering period. If well grown, the flower-scapes are 45–60 cm (18–24 in.) long, each carrying six to 10 nicely frilled, bright pink blooms. There is a softer pink form called 'Rosea', probably identical with the one listed in Europe as 'Fenwick's Variety'. This selected soft pink form, and also a pure white one known as 'Alba', are most desirable forms. 'Flavescens' blooms well into the winter, the heads of pale lilac-pink, frilly flowers held on 60–90 cm (24–36 in.) stems, remaining fresh for 10 days or more. 'Gigantea' is slightly larger flowered than the type, and produces very large bulbs.

N. bowdenii and its forms are the most prolific of all the larger-flowered nerines, increasing readily from division and the numerous offsets attached to the parent bulbs. Most of these offsets, if removed and planted out from autumn till spring, will produce flowering bulbs in one year.

A form or hybrid of *N. bowdenii* that was developed in the Channel Islands is known as 'Pink Triumph', and has proved a most valuable cut flower, blooming a month later than the type. It is similar in bulb, growth and bloom, except that the slightly narrower petals are a deeper shade of pink and more frilled. It is also known under the name of 'Bowden Frills'. Where happy, this variety is a prolific increaser, possibly because its dormant period is very short.

N. curvifolia var. *fothergillii* blooms freely if given hot, dry summer conditions, the flower-scapes being 40 cm (16 in.) tall, carrying six to 10 glittering, orange-scarlet blooms with a gold dust sheen. The much larger-flowered form, *N. curvifolia* var. *fothergillii* 'Major', is probably the largest flowered of all species, with bold umbels of dazzling, scarlet, gold-dusted blooms on 60 cm (24 in.) stems. In both forms the glaucous green foliage is depressed in the middle or curved at the edges, in contrast to the comparatively flat leaves of the other species, hence the name *N. curvifolia*. 'Major' is rather slow to increase, the large bulbs, 7.5 cm (3 in.) across, dividing up when mature only and not forming small offsets. Bulbs can be increased commercially by cross-cutting the largest bulbs through the base to half the depth of the bulb, in the same way as hyacinths are increased. Small bulbs will form along the cut edges.

If species and varieties are intercrossed, interesting new colours can be secured. *N. bowdenii* and *N. curvifolia* var. *fothergillii* 'Major' have been crossed on several occasions. One of the best of these hybrids is called 'Afterglow', with immense, bright salmon-rose heads of bloom on robust, 75 cm (30 in.) scapes, and another is known as 'Old Rose', the blooms of which are deep rose, attractively suffused with greyish mauve. They are all late bloomers, flowering during late autumn.

Nerine curvifolia var. *fothergillii* 'Major'

N. x *erubescens* is a distinct species, which can be briefly described as a pale pink form of *N. filifolia*, slightly taller growing and producing small, round bulbs about 2.5 cm (1 in.) across. It is a lovely soft shade of pink, very suitable for decorations and florists' use.

N. filifolia (syn. *N. filamentosa*) is probably the most prolific and best known of the low-growing species, and one that is deservedly popular as a border plant. Although easily grown except in the coldest of districts or in heavy wet soil, it seems to be happiest in a light ground with a shingly base, or else in a free volcanic medium. Basal root rot seems to develop only when drainage is poor or delayed. In this species the foliage, 15–25 cm (6–10 in.) long, is slender and grass-like, while the numerous flower-scapes, 20–40 cm (8–16 in.) tall, carry eight to 10 small, spidery, light rosy red flowers about 2.5 cm (1 in.) across, freely produced during late summer and autumn. Bulbs are small and elongated, about 1 cm (0.5 in.) in diameter at the base, and these develop numerous offsets.

N. flexuosa 'Alba' is the only white-flowered nerine in general cultivation. The flower-scapes, 45–60 cm (18–24 in.) tall, produced during autumn, carry six to 10 heavily crimped, reflexed flowers, each about 5 cm (2 in.) across. Unlike most other nerines, the broad, soft, yellow-green foliage is well in evidence before the flowers appear; in fact, its dormant period, except in hot, dry districts, is very short. The roundish, pale straw-white bulbs are often up to 7.5 cm (3 in.) across and increase more slowly than other species, seldom forming small offsets.

N. krigei, well known in South Africa, is hardy and easily grown. It somewhat resembles *N. bowdenii*, but the 40 cm (16 in.) tall scape of pink flowers is somewhat smaller, and the bulbs are large and roundish. It blooms from mid-summer into early autumn, commencing and ending the flowering season of nerines. The narrow, 1 cm (0.5 in.) wide leaves are always spiral twisted, an unfailing distinguishing feature. As the bulb is dormant during winter, it may prove just as hardy as *N. bowdenii* in cold districts.

N. masonorum, a low-growing species, closely related to *N. filifolia* and likewise a most useful border plant, is one of the first to bloom. The flat-topped, 7.5 cm (3 in.) wide heads of small,

Nerine filifolia

frilly, starry blooms, usually 12 on 22.5 cm (9 in.) stems, appear during late summer. The narrow, grassy foliage sets off the numerous bright, rosy-pink flower-scapes, which appear freely on well-established clumps. The bulbs are small and elongated, producing numerous offsets.

N. sarniensis, commonly called the Guernsey lily, was so called because bulbs were washed up during a seventeenth-century shipwreck and flowered so well there that botanists first thought that this was their natural home. This nerine with its different forms is one of the best large-flowered species, but it demands several months of hot, dry baking before blooming. The type is described as a bright salmon-red, while a brilliant orange-scarlet form is called 'Corusca'. Although the individual flowers of the latter form are smaller and its stems only 22.5 cm (9 in.) tall, the umbel carries up to 30 flowers. It is hardier than the type, withstanding quite heavy frosts. A paler, rosy red form called 'Plantii' is identical with the type except in colour.

N. tardiflora produces a large bulb, like *N. curvifolia* var. *fothergillii* 'Major' but more elongated, and when well established, produces 60 cm (24 in.), bold scapes topped with rather narrow-petalled, rosy-red flowers, appearing in late autumn.

For many years growers have been hybridising nerines, but because the bulbs normally increase very slowly, very few of the new hybrids have been made available to the public. Tissue culture has produced about 10 new cultivars; of these the following five can be recommended as outstanding:

'Mother of Pearl'—large, tall white with a flush of
   pink.
'Radiant Queen'—frill rose, overlaid with lavender.
'Salmon Supreme'—tall apricot-salmon with a red
   eye.
'Sunset Frills'—tall, frilled salmon-red.
'Virgo'—magnificent pure white.

Increase is usually from division of parent bulbs,
and in some species such as *N. bowdenii*, seed sets
freely and is quite easily raised. Seeds of nerines are
soft and fleshy, so should be sown at once in pots or
seed trays, and kept under glass or frames for two
years until they are large enough to plant out permanently, usually blooming the fourth or fifth year.

All species and hybrids of nerines are best
replanted as soon as possible after the foliage has
died down, usually from early summer until
autumn. *N. bowdenii* and its various forms are
dormant from late autumn till early spring so can be
planted much later.

NIEREMBERGIA
Solanaceae

This genus consists of about 35 species of perennials,
creeping plants or low shrubs, natives of America.
All seem to be particularly suitable for growing in
light, sandy soils in coastal areas, or on poor, dry
banks, although they are equally at home in good
soils. They provide a wealth of bloom in the spring
and again in the autumn if plants are cut back.

N. caerulea, usually offered as *N. hippomanica*, is
the best-known species. It forms a small, bushy plant
15–30 cm (6–12 in.) high, with much-branched,
thin, stiffly erect stems, and narrow, linear, acute
foliage, deep green and slightly hairy. The 2.5 cm (1
in.), bell-shaped, open flowers, produced in abundance, are bright violet-blue with small darker lines
and yellow in the throat. A deeper violet-purple
form, which seems to come true to type from seed, is
called 'Royal Robes'. Both are readily increased
from cuttings taken in the autumn. Fresh seed germinates freely, and plants bloom the first season.
They are ideal for edgings and massed beddings,
and in very cold countries are grown as annuals.

N. frutescens var. *atroviolacea* is a taller, shrubby
species with thin, brittle, twiggy stems. It attains a
height of 60 cm (24 in.) and as much or more across.
The 4 cm (1.5 in.) bells of deep violet-blue are most
attractive. Planted on the top of a wall, the branches
hang down with the sheer weight of the blooms. The
flowers of the ordinary form of *N. frutescens* are delicate pale blue shaded to white at the margins. There
is also a pure white form. Plants are increased by
autumn or spring cuttings. Heavy pruning is necessary after blooming, but they are short-lived plants
so fresh stock should be raised every two or three
years.

Nierembergia caerulea

NOMOCHARIS
Liliaceae

This genus of 16 species is closely related to the
liliums and fritillarias, and is distributed from the
Himalayas through upper Burma to western China.
The bulb is composed of elongated scales, and the
leafy flower-stems, 45–90 cm (18–36 in.) in height
according to the species, carry a number of nodding,
fringed and open flowers of outstanding beauty,
some resembling choice odontoglossum orchids.
Plants are not common in gardens, probably
because their culture is not generally understood.

Nomocharis mairei

N. thomsonianum is a native of Afghanistan. The bulb produces in spring, from a rosette of 30 cm (12 in.) leaves 2.5 cm (1 in.) wide, a straight spike 1 m (3 ft) high, bearing up to 30 rosy lilac, funnel-shaped, fragrant blooms 5–7.5 cm (2–3 in.) long, held nearly horizontally on the strong stem. This plant appears to withstand only moderate cold, particularly resenting late spring frosts when in growth, and preferring a well-drained but cool, moist, peaty soil. The bulbs form numerous small bulbs around the base and at the crown just below the leaves, and these, if planted out separately, can be brought into flowering size in two or three years. The mature bulbs are approximately 4 cm (1.5 in.) wide and up to 10 cm (4 in.) long. It is a little-known, attractive plant, which is quite easily grown, although it does not bloom freely unless conditions are to its liking.

Two other species, *N. bulbiferum* and *N. macrophyllum*, have flowers that are rosy lilac to pinkish mauve, while *N. campanulatum* is a desirable, dark red-flowered species, tipped green on each segment.

Bulbs are dormant from mid-summer until autumn, when they should be transplanted.

Stocks are best raised from seed in shallow trays, the mixture being composed of equal parts of coarse sand, leaf mould and loam. They should be grown in boxes or pots for two years and then planted out into a similar prepared mixture. Seedlings bloom the third or fourth year after sowing, but are well worth waiting for. A semi-shady, cool spot with sharp drainage is necessary, and bulbs are quite hardy, withstanding frost and snow during the winter.

N. mairei has 7.5 cm (3 in.), rose-coloured flowers, heavily blotched with reddish purple. Flower-spikes 60–90 cm (24–36 in.) high, with whorls of 15 cm (6 in.) leaves on the lower portion, often carry a dozen or more or these arresting, wide-open blooms, produced in early summer.

NOTHOLIRION
Liliaceae

This genus of six bulbous species from India, China and North Africa differs from the liliums in that the non-scaly bulbs are covered with a brown tunic.

Notholirion campanulatum

NYMPHAEA
Nymphaeaceae   Water-lilies

This is a genus of about 50 species of aquatics with fleshy or tuberous rootstocks, natives mostly of the Northern Hemisphere or the tropics, with a few in South Africa or Australia. Most of the species and varieties are hardy and easily grown, provided the directions given below are followed.

Three distinct types are grown. The first and most plentiful are the large-flowered, robust-growing species and varieties, of which a dozen or more are generally grown, including flowers of white, cream, yellow, bronzy yellow, coppery red, pinks, reds and crimson. Second are the miniature or pygmy types, with comparatively smaller blooms and general growth, available in about six shades from white through yellow and pink to red. This class is eminently suited for planting in small pools such as in rockery ponds and for tub culture. These varieties are mostly forms of *N. pygmaea* or *N. tetragona*. Third are the blue-flowered water-lilies of the *N. stellata* type, and these form distinctive, small, hard, black, cone-like roots, which are quite dormant during the winter, all fibrous roots disappearing completely. The colour of the usual species is pale blue. The flowers are 10 cm (4 in.) across, and in contrast to the blooms of the other nymphaeas, which rest on the surface of the water, they are held up to 15 cm (6 in.) above the pond level. Reddish purple, deeper blue, and even pinkish mauve forms and hybrids of *N. stellata* occur. This species and its varieties can be successfully grown only in a district where a hot summer is enjoyed. In places where there is a danger of being damaged by heavy winter frosts, it is advisable to lift the completely dormant roots in winter and store in damp moss till the spring, when they can be replanted. Most tropicals, however, will stand up to 15 degrees of frost when dormant in water.

Most water plants, particularly water-lilies, prefer full sun to enable them to flower freely, so a suitable site should be chosen, away from the shade of trees or buildings. If a concrete base is provided throughout, the pond should receive a layer of heavy loam to a depth of 10–15 cm (4–6 in.). This must be firmly rammed or the soil and plants will work loose as soon as the water is added. When planting, allow just sufficient water in the new pond to cover the plants and the soil, and leave this for several weeks before filling up the pond completely. Most water-lilies thrive best in water 30–60 cm (12–24 in.) deep, but it is better to err on the shallow side as the nearer the roots are to the rays of the sun, the freer they will bloom. Some people prefer to plant their lilies in wire baskets, which are lowered into the required position. These are preferable to other containers, as the roots will penetrate into the surrounding sediment and maintain the plants for much longer. Water-lilies are gross feeders, usually more than doubling their size each season, and the soil in the containers quickly becomes used up or impoverished, so fresh plantings should be made every two or three years. An addition of cow manure or bone meal with the soil will help to sustain plants in vigour longer. A layer of small stones placed on the top of the soil after the plants have been set will help to anchor the container on the bottom and also to prevent the soil becoming loosened with the water and washed away.

Spring planting is best, any time after the newer leaves have appeared, as plants seem to establish themselves more readily when the new growth is taking place. A simple way to establish water-lilies in lakes and ponds, or where it is not possible to drain out the water before planting, is to ball up the crowns tightly in turfy loam, leaving the green shoots protruding and adding a heavy stone to the

Nymphaea cultivar

ball. These can then be dropped into the required position and will remain undisturbed until the new roots push through the sacking to attach themselves in the mud bottom. It must be remembered that water-lilies prefer almost stagnant conditions and, therefore, do not thrive in running water such as streams. They do not, as a rule, flower until the water becomes warm with the sun's rays in late spring or summer. Hardy varieties of water-lilies with creeping rootstock should be planted horizontally and tropicals with cone-shaped rootstock should be planted in an upright position.

Nymphaea cultivar

O

OENOTHERA
Onagraceae   Evening primrose

This genus comprises over 200 species, mostly herbaceous plants or low shrubs, natives of extratropical America.

O. acaulis is a perennial trailer, which flowers mainly in the evening with white flowers. *O. odorata* is a perennial, with large, yellow flowers opening in the evening and growing to 45 cm (18 in.).

O. biennis is a showy plant, growing over 1 m (3 ft) tall and opening its large, yellow, scented flowers in the evening. It is biennial, as its name implies.

The following species and forms open their flowers by day. *O. fruticosa* produces an upright bush of twiggy stems from a basal tuft of purplish green leaves, and an abundance of large, yellow flowers throughout late spring and summer. 'Youngii' is decidedly the best of several varieties grown, and extremely free-flowering. The growth, however, is semi-lax and spreading, the plant seldom exceeding 30 cm (12 in.) high, but the prolonged display of canary-yellow flowers is truly remarkable. Another good form is 'Fireworks', the buds of which are dark red, with masses of yellow flowers on 30 cm (12 in.) stems.

O. missouriensis has prostrate growth and large, 10 cm (4 in.), canary-yellow flowers for months. It is an excellent wall plant in the sun, growing 30 cm (12 in.) tall and about 60 cm (24 in.) wide.

O. speciosa has pink-tinted, white flowers in profusion in the summer, and grows 60 cm (24 in.) high. It is an excellent perennial with running rhizomes on medium to light soils but is less perennial on clay soils.

O. tetragona is a very similar species, with minor botanical differences. *O. tetragona* var. *riparia* is a low-growing form, to only 25 cm (10 in.), with a profusion of yellow flowers in summer.

Oenothera fruticosa

It is interesting to watch the buds of the oenotheras open in the sun. The sepals separate and then the petals stir, unfold and, as if by magic, shake out their wrinkles in a very short time. All species resist dry conditions and prefer full sun, but are also quite easy to grow in any well-drained soil. Clumps can be broken up and transplanted during the winter months or early spring.

OMPHALODES
Boraginaceae

This genus of 28 species, annuals and perennials, natives of the Mediterranean region, east Asia and Mexico, is related to the cynoglossums. Most of the herbaceous species are attractive, low-growing

Omphalodes cappadocica

plants suitable for the rockery, woodland planting or the front of borders.

O. cappadocica is a desirable, tufted perennial with deep green leaves 7.5 cm (3 in.) long, puckered or indented in an interesting manner, and 30 cm (12 in.), graceful, loose racemes of forget-me-not-like, bright blue flowers in early spring. It is lovely associated with the creamy yellow erythroniums and other early spring bulbs. Some of the species are difficult to grow, preferring shade, good drainage and lime, but this species seems happy in any position that is not too dry. Other blue-flowered species worth securing are *O. luciliae* and *O. verna*, particularly the latter, which is a grand plant for carpeting woodlands.

Increase of all species is from divisions of old clumps during winter or spring, or from fresh seed if available.

OPHIOPOGON
Liliaceae   Mondo grass

This is a genus of evergreen perennials with grass-like foliage. They are suitable for a position in sun or partial shade and are often seen growing under deciduous trees.

O. planiscarpus grows up to 30 cm (12 in.) tall,

with white flowers in sprays. *O. p.* 'Arabicus' has black foliage, against which the flowers contrast well.

O. japonicus is a mat-forming perennial, with glossy green foliage to 30 cm (12 in.). It has spikes of lilac flowers in summer, followed by blue-black berries.

Propagation is by division of plants in spring.

ORCHIS
Orchidaceae

O. mascula is native to Britain, and is widespread in Europe, often found in scrub or open woodland and on grassy roadside banks on clay soils. It has been grown successfully in the Southern Hemisphere. The three to five leaves are oblong and plain green, sometimes spotted. The flowers are numerous in a loose, blunt spike from pink to dark purple, the lip having dark spots on a pale centre.

Orchis mascula

ORNITHOGALUM
Liliaceae

This genus consists of 150 bulbous species belonging to the lily family, natives of Europe, Africa and Asia. Most species produce small to large, round, smoothish bulbs, nearly all hardy and easily grown.

0. arabicum is probably the most common species, called the Arab's eye because of the jet-black eye in the centre of the pure white flowers, six to 12 on a roundish raceme. The scape is about 60 cm (24 in.) long, and the cut blooms last quite well.

0. nutans is a useful hardy species producing ovate, white bulbs about 4 cm (1.5 in.) thick, and one-sided racemes of drooping, white flowers, green on the outside, each 30–45 cm (12–18 in.) stem carrying up to 12 on a 15 cm (6 in.) scape.

0. pyramidale produces an ovate bulb about 4 cm (1.5 in.) thick, with four to six linear, rather fleshy leaves, usually withering before flowering finishes. The white flowers with a green keel on the back, the bracts also coloured, are held in compact, 20–50-flowered racemes, about 20 cm (8 in.) long, on 45–60 cm (18–24 in.) scapes. A species related to and often confused with this is *0. narbonense*, the flowers of which are milk-white, with a narrow green keel outside and leaves much longer.

0. saundersiae is perhaps one of the most attractive species, in which the massive, many-flowered scapes reach a height of 1.2 m (4 ft), and the large, rounded bulbs are 7.5 cm (3 in.) across. The stately spikes of waxy, creamy flowers with blackish green centres are attractive for group planting in the back of the herbaceous border and also for indoor decorations, lasting several weeks in a fresh condition. In contrast to the other species, which bloom in early summer, *0. saundersiae* is at its best in the late summer, the bulbs being dormant and planted out during the winter. It is hardy and easily grown, and stocks are readily increased from the abundant seed crop ripening in late autumn. Bulbs do not reach full blooming size for three years.

0. speciosum is a lovely, dwarf-growing species, which seldom exceeds 30 cm (12 in.) in height when in bloom in spring. Another similar species, rather taller growing with golden yellow flowers with greenish brown centres, is called *0. flavissimum*. A sunny, well-drained position free from frosts over

Ornithogalum saundersiae

eight degrees is essential for success.

0. thyrsoides is commonly known as 'chincherinchees'. A form of this hardy species is grown by the million in South Africa as a cut flower. The common type produces four to six basal, fleshy leaves, 15–30 cm (6–12 in.) long, 4 cm (1.5 in.) wide, and 12–30 pure white flowers with pale greenish brown eyes in a densely set raceme, 15–20 cm (6–8 in.) long, on a 45–60 cm (18–24 in.) scape. Large bulbs, over 4 cm (1.5 in.) across, produce several spikes of bloom. A much taller-growing form, known as *0. thyrsoides* 'Major', is larger in all its parts and grows up to 1.2 m (4 ft) tall, but the ordinary form seems to be preferred. There are six distinct forms of *0. thyrsoides* recognised by botanists, and a double-flowered variety is also grown.

0. umbellatum, commonly known as Star of Bethlehem, produces roundish bulbs up to 4 cm (1.5 in.) wide, with six to nine narrow, ascending leaves, 15–30 cm (6–12 in.) long. A broad corymb about 15 cm (6 in.) long on a 30 cm (12 in.) scape carries six to 12 satiny, white flowers, greenish striped outside. This species is hardy, easily grown and increases

Ornithogalum montanum

freely. It is useful for cutting. *O. montanum* is very similar in growth to *O. umbellatum* but is usually shorter.

Ornithogalum species can be increased by seed or by offsets.

ORTHROSANTHUS
Iridaceae

This genus of perennials is closely allied to *Sisyrinchium*. *O. multiflorus* is an Australian species with a woody rhizome, bold, grassy foliage to 60 cm (24 in.), and 90 cm (36 in.) spikes of sky-blue flowers in late spring. Propagation is by division in spring.

OSTEOSPERMUM
Asteraceae

These shrubby perennials, previously listed under *Dimorphotheca*, are native to South Africa, where they are known as veldt daisies. They are hardy to frost of five degrees, and while some are bushy and compact, others are spreading. The daisy flowers are either solitary or in loose panicles.

O. barberiae is a spreading plant with purplish pink daisies continuously flowering throughout spring and summer.

O. ecklonis is a shrubby perennial and a popular garden plant. It grows up to 75 cm (30 in.) tall with 7.5 cm (3 in.) daisies, glistening white with deep blue centres and streaked with bluish mauve underneath the petals.

'Tresco Peggy' has very rich, dark purple flowers for many months. 'Whirligig', sometimes named 'Starry Eyes', is another ground-hugging plant ideal for covering banks or walls in full sun. Several other cultivars are grown, with pink daisies in various shades.

All the osteospermums are readily increased by cuttings, and can be maintained in areas where frosts are severe by retaining cuttings under glass in winter.

Osteospermum 'Tresco Peggy'

Osteospermum 'Whirligig'

OSTROWSKIA
Campanulaceae

This genus of a single species, *O. magnifica*, was introduced from central Asia in 1887. It is a real aristocrat but can be grown successfully only by expert gardeners, or those who can provide the conditions desired. It is a near relation of the campanulas, and the large, wide-open, saucer-shaped bells are a lovely shade of soft mauve, usually four to six on a 1 m (3 ft) stem. It is quite hardy in warmer climates, resisting cold in winter when dormant, but will not tolerate excessive moisture. It prefers full sun in very sandy, loose, free soil, and any failure is due to poor drainage, with excessive moisture rotting the heavy, fleshy roots. Plants are seldom available, but they travel well as the roots remain dormant for nearly six months. If fresh seed is available, this germinates freely and plants are not difficult to raise, but they usually take three or four years to reach flowering size. Transplant during winter.

OTANTHUS
Asteraceae

Otanthus maritimus is a coastal herb from the Mediterranean. It has very silvery foliage and grows to about 50 cm (20 in.). The growth is bushy and erect,

Otanthus maritimus

with small terminal heads of yellow. A sunny, well-drained situation is required, and the plant remains in flowers for weeks in early summer. Propagation is from seed or cuttings.

Othonnopsis cheirifolia

OTHONNOPSIS
Asteraceae

This is a small genus of South African sub-shrubs. *O. cheirifolia* grows about 30 cm (12 in.) tall, with bushy growth, fleshy grey leaves, and bearing bright yellow daisies like a senecio, continuing to flowers for many months. It prefers a situation in full sun with well-drained soil, and can be propagated by cuttings in summer.

OURISIA
Scrophulariaceae

Several species of these small plants from South America and New Zealand are suitable for rock gardens and borders in cooler districts and in part-shade.

　　O. coccinea has erect, 30 cm (12 in.) stems bearing

Ourisia coccinea

pendulous, red trumpets about 4 cm (1.5 in.) long in loose clusters. The attractive, oval, toothed foliage forms a spreading clump up to 25 cm (10 in.) across.

O. macrophylla has 30 cm (12 in.) stems bearing clusters of white flowers, but it is not tolerant of warmer climates.

OXALIS
Oxalidaceae

This genus has over 800 species of annual, perennial and bulbous plants distributed over South Africa, tropical and sub-tropical America.

Some species should not be planted in the garden because they may spread excessively and be difficult to eradicate. Others are generally well behaved and increase slowly. Many flower in autumn and winter, giving a bright display on sunny days. They can also be easily grown in 15 or 20 cm (6 or 8 in.) pots in the open and brought into a sunny patio or conservatory to flower. Sun is essential both for the initiation of flowers and for their opening.

In most cases the leaves are divided into three leaflets, sometimes resembling clover. *O. acetosella*, also known as Irish shamrock, has white flowers. It should not be planted in rock gardens but can be grown as a ground cover among shrubs. It is difficult to eradicate. *O. adenophylla* is a low-growing plant from the Andes. It has grey-green leaves and pink flowers with a darker eye. It is good for the rock garden and in colder areas.

O. deppei has four large leaflets stained with black and red flowers.

O. fabifolia will spread slowly but is low-growing, with bright yellow flowers in early winter. It is very free-flowering.

O. hirta has leafy stems to 20 cm (8 in.) and bright pink flowers towards the top in winter. The corms are bright orange and easily found, but they spread slowly.

O. lobata is very small but makes a bright display of yellow flowers in early spring.

O. luteola has bright yellow flowers in winter, and is very slow to spread.

O. pes-caprae is taller, to 25 cm (10 in.), with sprays of yellow flowers, three to 20 on each stem. Although attractive, it spreads by seeding and should not be regarded as a garden plant.

O. purpurea has clover-like leaves and 5 cm (2 in.), bright pink flowers in winter. It can be used as a ground cover as it spreads freely. There is also a handsome, purple-leaved form with the same rich pink flowers. *O. purpurea* 'Alba' makes an excellent show of white flowers in mid-winter.

Bulbs, corms or rhizomes are transplanted when dormant in early autumn.

Oxalis fabifolia

Oxalis purpurea 'Alba'

OXYPETALUM
Asclepiadaceae

Although there are more than 100 species from Brazil and Uruguay, only one species is commonly grown. *O. caeruleum* (syn. *Tweedia caeruleum*) is a sub-shrub seldom growing over 60 cm (24 in.) but becoming quite bushy. The starry flowers are a most attractive, light blue, in small heads, and are produced over a long period in summer. They are followed by 15 cm (6 in.) long, boat-shaped seed-pods. Being of the same family as the swan plant, it is sometimes a source of food for the monarch caterpillar.

Oxypetalum caeruleum

P

PACHYSANDRA
Buxaceae

This is a genus of three species of creeping perennials and sub-shrubs with tufted foliage.

P. terminalis makes an excellent ground cover for cooler districts. Native to Japan, it grows up to 30 cm (12 in.), and produces spikes of greenish white flowers in the spring. The form 'Variegata' has attractive silvery variegations. Propagation is usually by division in the spring or from cuttings in the autumn.

PAEONIA
Paeoniaceae

This genus of 33 species, most of which are herbaceous, is distributed over most parts of the Northern Hemisphere. The wide selection of hardy perennial varieties offered and grown today has been derived from the Chinese species *P. lactiflora*, also known as *P. edulis* and *P. albiflora*. Both single and double-flowered varieties are available in all shades of soft and deep pinks, salmon, rose, white, crimson and purple, many displaying attractive central cream or yellow stamens.

Double-flowered varieties:
'Albert Crousse'—fully double blooms of soft apple-blossom pink.
'Blush Queen'—pure white, double flowers flushed pink in the centre.
'Bunker Hill'—large, deepest mahogany-red, early flowering.
'Duchess de Nemours'—free-flowering, pure white, richly scented.
'Edulis Superba'—bright pink, early flowering, strongly scented.

Paeonia 'Festiva Maxima'

'Festiva Maxima'—pure white with a few carmine spots, scented.
'Karl Rosenfield'—very showy, rich rose-red, fully double.
'M. Jules Elie'—huge, bright lilac-pink on tall stems.
'Pink Formal'—very large heads of soft pink.
'Sarah Bernhardt'—very popular; 1 m (3 ft) stems with large, soft pink, scented blooms.
'Solange'—very large double, icy white, scented.
'Torpilleur'—lovely rose-red semi-double with creamy centre.

Single-flowered varieties:
'Bowl of Beauty'—pink outer petals with large centre of cream petalodes.
'Jan Van Leewen'—large, pure white with golden stamens.
'O-Sho-Kum'—dark red with long stems.
'Queen Mary'—pale apple-blossom bowls of pink flowers on 50 cm (20 in.) stems.

Occasionally paeonies may be seen flowering in warmer climates, but generally they prefer cooler conditions. Any good garden soil can grow and

Paeonia 'Sarah Bernhardt'

flower paeonies, provided it is very deeply dug and well enriched with decayed animal manure. Good drainage is essential, although a soil a little on the heavy side is to be preferred, a partial clay subsoil being ideal. Paeonies are gross feeders and when established should be heavily topdressed each season soon after the crop of blooms has finished. Do not manure in the winter or spring when the new growths are appearing, as a fungous foliage disease

Paeonia 'Bowl of Beauty'

called *Botrytis paeoniae* may occur. This is sometimes called bud rot or bud blast, and causes the foliage to turn black. If desired, this can easily be controlled by a fungicide spray in the spring.

P. officinalis, with its varieties and forms, is a well-known favourite in Europe, blooming several weeks ahead of the better-known Chinese varieties. The common type (a native from France to Albania) produces 12.5 cm (5 in.), red flowers, the single petals enclosing a central bunch of bright red stamens. These blooms are produced singly on 45–60 cm (18–24 in.) stems. A form called *P. officinalis* 'Anemonaeflora' has bright crimson flowers with rich crimson, twisted filaments edged with yellow, and is particularly valuable because it blooms about a month before the hybrids of *P. lactiflora*. The following are all fine cultivars of *P. officinalis*:

'Alba Plena'—pure white, double flowers, not scented.
'Rosea Splendens'—bright pink, double flowers, not scented.
'Rubra Plena'—most popular double crimson.

Another dainty little species, which should be grown more, is *P. tenuifolia*. The dense, much-divided, deep green foliage, glaucous beneath, is topped with solitary, cup-shaped, rich crimson, single flowers 7.5 cm (3 in.) across with central yellow stamens. Other forms, including a double red, are also grown.

Small, poor or even no blooms are to be expected the first year after planting, but each succeeding year should provide larger and better blooms. When once established, plants should be allowed to remain undisturbed for years. As a rule, however, clumps will benefit from being broken up or divided from five to 10 years after planting. When dividing clumps, be sure to allow two or three eyes to each root, shorten the fleshy roots to 15 cm (6 in.), and plant the top of the crown about 5 cm (2 in.) below the surface, firming the ground afterwards.

Some people complain that they cannot get their paeony roots to flower freely, while others secure no blooms at all. This can usually be traced to impoverished soil conditions, which can be rectified with heavy topdressings of well-decayed cow manure. If the soil is very light, such as volcanic soil, an addition of clay soil will help, but usually liberal dressings

Paeonia officinalis 'Rubra Plena'

of manure will eventually bring the desired results. It must be remembered that with continual rains, light soils leach out and become impoverished much more quickly than heavier soils. Paeonies also prefer a good hot, dry autumn to develop the flower buds for the following spring, while they seem to flower all the more freely after the experience of a cold winter.

All paeony species can be easily raised from seed, blooming the third or fourth year after sowing.

PANCRATIUM
Amaryllidaceae   Sea daffodil

The bulbs of these uncommon plants from the Mediterranean region are large and once planted or potted, should not be disturbed as long as they are healthy and thriving.

P. canariense grows 60 cm (24 in.) tall, with white flowers in early autumn.

P. illyricum has fragrant, white flowers in early summer, and grows to 45 cm (18 in.) tall.

P. maritimum has fragrant, daffodil-like flowers in summer. They grow to 60 cm (24 in.) and are greenish white and funnel-shaped.

The bulbs prefer a light soil in sun, with about 10 cm (4 in.) of soil covering them. The are dormant in winter, when they should not be subjected to excessive moisture. Propagation is by seed or from offsets of the older bulbs.

PAPAVER
Papaveraceae   Oriental poppy

This genus comprises about 100 species of annuals and perennials with milky sap, natives of Asia, Europe and North Africa. There are a number of different varieties and hybrids of the species *P. orientale*. These giant poppies with blooms 15–20 cm (6–8 in.) across, on stems up to 1 m (3 ft) long, provide a bold splash of colour in the spring. They are useful cut flowers, lasting several days in water if the stems are scalded or bruised. The colours available range from pure white through lilac, heliotrope, pink, salmon, orange, red and crimson to deep maroon. Cultivars worth growing include:

'Allegro'—large, bowl-shaped flowers of bright orange-scarlet, growing only 50 cm (20 in.) from a very compact rosette.
'Beauty of Livermere'—scarlet, frilled flowers.
'Dubloon'—fully double orange, large bloom, early.
'Princess Victoria Louise'—showy cerise-pink.

Oriental poppies prefer a cool climate, loose, free soil and raised beds if the ground is inclined to be damp or heavy. Naturally they prefer a good hot, dry autumn, which ripens the roots, resulting in a good crop of bloom in the spring. Plants are dormant from autumn till early winter, and are best transplanted in autumn, although they can be successfully shifted until late spring, but will not bloom that season.

Increase commercially is from pieces of roots 5 cm (2 in.) long inserted upright in boxes of sand and planted out in the spring, by which time the foliage will have appeared. Old clumps are best broken up and replanted every two or three years, otherwise the crowns are liable to rot. Plants are easily raised from seed, and if sown in the autumn these will bloom the following summer. A good range of colours can be expected from these seedlings, but they will not equal in quality of blooms the named varieties, increased vegetatively. Some of the older red, orange and pink sorts come reasonably true to type from seed. Remove old foliage as soon as it fades so as to keep the crowns healthy and exposed to full sunlight.

Papaver orientalis

PELTIPHYLLUM
Saxifragaceae

This genus has only one species. *P. peltatum* is a handsome perennial from North America, suitable for the banks of ponds or streams. In such places the large, peltate leaves give a fine effect, growing up to 1.2 m (4 ft), with a diameter of 60 cm (24 in.). The flowers, in large umbels, appear in early spring before the leaves have developed. This plant will grow well in a moist loam that is never allowed to dry out. Propagation is by seed or division.

PENSTEMON
Scrophulariaceae

About 250 species of herbaceous plants belong to this genus. These are mainly woody at the base, and are native to North America and Mexico. Many species are really attractive border plants, but few are widely known in warmer climates. A staminode representing a fifth stamen distinguishes this genus from its close allies.

P. barbatus, sometimes listed as *Chelone barbata*, is a hardy, easily grown, desirable perennial, preferring a position that is not too dry. It produces long, narrow, slightly branching, 1 m (3 ft) spikes of slender, tubular, pendant flowers, usually carmine-pink. In moist, rich soils plants may produce spikes up to 1.5 m (5 ft) tall. A brilliant scarlet-flowered form, *P. barbatus* 'Coccineus', is also worthy of cultivation. If raised from seed, some variations and interesting shades may be secured.

P. digitalis has spikes of slender, white trumpets, and grows to 1 m (3 ft).

P. fruticosus subsp. *scouleri* somewhat resembles in habit of growth and appearance *P. heterophyllus*, except that the stems, flowers and leaves are larger and rather coarse in growth. The flowers of the type are a cool lilac shade, although mauve-blue and pink forms are also known. Some variation in colour can be expected from seedlings. This is a good, hardy garden plant, which would succeed where *P. heterophyllus* might fail with wet or cold.

P. heterophyllus is a lovely species from California. From the semi-prostrate, evergreen, woody rootstock, numerous erect, 35 cm (14 in.) stems, with 2.5 cm (1 in.) long flowers, loosely arranged on the pedicels, appear in the late spring. These tubular flowers, narrow at the base, funnel-shaped and somewhat inflated, are a lovely shade of bright blue, somewhat tinged pink. Plants are increased from seed if available, or from spring or autumn cuttings of unflowered green shoots.

Penstemon digitalis

P. hirsutus grows up to 60–90 cm (24–36 in.) tall, with tubular, lilac-coloured flowers at its peak in mid-summer. A dwarf form, *P. h.* 'Pygmaeus', has the same colouring and is suitable for the rock garden.

P. richardsonii grows to 60 cm (24 in.), with violet-coloured flowers over mats of glaucous foliage. *P. venustus* is a sub-shrub to 75 cm (30 in.), with long leaves and short flowers of light violet to violet-purple.

Penstemon hybrids come in a good range of colours, from near whites to light and deep pinks, crimson and purple in self-colours, and also some with spotted throats. The following varieties are all reasonably perennial, except in colder districts. They are very showy and soon form strong bushes 60–90 cm (24–36 in.) tall. All will grow readily from cuttings, and it is wise to replace stock with young plants whenever they appear less than vigorous. In colder districts cuttings can be taken in the autumn and held in frames over the winter. These plants will bloom throughout the following spring and summer.

'Evelyn'—forms a neat, bushy plant with slender spires of slim, rose-pink flowers, which continue all summer.

'Firebird'—a splendid variety, with 90 cm (36 in.) stems of large, deep red bells for most of the summer.

'Garnet'—deep red trumpets on 75 cm (20 in.) stems.

'Pink Cloud'—many deep pink flowers with white throats.

'Purple Passion'—dark purple flower-heads atop each stem, 90 cm (36 in.).

'Redcoat'—many spikes of rather smaller, bright red trumpets; flowers very freely.

'Susan'—very large, tubular, soft pink flowers, deeper on the edges.

Fresh plants are usually increased from divisions of older clumps, which are transplanted during winter and spring. Cuttings can also be taken during the autumn.

Penstemon 'Susan'

PENTAS
Rubiaceae

One species of this genus is grown in gardens. *P. bussei* (syn. *P. coccinea*) is a soft-wooded, shrubby plant with heads of scarlet flowers appearing through summer and autumn. It grows to about 60 cm (24 in.), and is suitable only for gardens free from frost. It will succeed in partial shade. Propagation is by softwood cuttings taken in summer or by seed sown in spring.

PEROVSKIA
Lamiaceae   Russian sage

This genus consists of seven species, of which the best known is *P. atriplicifolia*. The plant grows erectly to a height of 1.5 m (5 ft), branching near the top and carrying panicles 30 cm (12 in.) long, arranged in a series of opposite spikes, of small violet-blue flowers, two-lipped and tubular at the base. The grey-green foliage, downy at first, possesses a sage-like odour, while the shoots and stems are covered with a close, whitish down. It somewhat resembles a giant-growing catmint, or is reminiscent of some of the taller-growing salvias. The plant blooms during late summer and autumn when flowers of this colour are scarce. It is a valuable perennial for associating with the taller-growing heleniums, rudbeckias and helianthus.

The only other species of garden value, also from Afghanistan, is known as *P. abrotanoides*. In contrast to *P. atriplicifolia*, this species is much-branched, growing 1.2 m (4 ft) high, but otherwise it is similar in bloom and foliage. Both are desirable, shrubby perennials worthy of much wider cultivation.

Neither species is quite hardy in cold districts, but unless the winter has been unusually severe, they will come away from the base in the spring after being reduced to ground level. *P. atriplicifolia* is quite easy to propagate from green-wood cuttings with a heel, taken in the spring; otherwise the hard, woody rootstock is difficult to break up into divisions. Transplant when dormant during winter.

Perovskia atriplicifolia

PETRORHAGIA
Caryophyllaceae   Tunic flower

Only one species of this genus is commonly grown. *P. saxifraga* (syn. *Tunica saxifraga*) produces a cloud of pale pink flowers like a small gypsophila. It grows to 20 cm (8 in.) high, and two double forms are available. 'Alboplena' is double white, and 'Rosette' is double pink. Propagation is by cuttings or division.

PHLOMIS
Lamiaceae   Jerusalem sage

This genus consists of about 100 species of herbaceous perennials and shrubs from southern Europe and the Mediterranean region. They are sage-like with woolly leaves.

P. cashmeriana has light lilac flowers in summer, growing 60 cm (24 in.) high.

The best-known species is the sub-shrubby *P. fruticosa*, which grows to 60–90 cm (24–36 in.), with heads of curious yellow flowers.

P. russeliana (syn. *P. viscosa*) has large, golden

Pentas bussei

Phlomis russeliana

yellow flowers and grows about 1 m (3 ft) high.

P. tuberosa may grow to 1.5 m (5 ft), with rosy purple flower-heads.

All prefer well-drained situations in full sun and will thrive in dry climates. Plants can be increased by cuttings taken in autumn.

PHLOX
Polemoniaceae

This genus of 60 species of annuals and perennials is confined to America. The only annual species in cultivation, *P. drummondii*, with its present strains and varieties, is among our finest bedding plants. The perennial phlox have been derived from the herbaceous, deep purple species *P. paniculata*, previously known as *P. decussata*. Rose and white forms of this species also exist and were used in the breeding of the present-day varieties.

Good cultivars of *P. paniculata* include:

'Border Gem'—deep violet-purple; 90 cm (36 in.).
'Bright Eyes'—white with a crimson eye; 90 cm (36 in.).
'Caroline Van den Berg'—heads of mauve, a self-colour; 90 cm (36 in.).
'Le Mahdi'—strong growing, violet-mauve; 90 cm (36 in.).
'Leo Schlageter'—rich, velvety, dark red; 90 cm (36 in.).
'Lord French'—cerise; 90 cm (36 in.).
'Mies Copyn'—lilac-pink, good in warmer areas; 90 cm (36 in.).
'Prince George'—orange-salmon, very bright; 90 cm (36 in.).
'Sir John Falstaff'—rich salmon-pink; 90 cm (36 in.).
'Snowman'—more dwarf, icy white with green eye; 60 cm (24 in.).

P. maculata provides us with two good cultivars similar in growth habit to *P. paniculata*. The plants have erect growth and tall, cylindrical spikes, which are quickly followed by others, especially if the spent heads are removed. 'Alpha' has fragrant heads of rosy lilac, and 'Omega' has similar heads of white flowers with a small, lilac eye. Both will grow to 90 cm (36 in.).

These indispensable hardy perennials, with their marvellous range of shades, will grow in almost any soil, but will not flower long if subject to very dry conditions. In warmer districts partial shade and generous mulching are recommended. If ample water is available, a second crop of blooms can often

Phlox paniculata 'Mies Copyn'

be secured by snipping off the flower-heads as soon as they are finished and not allowing the plants to set seed. It is also a good idea, if planted in exposed positions or dwarf plants are required, to snip out the centre of the shoots in the spring when 15 cm (6 in.) high. This will keep the ultimate flowering height down to 45 cm (18 in.). Most of the newer varieties are dwarf or semi-dwarf, but some will grow about 1 m (3 ft) in sheltered spots.

Another smaller phlox is *P. stolonifera*, so named because of its growth habit. The cultivar 'Adrienne' is about 30 cm (12 in.) tall, with elegant, cylindrical heads of bright lilac-pink in mid-summer.

There are several prostrate-growing species of phlox, the best known being *P. subulata* and hybrids between other trailing or tufted species such as *P. nivalis*, *P. bifida* (*P. stellaria*) and *P. stolonifera*. These are of the greatest value for rockeries, banks and rock walls, while many are very suitable as trailing plants. During late spring they burst into a blaze of colour, entirely covering the plants. They resist dry conditions and thrive reasonably well in poor or sandy soils. The many uses of these hardy plants make them a first-rate subject for small or large gardens. A few of the best species and hybrids are:

P. amoena variegata—forms rosettes of pink, green and white, with bright pink flowers.
'Betty'—deep pink.
'Blue Ridge'—soft lavender-blue.
'Camla'—soft pink.
'G.F.Wilson'—lilac-blue.
'May Snow'—pure white.
'Scarlet Flame'—scarlet-red, vigorous.
'Temiscaming'—purple-red, vigorous.
'Vivid'—pink with darker eye.

Plants are sometimes affected by a form of eelworm. It attacks the young shoots, giving the leaves a much wrinkled or curled-up appearance. Affected portions should be cut off and burnt, as this may allay the infection, but once this trouble appears in a bed it is hard to eradicate. A black leaf spot sometimes attacks the young shoots when nearing flowering stage, but this does not materially affect the blooming of the plants. It can, however, be controlled with a fungicide spray.

Increase can be from divisions of old established clumps if healthy, or from root cuttings 5-7.5 cm (2-3 in.) long, which should be inserted upright in

Phlox subulata 'Temiscaming'

sand, the tips just protruding above the surface. If taken in late autumn or early winter, these root cuttings will have formed eyes and a single shoot in time for planting out in the spring, and will flower freely during the autumn months after the older clumps have finished.

PHORMIUM
Phormiaceae   New Zealand flax

The genus consists of two species, both native to New Zealand. The common *P. tenax* is to be seen growing wild in most of the damp or swampy lands, particularly in the North Island.

P. cookianum 'Tricolor' is a most attractive variegated form of the hardy mountain flax. The striking green leaves up to 60-75 cm (24-30 in.) long are striped with cream and edged with red. The flowers of *P. cookianum* are always pendulous, which distinguishes them from the erect flowers of *P. tenax*. It makes a fine tub plant and will tolerate drought as well as wet conditions. Numerous cultivars of this species have been raised, some of which are hybrids with *P. tenax* forms.

'Bronze Elf'— a low-growing, bronze-leaved plant.
'Cream Delight'—attractive soft cream variegation; to 1 m (3 ft).
'Dark Delight'—fairly erect to 1 m (3 ft), deep purple-bronze, deepening with age.
'Dazzler'—drooping bronze leaves heavily striped with red, apt to revert to all bronze; grows to 1 m

Phormium cookianum 'Duet'

(3 ft) slowly.

'Duet'—growth erect and spreading, leaves green with creamy white variegation, 1 m (3 ft); exceptionally free-flowering.

'Maori Chief'—this and others in the Maori series have bronze leaves striped with pink and red in various ways.

'Rainbow Red'—similar to the Maori series but in time develops pink leaves that fade to cream when old. Young plants show rich red colour.

'Rubrum'—the best dark reddish purple cultivar; 1 m (3 ft).

'Thumbelina'—very narrow, bronzy purple leaves; to 30 cm (12 in.).

'Yellow Wave'—spreading growth, leaves strongly variegated with yellow; to 1.2 m (4 ft).

P. tenax is the common native, green-foliaged flax, growing 1.8–2.4 m (6–8 ft) tall. The various variegated and coppery red-foliaged forms are particularly useful in modern gardens. Cultivars of *P. tenax* include:

'Goldspike'—vigorous and erect, with yellow-striped leaves to 1.5 m (5 ft).

'Guardsman'—very erect to 1.5 m (5 ft); bronze leaves are striped with red and deep pink; very striking.

'Radiance'—very striking, erect foliage with broad bands of yellow; to 1.2 m (4 ft).

'Williamsii'—an erect-growing form with 15 cm (6 in.) wide green leaves, heavily veined with yellow; distinct from the more common 'Radiance' in that the tips of the leaves droop grace-

fully; foliage grows 1.5 m (5 ft) tall; flower-spikes to 3 m (10 ft).

These various forms of *P. tenax* can be put to a number of uses, as they are most accommodating plants. The smallest are happy in the rockery, adding quite a distinctive note, while they make excellent long-suffering tub or pot plants. Increase is from divisions during winter or spring, while there is quite a chance of securing something different from seed.

Phormium tenax 'Williamsii'

PHYGELIUS
Scrophulariaceae   Cape figwort

These are South African shrubby perennials, of which *P. capensis* seems to be the best known. An erect-growing plant 1 m (3 ft) high, with glabrous, deeply veined, fuchsia-like leaves, it produces terminal heads of narrow, tubular, pendant, scarlet, penstemon-like flowers in pairs, with protruding stamens. This plant flowers freely during summer and autumn, providing its best display during the hot weather. In its wild state the plant is said to be variable in colour, and a selected scarlet-flowered variety is known as 'Coccineus'.

P. aequalis is an erect-growing, shrubby perennial, similar to *P. capensis* except that the flower-

PHYSALIS
Solanaceae   Bladder cherry

There are about 100 annual and perennial species, mostly American, but few are of any horticultural value. The best-known and most attractive is *P. alkekengii* (syn. *P. franchetii*), commonly called the Chinese lantern plant. This produces whitish underground stems, which spread quickly in light, moist soils, throwing up numerous unbranched, 60 cm (24 in.) stems, well furnished with large, light green leaves and small, whitish flowers at the axils. In the autumn an ornamental bladder-like calyx 5 cm (2 in.) across develops from the insignificant flowers, and finally reaches a brilliant shade of coral-red or orange-scarlet. These attractive fruits remain on the stems after the leaves have fallen, when they become most decorative, retaining their colour throughout the winter. When the bladders are all coloured, the stems may be cut and hung to dry in an airy shed.

Plants will thrive to perfection in semi-shade and any odd corner where other plants may fail. They can be readily increased from seed sown in the spring, or by root divisions any time during winter. In very light soils the plants may need to be kept in bounds by a band of tin or similar barrier, but the surplus roots can easily be removed, and there is no need for the plants to become a pest. Transplant while dormant during winter.

PHYSOSTEGIA
Lamiaceae   Obedient plant

The common name is derived from the fact that the hinged flowers remain at the angle at which they are turned.

The genus consists of 15 herbaceous species native to North America. The best-known species, *P. virginiana*, is apparently the only one of any garden value. The pretty foliage surrounds the graceful spikes about 1 m (3 ft) high, lightly branched at the top, carrying numerous pale orchid-purple flowers. It is also sometimes called false dragonhead, as the tube-shaped blooms resemble a small snapdragon. The buds and flowers grow on a stem as if arranged on the four sides of a square. A

Phygelius aequalis 'Yellow Trumpet'

heads are more compact and larger, and the tubular blooms are larger. The form commonly grown is a dull salmon on the outside and orange touched with purple inside. This species is quite hardy, growing about 1 m (3 ft) high and across. A new cultivar called 'Yellow Trumpet' has shiny, green leaves on a compact bush. The long, creamy yellow flowers hang down in clusters, similar to a penstemon, and they continue from summer until winter.

Phygelius is grown as a pot plant in very cold countries, and is also used for bedding out in the spring. It seems to be fairly hardy, even in cold districts, although heavy winter frosts usually cut plants to the ground. In warm districts the bushes are best pruned back heavily in the spring so as to keep them from becoming ragged in appearance, treating them as herbaceous perennials. Increase is best from spring or summer cuttings, which can be set out any time from autumn until early summer. Older roots can be divided up in the winter or early spring.

Physostegia virginiana 'Vivid'

broad foliage, making an attractive rosette. The flowers are inconspicuous. Plants can be increased by division or raised from seed in spring.

PLATYCODON
Campanulaceae   Balloon flower

The platycodon, a monotypic genus, is very closely allied to the campanula, and was at one time known as *Campanula grandiflorus*. The 7.5 cm (3 in.) flowers have five petals, opening out rather flat, but when in bud they resemble inflated balloons, hence the common name. The flowers, which are single, rarely double, are mostly in shades of blue, some being beautifully veined either with white or a deeper blue, while pure white forms occur. They begin flowering in early summer and continue over a long period. The thick, fleshy roots give an indication that plants resent wet feet and will tolerate dry conditions, preferring a sunny open border. They are not at all rampant, as the flower-spikes are confined to the original rootstock, which increases slowly.

The only satisfactory method of increase is from seed, which germinates freely in the spring, the seedlings blooming the same year. The only recorded species, known as *P. grandiflorus*, is considerably variable, but the form usually grown reaches a height of 45–60 cm (18–24 in.). A dwarf-growing and more compact form is known as *P. g. mariesii*,

deep pink form called *P. virginiana* 'Vivid' is the most popular. A pure white-flowered variety is also grown, and a pale pink variety is called 'Rose Bouquet'.

This interesting, easily grown perennial will do well under almost any conditions, although it does better in a moist soil and will always thrive in the shade. All are suitable as cut flowers, remaining in a fresh condition for quite a long period.

In light, free soils these plants spread rapidly and should be divided up every year or two. The flowering period is from late summer until late autumn. Easily increased from divisions, plants should be set about 45 cm (18 in.) apart and planted out during winter.

PLANTAGO
Plantaginaceae

Plantains are not usually welcome on the lawn or in the garden, but one species is grown for its handsome purple foliage. *P. major* 'Atropurpurea' has

Plantago major 'Atropurpurea'

Platycodon grandiflorus

while a small-flowered type growing up to 90 cm (3 ft) high used to be listed as a distinct species, *P. chinensis*. These and other forms have been isolated and raised from seed through several generations and now come reasonably true to type. 'Snowflake' is a very attractive, semi-double white; 'Mother of Pearl' is another in pale pink; and a deep blue selection is named 'Apoyama'. Double-flowered forms do not set seed and must be increased from cuttings taken in the spring when the new shoots are 5 cm (2 in.) long. Transplant when dormant during the winter months.

PLECTRANTHUS
Lamiaceae

This is a genus of trailing or bushy perennials grown primarily for their foliage. They come from various sub-tropical areas and are not hardy in cooler climates, although they grow freely where frosts are not heavy. If cut back by frost, they will shoot again in spring. They prefer a position in moist soil in partial shade.

P. coleoides has purple stems and spikes of lilac

flowers in the autumn. It spreads quickly but is too vigorous for ground cover.

P. fruticosus (syn. *P. saccatus*) is shrubby, up to 80 cm (32 in.), and in the autumn has quantities of mauve-blue flowers.

P. mahonii grows to 90 cm (36 in.) and has lovely spires of soft pink flowers over fresh green foliage, maroon on the undersides. It flowers in the autumn, making an excellent contribution at this season. This species is hardy in most coastal districts.

Propagation is by division or cuttings in spring.

POLEMONIUM
Polemoniaceae Jacob's ladder

This is a genus of hardy herbaceous perennials, several of which are good garden plants.

P. caeruleum has fern-like foliage and grows to 60 cm (24 in.) or more, bearing numerous spikes of small, blue flowers.

P. foliosissimum has more foliage on the flower-stems and deeper blue flowers. A good cultivar with bright blue flowers, to 45 cm (18 in.), is named 'Sapphire'.

P. pauciflorum is an uncommon species, with tall stems of yellow, drooping flowers. It appreciates a moist soil in sun or partial shade.

Propagation is by division of plants in spring or by seed sown in autumn.

Polemonium caeruleum

POLIANTHES
Amaryllidaceae   Tuberose

This old-time, sweet-scented, tuberous perennial, a native of Mexico, was first introduced into England in 1629. The waxen appearance and the exotic fragrance of the flowers of *P. tuberosa*, the only species in the genus, may give the impression that it requires hot-house conditions to be grown successfully, but anyone can bloom this plant freely if a few simple instructions are followed.

The most popular variety is a double, creamy white form called *P. tuberosa* 'The Pearl'. A single-flowered variety with trumpet-shaped blooms is also attractive and less heavy in appearance. The leaves are long and grass-like.

Once a crown of tuberose has bloomed it will never bloom again, and many gardeners throw them out in disgust. The secret of success is to plant fresh side shoots each year, discarding the old crowns. These offsets should be grown in a nursery bed for the first season, then lifted the following autumn or winter, stripped of their numerous side shoots, and planted in the garden. They should bloom the season after they reach full size, although under ideal conditions and in warm districts, the selected largest offsets are likely to flower in the late autumn, and even during winter, after being planted out. If left attached to the parent clump, the offsets are usually too numerous and crowded to reach full flowering size, although occasionally small, poor-quality spikes are produced. Crowns or roots are usually transplanted when dormant during winter.

POLYGONATUM
Liliaceae   Solomon's seal

This genus comprises 50 species, most of which are attractive, hardy, herbaceous plants, widely dispersed over the northern temperate regions.

P. multiflorum is a popular and easily grown herbaceous plant, with arching stems, 60–90 cm (24–36 in.) long, furnished with light green leaves on either side. From the axils of these, small, drooping, tubular and bell-shaped, white flowers, up to 5 cm (2 in.) long, appear in spring. The flower-stems are particularly suitable for large, indoor decorations. There is also a double-flowered form and one with attractive, variegated foliage, but they are not very vigorous.

While the plant will thrive in almost any soil, bold clumps are seen at their best under tall trees. In some climates the flowers are followed in the autumn by black or purple berries. Plants are easily increased by dividing up the long, fleshy rootstocks.

There are quite a number of other hardy species worth cultivating. *P. oppositifolium* has white flowers ribbed with red; *P punctatum* has white flowers with lilac spots; and *P. roseum* is a dwarf-growing, pink-flowered species.

All species are dormant during the winter, and should be transplanted at this time. The thick, fleshy rhizomes lie just under the surface of the ground and care should be taken not to damage the new season's shoots.

Polygonatum multiflorum

POLYGONUM
Polygonaceae   Knotweed

This large and varied genus of annuals and perennials includes a perennial that is valuable for cooler districts. *P. bistorta* grows to 45 cm (18 in.), with oval

Polygonum campanulatum

leaves and soft pink flower-spikes. It does particularly well in a damp position. The variety 'Superbum' sends up numerous 1 m (3 ft) spikes of clear pink flowers in early summer.

P. campanulatum has narrow, oval, velvety leaves up to 15 cm (6 in.) long and elegant, branching heads of pale pink, fragrant, bell-shaped flowers in summer.

Propagation is by seed or division in autumn or spring.

POTENTILLA
Roseaceae

This large group of perennials, herbs and shrubs comprises 500 species, which are found throughout the northern temperate and frigid zones. There are a number of attractive shrubby species, but in the herbaceous section the lovely varieties available are mostly hybrids of *P. atrosanguinea*, which has 2.5 cm (1 in.), single, scarlet flowers, freely produced on 45 cm (18 in.), branching stems, and *P. nepalensis*, which is rather variable in colour, but usually orange-scarlet to purplish crimson. *P. argyrophylla* is the parent species of the yellows. A single-flowered, cerise-pink with a deeper eye, called 'Miss Willmott', is a form of *P. nepalensis*, and probably the best.

An interesting, lower-growing species with bright yellow flowers on loose, terminal clusters is called *P. recta*. A selected form of this species and an excellent garden plant, seldom exceeding 30 cm (12 in.), is called 'Warrenii'.

P. rupestris is an early-flowering species, with white flowers with yellow eyes. These are carried on branching heads over a dense cluster of leaves. *P.* 'Firedance' is a splendid cultivar that is quite easily grown. It is semi-prostrate with a long succession of single flowers in which shades of orange, salmon and red are intermingled.

There are a number of double-flowered varieties and these are most desirable border plants. The variety 'William Rollison' has rich orange flowers with yellow centres, while 'Mons Rouilliard' is a deep blood-red with a golden seam running through the double blooms. 'Vulcan' is a dark crimson-maroon.

One reason these plants are not as popular as they might be is that the flower-stems are inclined to sprawl, lying almost flat on the ground instead of being held erect. However, this can be avoided by supporting plants with wire hoops.

Potentilla recta 'Warrenii'

The single varieties increase from runners, like strawberries, and also grow readily from seed. The hybrid doubles must be divided up from old clumps. Plants can be shifted during the winter months.

PRIMULA
Primulaceae

The genus *Primula* has a wide natural distribution and species are diverse. Some are adapted to moist, shady situations while others are best treated as alpines. Most species prefer a cold winter and cool summer, dying out if extended drought and excessive heat prevail.

Plants of many primula species are completely dormant in the winter, and can be transplanted during the winter months or when plants are just commencing top growth in the spring. They need to be well established at least one season before good blooms can be expected. Large roots resent disturbance.

Auriculas
P. auricula is a hardy perennial from the mountain regions of Europe and can be easily grown in cooler climates. Border or garden auriculas are very hardy, with leathery leaves and purple and yellow flowers. Almost every conceivable shade and combination of colours exists, although the tendency is towards deep violet-blue and rich maroons, with yellow or cream centres. Pure self-colours are much sought after. Plants grow to 25 cm (10 in.) and flower in early spring. The foliage is smooth and leathery, and many varieties are heavily powdered with a fine, mealy substance called farina. This substance, which is also present on most of the garden hybrids, has given rise to the common name of 'dusty millers'. In England, where these plants thrive to perfection in the cooler conditions, they are divided into two sections, the show auriculas and the alpine auriculas. Both sections are very fine, although the show auriculas provide the greatest range of colour combinations. Fresh seed germinates well but requires rather cool conditions. Plants need careful attention and must never be allowed to dry out.

Auriculas delight in leaf mould, good turfy loam, and plenty of coarse sand for drainage. Grass grubs

Primula aurantiaca

and other insects are rather fond of the roots, but this can be controlled by dusting the plants in their permanent position with a suitable insecticide.

Candelabra primulas
Perhaps the easiest of these 'cold climate' primulas to grow are the candelabra primulas, which produce whorls of umbels of bloom or tiers of flowers, one above the other, on 60–90 cm (24–36 in.) stems. The large, deeply wrinkled leaves on the ground around the central crown produce in the spring several of these most attractive scapes of bloom. The roots are quite dormant in the winter when all the foliage dies away completely. As a rule, seedlings require a full summer's growth to produce large enough crowns to flower freely the following spring, and it is difficult to provide suitable growing conditions throughout the summer in hot districts. A semi-shady situation that never becomes dry is desirable. Plants of this type can be very easily grown on the edges of ponds or banks of streams. These primulas are intolerant of

lime, delighting in acid conditions provided by peaty soil or leaf mould.

The following species include the better-known and more easily grown, hardy, taller primulas, which present no difficulty in moist climates. Remember that the main requirements are peaty or acid soil, semi-shade in hot districts and ample water in summer.

P. aurantiaca grows up to 50 cm (20 in.), with whorls of flowers in various shades of orange to reddish orange. It hybridises easily, so the seedlings are variable.

P. beesiana. The true species is now difficult to obtain because it crosses readily with other species of the candelabra primulas that come within range. This is hardly to be regretted because the hybrids are more attractive, less coarse in growth, with flowers in a wider range of shades. The true type is a shade of rosy mauve with a yellow eye, while the 'Beesiana Hybrids' range in colour from pink, rose, orange-red to mauve and purple, the whorled flower-stems being 60–75 cm (24–30 in.) tall.

P. bulleyana resembles *P. beesiana* and other species in this group, requiring the same moist, preferably semi-shady, conditions. The colour is usually deep orange, but in the hybrids or strains the range of colour varies from deep yellow to almost tangerine. Increase, as with similar species, is from fresh seed, preferably sown in the autumn on finely chopped-up moss, kept damp in a shady spot until seedlings appear.

P. burmanica is closely allied to and often confused with *P. beesiana.* It does not cross readily with other species in the candelabra group, so true stock is easily secured from seed. The flowers, which are borne in three to six tiers on 60 cm (24 in.) stems, are usually a brilliant shade of reddish purple with a yellow eye. This species is most attractive when planted massed and grouped with the orange-yellow species *P. bulleyana.* Moist, semi-shady conditions or a cold winter climate are preferred.

P. heladoxa is probably the easiest of the candelabras to grow, and it is also the tallest, growing to more than 1 m (3 ft) in moist conditions. It is also the

Primula japonica 'Millers Red' (left) and 'Postford White' (right)

only one with evergreen foliage; all the others lose their leaves in winter. This species may develop up to 10 whorls of bright yellow flowers from spring until early summer. It seems to enjoy warmer areas.

P. japonica is probably the oldest and best known of the tall-growing candelabra type, having been in cultivation in Europe for centuries. It does not require as much moisture as other species of this kind, but it is a shade-lover and prefers a mixture of loam and leaf mould. The leaves are large and the flower-scapes tall and strong. The best types are a deep red colour, but it is a most variable species, and pale shades also occur, some being rather dull or unattractive. Seedlings reproduce almost invariably true to the parent type, and if seed is saved from a select stock, good colours should result. 'Postford White' has pure white, drumstick flowers, and 'Millers Red' is a really bright crimson.

P. pulverulenta is one of the easiest species to grow and a true perennial, the clumps of which can readily be divided as older roots seldom die out. The

colour is usually crimson-red with a purple eye, the robust, tiered flower-scapes reaching a height of 75 cm (30 in.). It is a particularly suitable species for massing in moist, shady woodlands or beside water. A strain of beautiful pink shades is known as *P. pulverulenta* 'Bartley Strain'.

Sikkimensis primulas
This is a group of fragrant primulas, often referred to as cowslips.

P. alpicola is a variable, cowslip-like, plant with fragrant flowers in shades of yellow, violet or white in early summer.

P. florindae, the Himalayan cowslip, is another species that grows and flowers best in colder areas. It is vigorous, usually reaching 60–75 cm (24–30 in.) tall, with heads of yellow, dangling flowers. Most seed strains include shades of orange and red. This species flowers later than other tall primulas, thus extending the season.

P. sikkimensis, sometimes called the giant cowslip, is never happier than when growing alongside a stream, with its 'toes' in the water. It is sweet-smelling, with fresh green foliage, and 60–90 cm (24–36 in) stems surmounted by drooping, citron-yellow flowers, and is another choice plant for a moist place in cooler districts.

Other species
P. capitata mooriena has large, fragrant, white flowers in bunches atop stout stems 25–60 cm (10–24 in.) long. It is quite easy to grow and flowers in spring.

P. cockburniana is like a small candelabra with dainty whorls of dark orange in late spring. It is charming but not long-lived, so seed should be collected.

P. denticulata is perhaps the best-known and most popular of all the Asiatic primulas. Although delighting in water-side conditions and a cold climate, it is equally at home in partial sun as in the shade, provided the shallow roots do not become dry during the summer. The leaves are comparatively narrow and crinkly, while the spherical, ball-shaped flower-head, composed of numerous florets, is held on a short, stout scape, usually 25–35 cm (10–14 in.) long. The plant commences to bloom early in the spring, as soon as the weather begins to warm up, several scapes of bloom appearing on a single clump. The usual colour is pale lilac to bluish mauve, but all

Primula sikkimensis

Primula denticulata 'Alba'

the tones are attractive and never washed out or faded. Several selected forms have been raised, including a pure white variety and a deeper-coloured form known as 'Viscount Byng'; the nearest to red is called 'Ruby'. Unfortunately, none of these forms will bloom freely in warmer districts where there is little or no frost.

P. juliana includes a number of hybrids, of which 'Wanda' is the best known. It grows as a primrose and has claret-purple flowers in spring.

P. x *kewensis* is a hybrid raised at Kew. It has primrose-yellow heads of flowers to 30 cm (12 in.) in winter and early spring. It can be grown in open shade in milder coastal gardens.

P. malacoides is a popular bedding plant but will be perennial if the flowered stems are removed before seeding. The modern strains breed true from seed and should be sown in summer under cover for winter flowering outdoors, or under glass in cold districts. Pure white, lavender, rose and crimson strains are grown. 'Nobel Rose Eye' is a new form with rounded heads of soft pink flowers, each with a deep rose centre. It reaches 18 cm (7.5 in.) and flowers profusely. 'First Love' is another mixed strain, growing to only about 15 cm (6 in.).

P. obconica is frequently grown as a pot plant but is successful outdoors in shady places that are free from frost. The leaves are broad and hairy on the underside, and the flowers are up to 4 cm (1.5 in.)

across. Colours include pink, red, blue and white.

P. rosea 'Grandiflora' is a low-growing plant for moist places in a cold climate. The flowers are a bright carmine-rose, appearing in early spring before the leaves, and growing up to 25 cm (10 in.). It is lovely in a mass planting.

P. sieboldii has tufts of soft, heart-shaped leaves and loose heads of attractive flowers in various colours—white, rose-pink, rosy magenta and inter-mediate shades. This species can be grown from seed or increased by division. It does best in cool climates.

P. vialii is a Chinese species quite unlike other primulas, with pointed spikes to 45 cm (18 in.), with red buds opening to lavender. It may be grown quite successfully in cooler climates in half-shade.

Primroses and polyanthus

Primroses have been derived from *P. vulgaris* and, strictly speaking, have short flower-stems. Poly-anthus have been derived from a cross between a primrose and a cowslip, and flower-heads are borne on a single stem held clear of the leaves.

Over the last 20 years, these plants have been sub-ject to intensive plant breeding, and both primoses and polyanthus occur in a range of colours covering the full spectrum, including blue and green. Because of the intensive breeding, the distinction between primroses and polyanthus is arbitrary and the two

Primula sieboldii 'Mikado'

types grade into each other. Some strains developed with very large flowers, and these are best suited as pot plants to be grown under cover. Others with smaller flowers have been developed as bedding plants that will stand up to the weather. Two features in the development of modern primroses/polyanthus have been the change from biennial to annual habit, allowing the plants to flower more quickly from seed, and the ability to flower from late autumn right through winter, making them important winter bedding plants. While these changes have been going on, some specialist growers have maintained more traditional forms.

The Cowichan strain is characterised by a lack of any marked eye colour. It comes in rich, glowing colours, and unlike the modern bedding types, individual plants will survive in the garden for many years.

Double forms of both primrose and polyanthus have been known for many centuries. However, because doubleness has been achieved by the con-

Polyanthus, Cowichan strain

version of all sexual parts of the flower into petals, they are not normally propagated by seed. This century, Florence Bellis, at her Barnhaven Nursery in Oregon, was able to produce a seed strain that gave a population of plants approximately 25 percent double flowers and 75 percent single. The maintenance of the Barnhaven strain was continued until recent times in Britain, and superior selections have been made and propagated vegetatively in a number of countries.

The gold-laced polyanthus is a very striking and distinct type of polyanthus. It was developed over several centuries by artisans in the north of England, who grew plants in pots for competitions. It was dis-

Primula vialii

Gold-laced polyanthus

tinguished by having a scarlet or chocolate-maroon ground colour with a very precise gold edging to the petals. The edging joined up with a large, circular eye of the same colour. The lacing makes the five or six petals appear to be 10 or 12. As with the double primrose/polyanthus, highly desirable plants were maintained by vegetative propagation, and only enthusiasts produced seed for their own use. In recent years a good-quality seed strain was made available by Barnhaven, and selected plants can now be more easily obtained. A double gold-laced form called 'Inca Gold' was produced in New Zealand.

PTEROCEPHALUS
Dipsacaceae

This is a genus of compact annual and perennial plants with scabious-like flowers and feathery seedheads. From Greece we have *P. parnassi*, a low-growing perennial with crinkled leaves and large, cream-coloured flowers flushed with purplish pink, suitable for the front of the border or the rock garden in full sun. It is easily grown from seed or cuttings.

PULMONARIA
Boraginaceae   Lungwort

These are attractive dwarf or low-growing perennials, admirably adapted for growing in shady nooks or rock gardens. There are 10 different species, all of which are attractive garden plants. The foliage is rough and sometimes speckled with white, forming a neat, attractive clump even when the plant is not in bloom. They are very hardy and easily grown, and the abundance of blooms in the spring makes them worthy of more attention. Plants somewhat resemble mertensias in habit of growth and flower.

P. angustifolia opens pink at first and then changes to azure-blue, the leaves being unspotted. Two selected named varieties are worthy of mention, namely 'Munstead Blue', with lovely, gentian-blue flowers, and a deep red form known as 'Rubra'.

P. longifolia is a recent introduction. It has long leaves and rich blue flowers from mid-winter to spring.

P. saccharata produces an abundance of soft pink flowers, which change to blue as they fade in spring, and when finished the attractive silvery, mottled leaves form a neat and interesting clump.

Transplant or divide up roots in the late autumn or early spring.

PUYA
Bromeliaceae

This genus embraces about 120 species. Most are woody or herbaceous plants that die out after seeding; others are frost tender, being suitable only for growing in greenhouses or very sheltered spots.

P. berteroniana (previously *P. alpestris*) is one of the rarest and most curious plants in cultivation. In its young stage the plant resembles a young pineapple, with its rosette of greyish green, symmetrically arranged, toothed leaves 40–60 cm (16–24 in.) long.

Puya chilensis

For several years the plant changes little, except in size, and then a 5 cm (2 in.) thick, fleshy, naked spike, straight as a lance, emerges from the centre, ultimately reaching 1.2–1.8 m (4–6 ft) in height. The top half of this stem radiates with other 25 cm (10 in.) spikes, clothed with wax-like flowers 2.5 cm (1 in.) wide and 5 cm (2 in.) long, of a shade of iridescent, peacock-bluish green, a combination that is impossible to describe and defies any colour chart. These fascinating flowers are enhanced by the brilliant orange-yellow anthers. Each bloom lasts about three days, but the other buds open up in succession on these side spikes. The stiff, tough foliage suggests that it is hardy in most warmer climates. It demands full sun and prefers a loose, freely drained soil.

P. chilensis is a very large plant from Chile. The leaves are 1 m (3 ft) long, 5 cm (2 in.) wide, in huge, dense rosettes. The flower-stems, 20 cm (8 in.) thick, rise to 5 m (16.5 ft) high, with flowers, similar in shape to *P. berteroniana* but yellow, appearing in spring. This species is suitable only for parks and very large gardens.

Increase is from seeds only. Seedlings are easy to raise, but it is four to five years before the plants, which are best pot-grown, are large enough for planting out, and 10 years before they bloom. Apparently, *P. berteroniana* will seldom set seed from its own pollen and therefore needs to be crossed with the pollen of another plant blooming at the same time.

An unusual and striking juxtaposition of colours—*Alchemilla mollis* (left) and *Geranium himalayense* (right).

R

RANUNCULUS
Ranunculaceae

The genus comprises about 400 species of annual and herbaceous plants, widely distributed over the globe but mostly numerous in temperate and cool regions of the Northern Hemisphere. As well as the strains of popular garden ranunculus, of which millions are planted every year, a few species are grown. There are also several attractive, low-growing, perennial species very suitable for growing in rock gardens, but these are not described here.

R. acris is the common buttercup, but a free-flowering, full double, bright yellow-flowered form called *R. acris* 'Flore Pleno' is cultivated and is a showy, spring-blooming perennial. It is commonly called the yellow bachelor's buttons. There is also a double, white-flowered form.

R. insignis is a New Zealand native species related to *R. lyallii*. It has brownish, hairy, round and kidney-shaped leaves, and 5–7.5 cm (2–3 in.), golden yellow flowers, 10–40 on a 90 cm (36 in.) stem. Although somewhat easier to grow than *R. lyallii*, cool growing conditions are essential for success. Increase is from fresh seed sown as soon as it is ripe.

R. lyallii. This glorious Mount Cook lily, plentiful in the alpine regions of the South Island, is the giant of the race, established plants throwing up stately, branching flower-heads 1.2 m (4 ft) tall or more. The rhizome or rootstock is thick and spreading, the attractive leaves up to 30 cm (12 in.) across, and the beautiful, bowl-shaped, single flowers, sometimes duplexed, are 10 cm (4 in.) across. Unfortunately, this lovely summer-blooming plant is not happy in any but a cool climate. *R. lyallii* is greatly prized by English gardeners. The best means of increase is from fresh seed sown in the autumn or spring.

The various strains of garden or florists' ranun-

Ranunculus lyallii

culus bloom in the spring and become dormant during the summer, forming claw-like, pronged roots. There are quite a number of strains, all of which have been derived from the variable species *R. asiaticus*, which was introduced from the Orient and grown in France as far back as the thirteenth century. Most gardeners believe that, like the common buttercup, these ranunculus prefer damp or wet ground. However, if drainage is poor, it is often the case that the first or central bloom of each root will be reasonably good, but the remaining side shoots will carry smaller, inferior blooms, and the length of display will be comparatively brief. The roots of these ranunculus are fine or hair-like, and if the drainage is adequate, these roots will spread out and penetrate to a depth of 60 cm (24 in.), thus providing a rich and full supply of nutrients to sustain the plants in full vigour. If growing conditions are unsuitable, good-quality, double-flowered ranunculus will yield only semi-double or inferior single-flowered blooms.

If drainage is questionable, remove the soil or trench it to a depth of 60 cm (24 in.) and provide a layer of tree branches, old rubble or similar material so surplus water can quickly drain away. In light sandy or volcanic soils, poor-quality blooms may be due to impoverished conditions, and suitable fertilisers should be applied. Any average garden soil rich in compost or decayed vegetation will grow good ranunculus.

Stocks for sale are all raised from seed sown in autumn; the bulbs that flower in the spring are not allowed to set seed, the flowers being mown off as they appear. Bulbs should be planted with the claws downward, 5 cm (2 in.) deep and 15 cm (6 in.) apart. Larger bulbs usually indicate extra vigour and should be chosen for preference. If small bulbs are planted, these should be set out early in the autumn so they can become well established before the winter. In very cold districts and places with a prolonged wet spring, spring planting is recommended.

The best and largest-flowered strain is the Californian 'Tecolote Strain', which is available in eight colours, all fully double. The Australian 'Hadeco Strain' has large, double flowers.

REHMANNIA
Scrophulariaceae

This is a genus of five species, natives of China and Japan.

R. elata is a lovely perennial but it has a tendency to spread in light, free soil. The deep green, lance-shaped leaves, notched and irregular in outline, form decorative rosettes lying flat on the ground, and from their centres rise the dainty, 1 m (3 ft) spikes of 10 cm (4 in.), rosy purple flowers, each with a yellow throat and spotted red like delicate incarvilleas, marked in the throat like penstemons. It flowers for several months during summer, and should be watered frequently in the hottest weather.

Several interesting hybrids have been raised, including 'Kewensis', a creamy yellow with purple blotch, and 'Briscoei', a soft pink with dark veining.

Propagation is by seed sown in autumn or root cuttings taken in winter. Plants should be set out during winter or early spring.

REINECKIA
Liliaceae

There is only one species in this genus, *R. carnea*, from China and Japan. It grows about 30 cm (12 in.) tall from a creeping rhizome, with linear leaves that form a clump. Early in spring it puts up spikes of red flowers. There is also an attractive variegated form. Plants prefer a shady situation and will often burn if planted in full sun.

REINWARDTIA
Linaceae

The sub-shrub *R. indica*, from the mountains of northern India, has yellow flowers and is sometimes known as yellow flax. It grows 60 cm (24 in.) or more, and in frost-free gardens it is a valuable and showy, winter-flowering plant, growing to perfection against a sunny wall. In cold districts it may be grown in a glasshouse. Plants should be cut back after flowering, and young plants should be pruned to encourage branching. Propagation is by softwood cuttings taken in spring.

Rehmannia elata

Rheum palmatum 'Bowles Crimson'

RHEUM
Polygonaceae

These are plants of the rhubarb family, mostly grown for their handsome foliage. All are natives of Asia.

    R. alexandrae is a most unusual and striking plant, with large leaves and 90 cm (36 in.) flower-spikes covered with papery, yellow bracts. *R. australe* (syn. *R. emodi*) has large leaves with wavy margins, and tall spikes of white flowers to 3 m (10 ft). *R. palmatum* is an imposing plant, growing to 2 m (6.5 ft), with large leaves, palmately lobed. This feature is more pronounced in *R. palmatum* var. *tanguticum*.

    Rheums need ample space and good fertile soil. *R. alexandrae* needs a cold climate and very well-drained soil. Propagation is by division in spring or seed sown in autumn.

ROCHEA
Crassulaceae

This is a genus of succulent plants. *R. coccinea* has leafy stems to 50 cm (20 in.), with bright scarlet, flattish flower-heads in summer. *R. impressa* grows to 20 cm (8 in.), with smaller heads of rosy red flowers, and is quite suitable for the rock garden. Both species require sunny, dry conditions, on a wall or similar situation. They will be hardy in most coastal gardens but not inland. Increase is by seed or cuttings in spring or summer.

Rochea coccinea

RODGERSIA
Saxifragaceae

The six species of hardy, herbaceous perennials in this genus are from China and Japan. They enjoy moist situations or semi-shade, and all have handsome foliage. *R. aesculifolia* has deeply cut leaves up to 45 cm (18 in.) across, resembling horse chestnut leaves. The flowers are spikes of blush-white.

    R. pinnata 'Alba' has white flower-spikes to about 1 m (3 ft), and *R. pinnata* 'Superba' is a lovely form with bronzy leaves and deep pink flower-spikes.

    R. sambucifolia has pinnate, elder-like leaves and

Rodgersia pinnata 'Superba'

white flowers in rather dense panicles to 90 cm (36 in.).

R. tabularis has large, umbrella-like, apple-green leaves on 90 cm (36 in.) stalks, and the creamy white spikes grow more than 1 m (3 ft) tall.

All species flower in summer, and propagation is from seed or division of the rhizomes in spring. Plants prefer a well-sheltered location in moist, peaty soil.

ROMNEYA
Papaveraceae   Tree poppy

This is a genus of only one species. Its flowers have been described as 'a glorious miracle', with their semi-transparent, delicate, crinkled petals, resembling in texture the finest white silk crepe. Each flower, large and single, rather like a white paeony,

is 15 cm (6 in.) across, with a mass of golden yellow stamens in the centre. Flowers are produced in late spring and summer, borne on long stems branching near the top, and carrying 15–20 flowers, which open up in succession. The leaves are bluish green and very deeply cut.

This poppy is a semi-shrub, reaching 1.2–1.8 m (4–6 ft) in height, spreading and rather untidy in habit, but it is best treated as a herbaceous perennial and cut back near the ground each winter. The species *R. coulteri* is perhaps not as fine, or as beautifully ruffled, as its variety *R. coulteri* var. *tricocalyx*. The flowers of both are quite useful for home decorations.

These aristocrats must be planted in full sun with ample drainage, preferring sandy loam or shingly soil. It is useless to attempt to grow them in heavy, clay soils. The fleshy roots tend to decay in the winter when the plant is dormant, so a dry, sunny spot is ideal.

R. coulteri can be propagated from seed, though it is difficult to germinate, and the easiest method is from root cuttings 5 cm (2 in.) long, covered with coarse sand until the leaves appear. Spring is the best time to shift plants, and as the roots produce very little fibre, they need firm planting and a little attention until established. When well rooted, the plants should not be disturbed or dug round deeply, but otherwise they are easy to grow.

Romneya coulteri

Romulea rosea and *R. rosea* 'Alba'

ROMULEA
Iridaceae

Closely related to the crocuses, this genus of about 50 species is distributed over western Europe, the Mediterranean region, and also South Africa. They differ from crocuses in that the stem appears above the ground and the corm has a hard, brown, crust-like, leathery tunic.

R. bulbocodium is the best-known species. It grows about 15 cm (6 in.) high, and in early spring each corm produces several bright violet, bell-shaped blooms 5–7.5 cm (2–3 in.) across, with conspicuous yellow centres.

R. requienii produces a rather small corm but gives a brave display of deep violet-blue flowers with yellow anthers during winter. It is a splendid subject for the rockery when planted in a mass.

R. rosea is perhaps the strongest growing and tallest of all the species, with numerous 30 cm (12 in.), thin, rush-like leaves and rosy cerise flowers on 25 cm (10 in.) stems during late spring. It is the last to bloom. These is also an excellent white form, *R. rosea* 'Alba', which is equally easy to grow. They both open their flowers with the sun. It is advisable not to let the seed ripen on the plants to avoid unwanted seedlings.

R. sabulosa is the best of all the species and claimed by many to be the finest rock garden bulb in cultivation. The vivid cochineal-red flowers are 7.5 cm (3 in.) across, with three to four of these open bells to a bulb. A border in full bloom or a mass-planted pocket in the rockery presents a dazzling display. Unfortunately, this species is slow to increase and seldom sets fertile seed. The safest way to obtain seed is to hand-pollinate the flowers.

Romuleas have the advantage of thriving in hot, dry districts where most of the Dutch and wild species of crocuses would fail. Increase, except in some species such as *R. rosea* and *R. bulbocodium*, is rather slow from bulb division as no smalls or 'pips' are produced, but all species seed freely if happy, and stocks can be quickly increased. Bulbs raised in this way will bloom in the second season.

RUDBECKIA
Asteraceae   Cone flower

The autumn golds are greatly enhanced by the different varieties of rudbeckias, especially the double-flowered forms, which yield a wonderful crop of bloom. Like the heleniums and heliopsis, they help to continue the interest in the herbaceous border until late autumn. They are easy to grow, requiring no special cultivation or situation, but like all plants of the sunflower family they prefer full sun and free drainage, while good or enriched soil will yield better blooms.

R. fulgida is one of our best semi-dwarf perennials, commonly called black-eyed Susan. It grows up to 90 cm (36 in.) high, and should be planted in groups like Michaelmas daisies. The plants carry a profusion of starry, 10 cm (4 in.), golden yellow daisies, each with a jet-black prominent cone. There are several forms, all flowering for many weeks from late summer until autumn. *R. fulgida* var. *speciosa* is probably the one originally grown in gardens, but we now have 'Goldsturm' and *R. fulgida* var. *deamii*, with similar flowers and rather larger foliage. Both grow 60–90 cm (24–36 in.) tall, and are claimed to be superior.

R. hirta and its hybrids, also commonly called black-eyed Susan, are attractive, free-flowering plants, which provide a prolonged display of bloom

The yellow of *Rudbeckia fulgida* 'Goldsturm' contrasts well with the vivid blue
of *Salvia patens*, the red of *Lobelia splendens* 'Queen Victoria' and a white verbena.

all summer and autumn. The yellow, gold or orange flowers are often attractively zoned or tipped with brown or coppery red. Seedlings raised in the spring bloom the first season, and plants are usually treated as biennials.

R. laciniata and its various garden forms are usually strong-growing plants, often attaining 2.2 m (7 ft) in height. The form *R. laciniata* 'Golden Glow' produces large, full double flowers, yellow tinged with green before they are fully matured. *R. laciniata* 'Goldquelle' has large, chrome-yellow, double flowers, but is the only dwarf-growing form in this species, seldom exceeding 75 cm (30 in.).

R. maxima is an uncommon plant, growing to 1.5–2 m (5–6.5 ft) tall. The lower leaves are 25–30 cm (10–12 in.) long, and it has large, drooping, pure yellow flowers with high, central, black cones.

R. nitida is a tall-growing, single-flowered species, of which the German-raised form *R.* 'Herbstsonne' is decidedly the best. The interestingly scalloped foliage is a glossy deep green, and the stately, branching heads of bloom, not overcrowded, carry 12.5 cm (5 in.) wide, primrose-yellow flowers, each with a high, bright green, central cone. It blooms acceptably during late autumn. It has strong stems and grows to 2 m (6.5 ft) tall.

R. purpurea and its varieties is described under *Echinacea*.

All the rudbeckias are easily increased by dividing up the old clumps in winter or spring.

RUELLIA
Acanthaceae

RUTA
Rutaceae   Rue

This is a very variable genus of 250 species. *R. ciliosa*, from the southern United States, is a perennial herb that forms a rosette of 7.5 cm (3 in.) leaves. This gives rise to several stems bearing tubular, bluish or lavender flowers.

R. macrantha is a sub-shrub from Brazil. It grows up to 1 m (3 ft), with purple-pink, tubular flowers opening in winter in the axils of the upper leaves. It is not very frost-hardy.

Propagation is by stem cuttings taken in spring.

R. graveolens is an evergreen sub-shrub from the Mediterranean. It has aromatic foliage and glaucous, divided leaves.

The cultivar 'Jackmans Blue' is a compact form, growing only 60 cm (24 in.), with deep glaucous blue leaves, usually evergreen, against which the yellow flowers make a pleasing contrast in midsummer. Another form, 'Variegata', has leaves bordered with white.

Propagation is by cuttings taken in spring.

S

SALVIA
Lamiaceae
Sage

This is a big genus of over 500 species, including annuals and shrubs. There are many attractive herbaceous species, without which our gardens would be the poorer, particularly as many of them provide shades of blue, violet or purple not frequently found in other plants. Most, if not all, of the attractive cultivated species are hardy in all but the very coldest districts, and are easily grown in any good, average garden soil. Some of the fleshy-rooted ones, as in *S. patens*, may suffer winter damage if the soil is frozen below the surface, but such plants can be lifted and stored, like dahlias, in sawdust or sand over the winter.

S. 'Alan's Maroon', known also as 'Burning Embers', is a shrubby plant that flowers continuously from late spring until the late autumn, with good spikes of maroon flowers. It is not very frost-hardy and succeeds better in warm areas.

S. argentea makes a lovely rosette of broad, silver foliage, and in its second season produces branching stems 60 cm (24 in.) tall, bearing a good display of white flowers.

S. azurea. This erect-growing plant, 1.5 m (5 ft) tall, has deep green foliage and terminal floral whorls of bright blue flowers in the autumn. It is useful for associating with heliopsis, heleniums and other yellow flowers.

S. 'Bethellii', a form of *S. involucrata*, is often seen in gardens during late autumn. It has terminal, whorled spikes of rosy crimson flowers, not unattractive despite the hard colour. It is a strong-growing bush 1.2–1.5 m (4–5 ft) high and 1 m (3 ft) across.

S. canariensis is shrubby to over 1 m (3 ft), with white, woolly stems and panicles of purplish rose flowers and bracts.

Salvia argentea

S. coccinea has splendid spikes of showy, scarlet flowers on black stems. It grows to 60 cm (24 in.) and does well in a sunny, warm position.

S. dichroa is a half-hardy, strong-growing species 1 m (3 ft) tall, with large, hairy leaves and comparatively large flowers, pale blue lateral lobes, and white, drooping mid-lobes. It is unusual and attractive, and a useful border plant, growing to 60 cm (24 in.).

S. elegans (syn. *S. rutilans*) is the pineapple sage. It is a strong-growing, shrubby species with terminal racemes, 15 cm (6 in.) long, of bright scarlet, narrow, tubular flowers, each about 5 cm (2 in.) long. It provides a bold display in the late autumn, when a well-established clump 1–1.8 m (3–6 ft) high will yield 50–100 heads of bloom. It increases readily from divisions in winter or cuttings in spring.

S. farinacea is an interesting introduction from Texas, growing 60–90 cm (24–36 in.). The attractive foliage and stems appear to be coated with a silvery white substance, which accentuates the terminal whorls of tubular, purple-violet flowers. A lower-growing type, 'Blue Bedder', is used as an annual. Both forms are easily raised from seed sown in the spring, blooming in the autumn.

S. guarantica (syn. *S. ambigens*) forms a shrubby bush 1–1.5 m (3–5 ft) high with four-angled stems and deep green, ovate leaves 7.5–12.5 cm (3–5 in.) long. The terminal and axillary racemes, composed of five or six whorls of 5 cm (2 in.) long, tubular flowers, appear throughout summer and autumn, usually until frosts come. The colour is an intense, deep blue, most valuable and elusive in perennials. In light soils the rootstock spreads underground but not to such an extent as to become a nuisance. The cultivar 'Black Knight' has strong, shrubby growth to 1.5 m (5 ft) and bears numerous very dark blue spires all through summer and autumn.

S. haematodes is regarded by many as belonging to *S. pratensis* but the form in cultivation differs in its appearance from that species. It is an attractive plant, growing about 1 m (3 ft) high, with large, hairy leaves in rosette form, and branching, terminal whorls of bluish violet flowers forming large panicles. It grows quickly, blooming the first season after seed is sown. In mild districts it is best treated as a biennial; fresh stocks are raised easily from seed or cuttings.

S. leucantha is one of the most valuable of the late autumn-blooming perennials, continuing in flower

Salvia leucantha

in mild districts right through the winter until damaged by frosts. With its dull, sage-green leaves, silvery underneath, and woolly, floral whorls of lavender-violet with conspicuous white corolla, this is a most attractive plant, useful for cutting and for associating with the late-flowering, bright yellow *Helianthus salicifolius*. Increase is from divisions during winter or by rooting of spring cuttings.

S. mellifera has shrubby growth and interrupted spikes of lavender-blue flowers. It comes from Mexico, as does *S. microphylla*, which grows bushy to 90 cm (36 in.), with 30 cm (12 in.) long racemes of red flowers.

S. mexicana, or Mexican sage, is a bushy plant to 1.5 m (5 ft), which produces in late summer numerous sulphur-yellow bracts followed two weeks later by long, deep blue flowers—a most unusual combination. It should be pruned after flowering.

S. microphylla var. *neurepia* (syn. *S. grahamii*) has shrubby growth to 1–2 m (3–6.5 ft) and bears showy, crimson flowers from summer until autumn.

S. officinalis is the common culinary sage, of which there are three forms that are splendid foliage plants for ground cover, bedding, or providing a solid break between lower-growing perennials. *S. officinalis* 'Icterina' has grey-green foliage, strikingly variegated with yellow; 'Purpurascens' has velvety, purplish grey-green leaves; 'Tricolor' displays cream and pink variegations over the green. All are

Salvia guarantica

Salvia mexicana

freely used massed under shrubs and roses, and for general bedding use.

S. patens is one of the best lower-growing, blue-flowered perennials, with dull, sage-green, oval leaves and 45 cm (18 in.) stems carrying 5 cm (2 in.), deep blue flowers with broad tubes. A pale blue variation, 'Cambridge Blue', is a lovely, soft cornflower-blue. These are most desirable plants, blooming freely in summer and late autumn, even the first year from seed if sown early in the spring. They set seed freely, but dormant roots can be transplanted in winter and early spring.

S. pratensis is a desirable bushy, hardy perennial, 60–90 cm (24–36 in.) high, with characteristic sage-like foliage and 15 cm (6 in.), terminal spikes of blue flowers, some forms being violet, rosy purple or white. A form of *S. pratensis* called 'Tenorii' gives us deep blue flowers. All have tuberous rootstocks like *S. patens*, and are usually transplanted during winter. Increase is from seed, cuttings or divisions.

S. sclarea var. *turkestaniana*, clary sage, is a strong-growing plant with heavy stems and broad leaves 30 cm (12 in.) long. The large flower bracts, 30–45 cm (12–18 in.) long and 10–15 cm (4–6 in.) wide, are an unusual shade of silvery lavender-pink, changing with age but remaining attractive over a long period. The plant needs room to be grown well, and is seen to best advantage planted in bold clumps in semi-shade. It increases quite freely from seed sown in the spring, usually blooming the following autumn.

S. splendens is the popular scarlet salvia used for bedding. It is really a half-hardy sub-shrub, and is now offered in several shades of white, salmon, purple and pink.

S. x *superba* (syn. *S. nemorosa*) is a much-branched plant 60–90 cm (24–36 in.) high and across, with glabrous, dull green foliage, finely pubescent beneath, and numerous terminal floral whorls of violet-purple bracts 30 cm (12 in.) long throughout the summer. It is a useful plant, remaining attractive after the flowers have fallen. A selected, dwarf-growing form 45 cm (18 in) high, known as 'East Friesland', has neat, upright spikes of violet-blue flowers. 'Lubecca' grows to 60 cm (24 in.). All are splendid, trouble-free, hardy perennials, easily grown in full sun and resisting drought.

S. uliginosa is a tall-growing, narrow-leafed species from Brazil, with many-flowered floral whorls of bright blue. It is a valuable late-flowering plant for the border. Increase is from divisions and cuttings during winter or spring.

S. verticillata grows to 1.2 m (4 ft), with arching spikes of small, violet-blue flowers. 'Alba' has white flowers with green buds, and greyish leaves.

Salvia uliginosa

Sandersonia aurantiaca

SANDERSONIA
Liliaceae Gold lily of the valley

Only one species of this genus is recorded, *S. aurantiaca*, from South Africa. Allied to the gloriosas and littonias, it requires similar treatment—loose, free soil, a sunny, sheltered spot and freedom from heavy frosts. It is a lovely bulbous plant, throwing up two or more stems 30–45 cm (12–18 in.) high, each bearing a number of brilliant orange-yellow lanterns about 2.5 cm (1 in.) long, branching out on single, semi-pendant pedicels from the axil of the leaves and stem. It has been grown to perfection in loose river sand, the plants blooming profusely and also seeding well. The fleshy, tuberous roots are completely dormant during the winter, so there is no reason why they cannot be grown in very cold districts, provided bulbs are lifted in late autumn and kept in sand, and replanted when danger of spring frosts is over. If good, sharp drainage is assured and winter frosts do not penetrate more than 5 cm (2 in.)

into the soil, they can be planted 10 cm (4 in.) deep and left undisturbed. New growth is from the tips of pronged tubers, not from the top; these should be planted prongs downward. Plants can be increased readily from divisions of tubers or from seed, and will bloom the second year after sowing.

SANGUINARIA
Papaveraceae Blood root

This is a handsome North American herbaceous plant, frequently grown in cooler districts. The species *S. canadensis* is a beautiful spring-flowering plant, thriving best in rather sandy, free soil or any semi-shady situation that does not become water-logged. The attractive, bluish green, heart- or kidney-shaped leaves, produced from each terminal point of the thick rootstock, are quickly followed by pure white, single flowers resembling an open, cup-shaped water-lily 7.5 cm (3 in.) across, the centre being filled with numerous stamens. Both leaves and flowers are carried singly on 15–30 cm (6–12 in.) stems. This is a lovely subject for establishing under large deciduous trees. Even more lovely is the rare form 'Flore Pleno' (syn. 'Multiplex'), which has double flowers of glistening white.

Transplant as soon as the leaves die down in late autumn or winter. Increase is from division of the fleshy, thick, horizontal rootstock.

Sanguinaria canadensis 'Flore Pleno'

SANGUISORBA
Rosaceae   Poterium

This is a genus of about 30 species, distributed over the north temperate zone. Most species are weedy and unattractive, an exception being the beautiful *S. obtusa*, better known as *Poterium obtusum*. It is a welcome addition to the herbaceous border because it flowers during late summer, the charming, rosy pink bottle-brushes nodding on their elegant, 75 cm (30 in.) stems. This hardy species presents no difficulty in any good garden soil and yet it, and the white-flowered variety, are not at all common.

Plants may be increased by division of old, well-established clumps. The thick, leathery roots are tough and difficult to break up, but every piece with an eye attached will usually grow with little trouble if planted firmly. Transplant during winter, making sure that the roots are firmly placed in the soil.

SANTOLINA
Asteraceae   Lavender cotton

This genus of about 10 species of aromatic sub-shrubs and herbs is native to the Mediterranean region. These dwarf shrubs are usually included in

Santolina chamaecyparissus

the perennial section, as they are largely used as foliage plants.

S. chamaecyparissus forms a neat, dense, aromatic rounded bush to 45 cm (18 in.) tall and across, composed of innumerable, silvery grey, felted shoots. In summer yellow, button-like flowers protrude just above the foliage. This is a useful plant for breaking up hard shades of red, purple and magenta flowers. Plants are easily increased from cuttings, and older bushes should be cut back to about 15 cm (6 in.) high early in the spring.

SAPONARIA
Caryophyllaceae   Soapwort

This is a genus of summer-flowering annuals and perennials, particularly well suited to rock gardens.

S. ocymoides is a vigorous trailer, growing 15 cm (6 in.) tall, with plentiful panicles of rose-pink flowers in summer.

A taller perennial is *S. offinalis*, and two double forms, 'Albo Plena' and 'Roseo Plena' (sometimes called 'Rose Dream') are grown. Each stem bears a large head of fully double, pink flowers on rather sprawling stems. It is a good plant for filling in gaps between shrubs.

Propagation is by seed sown in spring or cuttings taken in summer.

SAUROMATUM
Araceae   Manarch of East

This genus of four species comes from tropical Africa and Asia. The species *S. guttatum* var. *punctatum* seems to be the only one grown of this curious, hardy, bulbous genus. The large, roundish bulb produces in spring attractive, tall, marbled stems 45–60 cm (18–24 in.) long, resembling a giant fern frond or digitated, leafed umbrella. The flower spathe, which is like the bloom of an extenuated arum lily, is yellowish green with irregular purple spots, enclosing the central, 22.5 cm (9 in.) tongue of shining purple-black. Full-sized bulbs, which are often up to 12.5 cm (5 in.) across, produce flowers out of the dry bulb without any soil or water, and can

Saponaria ocymoides

be placed in a sunny spot inside the house. After blooming, they can be planted in the garden, and the leaves will follow soon afterwards. This is a plant that never fails to attract attention, and is easily grown in any free soil in full sun. Increase is from smallish bulbs that form around the leaf-stem, on top of the parent bulb. Plant out during winter.

SAXIFRAGA
Saxifragaceae   Saxifrage

About 400 species are known, most of which are rock plants. Many are very beautiful and indispensable to a well-planted rockery. Some form a dense mat or carpet, others tufted cushion-like clumps. A number of the most attractive species, with long, dainty sprays of bloom, arise from rosettes of silvery-encrusted foliage. Some of the hardy, strong-growing varieties have been reclassified under *Bergenia*, q.v.

S. cortusifolia var. *fortunei* 'Wada' has glossy green, maple-like leaves with ruby-red undersides, from which arise loose panicles of dainty, white flowers in late autumn. It is a very attractive plant.

S. moschata is an evergreen perennial, forming a mound to 10 cm (4 in.). From rosettes of small, toothed, green leaves arise star-shaped, creamy white or pale yellow flowers on thin stems.

S. umbrosa, known as London pride, is suitable for the front of the border. It has rosettes of foliage at ground level and spreads slowly. In late spring, every rosette throws up a spike of dainty, white flowers 30–40 cm (12–16 in.) high, rather like heuchera flowers. These come in pink and red.

Propagation is by seed sown in autumn or by rooted offsets planted in winter.

SCABIOSA
Dipsacaceae   Pin-cushion flower

There are about 100 species in this genus, mostly from Europe and Asia and some from Africa. The common annual pin-cushion flower has been derived from the species *S. atropurpurea*. There are several desirable perennials, some of which are worthy of more attention.

S. anthemifolia is a procumbent, strong-growing species, introduced from South Africa and sometimes listed as *S. columbaria*. It is particularly suitable as a bank plant, covering an area 1–1.5 m (3–5 ft) in diameter in a short time. It is a most variable species if raised from seed, ranging from lavender, blue-mauve, purple and rose to white. The most desirable, pink-flowered forms should be increased from

Saxifraga umbrosa

Scabiosa columbaria (rear) and *Nepeta* x *faassenii*

cuttings taken during the winter or spring. Plants need heavy pruning once or twice a year, preferably after each main crop of bloom.

The true *S. columbaria* is a native of England, quite attractive in its own way but not comparable to its South African cousin. The smaller flowers are lilac or rosy purple, shorter stemmed and not so strong growing.

S. caucasica is the best-known and most valuable species in that it remains in bloom all spring and summer, with an occasional flower during mild spells in winter. The flower-stems are usually 45–60 cm (18–24 in.) long, each carrying one to three flattish heads of light blue flowers, about 7.5 cm (3 in.) across. A pure white form is grown under the name of *S. caucasica* 'Alba'; there is also a range of blue and lavender shades of improved types. 'Clive Greaves' is a lovely lilac-blue, and 'Miss Willmott' is the best large-flowered pure white for cutting. *S. caucasica* 'Mountain Blue' has well-formed, nicely frilled flowers that are a lovely shade of deep sky-blue, without any suggestion of mauve or lavender. A very fine, deep violet-blue variety is called 'Amy Jeffrey'. All varieties of *S. caucasica* prefer lime, and well-drained soil is essential.

S. lucida grows to 60 cm (24 in.), with clumps of oval leaves and 4 cm (1.5 in.), dense heads of lilac to mauve flowers. Selected forms have rose-pink flower-heads.

S. ochroleuca (syn. *Knautia macedonica*) grows to about 70 cm (28 in.), with oval, dentate, grey-green leaves and pale yellow flower-heads.

S. rumelica is a vigorous, semi-prostrate plant, with dark green leaves and a profusion of 5 cm (2 in.) wide, very double, pure deep crimson flowers on curved, 60 cm (24 in.) stems. It is rather floppy in habit, but valuable on account of its colour and the quantity of bloom. It is hardy and easily grown, but good drainage is essential.

Increase of scabiosa is from seed sown in spring or from divisions of the selected forms of *S. caucasica*. It is usually fatal to transplant them in autumn or winter, but they can be moved quite safely in spring and early summer.

SCADOXUS
Amaryllidaceae

This is a genus of bulbs that delight in partial shade and rich, well-drained soil.

S. multiflorus (syn. *Haemanthus multiflorus*) grows to 75 cm (30 in.). It has pointed, basal leaves and a spherical umbel of flowers in summer.

S. m. subsp. *katherinae* (syn. *H. katherinae*), the blood flower, has bright, apple-green, erect leaves up to 1 m (3 ft) tall and a densely flowered, cylindrical umbel, up to 22.5 cm (9 in.) across, of brilliant scarlet-red, starry flowers.

Increase of scadoxus is by seed or offsets in spring.

Scadoxus multiflorus subsp. *katherinae*

SCHIZOSTYLIS
Iridaceae   Winter ixia

S. coccinea is the better known of the two species of this hardy perennial from South Africa. It is only half-hardy in the Northern Hemisphere, but in warmer parts of the Southern Hemisphere it has been seen growing wild, mostly in high-altitude peaty swamps, the clumps resting on tufts of vege-tation a few centimetres above the water level. The roots are half-bulbous, slightly thickened at the base, with miniature gladiolus-like foliage 30 cm (12 in.) or so high persisting all the year round. During late autumn, winter and spring each clump produces several spikes of six to 10 bright scarlet-red flowers about 5 cm (2 in.) across on 45 cm (18 in.) stems. If plants are not overcrowded and are divided up each season after blooming, the flowers are larger, keep longer and carry more blooms to the spike.

A much larger-flowered form, entirely super-seding the type, is called 'Gigantea'. A pretty pink-flowered form is called 'Mrs Hegarty', while a larger-flowered, soft pink is called 'Viscountess Byng'. 'Sunrise' is a new cultivar with larger, richer pink flowers and should be obtained in preference to other pink cultivars. A pure white-flowered form, 'Alba', is also available.

Old clumps can be divided almost any time of the year, but preferably in spring.

SCILLA
Liliaceae

This was once a fairly large genus but it is now reduced to about 80 species, widely distributed throughout Europe, Asia and Africa. It is distin-guished from the hyacinths by the shape of the flower segments. Some confusion exists in some of the trade names, particularly in the English and European species.

S. bifolia is a most charming little, early-flowering bulb, common in Europe. In most countries in the Southern Hemisphere, it is slow to increase, appar-ently needing cool growing conditions. It has two strap-like leaves, 15–20 cm (6–8 in.) long and 1 cm (0.5 in.) wide, and short scapes of four to eight,

Schizostylis coccinea 'Gigantea'

hyacinth-like flowers of an intense blue very early in the spring. Plants increase freely from seed, which blooms the second season, reaching full size in the third year. Plant bulbs in autumn, 6 cm (2.5 in.) apart and 7.5 cm (3 in.) deep. A natural hybrid exists between this species and *Chionodoxa*, called *Chionoscilla*.

S. hyacinthoides (syn. *S. parviflora*) produces a large bulb, 5 cm (2 in.) across, and a profusion of offsets. The leaves are spreading, strap-like, 25 cm (10 in.) long, and the erect flower-scapes are 45–60 cm (18–24 in.) high, with open, campanula-blue or lilac-blue flowers, while pure white and rosy red forms are known. Unfortunately, this lovely bulb is noted for its extreme shyness in flowering, and nobody seems to know the secret of making it bloom. Clumps left undisturbed will, however, reward one with odd spikes from time to time. Plant in autumn, setting bulbs 7.5 cm (3 in.) deep and 15 cm (6 in.) apart.

S. italica (syn. *Endymion italicus*) produces a conical spike of up to 30 small, fragrant, pale blue flowers, opening very early in spring.

S. peruviana is commonly called the Cuban lily, a misnomer as it was once thought to have come from Peru. This species produces a large bulb, 5–10 cm (2–4 in.) across, with a ring of offsets, which should be detached and grown separately. The plant forms a rosette of broad leaves 25–35 cm (10–15 in.) long, from which rises a robust, central scape, terminating just above the foliage in a broad, conical raceme, 10 cm (4 in.) across, of violet-blue flowers with white anthers. A pure white form is sometimes found. This bulb flowers in spring, and as it is dormant for a very short time only, it should be transplanted as soon as the leaves have faded. A complete year's rest seems to be needed as the same bulb never flowers two years in succession. Plants can be increased from offsets or seeds, which take three years to mature. Dormant bulbs can be planted in late autumn, about 20 cm (8 in.) apart and 7.5 cm (3 in.) deep. It prefers a sunny position but is also happy naturalised in semi-shade.

S. siberica, the Siberian squill, is an early-flowering, rich blue, hyacinth-like bulb, somewhat resembling the chionodoxa in bloom, growing about 15–25 cm (6–10 in.) in height, with two to six flowers on a stem. A bright blue form with taller stems is called 'Spring Beauty'. *S. siberica* and its forms seem quite happy in colder districts. Increase is usually from seed, with bulbs blooming the second or third season. Healthy, vigorous stock, free from disease, can thus be more easily secured than from divisions and offsets of parent bulbs. This species is rather subject to bulb mite and attacks of narcissus fly. Transplant in autumn, setting bulbs 5 cm (2 in.) apart and the same depth.

S. tubergeniana is a welcome early-flowering bulb for the rockery, blooming along with the snowdrops and winter aconites in late winter. The flower-stems are only 10 cm (4 in.) high, each bulb yielding three to four scapes carrying two to six wide-open, delicate, light blue flowers. A pocket in full bloom in the rockery is really delightful. It should be planted in autumn, 5 cm (2 in.) apart and deep.

S. verna is the smallest of the genus and is a native of Britain and northern Europe, occurring near the sea. The starry, mauve-blue flower-spikes grow to about 15 cm (6 in.) high, but it is rather too small for general cultivation.

Scilla peruviana

Scrophularia aquatica, variegated form, and *Lobelia splendens* 'Queen Victoria'

SCROPHULARIA
Scrophulariaceae   Figwort

Only one species of this genus is generally cultivated. *S. aquatica* (syn. *S. nodosa*) and its variegated
form have striking foliage but insignificant flowers,
which are best removed. The plant grows to 1 m (3
ft) or more, with showy, large leaves, half green and
half creamy white. It enjoys moist conditions and
will grow well in bog gardens, but it is also quite
happy in mixed borders in locations with a good
spring rainfall. Stocks can be increased by seed or
cuttings.

SCUTELLARIA
Lamiaceae   Helmet flower

This genus consists of about 300 species of annuals,
perennials and small shrubs, natives mostly of temperate regions and tropical mountains, but few are
in general cultivation.

S. baicalensis is distinguished by the fact that the
foliage stems and flowers are smooth instead of
downy, while the erect flower racemes are more
closely set, the plant forming a larger bush up to 45
cm (18 in.) tall and across. It is commonly called the
skull cap because of the shape of the flowers, and is
very suitable for the front of a border. Plants are
easily raised from seed and usually bloom the second
season after spring sowing. The hard, woody roots
are not easily divided, but plants can also be
increased from spring cuttings taken when the new
shoots are a few centimetres high. These are useful,
low-growing plants, which resist dry conditions in
the autumn, blooming in spring.

S. formosana is an erect, shrubby perennial to
1 m (3 ft) tall, with ovate leaves 5–7.5 cm (2–3 in.)
long and dark violet-blue flowers in loose terminal
racemes.

S. incana (syn. *S. canescens*) is a robust plant to 1 m
(3 ft), with oval, 12.5 cm (5 in.) leaves and showy
panicles of blue flowers.

S. indica var. *parvifolia* (syn. *S. japonica*) is a
shrubby species up to 30 cm (12 in.) high and more
across, with small, rounded, dark green, toothed
leaves, slightly downy, and numerous dense racemes

Scutellaria orientalis

of hairy, violet-blue flowers, held erect.

S. orientalis is rhizomatous, with creeping and
rooting stems. The leaves are oval and toothed,
and in summer the plant has yellow, tubular
flowers, to 10 cm (4 in.), with a brownish purple
lower lip.

SEDUM
Crassulaceae   Stone crop

This is a large genus of nearly 600 species, most of
which are prostrate rock plants with rosettes of fleshy
leaves, which resist very dry conditions. All are easy
to grow but prefer sandy soil, and most will fail in
wet or heavy ground. Many of these low-growing
species are used as a carpet for covering graves or
poor stony ground, and they are also interesting for
window boxes.

S. adolphi 'Variegata' is grown mainly for its
attractive, variegated foliage, up to 30 cm (12 in.).

S. sieboldii 'Variegata' makes a lovely pot and
hanging-basket plant, with yellow, variegated leaves
on trailing stems and terminal heads of purple-red
flowers in late summer. Both these variegated forms
are hardy enough for outdoor planting in most
coastal districts.

S. spectabile is used extensively in perennial
borders. It has fleshy, glaucous green leaves in

Sedum spectabile 'Autumn Joy'

whorls up the 60 cm (24 in.) flower-stems, topped with umbels of flowers 10 cm (4 in.) or more across. The common type is a lilac-pink shade, but a selected form, 'Brilliant', has bright purple-red flowers in late spring and mid-summer, lasting in bloom over a long period. Under glass it will flower almost any time of the year. This is one of the few hardy sedums that will thrive in heavy clay ground, which it prefers to very light or poor soil, remaining in bloom over a long period. Forms of this species include 'Autumn Joy', brick-red, 'Carmen', a light carmine-rose and 'Meteor', a glowing rosy red. *S.* 'Weihenstephaner' is a mat-forming plant with golden yellow flowers in summer.

S. 'Vera Jamieson' is a new hybrid with purplish foliage and heads of pale pink flowers in the summer. It grows to 25 cm (10 in.).

Increase stock in the spring by pulling apart and planting the new shoots, which root quickly. Year-old roots can be shifted during winter.

SENECIO
Asteraceae

This is probably the largest genus in the vegetable kingdom, containing about 3000 species, most of which come from South Africa.

S. cineraria (syn. *Cineraria maritima*), commonly called dusty miller, grows to 30 cm (12 in.), spreading to 60 cm (24 in.). It has very silvery foliage and yellow daisy flowers, and is used mainly for foliage effects. 'White Diamond' is the best form.

S. crassiflorus is a medium-hardy, rapid-growing trailer, useful for covering banks or bare patches. It trails over walls, rooting as it spreads. The leaves, shoots and stems are very silvery throughout. Masses of contrasting yellow daisies are produced during summer.

S. grandifolius from South Africa grows to 1.5 m (5 ft), with bold foliage and large heads of small, yellow flowers in late summer.

S. petasitis is a shrubby species suitable for the back of the border. It has large, roundish, downy leaves and panicles of bright yellow flowers with brownish centres.

S. pulcher is a little-known but interesting and hardy perennial, growing about 60 cm (24 in.) tall, happy in sun or shade. It produces dark green, leathery, toothed leaves, and large flower-heads composed of several finely rayed, rosy purple daisies, each with a central yellow disc.

Plants can be freely increased from seed or divisions of established clumps during winter. They prefer good, rich soil and a cool root run.

See also *Ligularia dentata*.

Senecio petasitis

SIDALCEA
Malvaceae   Prairie mallow

The eight species in this genus are natives of western North America. Some are annuals, but most are hardy perennials of erect growth, 0.6–1.5 m (2–5 ft) in height. The varieties in cultivation today are mostly hybrids of the better species. The deep green leaves are palmate and partly cleft, while the erect flower-spikes carry hundreds of single, mallow-like, crimped flowers, 2.5–5 cm (1–2 in.) across, on a pyramidal terminal raceme, usually 1–1.2 m (3–4 ft) tall. They are all very showy in the border, and are worthwhile, easily grown perennials. The flowering period can be greatly extended by removing the faded flower-spikes.

S. 'Bianca' is a new cultivar with spikes of pure white flowers growing up to 90 cm (36 in.); 'Party-girl' grows to 90 cm (36 in.) with spikes of bright, clear pink; 'Rose Queen' is an older, taller cultivar with bright pink flowers; 'Sussex Beauty' has paler pink flowers to 75 cm (30 in.)

Increase of sidalcea is by division in spring.

Sidalcea cultivar

SILENE
Caryophyllaceae

This is a genus of annuals and perennials, including some very fine rock garden plants. All species are easily grown in a sunny spot in fertile, well-drained soil.

S. *maritima* is a mat-forming species with glaucous leaves up to 3 cm (1.5 in.) long and white flowers on 10 cm (4 in.) stems. The double form 'Swan Lake' has large, creamy flowers on trailing stems, and is ideal for growing over a bank or wall.

SISYRINCHIUM
Iridaceae

This is a genus of 100 annual and perennial species.

S. *angustifolium*, sometimes known as blue-eyed grass on account of its grass-like foliage and bright

Sisyrinchium angustifolium

Sisyrinchium striatum

blue, starry flowers in spring, grows to 25–30 cm (10–12 in.) and is a good rock-garden plant.

S. macounii alba is a popular small plant, with iris-like growth and masses of cup-shaped, white flowers for many weeks in early summer. It grows to 25 cm (10 in.).

S. striatum has 60 cm (24 in.) stems bearing a long succession of cream flowers. It is quite happy in partial shade, but the soil should be light and need not be rich. *S. striatum* 'Variegatum' is similar but the foliage is attractively striped with cream.

Clumps of sisyrichium can be increased by division, but *S. striatum* is best propagated from seed.

SMILACINA
Liliaceae

This genus of 25 species is native to North America.

S. racemosa, a perennial of graceful appearance, is the species commonly grown. It bears sprays of creamy white flowers up to 90 cm (36 in.) in late spring, followed by red berries. It needs a good, rich soil in partial shade, with plenty of moisture in the growing season.

Plants may be increased by division in spring or by seed sown in autumn. Rhizomes may be transplanted in autumn or spring.

SOLIDAGO
Asteraceae   Golden rod

This is a genus of over 100 species of perennials, mostly natives of North America, with a few in the south. The golden rods and the wild perennial asters are among the glories of the American autumn, as they complement each other, one with shades of yellow and gold, and the other drifts of blues and purples.

S. canadensis is the common species of solidago, plentiful in old gardens, and sometimes naturalised in woodlands, where it makes a blaze of colour during autumn. It grows to 1.8 m (6 ft) tall, with branching sprays of hundreds of miniature, golden yellow flowers. It is suitable for the back of the herbaceous border.

The following hybrids are all superior to the type, daintier in habit, lower growing, and lasting longer in bloom. They are much slower to increase, are not prolific like the wild type, stand up to hot weather better, and are useful for cutting. All can be increased by division during winter or early spring.

Smilacina racemosa

x *Solidaster luteus*

'Baby Gold'—dwarf to 45 cm (18 in.); golden yellow flowers.

'Cloth of Gold'—dwarf to 45 cm (18 in.); deep golden flowers.

'Golden Wings'—to 2 m (6.5 ft); very broad, handsome panicles of golden yellow.

'Goldenmosa'—to 75 cm (30 in.); large heads of feathery, yellow plumes, flowering in late summer.

'Peter Pan'—to 75 cm (30 in.); large, bright yellow flower-heads.

S. odora is a species grown chiefly for its aromatic foliage, which has an aniseed-like perfume when rubbed.

S. virgaurea (often wrongly called *S. brachystachys*) is a charming little plant, growing only 25 cm (10 in.) high, in contrast to the somewhat coarse, rampant species. It forms a neat bush studded with stumpy spikes of yellow during autumn, and is good for the front border or rockery.

x *Solidaster luteus* is a hybrid between a solidago and *Aster ptarmicoides*, and produces rather floppy sprays of yellow flowers, paling with age.

Solidago and solidaster may be increased by division in spring.

SPARAXIS
Iridaceae

This genus from South Africa has six species of spring- and summer-flowering corms with bright flowers. They succeed best in a warm climate on a sunny, well-drained site.

S. bulbifera has unusual-shaped corms and maize or straw-yellow flowers, which have an almost transparent appearance.

S. elegans (syn. *Streptanthera cuprea*) is an attractive plant that readily hybridises with other sparaxis. It is a striking plant, with wide-open, orange flowers with purple, black and yellow markings in the centre, on 25 cm (10 in.) stems. There is also a white-flowered form. A lovely self-coloured, scarlet-red variety, named 'Scarlet Glory', is a splendid sparaxis for massing. Another self-coloured, rose-pink variety is called 'Harre's Pink'. To maintain these self-colours or selections, it is necessary to propagate only from the bulbils that form on the

Sparaxis elegans

Sparaxis hybrids

stems, and it is essential that seed is cut off before it ripens.

S. *tricolor* is the best-known species. Its flowers are usually red or pink and white with a yellow throat. This variable species has been crossed with the creamy white and purple-flowered forms of S. *grandiflora*, and natural hybrids have also been selected, so that today these bulbs are grown as mixtures, embracing a wide range of colours and combinations of colours, through white, cream, pink, rose and crimson to purple and maroon.

Propagation is usually by offsets. Plant bulbs or offsets of all sparaxis in late summer/early autumn. If seed is sown thinly as soon as it is ripe in early summer, some will bloom the following spring.

SPILOXENE
Hypoxidaceae

This is a genus of some 20 species of cormous bulbs or perennials, mostly natives of Tropical Asia, Africa and America, few of which are worthy of cultivation.

S. *capensis* is the best-known species, producing 25 cm (10 in.) tall, thin stems, each with one to four starry, snow-white, 10 cm (4 in.) wide flowers with purple-black centres. A clump in full bloom is daz-

zlingly brilliant. When closed at night or in dull weather, the long, pointed buds are stained or striped green on the exterior.

These species or forms of spiloxene intercross readily and provide some interesting colours, intermediate between white and deep yellow, with or without the peacock centres. A district with plenty of spring sun is essential to get the best out of these bulbs, as the flowers simply refuse to open up in dull, cold weather. Like ixias, sparaxis and many other South Africans, they are seen at their best in full sun, after a shower of rain.

The bulbs increase readily. They should be planted with the smooth side down, in groups of 10 or so, planted close together, in autumn.

SPREKELIA
Amaryllidaceae   Jacobean lily

S. *formosissima*, the only known species of this genus, is a very hardy, easily grown bulb, preferring a loose, free soil and good drainage. The interesting, orchid-like, vivid crimson-scarlet flowers, 12.5 cm (5 in.) long, never fail to attract attention. The bulbs, which are roundish, 5 cm (2 in.) across with a long neck, are pure white, enclosed in a thin black skin. The six-petalled flowers are most unusual in

Sprekelia formosissima

appearance, in that three of these elongated petals, 7.5 cm (3 in.) long, are held erect and the three lower ones enclose the stamens. The flowers are produced singly on 35 cm (14 in.) stems, and the deep green, strap-like leaves soon follow. The flower-scape is formed in the bulb the previous year, and it soon rushes into bloom when the bulb is replanted in the spring. Bulbs can be held back to bloom later if desired, like the zantedeschias. In very cold districts, bulbs can be lifted in the autumn and kept in dry storage over the winter. They can then be planted out again in spring, when the heaviest frosts are over. In general this is an easy bulb to grow, and it can be safely shifted or transplanted, even when in bloom.

STACHYS
Lamiaceae   Lamb's ear

This is a genus of spring- and summer-flowering perennials, shrubs and subshrubs. Most species prefer a sunny location but in general plants are tolerant of a wide range of conditions.

S. byzantina (syn. *S. lanata* and *S. olympica*) is a well-known plant with heavily silvery felted and softly downy, 20 cm (8 in.) long leaves. These leaves, which form a neat low mat, are quite attractive and make a useful carpet that grows easily in almost any situation. The flowers are not very attractive. 'Sheila McQueen' has particularly fine, woolly flower-spikes, which will store extremely well for dried flower arrangements if cut before they are fully developed. A non-flowering form, 'Silver Carpet', grows to about 12.5 cm (5 in.) tall and has foliage that remains attractive all season, making a very good ground cover. *S.* 'Cotton Ball' is a mutant of *S. byzantina* with curious 'bobbles' of flowers along the flowering stems.

S. grandiflora (syn. *Betonica macrantha*) is the herb betony, and grows to 30 cm (12 in.) tall, with plentiful pale purple flower-spikes in early summer.

Plants are readily increased from seed or division, and will tolerate dry conditions or grow in poor, sandy soil.

Stachys byzantina, with its downy grey leaves, is a useful plant for edging a herbaceous border.

STERNBERGIA
Amaryllidaceae   Autumn crocus

This is a desirable miniature section of the amaryllis family. The best-known species is *S. lutea*, which produces freely, in the autumn, several crocus-like, bright yellow flowers, 5 cm (2 in.) across, on 15 cm (6 in.) stems. The single, strap-like leaves follow quickly after blooming, and continue growing until late spring. The 5 cm (2 in.) wide, roundish bulbs, coated with a thin, black skin, delight in a well-drained or rather dry spot, and are usually happy planted at the base of old deciduous trees. They thrive remarkably well, increasing freely in loose sandy soil, and when really at home provide a most attractive border. Like all other bulbs of this family, they are subject to attacks of the narcissus fly.

There is also a miniature-flowered form known as *S. lutea* 'Graeca', with flowers and plant growing about half-size. It is a delightful subject for grouping under trees or for large pockets in the rockery. Transplant from late summer to autumn.

Sternbergia lutea

STOKESIA
Asteraceae   Stokes aster

This genus of only one species was listed at ŏne time under asters. It is one of the finest dwarf-growing, hardy perennials and worthy of more extensive

Stokesia laevis

planting. *S. laevis* (syn. *S. cyanea*) usually has large, lavender-lilac-blue, finely rayed, double, cornflower-like blooms, 12.5 cm (5 in.) across, on branched stems 30–40 cm (12–16 in.) long. It is somewhat variable from seed, occasionally giving purplish blue, mauve, rose and even pure white forms. A very fine selected variety, raised in America and called 'Blue Moon', produces immense, mauve-blue flowers up to 15 cm (6 in.) across, while a corresponding introduction from England is called 'Blue Star'. All forms are good cut flowers and most desirable border plants, blooming through summer until autumn. These plants are particularly drought-resistant but resent heavy, wet clay soils.

Increase is from seed or divisions of older clumps during the winter months. Seedlings can be planted out until early summer, often blooming in late autumn. Root cuttings 5 cm (2 in.) long can be grown in coarse sand early in winter.

STRELITZIA
Strelitziaceae   Bird of paradise

This small genus of half-hardy South African plants comprises five or six species, of which the best known and most attractive is *S. reginae*. The stiff, concave, canna-like leaves, about 30 cm (12 in.) long, are borne on 60–90 cm (24–36 in.) stems. The flower, which rests horizontally on its tall stem, like a bird poised ready for flight, is bright orange-yellow with luminous blue-purple, and a deeper purple-violet shade at the base. When fully out, the flower resembles a bird with half-opened wings.

S. reginae is a plant of striking appearance, thriving in any good, rich soil and a sunny spot. Except in hot districts, it does not bloom freely outside. The plant itself is fairly hardy, but the flower-spikes, which are usually developed during the winter, opening up in the spring, are often damaged by frosts, resulting in malformed blooms. The thick, fleshy roots, 1.5 cm (0.5 in.) across, grow deeply and conserve moisture, helping the plant withstand hot, dry conditions. It can be grown quite easily as a tub plant, preferring a rich, fairly heavy soil. Plants under glass do not bloom until well-established in large pots or small tubs. Blooms last in fresh condition for a long time.

A very strong-growing species called *S. nicolai*, with very large leaves up to 6 m (20 ft) tall, is grown in Australia. The flowers are white with a deep purple spathe. This species is grown mostly for its attractive foliage.

S. parvifolia. Until recently this species was considered to be merely a geographical form of *S. reginae*, in that the only apparent distinguishing features are that the leaves are reduced to small, thin blades on the end of tall, stiff stalks. Some Australian growers prefer this species, which in other respects is identical to *S. reginae*, as they claim it blooms more freely. Another species, *S. juncea*, has no leaves at all—just a spiky tuft of erect stems up to 1.2 m (4 ft) tall.

Strelitzia reginae

Increase is from divisions of established clumps in the spring, or else from fresh seed, although this does not always set. The seeds, which are as large as peas, black and hard, should be soaked overnight in warm water to hasten germination, otherwise they may not come up till the following spring.

STREPTOCARPUS
Gesneriaceae

This is a genus of about 100 species of perennials, the strains available today being the result of numerous crossings, many involving *S. rexii*. These are half-hardy greenhouse or conservatory plants, but they are also grown in shade-houses or cool spots outside in frost-free districts. The deeply veined, stemless leaves, 15–20 cm (6–8 in.) long, are handsome in themselves, and central flower-stems 20–30 cm (8–12 in.) tall carry one or more bignonia-like, trumpet flowers 5–7.5 cm (2–3 in.) across. They are mostly in shades of light and dark blues, pink and rose, usually with spotted throats. The streptocarpus are valuable winter- and spring-flowering plants, easily grown and continuing in flower over a long period.

Stocks are usually raised from seed, and although not difficult to germinate and handle, care is needed as the seeds are so tiny that they can be washed away during watering or they can be covered too deeply. They should be lightly scattered on finely sieved soil or chopped moss pressed firmly and lightly watered without any soil covering. Seedlings should be pricked out twice, and will commence to bloom 10–15 months after sowing. A mixture of turfy loam, leaf mould and coarse sand is the best potting medium, although any good compost soil will do. Plants are best transplanted or divided up during winter or early spring.

SYMPHYANDRA
Campanulaceae

This is a pendulous bell-flower from the Mediterranean region. One species, *S. hoffmanni*, is commonly grown. It reaches 30–60 cm (12–24 in.) and has large, white bells on dense spikes. It prefers sandy soil and may be propagated by seed or division in spring.

Other species worth growing include *S. cretica*, which grows 45 cm (18 in.) with lilac-blue flowers in summer, and *S. wanneri*, which grows to only 15 cm (6 in.) and has rich blue bells in summer. It is a good plant for the rock garden.

SYMPHYTUM
Boraginaceae

These are herbaceous perennials native to Europe and Britain.

S. grandiflorum grows to 45 cm (18 in.) tall, with cream, tubular flowers on drooping stems above the broad, deep green leaves in spring and summer. It is excellent, quick ground cover under trees as long as the ground is not too dry.

S. officinale, comfrey, is available in a dark blue form, which grows about 90 cm (36 in.). *S. o.* 'Variegatum' is a very striking form, with 10 cm (4 in.) leaves broadly variegated with white.

Propagation is by seed in autumn or division in spring.

Symphytum officinale 'Variegatum'

T

TANACETUM
Asteraceae

This is a genus of perennials, some evergreen, with daisy-like flowers and often with aromatic foliage. Species now included in this genus were previously classified under *Chrysanthemum* and *Pyrethrum*.

T. coccineum (syn. *Chrysanthemum coccineum*, *Pyrethrum roseum*), commonly known as pyrethrum, is a native of the Caucasus. Garden hybrids derived from this species are among the finest spring-flowering perennials and are valued for the constant supply of cut flowers they provide. Plants produce neat, compact clumps of much-divided, fern-like foliage, from which arise numerous large, highly coloured daisies, 7.5–12.5 cm (3–5 in.) across, either single or double, on long, firm stems. Every shade of red and pink is represented as well as pure white.

Cultivars include:

'Brenda'—magenta-pink flowers; feathery leaves; to 60 cm (24 in.).
'Eileen May Robinson'—light pink, single flowers with yellow centres; feathery, aromatic foliage; to 75 cm (30 in.).
'Harold Robinson'—single, rosy red flowers.
'James Kelway'—dark crimson-red.
'Lord Roseberry'—fine double rosy red.
'Mrs James Kelway'—beige-pink flowers.
'Mrs Wilson Barrett'—fine double old rose.
'Queen Mary'—best double pale pink.
'White Aster'—good double white.
'Yvonne Cayeux'—double cream.

Plants do best in fertile, well-drained soil in a sunny, open location. Flowering commences as soon as the warm weather starts, but the display of bloom is usually finished by mid-summer, unless ample water is given or older plants have been broken up in the spring, thus prolonging the flowering season.

Tanacetum parthenium

Blooms should be kept cut and flower-heads not allowed to set seed if a longer blooming period is desired.

Plants are best increased from divisions in spring. This is also the season for transplanting. Slugs and snails are very fond of the young shoots in the spring, often killing fresh plantings outright.

T. parthenium (syn. *Chrysanthemum parthenium*), the herb feverfew, is also known as pyrethrum. 'White Bonnet' is a useful ornamental variety. It grows bushily to 50 cm (20 in.) and carries small, double, white flowers very freely, making a good display all through summer in a front-row position. It is not long-lived on heavy soils, but can be easily propagated from cuttings.

Chrysanthemum mawii

Chrysanthemum mawii should rightly be classified as *Tanacetum*, but this change does not appear to have been formally recorded. It is a bushy little perennial up to 40 cm (16 in.), with 2.5 cm (1 in.), single, pink daisies on erect stems. It comes from the Atlas Mountains of North Africa, and is hardy in all areas.

TECOPHILAEA
Tecophilaeaceae

This is a Chilean genus consisting of two species of bulbs. The better species, *T. cyanocrocus*, forms a flattish bulb up to 2.5 cm (1 in.) across, fibrous coated, which produces three narrow leaves and one to three wide-open, six-petalled, crocus-like blooms 7.5 cm (3 in.) across. These blooms, held on 10 cm (4 in.) stems, appear in the early spring and are a glorious shade of deep gentian-blue, with a small white centre adding to the intensity of the colour. A border or a group of a dozen or so bulbs in full bloom

is a wonderful sight. They are hardy and easily grown, blooming freely even in warmer climates. Good drainage is important, as is a location that is dry in summer. Increase is from seed, and bulbs will reach flowering size in three years.

TELLIMA
Saxifragaceae

This is a genus of only one species. *T. grandiflora* 'Purpurea' makes a dome of scalloped, heart-shaped foliage and is good ground cover under trees if the soil is not too dry. It has numerous tall spikes of greeny yellow, bell-shaped flowers, and the foliage usually turns to ruddy bronze in autumn. Propagation is by division in spring.

THALICTRUM
Ranunculaceae   Meadow rue

There are about 150 species of this genus, only a few of which are generally cultivated. All species are interesting plants for the herbaceous border, with fern-like foliage and small flowers in loose, free-branching panicles.

T. aquilegifolium, commonly called the feathered columbine, is a desirable species, growing to 1.2 m (4 ft). The plumy, corymbose panicles carry hundreds of tiny, white flowers with numerous purple central stamens, the general effect being a rosy purple. A pure white form is called 'Album'; a lilac-rose form is sometimes listed as 'Roseum'; and a splendid, rich violet-purple, semi-dwarf form is known as 'Purple Cloud'. All forms are attractive and useful garden plants, with handsome, greyish blue foliage.

T. delavayi is a first-class perennial, with tall, stately panicles 1.2–1.8 m (4–6 ft) high, carrying hundreds of small lilac-mauve flowers with conspicuous creamy white, central tassels. The loose, dainty habit adds much to its charm, and also makes it good for mixing with other flowers for decorations. An attractive, pure white variety, 'Album', coming true from seed, is also grown. A double-flowered form called 'Hewitt's Double' has now been success-

Thalictrum delavayi

fully propagated by tissue culture and will become more readily available. The great advantage of the double-flowered form is that it does not set seed, and the flowers remain attractive over a long period. It resembles the type in foliage only, the immense pyramidal heads of bloom, 60 cm (24 in.) across and reaching a height of 1.8 m (6 ft), are in effect like a violet-amethyst gypsophila in full bloom. However, for general effect in the garden, the single-flowered type is nearly as pretty, and is easily raised from seed sown in the spring, flowering freely the second season, and apparently quite hardy anywhere.

T. minus var. *adiantifolium* has lovely, dainty foliage very similar to the maidenhair fern, growing to 60 cm (24 in.). In the summer it has tiny mauve flowers. It is quite hardy, but also makes an attractive pot plant.

T. speciosissimum (syn. *T. glaucum*) seems to be the best of the yellow-flowered species. It has greyish blue foliage and 1–1.2 m (3–4 ft) flower-heads composed of masses of fluffy, light yellow flowers. It is a valuable, easily grown plant, happy alike in sun or shade.

Many other species are well worth a trial. All are hardy and easily grown, and many are attractive and valuable additions to the herbaceous border. Increase is from seed if available. Established clumps or plants are best planted before the quick spring growth starts.

THERMOPSIS
Fabaceae

These plants from North America are very similar to the lupin. Most of the 30 species in the genus have yellow flowers, but *T. caroliniana* is the best for gardens. It has handsome, lupin-like, yellow spikes up to 90 cm (36 in.), and will do best on light, sandy or volcanic soil in a sunny place. Other species are shorter in height. All are propagated from seed.

TIARELLA
Saxifragaceae

Two species of this North American perennial are commonly grown. They are small plants with heart-shaped leaves, which turn reddish in the autumn. The flowers of both species have 30 cm (12 in.) sprays of creamy white flowers. *T. cordifolia* has more compact spikes. *T. wherryi* has golden green foliage and rather longer spikes, and is very free-flowering, more so than *T. cordifolia*. They are very attractive in the front of the border or in the rock garden.

Tiarella cordifolia

TIGRIDIA
Iridaceae   Jockey cap

This genus of a dozen species is native to Mexico and South America. The species *T. pavonia* is the best known. These hardy bulbs are easily grown in any free, loose soil with good drainage, preferring a hot, dry autumn or conditions where gladiolus are happy. The interesting, bowl- or cup-shaped centres and three-petalled, extended segments, in all 10–15 cm (4–6 in.) across, are held erect on 45–60 cm (18–24 in.) stems. The common type is bright red and orange, but many colours and combinations of colours now exist, through pure white, cream, orange, pink, lilac, rose, red and purple-red, in self-colours and also heavily spotted in the throat. Each flower lasts only one day but is followed the next day by another, continuing in bloom over a long period. Blooms are not suitable for cutting, but they are most attractive plants, particularly in bold groups, either in mixed colours or separate named varieties.

A stock of bulbs can easily be increased from seed, which comes fairly true to the parent plant, bloom-

Trachelium caeruleum

ing sometimes the following autumn if sown thinly. Usually seed is sown thickly the first season, and the small bulbs are replanted the following autumn to bloom the next summer. Transplant during winter.

TRACHELIUM
Campanulaceae

This is a genus of about seven species of alpine perennials native to the Mediterranean region.

T. caeruleum forms an erect plant 0.6–1.2 m (2–4 ft) high, with ovate, acute, deeply double-toothed leaves, sometimes hairy beneath. The terminal flower-heads are in the form of corymbose panicles composed of hundreds of tiny, violet-blue, tubular flowers. There is also a white-flowered form, 'Alba', and both are useful in the herbaceous border. Plants are quite hardy, and fresh stock is usually obtained from seed.

Tigridia pavonia

TRADESCANTIA
Commelinaceae   Spider wort

TRICYRTIS
Liliaceae   Toad lily

This genus comprises about 60 species of American plants including shrubs and trailers, but the only form in general cultivation is that known as *T. x andersoniana*, sometimes called 'Moses in the bulrushes'. At one time it was thought to be the species *T. virginiana* but it is now known to be of hybrid origin.

It has broad, grassy leaves, triangular flowers and conspicuous stamens. The plants grow about 60 cm (24 in.), high and the flower-stems are held well above the foliage. In the best forms the flowers may be over 5 cm (2 in.) in diameter. Although the flowers last only one day, the plants continue to bloom all through the summer. This plant is most variable, and a great many coloured forms are known. The best cultivars include:

'Alba'—white with large, snow-white flowers.
'Blue Danube'—the best mid-blue.
'Flore Plens'—double, sky-blue flowers.
'Isis'—a splendid, rich deep blue.
'J. C. Weguelin'—an excellent light blue.
'Purple Dome'—violet-blue.

The tradescantias are easily increased by division and may be transplanted during winter.

Tradescantia x *andersoniana* 'Purple Dome'

The genus consists of 10 perennial species, each with short, creeping rhizomes and erect or arching stems 60–90 cm (24–36 in.) high, carrying oblong, pointed leaves and flowers, usually between the upper leaf axils. They are natives of Taiwan, Japan and the Himalayas. Plants thrive in most gardens that do not experience early frosts, but they prefer sandy, peaty soil.

Tricyrtis hirta

The only species commonly grown is *T. hirta*, which has leaves covered with soft, white hairs, and a cane-like stem resembling a miniature bamboo. The flowers appear in groups of two or three at the top portion of the stem and are bell-shaped, about 2.5 cm (1 in.) long and 5 cm (2 in.) across, pale lilac or almost white, heavily spotted with purple. Plants bloom in autumn, and in very cold districts need a warm sunny spot to reach maturity. The long stems carrying leaves and flowers are quite attractive for decorative purposes.

All the other species are worth growing, particularly *T. bakeri*, yellow-flowered spotted red, and *T. macrantha*, deep primrose marked with chocolate. Several interesting hybrids have been developed in Japan, and some are more vigorous than the species. The 5 cm (2 in.), alstroemeria-like flowers are produced nearer the top of the lilium-like stems and are in shades of rosy violet to soft mauve, usually with pale centres.

Increase is from seed, or division of established roots when plants are dormant in the winter or early spring.

TRILLIUM
Liliaceae   Wood lily

These most desirable spring-flowering, hardy, perennials are common in the American woodlands, mostly in districts with cold winters. They prefer rich, moist soil, abundant in leaf mould, a cool root run, and semi-shade, and may prove difficult to grow in warmer climates.

The best way to raise seedlings is to mix the seed with damp sand and keep it frozen during the winter months, sowing it in the spring, outside in a shady, damp position. Plants are acid-loving, and will be happy in woodland conditions among rhododendrons and other shrubs preferring acid soil. Seedlings should bloom three or four years after germination.

T. cernuum has broad leaves and 5 cm (2 in.), nodding flowers on stems 45–60 cm (18–24 in.) tall. The drooping petals are white, sometimes pinkish.

T. chloropetalum is a striking plant, growing to 40 cm (16 in.), with white, red or maroon flowers.

T. decumbens has dark red flowers on prostrate stems, and is quite unusual.

T. erectum carries 5 cm (2 in.) flowers on slender stems to 30 cm (12 in.). The flowers are variable in colour—white, pale pink, yellow or maroon.

T. grandiflorum (the wake robin) is one of the largest species. The stout stems, 50 cm (20 in.) tall, carry 7.5 cm (3 in.) flowers, pure white with overlapping petals. It is vigorous and usually long-lived. A very rare double form called 'Snow Bunting' has large and lovely, double white flowers.

T. ovatum has 10 cm (4 in.), white flowers fading

Trillium grandiflorum 'Snow Bunting'

to pink, and rounded leaves. It flowers in early spring before *T. grandiflorum*, and prefers deep shade.

T. rivale has 2.5 cm (1 in.), white flowers with purple spots on 12.5 cm (5 in.) stems. It prefers alkaline soil.

T. sessile has 3 cm (1.5 in.) flowers, maroon-red, without a pedicel, on 30 cm (12 in.) stems. The oval leaves are marbled.

T. undulatum has large, ovate leaves and slender, 30 cm (12 in.) stems carrying white flowers blotched with purple.

T. vaseyi has very handsome, large, deep maroon flowers and 35 cm (14 in.) stems. It will grown to 60 cm (24 in.) and is late blooming.

The woody, erect rhizomes should be planted out in winter, when they are dormant.

TRITELEIA
Liliaceae

This is a genus of 15 species, a number of which have been transferred from *Brodiaea*. They are hardy bulbs, easily grown in full sun, preferably in light soil with good drainage.

T. hyacinthina is a prolific species, growing 60–75 cm (24–30 in.) tall, with a many-flowered umbel of

Triteleia ixioides

flowers, usually pale lilac-blue with white and some forms into deeper bluish purple. It is long-lasting and useful as a cut flower. Seed-heads should be removed after blooming, particularly if it is grown in the rockery, otherwise seedlings will take possession.

T. ixioides scabra is the best form of a delightful, bright yellow-flowered species. The thin, 30–45 cm (12–18 in.) tall stem carries a dozen or more expanded blooms. This is sometimes classified as *Ipheion ixioides*.

T. laxa (syn. *Brodiaea laxa*) blooms in late spring. The crowded heads of trumpet-shaped blooms, 10–30 on a scape, resemble miniature agapanthus, with deep violet-blue flowers. It grows 30–45 cm (12–18 in.) tall, and is useful as a cut flower. A selected, deeper purple-blue form is called 'Blue King'. This species increases freely from seed, and flowering-sized bulbs are produced in the second season. It is hardy and not fussy about growing conditions.

TRITONIA
Iridaceae

This genus of over 50 species of bulbous plants, all natives of South Africa, now includes some of the species previously listed under *Montbretia*.

T. crocata is the best-known species, with its several coloured varieties. It produces a hard, flattish bulb up to 2.5 cm (1 in.) across, covered with a fibrous tunic. The common type with its 30 cm (12 in.) scapes of 5 cm (2 in.), bell-shaped flowers, borne in two rows like freesias or sparaxis, is a brilliant shade of orange. Bright pink, salmon, deep orange, scarlet and purple-red forms are also grown. These are increased from bulbs, as stocks raised from seed show considerable variation. *T. crocata* and its forms are valuable late-blooming bulbs, particularly suitable for massed borders, providing a brilliant display in late spring and early summer. The flowers are quite good for cutting, lasting a few days in water.

T. hyalina is not so well known. The petals of the flowers are widely separated and rounded at the points. The predominant colour is deep salmon, and the centre of the flower has a light, transparent appearance. It is quite an attractive species, coming into flower shortly before *T. crocata*.

T. lineata has creamy buff flowers, more funnel-shaped than those of *T. crocata*, and on 30–40 cm (12–16 in.) stems. It is not as showy as other species but increases well and is easy to grow in any sunny position.

T. squalida is a deep shell-pink with wine in the throat. It is similar in many respects to the preceding species, but it has transparent petal margins.

Tritonia crocata

TROLLIUS
Ranunculaceae   Globe flower

This genus of neat, hardy herbaceous perennials comprises 24 or more species from the marshy places of the northern temperate zone. They are grown for the beauty of their rounded, golden and orange flowers, held on neatly branched stems above the

Trollius 'Orange King'

attractive, much-divided, rich, green, palmate foliage.

Most of the varieties are hybrids or selected forms of *T. asiaticus*, *T. europaeus* and *T. chinensis*. The best-known variety is 'Golden Globe', with 5–7.5 cm (2–3 in.), golden yellow balls on 60 cm (24 in.) stems, which may be up to 1.2 m (4 ft) in a damp spot. *T.* 'Earliest of All' is lower growing, pale orange-yellow, while 'Commander-in-Chief' is perhaps the best of the darker shades, being a rich tangerine-orange. *T.* 'Goldquelle' is a fine, large flower in an orange shade, while 'Empire Day' and 'Fire Globe' are also good rich orange sorts. All the named hybrids are attractive and well worth growing in cooler districts.

The best of the species is *T. ledebourii*, a brilliant persimmon-orange. The selection called 'Golden Queen' has bright orange-yellow flowers on strong, sturdy stems. The flowers of this species are less globular in shape, displaying attractive, central, tasselled stamens and wide-open blooms up to 10 cm (4

in.) across. It will tolerate a warmer climate.

Trollius are increased from divisions in the winter or early spring, before they come into growth. All species and hybrids prefer moist or almost boggy conditions, but can be grown in any moderately rich garden soil if not allowed to become too dry. They are splendid plants for establishing alongside streams or ponds, naturalising in damp spots in an open woodland, and they do quite well in wet, shady places. They commence blooming in late spring, and if planted in a moist position, will continue all summer into autumn, growing 1 m (3 ft) in height instead of 45–60 cm (18–24 in.) under average conditions.

Most of the species can be increased from seed, which should be sown as soon as it is harvested. Imported seed may take several months or even a year to germinate. Transplant during the winter month.

TULBAGHIA
Liliaceae

About 30 species come from tropical and southern Africa, and are mostly grown as greenhouse plants.

T. fragrans is used in its native country for bedding in masses under large trees. The fleshy roots are dormant in the summer, but from late autumn till spring, numerous umbels composed of 10–20 soft violet, tubular flowers appear on 30 cm (12 in.) stems. These are long-lasting when cut. This species

Tulbaghia fragrans

will not stand very heavy frosts, but it is happy on the sunny side of big trees, which usually provide sufficient shelter in cold districts. A pure white-flowered form is also available.

T. natalensis has narrow, 1 cm (0.5 in.) leaves and white flowers in spring. It is hardy in warmer climates, and is without the garlic smell.

T. violacea seems to be quite hardy outside in warmer climates. It produces a thick, fleshy rootstock, numerous grey-green, evergreen, narcissus-like leaves, and 30 cm (12 in.) scapes carrying a dozen or more narrow, tubular flowers, 5–7.5 cm (2–3 in.) long, in a shade of lilac-mauve. It lasts in bloom as a cut flower over a long period, but unfortunately the cut portions yield a strong onion or garlic smell.

Propagation is by division or seed in spring.

TULIPA
Liliaceae

The wild species of tulip are natives of central Asia, Turkey and the Mediterranean region. An important factor in the successful cultivation of tulips is a climate that is similar to that encountered in these native environments.

Tulip species
There is a peculiar charm about wild tulips. Many of them flower earlier, and they are ideal subjects for the rock garden, where they can be planted to come up through established mats of low-growing alpines, or plants such as thyme and mint. Unfortunately, stocks tend not to be widely available.

Most tulip species prefer fairly deep planting, 15–20 cm (6–8 in.), in light, free soil or in pockets in a well-drained rockery. Bulbs can be planted in late summer and early autumn. The best way to secure a good stock of bulbs of tulip species is to raise them from seed. They will be more vigorous and free from disease.

In climates that are cold in winter and dry in summer, the following species, and any of their hybrids, may succeed in permanent plantings: *T. clusiana*, *T. kaufmanniana*, *T. saxatilis* and *T. sylvestris*.

T. clusiana, commonly called the 'lady tulip', is a

Tulip praestans

very dainty, narrow-petalled species, growing 40 cm (16 in.) tall, with long, pointed, snowy white flowers, stained outside with rosy red, and with a dark blue base inside. It naturalises by self-sown seed in a well-drained rockery, if the surface consists of metal chips or scree. A desirable variety, *T. clusiana* var. *chrysantha*, has yellow flowers with red interiors and the tips of petals reflexed.

T. eichleri has large, crimson-scarlet flowers with a yellow and black centre. It grows 30 cm (12 in.) high, and is most effective when massed.

T. fosteriana is one of the best species, of which many desirable selected forms have been propagated, the most sought after being the variety 'Red Emperor'. It grows up to 45 cm (18 in.) tall, with large, elongated, crimson-scarlet flowers and a handsome, shining base bordered yellow. A new hybrid strain between this species and a giant Darwin tulip gives us the largest brilliant red tulips ever raised.

T. greigii is a spectacular species with large, cup-shaped, bright orange-scarlet flowers, with a black blotch on a bright yellow base. The 7.5 cm (3 in.) wide, glaucous green leaves are attractively striped with purple-brown.

T. hageri has small, starry, dull-red flowers with peacock-like, greenish black centres and narrow yellow margins. It has been seen naturalised so thickly under old trees that weeds could not grow, and yet it is not generally known.

T. kaufmanniana is called the water-lily tulip, as the expanding flowers resemble a nymphaea, blooming in early spring. It grows only 15–20 cm (6–8 in.) high, but the large, open blooms, creamy white tinted yellow, with pinkish exterior, are most attractive, particularly in the rockery. It seems quite easy to grow in most districts. Selected forms are available, some of which are combinations of orange, flame and red.

T. praestans, with its several forms, usually grows about 30 cm (12 in.) high, with three to five intense orange-scarlet blooms on each stem. Some types are from carmine-red to deep vermillion-scarlet. They are early flowering and most brilliant.

T. patens (syn. *T. persica*), also called *T. breyniana*, seems happy in districts with a hot, dry summer and good winter drainage. Small, long, pointed flowers, bronzy gold outside and yellow inside, are freely produced on 20 cm (8 in.) stems. They are shown to best advantage in a rockery.

T. saxatilis, from Crete, does well in light, free soil and warm climate. The deep green leaves appear very early, and it needs a sheltered spot in very cold districts. Each stem carries one to three lilac-pink flowers with conspicuous yellow centres. This species is very free-flowering if happy, but the bulbs 'run', or send out long shoots or droppers, thus spreading very quickly in light soils. Under such conditions, a band of iron or other barrier is necessary, sunk deeply into the soil to keep the bulbs in position.

T. sprengeri is the last of the species to bloom, with starry, uniform, scarlet flowers and conspicuous yellow anthers. This species grows up to 50 cm (20 in.).

Opposite: This attractive two-tier pool is surrounded by flowering shrubs and perennials in white and shades of pink and purple. On the left a large-flowered foxglove (*Digitalis*) stands next to a white *Zantedeschia aethiopica*, in front of which are a white feverfew (*Tanacetum parthenium*) and a pink valerian (*Centranthus ruber*). On the right, tall, deep purple delphiniums dominate, and beside the urn, a heliotrope cascades over the brick wall.

T. sylvestris is the golden yellow, fragrant tulip that exists in a wild state in some parts of England. It grows about 35 cm (14 in.) tall, blooming early in the spring. It needs a sheltered spot, but otherwise it is quite easily managed.

Hybrid tulips

There is a wide range of hybrid tulip varieties available today. Healthy, vigorous stock, adequate drainage, cool growing conditions and deep cultivation are essential for good results. The most beneficial fertiliser is bone flour or bone meal, but a mixture of blood and bone and superphosphate will also give good results. Tulips prefer an alkaline soil. Bulbs should be planted in late autumn, at a depth of 15 cm (6 in.), where the temperature will be lower than near the surface. After flowering, the foliage will die down in three to six weeks, and the bulbs should be lifted and dried in an airy shed, not in the sun.

Tulip bulbs are usually fairly free from disease and pests, but a fungus commonly known as 'fire' often occurs during spells of cold weather or after hail, late frosts or wind damage. The foliage has a scorched, greyish white appearance, in large spots or covering the entire leaf. It spreads rapidly under suitable conditions, spoiling the blooms and causing the bulbs to ripen off prematurely. Affected plants should be destroyed.

Striping, or the breaking of the pure or self-colour of a tulip into flakes or stripes, is due to one or more virus diseases. Once affected, the constitution of the bulb is weakened and it never reverts to a self-colour. The virus is rapidly spread by means of green fly or other aphis, which chew the stem, flower or foliage of affected bulbs and pass it on to other clean stock. The aphis usually begins to appear about the bud stage and can be controlled with any good insecticide.

The classification of hybrid tulips includes the following groups:

Darwin hybrids: This splendid class is the result of crossing some of the best Darwin tulips with *T. fosteriana* and its forms. Most of them are vivid reds, blood-red and orange-scarlets, with immense, 20 cm (8 in.), wide-open blooms on 60 cm (24 in.) stems. The following all flower in mid-season and are outstanding.

Tulipa kaufmanniana 'Heart's Desire'

'Apeldoorn'—orange-scarlet with black base.
'Creme Jewel'—lovely pure white.
'Dover'—oriental scarlet with purple-black base.
'Golden Parade'—large golden yellow.
'Holland's Glory'—a dazzling, brilliant orange-scarlet, claimed to be the largest-flowered tulip grown.
'London'—blood-red with black base edged yellow.
'Oxford'—orange-red with yellow base.

Double late tulips: This is a tall-growing class with quite attractive, full double or paeony-flowered types, on 45–60 cm (18–24 in.) stems. Although quite easily grown, blooming late in the season, bulbs are slow to increase. Four good cultivars are:

'Allegretto'—yellow over a bronze base.
'Edite'—white on a pink ground.
'Erin', huge, paeony-like flowers in pure white.
'Hermione', pink suffused with pale pink.

Dwarf tulips: These grow about 20 cm (8 in.) tall, with quite large flowers on stocky plants.

'Ancilla'—another dwarf with *kaufmanniana* blood; creamy white with a red base.

'Donna Bella'—petals half white and striped with red; it flowers late in the season.

'Golden Bay'—yellow streaked with red, flowers mid-season.

Fosteriana hybrids: Some excellent varieties of early-flowering tulips are the result of crossing selected forms of this species with the giant orange-scarlet species *T. greigii* and others. They mostly display a combination of colours such as creamy white, scarlet-red outside, soft yellow with red centre bordered black. Many possess the beautifully marbled and mottled foliage. The following large-flowered varieties are recommended for warmer climates:

'Big Chief'—coral-red.
'Orange Emperor'—rich orange shades.
'Princess Royale'—pure yellow'.
'Purissima'—pure white.

Greigii hybrids: These are similar to the Fosteriana hybrids but flower a little later and are taller. These are also suitable for warmer climates.

'Oriental Splendour'—striking red and yellow.
'Royal Splendour'—deep scarlet-red self-colour.

Lily-flowered tulips: Varieties in this section grow tall, with elongated petals that turn back at the tips, resembling a lilium bloom. They are among the last to flower, and are very dainty and most useful for decoration.

'Ballade'—carmine bordered with white.
'Lilac Time'—soft purple.
'Maytime'—crimson.
'Queen of Sheba'—dark red with yellow.
'Westpoint'—pure yellow.

Parrot tulips: These constitute a rather small but popular class of tulips, most of which are 'sports' from other well-known varieties. The petals of the parrot tulips are longer and deeply laciniated so that they curl and twist in all directions. Among the splashes of bizarres, usually scarlet and brown markings on yellow or white ground, will also be seen patches of green tissue. Most varieties grow 45 cm (18 in.) tall and bloom along with the main crop varieties.

Single late tulips: This class is also called 'cottage' tulips. It cannot really be accurately defined, being just a collection of later-flowering tulips that do not find a place in the other classes. On the whole they are long and pointed in the petal, in contrast to the well-rounded Darwin type. Varieties include:

'Attila'—deep mauve.
'Edith Day'—striking carmine edged with white.
'G. W. Leak'—deep red.
'Halcro'—bright scarlet.
'Ile de France'—rich crimson.
'Kees Nelis'—yellow and flame.
'Leen Van der Nark'—crimson and white.
'Little Queen Bess'—pink.
'Pandion'—deep mauve edged with white.
'Queen of Nights'—purple-black.
'Spring Green'—cream marked with green.

U

URCEOLINA
Amaryllidaceae

This is a genus of five species, only one of which is commonly grown. *U. peruviana*, also known as *U. miniata*, is a most desirable bulb from the Andes in Peru. It is quite hardy and easy to grow in any free, well-drained soil, withstanding quite heavy frosts, possibly because it is dormant in the winter. The roundish bulb, up to 5 cm (2 in.) across, has one to three scapes 40 cm (16 in.) tall, each carrying two to six pendant, coral-red, urn-shaped or tubular bells, 5 cm (2 in.) long, produced in late spring/early summer. The shining, strap-like leaves are mostly developed after the flowers have finished, so that there is nothing to hide the attractive display of bloom on a well-established clump. Bulbs can be lifted when the foliage dies down, stored in a dry place during the winter, and planted out in the spring. The flower-spike is formed in the bulb the previous season, like the nerines, and bulbs bloom without soil or moist material, transplanting quite readily while in flower.

The urceolinas increase readily from divisions of bulbs, which can be left undisturbed for several years until too crowded. Unlike nerines and other bulbs of the amaryllis family, which should be planted with the neck or half the bulb protruding above the soil, urceolinas should be set about 5 cm (2 in.) below the surface.

Two other species are worth obtaining if possible: *U. latifolia*, which has yellowish red flowers tipped with green, and *U. pendula*, in which the upper part of the yellow flowers is green margined with white.

Transplant bulbs while dormant during winter.

URSINIA
Asteraceae

This is a family of South African annual and perennial sub-shrubs. *U. chrysanthemoides* var. *geyeri* is a lovely shrubby plant with small leaves up to 45 cm (18 in.), bearing numerous orange-red daisies, 5 cm (2 in.) in diameter, all through summer. It needs full

Urceolina peruviana

Ursinia sericea

sun and good drainage. Although not usually long-lived, it can be easily maintained from cuttings, which root very easily. *U. sericea* is a similar plant, which bears yellow daisies in profusion.

UVULARIA
Liliaceae   Bellwort

These uncommon plants from North America have lemon-yellow bells hanging on the ends of leafy shoots and are quite hardy everywhere. They are easily cultivated in rich soil in a shady position, and flower in late spring.

U. grandiflora grows to 60 cm (24 in.), with 12.5 cm (5 in.) leaves and dangling, lemon bells.

U. perfoliata, up to 50 cm (20 in.) tall, has shorter leaves and smaller flowers. Both species are usually propagated by division of the rhizomatous roots.

Uvularia grandiflora

V

VELTHEIMIA
Liliaceae

These lovely bulbs from South Africa should be grown in all frost-free gardens with good drainage. There are two extremely variable species.

V. bracteata (syn. *V. viridifolia*) is the most commonly grown, resembling a giant-flowered lachenalia, growing about 45 cm (18 in.) tall and blooming during the late winter and early spring. Broad, shining, deep green, wavy-edged leaves surround a dense raceme of deep pink-red, semi-pendant, tubular flowers tipped with green. It is a splendid cut flower. The fleshy bulbs grow up to 7.5 cm (3 in.) across, but 2.5 cm (1 in.) bulbs will bloom. It is more quickly increased from seed, which sets freely and germinates readily if sown as soon as ripe, and the bulbs bloom the second or third season.

V. capensis (syn. *V. glauca*) can be distinguished from the previous species by its longer, narrower

Veltheimia bracteata

foliage. It has reddish purple flowers tipped with yellow. Good drainage and hot, dry summer conditions are essential. When well established, bulbs form large clumps resting on the surface of the ground like nerines. Transplant while dormant in autumn.

VENIDIUM
Asteraceae

The genus comprises about 25 perennial and annual plants, all natives of South Africa. They are closely allied to the arctotis, which they resemble except that they lack the pappus. Plants are only half-hardy and resent wet or heavy ground. The following species can also be grown as annuals; seedlings raised in the early spring will bloom the following summer and autumn.

V. decurrens forms a much-branched, low-growing bush with soft, hairy stems, 30–45 cm (12–18 in.) long. The leaves are lyre-shaped, with the terminal lobe the largest, cobwebby at first, later smooth above and hairy below. The 7.5 cm (3 in.), rayed flowers are bright yellow with a black or dark brown central disc.

V. fastuosum is similar in habit but forms a bush up to 1 m (3 ft) high and across, with 15 cm (6 in.) long leaves, grey and hairy on both sides. In the type the golden yellow rays carry a purplish blotch at the base of the petals, and the conspicuous, 2.5 cm (1 in.) wide disc in the centre is brownish purple or black. An interesting range of hybrids includes bright orange, pinks, salmons, lavenders and intermediate tones or bicolours, all of which show the conspicuous brown or purple central zonings. These are very showy, and if planted in a sunny well-drained position, provide a brilliant display. Plants of any species are not long-lived, so fresh stock should be raised, either from cuttings of selected types taken in the autumn, or from seed sown in the spring. Plants are best set out in the spring as soon as the ground begins to warm up.

VERBASCUM
Scrophulariaceae   Mullein

Of this genus of nearly 300 species, only a few are true perennials, most being biennial herbs. There are also a number of hybrid cultivars, which are excellent plants for the middle and back of the border, especially on lighter soils including alkaline soils. On lighter soils they are not so long-lived.

V. bombyciferum is a biennial, growing 1.2–1.8 m (4–6 ft) tall, with silvery leaves and slender spikes of golden yellow. The best form of this species is 'Silver Lining'.

V. dumulosum is a dwarf species no more than 20 cm (8 in.) tall, very suitable for the rock garden. *V.* 'Letitia', a hybrid with *V. spinosum* as the other parent, is a delightful bushy shrublet, well covered in summer with 2 cm (0.5 in.), light yellow flowers.

V. 'Gainsborough' has bold, 1.2 m (4 ft) spikes of clear, light yellow, and 'Cotswold Queen' grows about the same height, with branching spikes of an unusual coppery colour. 'Pink Domino' is similar, with spikes of rose-pink. All three are perennial.

V. nigrum is sometimes known as *V. vernale*, although some doubt exists as to the validity of both names. It is a splendid, tall-growing plant, suitable

Verbascum dumulosum

for the back of a deep herbaceous border. From the rosette of large, heart-shaped, 30 cm (12 in.) leaves, covered with tiny hairs, arise tall, pyramidal spikes, 1.2–1.8 m (4–6 ft) in height, composed of hundreds of 2 cm (0.5 in.), yellow flowers, each with a central filament of purple hairs. A group of well-grown plants is impressive, particularly if associated with deep purple-blue delphiniums.

V. phoeniceum is a native of southern Europe and is fairly perennial. The flowers are about 3 cm (1.5 in.) across, forming a long, slender raceme, sometimes slightly branched at the base. The typical colour is violet-red, but shades of pink, lilac, rose and purple also occur; there is a wider range among the hybrids. Plants raised from seed often bloom the first season after sowing and provide some interesting colour variations, with spikes of bloom 60–90 cm (24–36 in.) or more.

All species and varieties prefer a sunny, well-drained spot, but otherwise they are very hardy and don't need any special attention. Old clumps do not divide up readily, and named hybrids are best increased from root cuttings inserted upright in boxes of sand until the small leaves appear in the spring. These cuttings should bloom in the autumn. Larger roots should be planted out during winter.

VERBENA
Verbenaceae

A genus of about 250 species, the verbenas are chiefly natives of the Americas, and they provide many outstanding, low-growing subjects for the front of the border.

V. peruviana thrives on light, free or poorish soil also doing well in fairly exposed coastal areas, where it will cover a bank with a solid mat of growth, the stems rooting into the soil at every joint. In spring, and to a lesser degree during summer and autumn, the bank is transformed into a blaze of dazzling scarlet, and as the plant does not usually set seed, the flowering period is greatly prolonged. This species is hardy and easily grown.

V. rigida, previously called *V. venosa*, is a distinct species from Brazil. It has thick, fleshy roots, rough, hairy stems and foliage, and compact little heads of royal-purple blossom throughout the summer. Two

Verbena rigida

excellent cultivars of this species, 'Polaris' and 'Blue Whisper', make very free-flowering ground covers, with small, lilac flower-heads.

V. tenera var. *maonetti* is a low-growing plant, very dainty and free-flowering. The heads are a pleasing amethyst shade with a narrow white stripe on each petal.

There is a range of splendid hybrid verbenas that are outstanding carpeting plants. They flower continuously all summer and autumn in full sun, and do well on a bank, a wall or at the front of a mixed border. Many are scented.

'Candy'—soft pink with white stripes on each petal.
'Cardinal'—brilliant red.
'Driven Snow'—pure white.
'Mauve Queen'—soft mauve.
'Mulberry'—soft mulberry shade.
'Pink Lace'—rich pink.
'Prince'—purple.
'Rose Queen'—very good pink.
'Seaview Beauty'—deep lilac-pink.

Plants of verbena will develop into a 60 cm (24 in.) wide mound of flower and will root at each node as they spread. They are hardy in mild climates, but where frosts are heavy, cuttings can be overwintered under glass. Although they are perennial, the best results are obtained by replanting young plants each spring.

VERONICA
Scrophulariaceae   Speedwell

This genus consists of about 300 species of small trees, shrubs, herbaceous plants and annuals. The herbaceous plants and annuals are natives of cooler parts of the Northern Hemisphere.

V. grandis var. *holophylla* has thick, glossy foliage and grows 35–50 cm (14–20 in.) tall, with spikes of intense blue in mid-summer.

V. incana has greyish leaves with short spikes of deep blue, little more than 30 cm (12 in.) tall.

V. latifolia, previously *V. teucrium*, includes several low-growing forms with rich blue flowers in profusion in late summer. 'Blue Fountain' is vivid blue to 60 cm (24 in.); 'Shirley Blue' grows to 20 cm (8 in.); and 'Trehane' has golden foliage in pleasing contrast to the 20 cm (8 in.), blue spikes.

V. longifolia has slender spikes with pale blue flowers up to 90 cm (36 in.) in early summer. In the form 'Variegata' the leaves are partly cream and the flowers a deeper shade.

V. spicata will grow to 60 cm (24 in.) and has

Veronica longifolia

bright blue spikes in late summer. A white form is called *V. spicata* 'Alba'. There is also a wine-coloured form called 'Red Fox'.

All veronicas prefer cooler climates. Plants are easily increased from divisions or from spring cuttings when the new shoots are 5–7.5 cm (2–3 in.) long. They can be transplanted during winter and will bloom freely in early summer.

VIGUIERA
Asteraceae

This genus of about 150 species, mostly annuals and perennials, originates in the warmer parts of America. *V. trinerva* was introduced from the alpine ranges of Mexico. The plant soon forms a tufted clump of robust, deep green leaves, 15–20 cm (6–8 in.) long, from which arise branching heads of bloom on 60–90 cm (24–36 in.) stems, carrying a number of finely rayed, deep yellow daisies, 7.5 cm (3 in.) across. The heads and stems are a little coarse in appearance, but it is nevertheless a distinctive herbaceous plant worthy of inclusion in most borders, particularly as it blooms over a long period. Plants will withstand frosts of 15 degrees or more. Increase is from divisions during winter or early spring. Fresh seed is easily raised, and plants will bloom the second season.

VIOLA
Violaceae   Violet

Violets are so well known that they need little description. Best results are obtained by planting new beds each year during spring, using the strongest outer runners. They are not fussy about soil, but a cool, shady spot should be chosen under deciduous shrubs or trees. This will allow the winter sun to penetrate, and the result will be more flowers. Animal manure with straw is beneficial, particularly in heavy soils.

V. cucullata (syn. *V. obliqua*) 'Freckles' is a deciduous American species, plain white freckled with blue.

V. hederacea is the Australian ivy-leaved violet,

Viola cucullata 'Freckles'

with two-toned blue and white flowers. 'Blue Boy' has abundant flowers of pure medium blue.

V. 'Marie Louise' is a full double mauve, and it and the white form 'Swanley White' are often sold together as the parma violets. They are very suitable for massing under big trees in a position that is not too dry, but are also quite successful grown in the open.

V. odorata is a spreading, rhizomatous plant with heart-shaped leaves. It has fragrant flowers from late winter into spring, and self-seeds readily. Plants can also be propagated by division. 'Admiral Avellon' is the so-called red violet, but is more a shade of rich purple with a reddish sheen. It is a little smaller than other cultivars, but a neat flower and nicely perfumed. 'Count Dorcy' is an interesting, ever-blooming variety, which forms a neat, round clump with no side runners or shoots. The small flowers are a pinkish red shade. A clearer pale pink form is called 'Pink Pearl'. 'Jazz' is a full double with four outer petals of purplish blue, and three or four inner ones of striped purple and white. 'Princess of Wales' is the best commercial variety, and if transplanted in rich, well-drained soil every two years, a crop of bloom can be expected for nearly six months until early spring. The large, single, delightfully scented flowers are about 2.5 cm (1 in.) across and carried on 30 cm (12 in.) stems. 'Royal Robe' is a deciduous species, denoting its American origin. It forms tight clumps without many runners and has large, purple flowers without scent. 'Wedgwood Blue' is a pure sky-blue.

New varieties of *V. odorata* raised in New Zealand include: 'Flamingo', pale pink shading to a deep pink centre; 'Gothic', cerise-pink centre with dusky pink outside; 'Schubert', clear soft amethyst with darker centre; 'Vienna', pure pale lilac-pink; 'Kerry', rose-red with deeper pink centre.

The following popular cultivars were originally grown from cuttings but are nowadays often raised from seed. *V. tricolor* 'All Black' has larger flowers than the older 'Bowles Black' and is good in sun or partial shade in warmer districts. *V.* 'Irish Molly' is brown suffused with mustard. *V.* 'Arkwrights Ruby' is rich red with a black centre, and *V.* 'Jackanapes' is a bright yellow and brown bicolour.

Plants should be propagated by division in spring or by seed sown in spring or autumn.

Viola tricolor 'All Black'

WACHENDORFIA
Haemodoraceae   Blood root

This is a small genus of five species, two of which are cultivated. Both come from South Africa, and are easily recognised by their pleated, strap-shaped foliage and red rhizomes.

W. paniculata is dormant in winter, and in spring sends up 30 cm (12 in.) flowering stems, much branched and bearing pale yellow flowers shaded brown, which open in succession.

W. thyrsiflora is much taller, with broad leaves to 90 cm (36 in.) and stout, showy spikes to 2 m (6.5 ft), of 7.5 cm (3 in.), open, golden flowers. It is easily grown on most soils with ample moisture in spring. The height is variable, some growing little more than 1.5 m (5 ft).

Propagation is by division in spring or by seed sown in autumn.

WATSONIA
Iridaceae   Bugle lily

This genus comprises about 70 species. All produce a gladiolus-like corm covered with a tough, fibrous outer skin. Some flower in the spring and early summer, becoming dormant for a short period in late summer. They can be lifted, stored and replanted as late as early spring. This group includes most of the species and hybrids usually grown. Another group is evergreen, blooming from mid-summer onwards. This includes *W. beatricis* and the scarlet *W. galpinii*.

W. aletroides is a distinct species, easily recognised by the narrow, cylindrical, 7.5 cm (3 in.), coral-red flowers, narrowed at the mouth, produced freely on 60 cm (24 in.) stems. It flowers in early spring,

Wachendorfia thyrsiflora

several weeks ahead of any other species or variety, and is grown for early cut blooms. Rose, pale pink and cream-coloured forms exist in the wild. This species is sometimes wrongly listed as *W. coccinea* which is a bright crimson-flowered species with open lobes, rather sparsely flowered on 45 cm (18 in.) stems.

W. beatricis is an evergreen species reaching a height of 1.2 m (4 ft) and commencing to bloom in mid-summer but continuing during autumn and even into the winter months in milder areas. It is a narrow-tubed, orange-flowered species that hybridises easily and has given us a range of colours, including light and deep pinks and reds. This species seems hardy anywhere, withstanding heavy frosts and even snow, although it may be advisable to give some winter protection the first season after planting or transplant roots in the spring, after frosts have finished. Seed germinates freely, and corms will bloom in the second season.

W. bordonica includes those previously known as *W. pyramidata* and *W. ardernei*. This is the most popular cultivated species, with large flowers in a range of colours including white and shades of pink and rose. It is also a parent of many modern hybrids.

W. brevifolia is not widely available, but it can be easily grown from seed from South Africa. It grows to about 50 cm (20 in.), with short foliage and dainty spikes of pale pink, tubular flowers coming into bloom in spring. It hybridises easily, and seedlings may have apricot or deeper pink flowers.

W. humilis is a small-growing species up to 1 m (3 ft) tall. It has a fan of short, broad, twisted leaves at the base, and develops numerous spikes of pale magenta-pink flowers during late spring.

W. marginata is a distinct, hardy species with broad, bluish green leaves edged with yellow. In spring it produces flower-stalks 1.2–1.8 m (4–6 ft) high, and slender stems carrying numerous short-tubed, cup-shaped, lilac-coloured flowers, which give it the appearance of a giant ixia. There is also a white-flowered form, 'Alba', which is rather light and attractive.

W. meriana is the earliest flowering of the taller watsonias, coming into flower in spring. It grows to about 90 cm (36 in.), with tubular trumpets of various shades of pink. It flowers freely and makes a good garden plant.

W. tabularis has tall spikes, to 1.5 m (5 ft), of coral-red flowers in mid-summer. Although the flowers are smaller than the hybrids, they are plentiful, with

Watsonia aletroides

many side shoots. It is evergreen and capable of withstanding frosty conditions.

The large-flowered hybrids bloom from spring to early summer, and include:

'Adelaide'—salmon-orange.
'Auckland'—apricot-pink.
'Bright Eyes'—rich lilac-pink.
'Canberra'—deep rosy mauve.
'Hobart'—large pure white.
'Illumination'—rich rose-pink.
'Melbourne'—salmon-pink.
'Rubra'—rich wine-red.

Watsonias may be left in the ground from year to year, except in very frosty areas. Plant in groups of one variety, 15 cm (6 in.) apart. The bulbs will increase, producing more flower-spikes each season.

X

XERONEMA
Liliaceae   Poor Knights lily

This genus consists of two species. *X. callistemon* is an outstanding plant, native to the Poor Knights Islands off the coast of New Zealand. It has handsome tussocks of bright green, spikey foliage from which spring 90 cm (36 in.) flower-spikes, terminating in great trusses of scarlet bloom, 25 cm (10 in.) long. The flower-heads resemble giant bottlebrushes with all the stamens on the upper side of the horizontal inflorescence. The flowers last for about a fortnight, but gradually change in colour from green to crimson.

It is quite easy to grow in any free, loose soil where it gets plenty of sunshine, but it must have perfect drainage. Well-established clumps may carry a dozen showy spikes. It also grows well outside in tubs. Plants may be raised from seed or by division, provided this takes place in the growing season and not in winter. It is advisable to transplant from pot-grown specimens.

Xeronema callistemon

Y

YUCCA
Agavaceae

There are numerous species of yucca that are ever-green shrubs, but two species do not make stems, growing rather like New Zealand flax (*Phormium* spp.), spreading slowly by suckers at ground level.

Y. filamentosa has sword-shaped leaves and produces, in mid-summer, imposing spikes of creamy white bells to a height of 1.5 m (5 ft).

Y. flaccida has greyish leaves that are more limp and less erect, with similar flower-spikes to *Y. filamentosa*. The form 'Variegata' has white-striped leaves, which make a very handsome rosette of white and green foliage, very effective even when the plant is not in bloom. 'Garlands Gold' has green and gold foliage. All these yuccas have sharp, pointed leaves, which have small, drooping, loose threads or filaments along the edges.

Varieties of *Y. aloifolia* such as 'Tricolor' and 'Quadricolor' are striking plants with spreading rosettes of thin leaves, variegated in green, cream and red. They should be carefully positioned because the leaves have very sharp points. They will grow very tall, with very large flower-spikes in time.

Propagation is by division of plants in spring.

Yucca filamentosa 'Variegata'

Z

ZANTEDESCHIA
Araceae   Calla lilies

The eight species in this genus used to be classified as *Arum, Calla* or *Richardia*.

Z. aethiopica is the common, white so-called arum lily, which grows wild in northern parts of New Zealand, alongside streams or in wet places. It is much prized in England and Europe, where the rhizomes are flowered under glass, the large white blooms being valued for indoor decorations. A splendid dwarf cultivar, *Z. aethiopica* 'Childsiana', grows to about 60 cm (24 in.) and is very free-flowering, making an excellent cut flower and a good garden plant. The flowers are pure white of medium size. In warmer areas it will continue flowering

Zantedeschia aethiopica 'Green Goddess'

throughout spring and early summer. A vigorous form named 'Green Goddess' will grow to 2 m (6.5 ft) in moist conditions. The flowers are heavily splashed with green and held on strong stems. Seedlings usually come true to type.

Z. albomaculata (syn. *Z. melanoleuca*) is a most variable species, growing about 60 cm (24 in.) high, with arrow-shaped leaves heavily spotted with white. The flowers are usually pale lemon, tubular in shape, revealing a purple-black base. The best forms raised from seed have yellow spathes flushed with apricot to peach pink and are generally described as sunset shades.

Z. elliottiana is the well-known and deservedly popular golden arum lily. It grows 60 cm (24 in.) tall, with large, deep green leaves, showing transparent, silvery white markings, giving a speckled effect. The bright golden yellow spathes, 15 cm (6 in.) long and 10 cm (4 in.) across, are nicely rolled back at the edges and not tubular, as with some species. It has never been found growing in the wild and is considered to be a selected form of the variable species *Z. albomaculata*. The true form should be a pure deep golden yellow without any black patch inside.

Z. pentlandii is a magnificent species resembling *Z. elliottiana* except that the arrow-head shaped leaves are unspotted deep green, and the spathes, 10–17.5 cm (4–7 in.) long, are several tones deeper in a rich orange-yellow. Its tendency to collapse in winter could be overcome by lifting and storing the bulbs when dormant.

Z. rehmannii is also a variable species, easily distinguished by its slender, spear-shaped leaves. It grows 30–45 cm (12–18 in.) tall, and the usual type produces 10 cm (4 in.), pale pink spathes, nicely rolled back at the edges. A deep violet-purple-flowered form is known as *Z. rehmannii* 'Violacea', and a tall, soft pink is known as 'Gigantea'. Many intermediate shades will appear in a batch of mixed

Zantedeschia elliottiana

seedlings, but the forms listed above usually breed true to type from seed.

New hybrids in a range of wonderful colours are now available, including:

'Afterglow'—rich orange with dark throat.
'Aztec Gold'—orange shaded gold.
'Black Magic'—clear yellow with black throat.
'Dusky Pink'—cream shading to mauve pink and
  dark throat.
'Golden Affair'—clear bright yellow self-colour.
'Majestic Red'—deep red, much admired.
'Pacific Pink'—lovely bright pink self-colour.
'Pink Persuasion'—rich deep pink.
'Pixie'—golden yellow to orange.
'Regal Charm'—golden centre shading to orange.
'Velvet Cream'—pale off-white cream.

Many of these hybrids change colour considerably as the flowers mature.

Fresh stock can easily be raised from seed. The large seeds are usually set out thickly in beds for one growing season, and the small corms, by then 2.5 cm (1 in.) across or less, will reach flowering size the following autumn. Corms are usually planted in spring, but if the soil is loose and free with good drainage, these do not need to be lifted each autumn and can be left undisturbed for several years. The blooms appear in late spring/early summer, but a succession of blooms can be obtained by planting over a period of weeks.

ZAUSCHNERIA
Onagraceae   California fuchsia

This genus has four species of dwarf perennials or low shrubs, natives of western North America.

Z. californica is valued for its long period of blooming, tolerance to dry conditions and poor soil, and its ability to thrive near the sea coast. The plant forms a rather dense bush, rather woody below, and the crowded, grey-green, rather hairy foliage is topped with short spikes of brilliant salmon-scarlet, small, fuchsia-like flowers, continuing in bloom until late autumn. A well-established plant will attain a height of 45 cm (18 in.) with a spread of 60 cm (24 in.).

Z. cana (syn. *Z. microphylla*) has narrower, more grey foliage but the flowers and the habit of growth are similar.

Z. garrettii is quite prostrate, forming a mat of foliage with scarlet flowers through late summer to autumn.

Zauschneria californica

All species seem hardy on well-drained soil in almost any situation, although they will not thrive in very wet or shady places. Increase stock while plants are dormant during winter from divisions of older plants; early spring cuttings will root readily.

ZEPHYRANTHES
Amaryllidaceae   Zephyr flower

Zephyranthes candida

This is the baby of the bulbous amaryllis family. There are 35 or more known species, all natives of the warmer parts of America. The bulbs are usually round, about 2.5 cm (1 in.) across. The leaves are mostly linear, narrow and rather fleshy, but some are broader and strap-like, about 15–30 cm (6–12 in.) long. In some species, notably the white *Z. candida*, the foliage is persistent all the year round, but with most it dies down completely during the colder winter months. The funnel-shaped flower, not unlike a crocus and composed of six segments, is produced singly on 10–30 cm (4–12 in.) stems.

Z. candida is the best-known and most commonly grown species, often called the white autumn crocus. It produces an abundance of pure white flowers about 5 cm (2 in.) long and 4 cm (1.5 in.) across during autumn, although odd blooms appear earlier. When the flowers are fading they carry a pinkish tinge, while the yellow central stamens are attractively conspicuous. Most other species bloom in the spring, continuing to a lesser degree during the summer and autumn, usually after a dry spell followed by warm rains. A garden hybrid between *Z. candida* and a golden yellow-flowered species from Guyana called *Z. citrina* is also quite common and apparently just as hardy as the white-flowered parent. It has pale primrose-yellow blooms and is called *Z. ajax*.

Z. grandiflora (syn. *Z. carinata*) is a pink-flowered species with blooms up to 10 cm (4 in.) wide, with leaves, bulbs and flower-stems proportionately larger. It is only half-hardy, requiring free, loose soil and a sunny spot.

Z. pendunculata, previously *Cooperia pedunculata*, has 30 cm (12 in.), linear, glaucous-green foliage, resembling a nerine in growth. The white, crocus-like, primrose-scented flowers, 5 cm (2 in.) or more across, slightly flushed pink with a red-stained tube, are held erect on 30 cm (12 in.) stems, and bloom in late spring or early summer. Bulbs increase reasonably freely from offsets, and stock can also be obtained from seed, with bulbs blooming the third season after sowing in autumn. The large seed-pods are interesting and decorative. Transplant during autumn or winter.

Z. rosea is a small, pink-flowered species from Guatemala. It is easily grown in light, free soils with frosts up to 12 degrees, but may withstand more winter cold if planted deeper. It is a lovely bulb for permanent edgings or for pockets in the rockery, providing several displays of bloom throughout spring and summer.

Increase of zephyranthes is by seed sown in autumn and spring.

Glossary

Adventitious: developing in an abnormal position.

Axil: the place where the upper side of a leaf or stem meets the supporting stem or branch.

Axillary: relating to or growing from the axil (q.v.).

Bipinnate: twice pinnate (q.v.); a pinnate leaf whose divisions are also pinnate.

Bract: a specialised leaf with a flower or arrangement of flowers growing in its axil (q.v.).

Calyx: the outer part of the flower that protects the developing flower bud.

Composite: having flower heads composed of many small flowers.

Cordate: heart-shaped.

Corm: the fleshy, enlarged, underground base of a plant's stem, by which the plant reproduces.

Corolla: the petals of a flower collectively.

Corymb: a flat-topped cluster of flowers flowering from the outside inwards.

Corymbose: arranged in corymbs (q.v.) or resembling a corymb.

Cultivar: a variety (q.v.) of a plant produced from a natural species and maintained by cultivation.

Dentate: toothed.

Genus: a clearly defined group of species (q.v.).

Glabrous: not hairy.

Glaucous: of a distinctly bluish green colour.

Hybrid: a plant resulting from a cross between two species.

Imbricated: overlapping.

Inflorescence: an arrangement of flowers on a plant.

Laciniated: jagged.

Lanceolate: shaped like the head of a lance.

Monocarpic: flowering or fruiting once before dying.

Monotypic: a genus comprising only one species.

Offset: a short, lateral shoot by which certain plants are propagated.

Ovate: shaped like the longitudinal section of an egg.

Palmate: shaped like an open hand.

Panicle: a loose, irregularly branched arrangement of flowers on a plant.

Pappus: a ring of hairs surrounding the fruit in members of the Asteraceae family.

Pedicel: the stalk bearing a single flower in an arrangement of flowers on a plant.

Perianth: the outer part of a flower.

Pinnate: a leaf with leaflets growing opposite each other in pairs on either side of the stem.

Procumbent: growing along the ground.

Prostrate: growing along the ground.

Raceme: an arrangement of flowers where flowers are borne along a main stem.

Rhizome: a thick, horizontal, underground stem whose buds develop into new plants.

Scape: a leafless flower stalk rising from the ground.

Sepal: a division of the calyx (q.v.) of a flower.

Sessile: having no stalk.

Spadix: a spike of small flowers on a fleshy stem enclosed by a spathe (q.v.).

Spathe: a specialised leaf enclosing a spadix (q.v.).

Species: a group of individual plants possessing the same constant and distinctive characters; a subdivision of a genus.

Sport: a plant that differs conspicuously from other members of its species, usually because of a mutation.

Stamen: the male reproductive organ of a flower, which produces pollen.

Staminode: a sterile stamen (q.v.) or a part resembling such a stamen.

Stolon: a runner; a slender, horizontal stem that grows along the surface of the soil and propagates by producing roots and shoots.

Tuber: a fleshy, underground stem or root of a plant, by which the plant reproduces.

Umbel: an arrangement of flowers where several flowers arise from the same point on the main stem and have stalks of about the same length.

Variety: a subdivision of a species.

Index

This index includes genera and common names. It was decided to include an alphabetical listing of genera—which may seem unnecessary in an alphabetical book—because of the numerous changes in plant nomenclature in recent years.